# THE MORAL MENAGERIE

MARC R. FELLENZ

*The Moral Menagerie*

PHILOSOPHY AND

ANIMAL RIGHTS

UNIVERSITY OF ILLINOIS PRESS

URBANA AND CHICAGO

Library of Congress Cataloging-in-Publication Data

Fellenz, Marc R., 1963–
The moral menagerie : philosophy and animal rights / Marc R. Fellenz
p. cm.
Includes bibliographical references and index.
ISBN-13: 978-0-252-03118-2 (cloth : alk. paper)
ISBN-10: 0-252-03118-0 (cloth : alk. paper)
ISBN-13: 978-0-252-07360-1 (pbk. : alk. paper)
ISBN-10: 0-252-07360-6 (pbk. : alk. paper)
1. Animal rights—Philosophy.
I. Title.
HV4708.F35          2007
179'.3—dc22          2006029386

*For Juliana and Sophia,*
*my two favorite animals*

# Contents

# Acknowledgments

Many students, teachers, and colleagues helped this work come about. I'd like to extend special thanks to the following:

Maxim Mikulak encouraged me to begin this work, and without his spurring me to do so I probably would not have undertaken it. Juliana Podd of the Longwood Library provided invaluable research assistance throughout the preparation of the manuscript. Phil Cafaro, Daniel Conway, Phyllis Deutsche, Harlan B. Miller, Shannon Sullivan, and Grace Wang provided valuable criticism on various drafts of the manuscript. Carl Mitcham was inexplicably generous with his time and encouragement to see me complete this work and bring it to publication. Finally, my gratitude to Liz Dulany of the University of Illinois Press, who worked very hard to see this work published.

# Introduction

## The Debate over Animals

Suppose you are walking through the woods on a path familiar to you. You come to a point where the path forks, yielding two routes that you know to be equally convenient for your purposes: both are wide enough for you to pass, neither is out of the way of your ultimate destination, and so on. For no particular reason you begin to head toward the left route, when you see that the trees at its entrance hold an elaborate spider's web that you will surely destroy if you try to pass. Assuming *ceteris paribus* (no mortal danger will present itself on the route to the right, no lives will be saved by quickly dashing through the one to the left, you are not allergic to spiders, and so on) should you change direction and bear to the right? The issues I mean to raise here are *ethical* ones: Would you be morally obligated to consider anything more than your own interests in this situation? Is there anything else morally relevant to be considered? A spider's web is indeed a remarkable structure, and one is tempted to credit its builder with humanlike ingenuity and cunning. Nevertheless, is it possible that something as alien from us, as primitive and "icky" as a mere spider, may possess morally relevant interests and a right that those interests be counted in our deliberations?

Many in the modern West will consider such questions absurd on their face. While Eastern mystics and sentimental children may muse about the moral claims of animals and insects, it is not a project one expects to occupy the Rational Mind. Nonetheless, the attempt to understand our relationship to other animals has been a universal concern among human cultures, and it raises fundamental philosophical questions that have been debated throughout the history of Western thought. Moreover, as students of applied ethics know, the past thirty years have seen fresh efforts among Western philosophers and other scholars to clarify the moral standing proper to nonhuman life forms and an intense debate over the moral evaluation of our treatment of animals. One result of this recent debate is a growing consensus that moral concern for animals cannot be dismissed out of hand. Many ethicists now contend that such concern is philosophically legitimate, and some, including philosopher Bernard Rollin (an important figure in this debate whose work is analyzed in detail in Chapter 5), argue that it should not be limited to other primates and mammals, but must extend even to animals as far removed from us as spiders:

> It is enough that we, as moral agents, can sensibly assert that the spider has interests, which are conditions without which the creature, first of all, cannot live or, second of all, cannot live its life as a spider, cannot fulfill its *telos*. And thirdly . . . it is necessary that we can sensibly say of the animal that it is *aware* of its struggle to live its life, that the fulfilling or thwarting of its needs *matter* to it . . . Further we are aware that it is in our power to nurture or impede these needs and even to destroy the entire nexus of needs and activities that constitute its life. And once this is recognized it is difficult to see why the entire machinery of moral concern is not relevant here.[1]

From those thinkers who concur with Rollin that our treatment of animals is an appropriate matter for moral evaluation, there has come a barrage of arguments to challenge the concepts of animals that have been dominant in Western cultures: the religious concept of animals as part of the *human dominion;* the legal concept of animals as *property;* the economic concepts of wild animals as a *resource* and of domestic animals as live*stock*—all of which presuppose the ethical judgment that animals cannot be the direct objects of moral duties because they exist as mere *means* to human ends. Such arguments frequently employ the claim that if nonhumans possess morally relevant interests and capacities—including analogs to human sentience, cognitive ability, and subjectivity—then our traditional ways of conceiving the animal rest on arbitrarily anthropocentric metaphysical and ethical foundations. This premise is both philosophically and practically significant, for once granted it would seem to follow that the systematic—and generally accepted—exploitation of animals is in need of serious moral reevaluation.

And contemporary efforts toward practical reform are indeed in evidence. While to my knowledge animal activism has yet to take the form of advocacy for arachnids, the familiar humane societies that date back to the 1800s have multiplied and taken novel forms in the past several years, reflecting a growing desire to make our moral machinery produce practical benefits for animals. This is seen not only in efforts to promote the welfare of farm animals and experimental subjects, but in such radical and overtly political movements as the Great Ape Project, which works internationally toward the goal of establishing legal personhood for nonhuman primates. Indeed, Rollin entertains the prospect of a new "monkey trial" in which the extension of legal rights to our closest relatives could be put to the test in dramatic fashion.[2] Nineteenth-century British laws criminalizing animal cruelty are modest compared to the body of animal law that is growing in Western democracies today. In the United States, there are continuing efforts by animal advocates to strengthen established legal protections for laboratory animals (codified in the 1967 Animal Welfare Act), and extend them to pets, zoo specimens, and the like; in Sweden, Switzerland, the Netherlands, New Zealand, and Australia one finds even more progressive animal legislation in place. All told, it seems that startling changes in our thinking about animals are under way.

Nonetheless, one cannot deny that on today's "animal farm" some animals are still more equal than others. On the level of practice, even while the "humane" treatment of domesticated animals is discussed as seriously today as ever, their systematic exploitation is still ubiquitous; and although much attention is paid to the plight of endangered wild species, there seems to be little will for the radical economic and cultural changes that would be necessary to ward off further extinctions. Likewise on the level of theory, while the issue of the moral status of animals has gained legitimacy, few ethicists today embrace as strong an animal-advocating stance as Rollin. Indeed, the recent debate is an active one because several thinkers have offered to defend the West's tradition of moral and intellectual anthropocentrism, including its refusal to extend genuine moral attention to nonhumans. Those who try to make this case will note the obvious and important differences between humans and nonhumans: as marvelous as other creatures may be, they do not exhibit the type or degree of deliberative reasoning, emotional complexity, and responsible agency that defines humans as self-reflective moral persons. Further, since our interests will inevitably conflict with those of other species, some will argue that human stewardship over animals is necessary for our own well-being. Few in this school will deny that there are grounds for affording sentient animals humane treatment, and most who persist in conceiving of the nonhuman world as a resource nonetheless recognize a duty to see to its wise use. But, they insist, to accommodate animals with the type of treatment that morality dictates we owe our fellow humans is a sign of ethical and political confusion that may be detrimental to humanity's own moral situation. As political philosopher Tibor Machan argues, "animals have no rights and need no liberation . . . To think that they do is a category mistake—it is, to be blunt, to unjustifiably anthropomorphize animals, to treat them as if they were what they are not, namely, human beings."[3]

## Objectives of the Present Analysis

This recent debate over animals and their possible claim to our moral attention, now in its fourth decade, is well established. But while it has caught the attention of many, both within and without academic philosophy, its value and importance has yet to be investigated fully. Ostensibly, its value lies with its practical effects, and will be found by determining what light it has shed on our duties to animals. However, there is also a broader theoretical issue that is raised by the debate: What exactly are we seeing when we examine the menagerie of moral arguments the debate has produced, and what does its presence today mean for philosophy and the culture at large? This book offers an analysis of the debate with a view to addressing both the practical and the theoretical concerns. I will not be presenting my own arguments for or against ethical vegetarianism or the use of animals in scientific research. Instead, I here attempt to retrace the grounds over which modern Western philosophers have been led in their hunt for the animal's proper moral standing. I focus on efforts to apply the major theories of Western ethical thought to our treatment of animals, examining both the principals in the recent debate and their predecessors among the major figures in the Western tradition. In addition, I make use of important perspectives from outside philosophy, including those of literary critic Marian Scholtmeijer, cognitive ethologist Donald Griffin, and ecologist Paul Shepard. In undertaking this analysis, I seek to make explicit the historical and philosophical backgrounds of the recent debate, to produce an assessment of the debate's results heretofore, and—what has been wanting in previous analyses of the debate—to offer an interpretation of what this phenomenon in Western ethical thought means for both philosophy and the animal. Let me elaborate on these objectives.

First, as will become clear over the following chapters, the philosophical, cultural, and biological histories that have been recalled in the debate are compelling narratives that are worthy of attention in their own right.

The breadth of information and speculation relevant to clarifying our relationship to the animal indicates that such clarity will not be had without undertaking a wide-ranging exploration of humanity's social and evolutionary origins, and ultimately of our place in the wider reality. Thus, it emerges from the debate that analyzing the moral standing of animals is neither a tertiary philosophical concern nor a passing fad; rather, it is a project that honors philosophy's essential mission to examine fundamental questions systematically. At a minimum, my analysis of this project establishes a relationship of mutual importance between philosophical thought and animal reality: metaphysics, epistemology, and philosophical anthropology have much to gain from a clarification of the animal's nature and its relationship to our own; and the current ecological crisis speaks to the need for philosophical reflection to inform our practices that affect other animals and their world. A principal objective of the present work is to convince those philosophers who may not have been moved to study the debate over animals to reconsider their inattention.

Second, while its philosophical implications are far reaching, the debate over animals is clearly of most direct significance for philosophical ethics. And this is so not only for the ingenious techniques of applied ethics that have been produced in the debate, but also for the more fundamental ethical questions that the debate raises. In analyzing the arguments in the debate, one may consider not only what they establish about the moral status of nonhuman animals, but also *what they reveal about the ethical theories they employ, and about ethics itself.* For the most part, these arguments are not the products of recent innovation in ethical theory, but rather the extension of standard frameworks of moral reasoning. As Rollin makes this point, "society has begun to 'remember' the extension of our consensus ethic for humans to animals . . . This has occurred by articulating the implicit, in an incremental fashion, rather than by imposition of radically new ideas totally discontinuous with our social-ethical assumptions."[4]

It therefore is reasonable to ask whether these arguments represent successes or failures for these assumptions. Do we emerge from this debate with clear and convincing prescriptive conclusions concerning our treatment of other species? Or are the results less impressive, providing more uncertainty than clarity, perhaps indicating cracks in their theoretical foundations? It is at very least a curiosity whether and to what extent nonhumans possess morally relevant properties, and how effectively our most prized ethical ideas can assimilate them. When we indulge this curiosity and leap to the otherness of the animal, what truths do we see in this mirror? What will their success or lack of success in clarifying the moral standing of nonhuman animals tell us about our ethical ideas, and about the human animals who depend on them? If thinkers like Rollin are correct and the exploitation of animals turns out to be unjustified, what will that say about the ethical models that have been used for so long to defend it?

Third, in searching for the answers to these questions, one finds that the debate over animals is an instructive instance of what Friedrich Nietzsche termed the *self-overcoming of morality*. Those in the debate who have argued for elevating the moral status of animals have done so largely on grounds that are relevant by the standards of traditional moral thought: if it can be objectively demonstrated that nonhumans possess morally relevant attributes, then rational consistency demands that they be granted commensurate moral respect. However, other thinkers have argued that the value of animal reality lies precisely in the fact that it transcends the boundaries of human civilization, and that therefore the appropriate evaluation of the animal cannot be accurately translated into the language of the standard ethical theories. The animal thus leads us down the following path: by the criteria of traditional ethical thought we are compelled to acknowledge that animals are to be valued as more than mere things; yet to the extent that this value cannot be adequately accommodated by traditional models, our pursuit of the animal requires that we explore alternative—perhaps extra- or post-ethical—forms of thinking. In this way, the animal highlights a connection between the canonical ethical thought of the West and its post-traditional critics, and in turn crystallizes the critical issues with which philosophy has been grappling for the past century. If traditional thought is forced to overcome itself, what lies on the other side of this overcoming is the challenge philosophy must face in the coming century. As I show, recent reflection on the animal sheds light on the direction this future thinking might take.

Let me be clear that my emphasis throughout this analysis is on breadth rather than depth. All the issues I touch on can and should receive more thorough treatment than I afford them here—in many cases they have. My goal is to highlight the importance of tracing the path that connects these issues; I make no pretense to bringing any of them to a firm resolution.

## Outline

My analysis proceeds in four parts. In Part I, I explore the historical and philosophical foundations to the recent debate over animals, and conclude that they provide a reasonable footing. While there are many cultural contingencies that have helped bring the animal to the attention of modern philosophers, I argue in Chapter 1 that there also are solid philosophical grounds for reflecting on animal reality. Such reflection is especially valuable for ethics; as I demonstrate, the question of the animal's proper moral standing provides an ideal test for an ethical theory. This is not to deny that substantive philosophical concerns shadow the extension of moral categories to the animal; in Chapter 2, I briefly survey these concerns and conclude that none is sufficiently strong to rob the recent debate of its meaningfulness.

In Part II, I survey several important arguments that have been offered in the debate. Since these arguments are, in the main, extensionist[5]—that is, attempts to extend traditional ethical ideas to cover our treatment of animals—I dedicate one chapter to each of four major theories in Western ethical thought: utilitarianism (Chapter 3), deontological rights theory (Chapter 4), Aristotelian ethics (Chapter 5), and contractarianism (Chapter 6). I do not purport to produce an exhaustive analysis of the individual arguments, but instead use them to assess what their underlying ethical theories imply for the animal. There is, of course, a wide variety of practices that involve animals, and the moral evaluation of each raises unique challenges. For the purpose of testing these ethical theories, I focus on what the arguments that employ them can establish concerning two institutionalized forms of animal exploitation: the use of animals for food (the most common) and the use of animals in medical and other scientific research (the most vaunted).

In Part III, I address a tension that emerges between the first two parts of the work. If the argument in Part I is sound, then it is incumbent on an adequate ethical theory to accommodate the proper valuation of the animal. But as I argue in Chapter 7, a review of the arguments analyzed in Part II suggests that none of the theories they employ succeeds at this task. While these theories are able to accommodate common moral intuitions about animals, and to establish that humans have at least some moral duties to nonhumans, none produces a completely adequate assessment of animal exploitation per se, especially in the context of domestication in which much of it occurs. Thus, we are forced to choose between the animal and the good: Do we heed the animal's demand for attention, or do we remain allied to the traditional ethical models that are unable to answer this call? I argue that the results of twentieth-century continental thought (Chapter 8) and ecophilosophical thought (Chapter 9) make a strong case for the former: these apparently disparate movements are allied in associating respect for the animal with a broader critique of the Western tradition. From these perspectives the value of the animal lies with its ability to illuminate the broader reality left unthought by traditional systems. Thus, extensionist attempts to subsume the animal within such systems are necessarily inadequate: by valuing only those aspects of animal reality that can be assimilated to human civilization, they thereby obscure the path to other cultural possibilities along which the animal can lead us.

Finally, in Part IV I explore what the preceding analysis implies for the relationship between human culture and animality. Making use of the critiques of civilization offered by Nietzsche and ecologist John Livingston, I argue in Chapter 10 that since our ethical theories are most successful at addressing those animals that are assimilable to domestic civilization, these theories are inherently linked to the processes of domestication themselves.. If the extensionist approach is unable to clarify the systematic exploitation of animals, it may be because in extending moral respect to animals it simultaneously binds them to what deconstructionist Jacques Derrida terms the "sacrificial structures" designed to justify their exploitation. The search for a cultural framework in which animality is valued as something more than the material for domestication leads to a conclusion that may strike some as paradoxical. As I explore in Chapter 11, diverse thinkers have made the case that such authentic appreciation of animals is to be found in hunting cultures—which institutionalize human participation in the world of the animal—and not in the peaceable vision of the humane animal advocate. Yet, no matter how compelling this case is, practical considerations make the replication of the hunter's world an improbable fantasy. I propose that constructing a viable surrogate may require a suspension of the ethical in favor of the aesthetic. In recent artwork, as well as our informal aesthetic intuitions, the animal is left free to act upon us, and to impel us to explore the wider reality that lies beyond the comforts of domesticated civilization. Cultural institutions built around this power, rather than the alleged rights of nonhumans, are needed to do full justice to the place of animals in our world.

## PART I

*Foundations of the
Recent Debate*

# I  *Why Care about Animals?*

## *The Uses of the Animal*

As outlined in the Introduction, this work is an analysis of the attention Western philosophy has paid to the issue of the moral standing of animals. In this chapter, I address the question of why the nature of animals and their possible claim to our moral attention constitute a topic worthy of philosophical exploration. The path to answering this question begins with an intriguing thought experiment proposed by medievalist Dorothy Yamamoto: "Suppose (in a parallel universe) *Homo sapiens* was the only animate species on a planet. What sense of their 'humanity' would the people on that planet have?"[1]

Yamamoto's query brings attention to the fact that interaction with other animals has been a constitutive part of the human species' entire history, in spite of some persistent efforts to stress the distance between humans and nonhumans. Worked, farmed, and hunted, the animal has always provided human beings with material benefits. But as recorded culture bears witness—from Paleolithic cave art to twenty-first-century science—the animal also has always fascinated the human mind. The world's mythological, religious, and literary traditions are steeped in our ancestors' attempts to understand and define this mysterious other. To this day, human iconography is pervaded by animal themes: we see them in the constellations, inscribe them on our children's toys, invoke them in the names of our athletic teams and social clubs, and use them for hundreds of idioms in every language. Invariably, throughout its various cultural manifestations, humanity has incorporated its relationships with other species into its understanding of itself and the world. Thus, while Yamamoto terms her question "unanswerable," one plausible response (to be defended later in this chapter) is that a humanity unconnected to other animate life would not be recognizably human.

Understanding *why* humans are so bound to other animals proves to be challenging. An appeal to biological need will not settle the matter. Strictly speaking, few humans in the developed world today *need* to use animals for sustenance; indeed, in the Information Age it seems anachronistic to rely upon animals for material goods. Nonetheless, in the West alone billions of animals are still slaughtered every year for food, the fur and leather industries are booming, and hunting and fishing (and other blood-sports, such as cock-fighting) continue to attract a following. Even allowing that the exploitation of animals is still a material necessity in some societies, the relationships between humans and other animals are rarely comparable to those exhibited between other species. In the modern world there are very few extant hunting cultures, so the human/animal dynamic is only infrequently analogous to a predator's pursuit of prey. Likewise, scavenging and parasitism are occasionally practiced by humans (carrion is in some quarters an accepted food source, and some herding peoples bleed rather than slaughter their stock), but they are not typical of human beings' general comportment toward the animals they use.

The uniquely human manner of relating to other animals through *domestication*—the context in which much of our contact with other animals occurs today—is occasionally analogized to symbiosis, inasmuch as most domesticated animals receive their sustenance from the humans who use them. But in truly symbiotic relationships there is a roughly equal exchange of benefit, which is something either impossible to assess or clearly lacking in our use of draught animals, pets, and agricultural livestock. Indeed, the very nature of domestication—the attempt *to make the animal our own*, to transmute animal reality into *a creature of our own design*—is emblematic of the fact that something more than material need and desire is at work in our use of animals. The exploitation of the animal provides a perennial source of *meaning* for human cultures, where the animal functions as an object with as much symbolic psychological value as material use-value.

For example, when Native American peoples fight against environmentalists and government bureaucrats for the right to hunt whales or other endangered species, doubtless they are seeking something more than an efficient means of meeting their protein requirements. Likewise, one suspects that the derision with which animal advocates are often met indicates something besides the preference most persons have for the taste of beef over soy, or the feel of fur over polyester. Human beings certainly desire the various material goods that animals provide, but the use of animals as the means to these pleasures is itself enjoyed as a good. As literary critic Marian Scholtmeijer argues, human exploitation of the animal "is in all likelihood foundational to culture and civilization";[2] as a result, the continued use of the animal gives expression to drives that are deeply embedded in culture and perhaps human consciousness itself, and which therefore will resist both pragmatic and morally based efforts to displace them.

The author and critic Maureen Duffy explains this phenomenon by asserting that "we have always used animals not simply for practical purposes but as *metaphors for our own emotional requirements*, and it's this that we are unwilling to give up by considering them as creatures with rights and lives of their own."[3] However, while we may try to justify the practical use of animals by noting their otherness, the exploitation of the animal cannot be *psychologically* effective in the way Duffy describes if its existence is completely alien; the consideration that animals *do* have lives of their own must always shadow the exploitation. That the animals we use must therefore be other-than-human but also similar-to-human is seen in many examples that underscore how thoroughly ambiguous our relationship with animals is. As philosopher Mary Midgley notes concerning the domestication of animals, exploitation *requires* sympathy: one cannot successfully elicit the desired compliance of another animal without recognizing and exploiting its innate sociality and subjectivity.[4] Critic René Girard sees this complex emotional connection between humans and domesticates as pointing toward an improbable explanation of the institution of animal domestication itself: namely, that it arose not out of material necessity, but rather the psychological requirements of religious sacrifice. For a sacrifice to be effective, the sacrificial victims must be similar to the sacrificer, and so the animals to be offered first had to spend time assimilating with the human tribe.[5] If this explanation is highly speculative, Girard's point nonetheless finds resonance in the modern sacrifice of animals for the sake of science: medical—especially psychiatric—research involving animals is dogged by the inherent dilemma that the validity of its results and the moral questionableness of its practice are both proportional to the physiological and psychological proximity of the research animals to human beings.

Whether sacrificed or made to perform, subjected to our noblest experiments or our whims, animals are thus not simply used as material media but also as institutionalized victims—the *workhorse*, the *scape-goat*, the *guinea pig*—a role they can fill only *if they are capable of being victimized*. Witness such spectacles as the bullfight, the rodeo, and the circus: the sense of conquest humans feel in the death, defeat, or dispiriting of the animal depends on the prospect that the animal can *feel* our victory and its own loss. But if it is possible in this way to assimilate the animal with our own emotional experiences, then our use of the animal—both practically and psychologically—can never be one-dimensional, but must reflect the full complexity of our own affective lives. The human hunter tracks the animal as prey, but is also known to respect the animal as a compeer; in totemic cultures animals are sacrificed and eaten, even while they are considered ancestral kin worthy of piety; and if the farmer perceives the wild animal as an enemy to be vanquished, it is only in the context of domestication that there arises the institution of companion animals that are treated as objects of affection. In the animal world we find metaphors for the full range of human emotion.

Functioning in this capacity as emotional metaphor—and being both related to us yet different—the animal emerges as an *empathetic* object. As cognitive ethologist Donald Griffin argues: "We are challenged by the very difficulties of putting oneself in the skin of another animal, but we are also searching for empathy, a consideration that has not received nearly the attention it deserves. We like and admire other animals to a considerable extent because we enjoy trying to imagine what their lives are like *to them* . . . This curiosity forms a continuum with the desire to understand people of different cultures whose lives differ from ours. In both cases it is a fundamental, and I believe significant, impulse to try to put ourselves in other shoes, or skin."[6]

But such curiosity is not simply a matter of idle enjoyment. Just as the different lives led by other humans shed light on the contingencies of our own, the different reality occupied by the animal provides a valuable mirror in which to view *our humanity*. In addition to fulfilling our material desires and emotional needs, the ability of animals to illuminate human reality and its relationship to the broader world underlies our inter-specific connection. As Scholtmeijer argues, animals can cement this link because they "provide a stance outside of culture from which culture may look at itself."[7] Art critic Steve Baker adds that animals—especially wild animals—being in themselves free of mythology and ideology, exist in "*unmeaning thereness*": an objective and unmediated perspective on reality that operates independently of the meanings with which culture is comfortable.[8] Thus, while the otherness of animals is often cited to justify their material exploitation, the most philosophically interesting uses of animals take advantage of their objective, extra-cultural nature as the means to human self-understanding.

## The Ambiguous Mirror

At first, the suggestion that the animal can offer "objective" insight into our human selves may elicit a skeptical response. If Scholtmeijer and Baker are correct in identifying the animal's proper domain as a kind of extra-cultural space, will culturally constituted human beings be able to appreciate that reality? When we stare into the eyes of the wild animal, are we capable of deciphering what is reflected back without corrupting its message? Rather than functioning as a reflective mirror, is it not inevitable that the animal must serve as a receptive canvas on which humans will inscribe their own meanings? If so, in the animal we are likely to find confirmation of our established self-concepts, and not a source of new truths. Consider, for example, the depiction of animals in myths, fables, and cartoons: enmeshed in thoroughly human situations, living out human anxieties and hopes. There the concerns of human civilization are projected onto the nonhuman world, and the animal—far from providing a critical view of culture—is exploited precisely as the vehicle for *naturalizing culture*.[9] The same may be said of our treatment of real animals: witness circus animals trained to caricature human behaviors, or the spectacle of pets sporting coiffed hair and clothing. Such absurd situations have the effect of ascribing to animals desires and attitudes that simply reinforce those of their human spectators, and are only infrequently appreciated for the satirical perspective they might provide (as, for example, in the photography of William Wegman).

While these objections dovetail with the preceding discussion of the psychological usefulness of the animal, it does not follow from them that for human beings the animal can never be more than a domesticated construct. Such a conclusion is militated against by the fact that, in addition to occupying a place outside of culture, animals (at least some) may also be said to occupy a *perspective*—a consciousness, a way of life, a form of subjectivity that contrasts with our own—and this renders them more resistant than other natural entities to the meanings that human beings may project upon them. Although the recognition of this fact by no means guarantees that humans can leap out of culture and assume the animal's perspective as a source of objective insight, history demonstrates that cultural institutions have embodied varying degrees of receptivity to that possibility. Griffin's analogy to human cultural interaction is instructive: some cultures are overtly racist (leading to genocide), some are more mildly xenophobic (emphasizing assimilation), and some embrace diversity as a source of enrichment; likewise, some cultures overtly practice misothery (leading to extinction), some are more mildly anthropocentric (emphasizing domestication), and some embrace the animal as a source of enrichment—creating institutions that honor the animal's perspective on the broader reality beyond the confines of human culture, and the insight into human existence it can make possible.

Thus, we find that the reflexive quality to our experience of the animal has been institutionalized in various ways as a source of human self-understanding. Historically, the most animal-embracing institutions are found in pre-agricultural societies. For example, in totemic cultures the animal is institutionalized as ancestral kin, and different clans identify with different totem species; in this way, human self-identity is effected precisely by means of identification with the animal world. Likewise, in various hunting cultures, assuming the animal's perspective is made a lived experience through the religious ritual of *metamorphosis*. During the sun dance of the Oglala of North America, for example, the ecstatic participants cut and impale themselves while dressed as various animals: the hunters thereby embody the vulnerability of their prey, a bond that forcibly alerts them to *their own* animality and the physical mortality that it includes.[10] Moving beyond simple empathy, such metamorphic ecstasis suggests an inter-specific example of the type of radical objectivity that anthropologist Clifford Geertz describes in this way: "To see ourselves as others see us can be eye-opening. To see others as sharing a nature with ourselves is the merest decency. But it is from the far more difficult achievement of seeing ourselves amongst others, as a local example of the forms human life has locally taken, a case among cases, a world among worlds, that the largeness of mind, without which objectivity is self-congratulation and tolerance a sham, comes."[11]

Images of metamorphosis pervade the world's body of myth and fable, but in post-agricultural societies such inter-specific allegories are more likely to affirm the primacy of human culture than the "largeness of mind" that would see human existence as but a "local example" of animal life. In ancient Western mythology, for example, the transformation of human into animal is often presented as a fitting punishment for reprehensible conduct: the God of the Hebrew Bible turns the prideful Nebuchadnezzar into an ox, Arachne's arrogance causes Athena to turn her into a spider, and so on. Yet in later Western literature the metamorphic "leap into otherness" occasionally emerges as a critical tool for exploring what it means to be human; the animal mask serves to unmask, bringing into acute focus a human characteristic more easily discerned in another species.[12] And in post-agricultural societies, more profound possibilities exist for the phenomenon of becoming-animal. For example, as the poststructuralist critics Giles Deleuze and Felix Guattari offer in their interpretation of Franz Kafka's use of metamorphic themes, the transformation into animality can complete a *deterritorialization* of human reality, a collapse of the hierarchical boundaries between culture and nature.[13] Thus, even though the juxtaposition of human and animal is often used to reinforce culturally useful meanings, the non-symbolic, non-metaphorical, asignifying perspective of the animal may also be used to illuminate the limitedness of human culture and meaning per se, and thereby point toward the broader extra-cultural reality.

These various attempts to exploit the animal's perspective demonstrate that the usefulness of animals is not exhausted by the material and emotional needs they can serve. Whether to confirm the superiority of human beings or to shatter that hubris, humans have perennially turned to the point of view of the animal in order to complete their anthropological conceptions. That this reflexive dimension is fundamental to the relationship between humans and other animals is suggested by *biophilic* thought, which holds that we are drawn to animals because experience of them was essential to the evolution of human consciousness and intelligence.[14] As ecologist Paul Shepard makes the case, "there is a profound, inescapable need for animals that is in all people everywhere, an urgent requirement for which no substitute exists. It is no vague, romantic, or intangible yearning, no simple sop to our loneliness or nostalgia for Paradise . . . Animals are among the first inhabitants of the mind's eye. They are basic to the development of speech and thought. Because of their part in the growth of consciousness, they are inseparable from a series of events in each human life, indispensable to our becoming human in the fullest sense."[15] Shepard defends these assertions by arguing that what we take to be distinctive in our human consciousness has its evolutionary origin in the minds of early omnivorous primates who moved from the forests to the plains. These beings required a synthesis of the consciousness of the plains predator—which must recognize the otherness of prey species—and the consciousness of the arboreal primate—a highly social being that defines itself in terms of its social relations to others.[16] This combination of intelligences in our early ancestors allowed them to appreciate other animals as both objects and subjects—as *related others*. This in turn made possible what we value today as *self-consciousness*, for these hominids found in their images of other animals concrete objects that *reflected parts of themselves*.[17] Thus, Shepard concludes, the ecology of the animal world is the irreplaceable archetype for the "ecology" of the world of the human mind.[18]

All anthropological theories of human evolution are necessarily speculative to some degree, and I do not propose to offer an exhaustive defense of the biophilic approach. Nonetheless, I believe the suggestion that the human capacity for self-understanding is dependent on animals—ambiguous related-others—is a philosophically compelling one, in part because of the plausible explanation it provides for the reflexive nature of our experience of the animal. If human consciousness was formed in the presence of other animals, we will inevitably be drawn in empathy toward the otherness of the nonhuman animal; from this objective perspective we have the opportunity to achieve a valuable type of self-awareness. Herein lies the key to Yamamoto's thought experiment: what makes *Homo sapiens* on her imaginary planet so unthinkable is that it would be deprived of this source of self-understanding, and its members might well have *no* sense of their own "humanity"—such as it would be—so vital is this connection between human and animal.

Because the biophilic explanation of this reflexive relationship plays upon both the otherness *and* the relatedness of the animal, it predicts what has indeed been the case: that our attempts to conceive our relationships with other animals in rational terms, and to define the correlative concepts of *animality* and *humanity*, have been on the whole uneasy. If the biophilic explanation is correct, a simplistic categorical separation of human and animal—the deconstruction of which has been central to the recent debate over the moral standing of animals—cannot stand. Indeed, despite the ubiquitous animal presence in our thought and culture, and the conviction with which certain conceptions of animals have been held, a shadow of uncertainty has followed the relationship between humans and animals. As philosopher José Ortega y Gasset asserts: "Man has never really known exactly what an animal is. Before and beyond all science, humanity sees itself as something emerging from animality, but it cannot be sure of having transcended that state completely. The animal remains too close for us not to feel mysterious communication with it."[19]

Such agnosticism is tempting, yet if adopted uncritically it risks obscuring the very ambiguity to which it speaks: if it is impossible to know the true nature of the animal, then human beings may feel free to attribute to animals any meaning or value they choose. Scholtmeijer rightly criticizes that position for too easily serving as an excuse not to examine the morality of our treatment of animals;[20] indeed, she argues, the opposite conclusion is perhaps more justified: "The less secure we are in our conceptions of animals, the more hazardous it becomes to victimize them."[21] If so, an appreciation of the ambiguity and complexity of our relationships with animals makes the exploration of their moral status a necessity.

## Why Now?

This exploration has a long history in the West. As philosopher and classicist Richard Sorabji has demonstrated, the philosophical questions that surround the moral standing of animals—which largely have involved identifying and evaluating morally significant features of animal consciousness—were actively debated among the ancient Greeks and Romans.[22] Nonetheless, most philosophers in the Western tradition followed Aristotle in denying any direct moral standing to animals, by virtue of a presumed moral gulf between rational and non-rational beings. Aristotle held that the animal exists as the natural slave of the human,[23] and many subsequent thinkers conceived of animals as means to human ends with no possible moral claims of their own. Thus, in the West the animal has typically fallen under the scope of moral concern only indirectly: for example, because of the possible moral lessons that may be gleaned from looking at animal behavior, or because treating animals as if they were moral objects better prepares humans to fulfill their moral duties to each other.[24]

Of course, there have been exceptions to the rule—notably, Pythagoras and Porphyry in the ancient world, Hume, Rousseau, and Schopenhauer among the moderns—and very few have embraced the counterintuitive Cartesian position that animals are mere machines that humans may dispose of however they see fit. Still, it is only in the modern era—most important, among the English thinkers of the eighteenth and nineteenth centuries—that there emerges a sustained attempt by Western philosophers to develop a coherent alternative to the Aristotelian understanding of the relationship between humans and animals. As noted in the Introduction, the results of these efforts for recent applied ethics have included various attempts to articulate direct moral duties to animals—from modest animal welfarism, which holds that humans have a duty to improve the quality of life for the animals we exploit, to more radical attempts to reevaluate animal exploitation per se. Because this recent concern for the possible moral claims of animals contrasts so sharply with the dismissive posture that has characterized much of the Western tradition, we must ask what accounts for this dramatic change. Is this recent attention merely a "fashionable piety" that will evaporate with cultural change,[25] a psychologically and politically perverse indulgence,[26] or are substantial philosophical matters involved? A brief look at some of the cultural transformations of the past three centuries will shed light on these matters.

Among other reasons, the debate over animals is significant in that it represents what philosophers Paola Cavalieri and Peter Singer describe as "an encounter between ethology and ethics," and so stands as a clear example of how philosophy may be enriched by natural science.[27] Specifically, it reminds us that while prescriptive ethical disputes cannot be settled simply by appeal to our descriptive knowledge of the world, neither should they be insulated from it. Philosopher Martin Heidegger's caution against an "over-sophisticated" philosophy that would refuse to give attention to the facts that science reveals well applies to the debate over animals, where the modern sciences of biology, ethology, animal psychology, and ecology have much to add.[28] Of obvious importance in this regard is evolutionary biology, with its declaration of the continuity and common descent of species—*Homo sapiens* included. It is no exaggeration that "every philosophical problem appears in a new light after the Darwinian revolution,"[29] and the problem of the moral status of animals more so than others. Once it becomes evident that the taxonomic gulf between humans and other animals is neither as clear nor as wide as was traditionally held in the West, then the traditional moral distinctions made between the interests of humans and those of animals also become murky and demand clarification.

It is no surprise, then, that one finds a flurry of writings in the nineteenth century on the moral status of animals. However, there were many in the eighteenth as well, which indicates that Darwinism was not a solitary force in this movement.[30] Within biological science, Darwin certainly had eighteenth-century forerunners (e.g., Pierre Louis Moreau de Maupertuis and Georges Buffon); continuity—although not natural selection or common descent—was already a popular scientific concept in the eighteenth century, and Henry Salt finds continuity-type arguments for reevaluating animal exploitation as early as Bernard de Mandeville's *Fable of the Bees* (1723).[31] Outside the realm of science, we find that there were other intellectual forces at work prior to the eighteenth century that collaborated with the emergence of evolutionary biology. For example, literary scholar Alan Rudrum argues that a theological debate, active in sixteenth- and seventeenth-century England, over whether God's nonhuman creatures are restored along with humans through the incarnation of Christ was an important precursor to subsequent discussion of ethical vegetarianism.[32] The art world of this period also played a role: a powerful shift in seventeenth-century England opened new types of aesthetic appreciation for the natural world—a sense of the *picturesque* and the *sublime*—which presaged the Romanticism of the eighteenth and nineteenth centuries.[33] Clearly, Darwinism was part of a larger intellectual reassessment of the nature of nonhuman reality.

As Scholtmeijer argues, this rethinking was able to attain moral significance because of some important social factors of the eighteenth century.[34] Most especially, before Darwin the Agricultural and Industrial Revolutions created a surge in urbanization, and in turn unprecedented physical, mental, and technological distance between humans and wild animals. No longer a pressing threat to human safety, the animal thus becomes a more likely object of empathy for citizens of industrialized societies. That the Industrial Revolution first took hold in England may explain why ethical arguments opposing the exploitation of animals have been advanced largely by English-speaking philosophers. It may also account for the humane ethic that Ortega derides as "English zoophilia."[35] It is noteworthy that the modern practice of pet keeping may be traced to eighteenth- and nineteenth-century England; no doubt this familiarity with household animals helped inspire the creation of animal advocacy groups, which also originated in nineteenth-century England.[36] Add to this social reality the Enlightenment sensibility that suffering is not only a concern for theology but also for concrete political action—a concept reflected in the advent of rights theory[37]—and the ground for Darwin's impact on the ethics and politics of our treatment of other animals was well prepared. Thenceforth, one finds emotional and aesthetic objections to vivisection and other forms of animal exploitation supplemented by rational philosophical argument with increasing frequency and intensity.

The latter half of the twentieth century further cultivated this ground with some relevant social factors of its own. David Sztybel notes the importance of the various human liberation movements that evolved in the West, whose momentum may arguably have made the cause of animal liberation inevitable.[38] The point is an important one because some (e.g., Jeremy Bentham, Richard Ryder, and Peter Singer—all discussed in Chapter 3) have argued that the logic of animal exploitation is analogous to that of racism and sexism; it is perhaps not coincidental that in oppressive human societies, targeted groups are often the victims of derisive comparisons to other animals. Additionally, Sztybel identifies the greater documentation of widespread and ostensibly cruel practices involving animals; Ruth Harrison's exposé of factory farming, *Animal Machines* (1964), and Richard Ryder's *Victims of Science* (1975) are important examples. Philosopher Harlan B. Miller argues that the coincidental prominence of the abortion issue helped make space for the moral consideration of animals because the moral status of the human conceptus and the moral status of nonhuman animals are both meaningfully debatable only to the extent that it is possible to separate moral and legal personhood from genetic humanity.[39] Miller also notes the rise of the environmental movement, which invites moral concern for the whole range of nonhuman reality, animals included.

However, in addition to such cultural contingencies, both Sztybel and Miller acknowledge the fundamental importance of recent advances in scientific knowledge. Just as the culture of the eighteenth century paved the way for Darwin, the cultural transformations of the twentieth century prepared the ground for the social and philosophical impact of contemporary revolutions in biology. First, one must acknowledge the importance of recent developments in neuroscience and the understanding of the human brain. While the lack of a predictive psychology or a completely effective psychopharmacology is evidence that this field is still in its infancy, what progress it has made in understanding the genetic and biochemical influences on human behavior and thought pushes forward the case that the definitive features of human consciousness may have biological rather than transcendent foundations. That the mind may be explainable in purely natural terms forces us to rethink categorical distinctions between humans and other animals that are based on anthropological dualism (discussed further in Chapter 2), and adds weight to the argument for continuity with respect to morally relevant psychological and intellectual properties.

Second, and more important, is our expanding knowledge of animal physiology and psychology, and the blossoming of *ethology* as a science. Early in the twentieth century, Heidegger encouraged biologists to "restore autonomy to 'life,' as the *specific manner of being pertaining to animal and plant*," to appreciate life "as something that cannot be explained or grasped at all in physico-chemical terms," and thereby free the biological sciences from "the tyranny of physics and chemistry."[40] One may argue that this objective was fulfilled later in the century with the work of ethological researchers, who followed Konrad Lorenz in focusing on the behavior of wild animals in their natural context. In addition to providing exciting details of sophisticated animal behaviors—details that advance the principle of species continuity further still—this research invites an understanding of animals on terms appropriate to their own natures.[41]

The need for this ethological insight is underscored by the fact that our thinking about animals is often shaped by our familiarity with domesticated species, which is hardly an adequate foundation for understanding animality in general. The dog, for example, is often used in casual discussions of the nature of animals, cited as embodying remarkable, humanlike qualities, or, alternatively, as exemplifying animal ineptness. However, the modern dog is the product of millennia of interaction with humans, and thus is more informative of the process of domestication than of the nature of wild canids. Likewise, the environment and needs of other domesticated animals are so controlled as to eliminate the potential for genuine animality to surface.[42] As Paul Shepard argues, household and agricultural domesticates are so behaviorally and physically debased compared to their wild counterparts that they can only belie the true nature of the animal. Under conditions of domestication, he writes,

> the animal ceases to be an adequate representation of a natural life form. Its debased behavior and appearance mislead us and miseducate us in fundamental perceptions of the rhythms of continuity and discontinuity, and of the specific patterns of the multiplicity of nature. Interpretations of this debauched ecology were formulated for civilization by its "educated" members. Effete dabblers from the city looked over the barnyard fence at the broken creatures wallowing and copulating in their own dung, and the concept of the bestial brute with untrammeled appetites was born. This was the model for "the animal" in philosophy, "the natural" from which men, understandably, yearned for transcendent release.[43]

The science of ethology promises an alternative vision, replacing both anthropomorphic and anthropocentric conjectures about animal nature with a more objective insight. Of course, not all recent scientific thinking is so accommodating to Heidegger's entreaty: the behaviorism and reductionism of twentieth-century life science largely squelched the active scientific discussion of such topics as animal mentality that was inspired by Darwinism in the previous century.[44] As Donald Griffin writes, much of our recent science "has gradually slipped into an attitude that belittles nonhuman animals . . . Physical and chemical science is assumed to be more fundamental, more rigorous, and more significant than zoology. Modern biology revels in being largely molecular, and this inevitably diverts attention away from the investigation of animals for their own sakes."[45]

Griffin thus contrasts ethology with two other movements in modern biology that fail to address the animal as a whole: molecular biology, with its emphasis on biochemistry and genetics; and evolutionary biology, which seeks to uncover the adaptive value of particular structures and functions. It should be noted, however, that recent developments in these other movements also complicate the relative moral standing of humans and animals. First, the young science of genomics confirms our genetic relatedness not only to the higher primates but also to life forms as apparently different from us as mice, flies, worms, bacteria, and fungi, taking the argument for continuity in unexpected directions.[46] That this knowledge may undermine the exclusion of the animal from moral concern is an ironic result of a project that has been fuelled largely by the anthropocentric drive to control and manipulate other forms of life. Second, evolutionary psychology confirms the meaningfulness of continuity by attempting to make genuinely scientific inroads into the biology of human behavior. The results of this enterprise to date are hardly stellar, and there are still good reasons to respect the force of cultural evolution as something independent of deterministic biological principles; still, the promise remains that something more substantive than the social Darwinism of the nineteenth century may yet emerge from this work.

Nonetheless, it is only when combined with ethological observation that these insights of modern biology attain full moral relevance, for only then are we confronted with the whole animal, the subject of attributes that are of potential moral significance. This case is made by Bernard Rollin, who argues that ethological observation is effective at breeding sympathy, and thereby provides the means to actualizing genuine moral concern for the animal.[47] Of course, the subjective nature of sympathetic reactions leaves one vulnerable to deception; one may be moved to sympathy by cartoon animals, or machines that mimic animal behaviors, so it would be erroneous to infer an animal's appropriate moral standing from the sympathetic feelings it may evoke. However, there is a growing consensus among ethologists that something more stable than sympathetic feelings is to be gleaned from the careful observation of animals in their natural environments: the considered judgment that some animal behavior will be explained completely only by the attribution of cognitive ability and such morally relevant properties as self-awareness and pain-experience. This conclusion will be strongest in the case of our closest relatives, but as Griffin argues, it is not unthinkable that even insects and arachnids may possess something meaningfully describable as "consciousness."[48] As I explore further in Chapter 2, the evidence for such claims is of obvious importance for the philosophy of mind and ethics, revitalizes our understanding of other species, and has radical implications for our understanding of ourselves. Here we only need to note that the field of ethology is alluded to frequently in the recent debate over animals as a substantive source of inspiration.[49]

## A Challenge for Ethics

While the scientific and cultural trajectory of the past three centuries would seem to make the ethical analysis of the animal both important and inevitable, the skeptical may still opt for the "fashionable piety" explanation for the recent prominence of the issue. Two arguments that support this position deserve some attention. First, if the industrialization of the seventeenth century made it safe to empathize with the animal, such is even more so the case today when human conquest of the planet is exponentially greater. This conquest not only takes the form of ceaseless human encroachment into the wild and monopolization of natural resources, but also ceaseless scientific inquiry: the same biological advances we just noted—including the deciphering of some species' genetic codes—have served to rob the animal of some of its mystery and otherness, making even the wild animal seem tame. The extent of this demystification is reflected in recent popular culture, in which the fear of other species must find expression through the microscopic (the recent "germ phobia" over HIV, the Ebola virus, "mad cow disease," necrotizing fasciitis, etc.), the imaginary (aliens, monsters, vampires), and the manufactured (genetically engineered mutants of our own making). Those wild animals that are powerful enough to harm a human being are more likely to be portrayed sympathetically than menacingly, in part because their numbers have dwindled so at our hands. Indeed, the term *wild* is quite nearly an anachronism; *nature* has been so totally commodified that both its exploitation and conservation are packaged as marketable goods. The commodification of the animal defines the agriculture and pet industries, and will only increase with the further development of genetic engineering technology. In times past, voicing moral concern for the animal could rightly be viewed as a courageous act of conscience; in the present climate, it may instead represent the final stage in the humanization of the world, and nostalgia for an unrecoverable, innocent relationship with animals.[50]

There is another, more cynical sense in which the concern for animals is a "safe" expression of humanitarian zeal. While many obviously have vested psychological, political, and economic interests in the exploitation of animals, raising objections to exploitative practices is perhaps socially less explosive than other social causes can be. It has been argued that concern for animals was encouraged in the nineteenth century because it was more benign to the existing power structure than concern for human rights and economic justice.[51] A case could be made that something similar is at work today. In a world in which over 90 percent of the wealth is in the hands of less than 10 percent of the population, it may be less incendiary to express compassion for the animals skinned to make a fur coat than to voice outrage at the extravagance of someone owning one. As Jacques Derrida offers, the vegetarian may simply be seeking an expedient path to a peaceful conscience.[52]

One may respond to such arguments by setting aside transient cultural factors and inquiring into the debate over animals from a purely philosophical perspective. Do the questions surrounding our treatment of other species simply present us with intractable problems for applied ethicists to ruminate, or are these questions of more fundamental philosophical importance, with ramifications that affect ethics proper? There are, I believe, good reasons for accepting the latter. In addition to the scientific evidence for the continuity between humans and other animals, there are legitimate philosophical grounds for requiring that our ethical theories be able to clarify the moral status of nonhumans, and bring some conviction to the moral evaluation of our actions involving them. Indeed, several features of the moral questions raised by our treatment of animals indicate that this issue represents an ideal test for an ethical theory.

1. *This issue has obvious practical effects for virtually anyone who would consider it.* Ethics is not purely a theoretical science, but also a practical one, the conclusions of which concern real actions. Thus, in evaluating an ethical theory it is relevant to see how it will affect the practical conduct of our lives. Granted, this point generally will not be decisive; for example, an ethical ideal ought not to be abandoned simply because it may be difficult to live up to in practice. Still, given the ubiquity of animal exploitation, the issue of whether this exploitation is morally justifiable has obvious implications for innumerable actions and decisions we all undertake daily: what we eat and wear and purchase, which path we take in the woods, and quite generally how we conduct ourselves in the world. It clearly matters in very concrete terms whether animals are beings to which we have moral obligations, or things that we may work, experiment upon, kill and eat, or otherwise use as we see fit.

This contrasts sharply with other prominent moral controversies that occupy applied ethics. While a man's reflection on the morality of abortion may have some practical effects (on voting choices, responsibility for birth control, etc.), this reflection must always be somewhat theoretical because of the obvious facts of human biology. One's thoughts about euthanasia can also bear practical fruits (e.g., composing a "living will"), but for the young and healthy the real effects of their convictions are hidden by the indefinite future. In like manner, most of us may debate the justice of capital punishment protected by the statistical unlikelihood of ever having to participate directly in a capital case. For the vast majority of us, however, there is no such buffer to protect us from the implications of our thinking about animals. One would be justified in questioning the usefulness of an ethical theory that could not offer an unequivocal moral assessment of the common practices that involve them.

2. *This issue confronts us with strong, competing intuitions.* That a moral controversy will evoke "intuitions" or pre-reflective feelings and judgments is certainly not unique to the question of our treatment of animals, but it is noteworthy how frequently appeal is made to such extrarational considerations in the debate, and how sentiment and spirituality seem to shadow the philosophical discussion. As Alistair Gunn makes the point, the recent attention to nature ethics generally may amount to "a return to intuitionism, perhaps even a quasi-religious philosophical idealism."[53] What role, if any, intuitions should play in moral argument is a matter of some controversy, and at very least it seems clear that, as philosopher Annette Baier argues, moral theory should not merely systematize existing intuitions, but "deepen moral insight" and "correct moral error."[54] Nonetheless, neither can ethics simply ignore the practical reality that our moral judgments are often informed by pre-reflective intuitions. In the case of our judgments about the animal, two intuitions frequently surface. First, few (at least in the West) can deny having the sense that—whatever its justification—humans are simply more important than other species. None but the polemical will hesitate at hypothetical "lifeboat" choices between the life of a normal human being and that of a pig, and many only rarely feel the need even to consider the real effects of their actions on those animals that simply get in the way of their desires: the possum that crosses in front of the car, the cow whose flesh is craved, or the spider whose web blocks the path. But second, many also feel viscerally that animal suffering is something bad, and overt cruelty to animals is wrong—irrespective of ultimate reasons. We find ourselves shocked and repulsed by graphic descriptions of the use of

laboratory animals in toxicity tests and psychology experiments, or the conditions on factory farms and in slaughterhouses. Our guts tell us there is something wrong in such violence.[55]

While such sentiments are not necessarily mutually exclusive, they are often at the root of conflicting judgments about the moral worth of animals: the researcher who tests the toxicity of floor wax on caged rabbits and the animal activist who tries to free them obviously hold different feelings about animals.[56] More interesting is that contradictory intuitions about animals often are held simultaneously. For example, despite the efforts of animal advocates, most legal systems still categorize animals as right-less human property, yet criminalize their exposure to "unnecessary" pain and suffering.[57] Millions of pet owners in the West do not think twice about eating the flesh of animals just as emotionally and cognitively sophisticated as the cats and dogs they bathe with love and affection—and are repulsed by other cultures in which meat from dogs and horses is common fare.[58] And such oxymora as "wildlife management" reflect the often inseparable reactions of awe and disdain that arise when civilized humans confront the untamed world of nature.

As critic Steve Baker notes, these "contradictory and compromised" attitudes signal that most of us are content to live "inexpertly" with animals,[59] and so it falls to ethical theory to attempt a rational evaluation of our pre-reflective judgments. Baier makes the point well: "I see no point at all in having a moral theory unless it can serve to help us live together more successfully and, therefore, unless it *aims* at general acceptance . . . So I see as unavoidable the issue of how we can with good conscience discount the moral convictions of some of our fellows and adopt a theory that has implications they reject . . . Both to cure the instability and incoherence in my own beliefs and to attempt to face up to the real disagreement in the community of moral thinkers, I must raise the issue: When is there good reason to discount moral intuition, however recalcitrant and ineradicable it may be?"[60] It is therefore reasonable to expect an adequate ethical theory to either identify a rational ground for our most vivid moral intuitions and resolve any conflicts among them, or provide clear justification for excluding them from our moral deliberations. The case of animals provides an ideal test. Whose intuitions are correct: the vivisectionist's or the vegan's? Perhaps neither? If there is some truth to both, how much should they—and animals—count in our moral deliberations?

3. *We have sufficient knowledge to be able to reach at least some general conclusions.* Our knowledge of animal biology and psychology

is certainly not complete; as I discuss in the following chapter, there are inevitable limits to the understanding we can have of other animals' experience, and these in turn will limit the conviction with which we can hold certain moral judgments involving animals. Moreover, the exact nature of animate beings and their place within the universe is far from clear. The discovery of organisms in unexpected places on our planet (such as the upper limits of the atmosphere and the harshest depths of the ocean), and the detection of the precursors to organic compounds in places beyond support the hypothesis that life may be present throughout the universe, and may even be an inherent property of matter—a conclusion that might make moral attention to terrestrial animals a less compelling issue. Conversely, should the hypothesis that life is rare and perhaps unique to the earth prove correct, it could help to ground an obligation for humans to be "good shepherds" of other animals—although it might also reinvigorate humanity's pre-Copernican hubris.

These examples indicate that the debate over animals is not entirely free of epistemological and metaphysical imponderables; trying to define the boundary between animate and other beings, or between humans and other animals, may prove as intractable as the efforts in the abortion debate to pinpoint when the fetus attains moral personhood. Nonetheless, there is reason to expect that a resolution to the moral standing of at least some animals should be closer to hand. If our understanding of the animal per se is incomplete, we are certainly familiar enough with those species proximate to us and most frequently affected by our actions to address their moral relevance intelligently. We are doubtless in a better position to evaluate such institutions as animal husbandry and hunting than the very new issues raised by other bioethical questions, such as human cloning, genetic testing, and the like. While we may forgive an ethical theory that failed to navigate these uncharted waters, we should be less forgiving should it fail to produce clear and rational conclusions about practices that are cross-cultural and as old as civilization itself.

4. *Attention to animal ethics might illuminate other moral issues.* For example, Rollin argues that "realization that animals are not separated by ontological chasms from people might well help us to come up with a more rational, less tradition-bound approach to such human problems" as euthanasia and abortion, for it would encourage more biologically realistic interpretations of human life and death.[61] Of course, one should not expect consensus any time soon: philosopher Peter Singer's simultaneous support for abolishing animal exploitation and

legalizing physician-assisted euthanasia has drawn derision from the popular press and euthanasia opponents; likewise, abortion proponents are often critical of animal advocates, fearing that the arguments for extending moral consideration to nonhuman animals (which are not rational agents) might also imply a moral standing for the human fetus (which also is not a rational agent) that might mitigate a pregnant woman's right to self-determination.[62] Still, *if* agreement could be reached concerning what if any aspects of animal reality demand our moral attention, it could shed light on some human moral dilemmas, especially those involving so-called marginal cases, that is, human beings who are not moral agents, such as infants and the enfeebled.

5. *The need for a philosophical ground to social policy is especially pressing in the case of policies that concern the treatment of animals.* If philosophical ethics cannot completely resolve controversial moral issues, the policies a society adopts toward those issues may still gain some measure of moral legitimacy to the extent that they are products of a democratic political process—of course, only some measure, unless one is prepared to argue that majority opinion is the ultimate arbiter of right and wrong. However, this limited degree of moral legitimacy cannot be assumed in the case of policies that affect those who are not political agents, which is certainly the case with nonhuman animals. In other words, to assume the legitimacy of the (human) political process for handling animal interests is to beg the question of human priority, for in practice, as Gary Francione argues, this process will always work against the animal:

> There are important political dimensions that accompany our attempts to apply philosophical theories to "balance" animal interests against human interests. The philosophical "balancing" apparatus may be theoretically correct, but the process can almost never work fairly because of the political status of nonhumans. Animals are regarded as the property of humans, and incapable of having rights because they are property; similarly, humans have rights—and most notably, they have the right to own and use private property. In human/animal conflicts, the human is usually seeking to exercise property rights over the animal. In any "balancing" situation, the animal is almost always going to come out the loser. So the philosophy looks great, but the results are less than desirable.[63]

These facts place a greater onus on ethicists to form a clear understanding of the animal's appropriate moral status and how it compares to human interests and desires. To defer this issue to political venues is in effect to decide against the animal.

6. *Finally—and of most interest to the present analysis—the issue raises fundamental questions about the nature of ethics itself.* The traditional ethical models found in Western philosophy and theology have been premised on human uniqueness: the belief that as rational (perhaps ensouled) beings, humans have a putative value and destiny that surpass that of any other animal. Accordingly, ethics has been conceived as governing only behavior of and toward human beings—the very embodiment of anthropocentrism. To ask whether any nonhumans ought to be included in the moral community is to question both this premised human uniqueness and the conception of ethics that presupposes it. Scholtmeijer argues that genuine empathy for the animal goes hand in hand with skepticism at the value of those cultural and individual qualities traditionally taken to be definitively human.[64] If so, then—contrary to the conclusion of the preceding section—moral concern for the interests of animals emerges as more incendiary, more subversive than it may at first appear.[65] Those who would offer a reasonable ethical theory must address these fundamental philosophical concerns, either by defending the traditional anthropological and metaphysical ideas that radically separate humans from animals, or by rejecting them and attempting a reconstitution of ethics accordingly.

## Conclusion

A confluence of factors, then, brings the animal to the attention of modern philosophers. Our pre-reflective intuitions, our growing empirical knowledge of the biological world, the force of our recent history, and legitimate philosophical concerns all indicate that the animal ought not to be ignored. Against those inclined to believe that the recent attention to mere animals is a passing fad, we may argue instead that it is an unavoidable and inevitable concern. If we believe in science as a continual probing of physical reality, then it is authentic science that attempts to overcome the anthropocentrism of traditional biology and understand the animal ethologically. In a parallel manner, to the extent that the animal embodies a threat to ethical and metaphysical foundations of Western thought, it is a necessary concern for a philosophical age absorbed in a wave of self-examination. In the face of such forces, it becomes evident that ethics must deal with the animal.

Furthermore, if biophilic thinkers are correct in identifying our experience of other animals as fundamental and formative, the method employed in the present work—namely, to use the question of the moral standing of animals as the launching point for a broader examination of ethical theory—emerges as more than a mere contrivance. As Heidegger makes clear concerning metaphysics, a coherent hermeneutic must make explicit the nature of the questioner—in the case of the question of being, *Dasein*, understood as a being with a history and a finite biography. In ethics, we are concerned with the question of *how to live*, a problem that is meaningful only to *a living being*—that is, a being with an *evolutionary* history as well as a cultural and biographical one. As this evolutionary history is not ours alone, but one that we share with the animal, no ethic that is true to our condition may ignore the larger totality of life. As Henry Salt urged over a hundred years ago: "It is full time that this question were examined in the light of some rational and guiding principle, and that we ceased to drift helplessly between the extremes of total indifference on the one hand, and spasmodic, partially-applied compassion on the other. We have had enough, and too much, of trifling with this or that isolated aspect of the subject, and of playing off the exposure of somebody else's insensibility by way of a balance for our own, as if a *tu quoque* were a sufficient justification of a man's moral delinquencies."[66]

If ethics cannot answer this challenge by resolving whether and to what extent the animal must count in our moral judgments, such a failure would indicate more than another knotty problem for casuistry, but rather a deeper indictment of traditional ethical models. To determine whether such an indictment is warranted, I will survey the major extensionist arguments that have been offered in the debate over animals—that is, those arguments that result from extending traditional ethical theories to evaluate the interests of *both* humans *and* animals. But before proceeding, it must be established more firmly that these are not false concerns. Can we be certain that our original questions about the spider's web—and even more pressing questions about our treatment of farm and laboratory animals—are not absurd? If there are legitimate grounds for withholding properly moral attention from animals, then it is meaningless to ask what a given ethical theory would imply for our actions that involve them. In other words, it is possible that an ethical theory could incorporate proper moral respect for the animal simply by denying that any is due. Thus, this test will only be fair once we establish that there are no impenetrable fences that will keep nonhumans outside the scope of moral concern. Several such barriers have been erected in the history of Western thought. In the following chapter, we will see how effective they are at keeping the animal at bay.

## 2   *Broader Philosophical Considerations*

In the previous chapter I addressed the question: Why now?—that is, what accounts for the recent attention, paid by ethicists and laypersons alike, to the moral standing of animals? Let us here begin with the obverse and ask: Why not before? What positive forces may have prevented this recent attention from materializing sooner? Two possibilities deserve mention. First, there are powerful psychological and political factors that make moral attention to animals problematic. Whether or not it is ultimately defensible, it seems undeniable that a thread of anthropocentrism runs through Western culture, and some have argued that it may be inseparable from civilization itself. If it can be demonstrated that animals—the vanquished in the conquest of domesticated culture—are beings with interests, rights, or other morally relevant features, then the humanization of nature may no longer be pursued without reservation. To take the moral claims of animals seriously threatens to subvert the foundations of humanity's self-concept in the post-Neolithic world, and thus the effort has traditionally been taboo. Even in the modern world—replete with those cultural attributes (discussed in Chapter 1) that facilitate respect for animals—granting a substantive moral standing to animals raises significant problems for political culture. The moral and political liberalization that has defined the past three centuries depends in part on positing the moral worth of human beings *as a class*, rather than as a function of the individual's talents or achievements. But such categorical equality is ostensibly unworkable in the case of other animals, which are more fittingly extended moral recognition in proportion to the morally relevant attributes they possess. Thus, those who fear that such a quantification of moral standing could ultimately undermine human egalitarianism have been loath to explore the possible moral claims of animals.

Second, and perhaps because cultural anthropocentrism has helped to mold our ethical models, there are substantial logical and philosophical questions about whether the West's traditional ethical categories may be extended to nonhumans. These concerns, the focus of this chapter, could form a plausible justification for the lack of attention the animal has received from much of the Western philosophical tradition. It makes little sense to ask, for example, whether animals have rights or whether our actions toward them are just if such categories as "rights" and "justice" cannot be applied meaningfully to any but human beings. The arguments for this position cover broad philosophical territory: theology and metaphysics, philosophical anthropology, semiotics, epistemology, and philosophy of mind. Thus, my goal here is not to mount exhaustive refutations of all the arguments against extending moral consideration to animals, for such a task—if possible—would require a work of its own. Rather, I will show only that none of the most common is prima facie sufficiently strong to refute the commonsense judgment that animals clearly are more than mere things, or to invalidate the use of the animal in my subsequent examination of ethical theories in Part II.

## Ensoulment

The clearest philosophical ground for excluding nonhumans from moral consideration may be found in ontology. If it is possible to establish a categorical distinction between human and nonhuman reality, it may entail the argument that moral categories function for human beings but do not apply to the type of reality animals occupy. The most explicit approach of this type is theological in nature, employing the assertion that we humans are ensouled beings, created in the image of a God who made the world, including animals, for our use. If humans possess immaterial souls that transcend their physical bodies, but nonhumans do not, this metaphysical difference may be used to justify an ethical one as well: since our destinies lie beyond this world, the elements of the material realm— including soulless animals—can never count as more than the means to that end. As an instrument of divine and human will, the nonhuman animal is thus excluded from the scope of our moral concepts.

To the extent that this position is derived from revealed sources,[1] we may respond, first, that revealed religions are not unanimous in denying souls and moral standing to nonhumans; the Hindu, Buddhist, and Jain traditions of the East are obvious examples, and, as noted in the previous chapter,[2] Western theologians have not been of one voice on this matter. Second, even if that were not the case, philosophers are under no obligation to accept putative revelations that are not rationally supported. Even within the bounds of natural theology, however, the premises that might lead us to discount the claims of animals are more equivocal than they at first may appear. The most obvious problems are theodicean. Even assuming that other animals lack immortal souls, a minimal recognition of their needs and desires alerts us to many animals' apparent capacity for suffering. Believers who reserve moral concern exclusively for their human fellows must therefore either deny the reality of animal suffering (a problematic and counterintuitive option pursued by seventeenth-century rationalists such as René Descartes and Nicholas Malebranche, but few others[3]), or explain why a just god would deliver other animals for our use in the knowledge that this condemns them to suffering at our hands. With this problem in mind, some Christian theologians have argued for an extension of the "golden rule" to make room for moral consideration of animals; others have resorted to the ingenious argument that animals' lack of immortal souls makes cruelty toward them especially condemnable because they have no future lives in which to receive divine compensation.[4] Still others have deduced that the dominion God grants us over the animal world obligates us to be "good shepherds," and to tend to animals with care. At a minimum, therefore, there seems to be ample room in any reasonable theological framework for attaching at least some moral weight to the consideration of animal interests.[5]

Interesting attempts have been made at defending a more substantial ethical status for animals on other theological grounds. For example, Andrew Linzey has experimented with the concept of "theos-rights" for animals, which he defines as "what is objectively owed to animals as a matter of justice by virtue of their Creator's right." Using this ethico-theological concept, he argues that "animals can be wronged because their Creator can be wronged in his creation," and thus "man and animals form a moral community . . . because God elects them within a special relationship with himself."[6] In a similar vein, James Gaffney offers the devotional posture he terms "sacramentalism," which he defines as

> a disposition to discern in all material created things an authentic reflection of the presence and power of God, and to value the diversity of material creation for its suggestion of divinity's inexhaustible richness . . . In a material world so envisaged, every material thing becomes,

so to speak, an icon, and the more intricate and exquisite are material creatures, the more transparent are they to the glory of their Creator. In such a scheme of things, animals must occupy an especially hallowed place, and become, not merely legitimate objects of Christian care and compassion, but incentives to awe and devotion.[7]

Such alternatives to the anthropocentrism of Western theology are appealing, but in what follows we need not rely on them, nor become entangled in other theological complexities. Rather, I offer these examples simply to demonstrate that the premise of a theological framework—even ignoring the larger metaphysical and epistemological difficulties such a starting point presents—does not preclude moral consideration of other animals.

If we consider the issue of ensoulment philosophically, it again should be noted that the denial of souls to animals is not universal, and comes relatively late to the Western philosophical tradition. An obvious, if ironic, example is Aristotle, who argues that *psyche* refers to the "essential whatness" of any natural, organized body—human, animal, or plant—with the potential for life; the ancient Greeks in general did not deny souls to nonhumans.[8] Those later thinkers who considered other animals soulless generally appealed to the animal's lack of attributes traditionally understood to be definitively human: free agency, rationality, and language use. While the behavior of nonhuman animals is putatively explainable by principles of biology and physics alone, the rational consciousness and free behavior of humans evade mechanistic explanation. Thus, some have argued that these human attributes must be the products of a reality that transcends the material.[9] The moral relevance of these attributes themselves will be considered subsequently; to the argument that they indicate a fundamental ontological difference between humans and animals, several responses are possible.

First, while it may be difficult to experience our consciousness and sense of self as epiphenomena of purely physiological processes, as discussed in Chapter 1 the modern neurosciences—framed in a context of evolutionary biology—make a naturalistic explanation of human consciousness more plausible now than ever before in the history of the study of the mind. Correlatively, the more that is learned about the complexity of animal consciousness and behavior, the less absolute the boundary between rational and animal consciousness becomes, and the more plausible the Darwinian assertion of continuity of mental faculties. Independent of the scientific advances of the twentieth century, anthropological dualism has always been plagued by metaphysical and epistemological problems. For example, how does the allegedly spiritual event of my deciding to have a drink cause my arm to move and pick up a glass? In turn, how can the alcohol molecules I consume affect the psychic events of my consciousness? Such mystical stopgaps as Descartes' pineal gland provide inadequate solutions to these difficulties. A full exploration of all these issues would take us far afield into the complexities of the philosophy of mind and consciousness studies. For present purposes, it is sufficient to state that—while it faces difficulties of its own—an explanation of consciousness that revealed it to be neither psychic in nature nor uniquely human is theoretically possible, and a desirable scientific and philosophical objective. Apprehension at this prospect might well reflect an intuition that human and animal are ontologically distinct, and thus runs the risk of circularity when offered as support for that conclusion.

## Species Essentialism

While the argument that ensoulment essentially divides the human from the animal—even assuming that it could validly debar animals from moral consideration—may be tenuous, the ontological separation of humanity from the rest of the natural world is such a central idea to Western culture that its incarnations are not exhausted by such metaphysical arguments. It is clearly reflected in the history of life science, which, like Western science generally, had until recently been the handmaiden of theology. As late as the early nineteenth century, the West's understanding of the natural world had been haunted by the metaphysical idea that the various forms of animate life are exemplars of divine archetypes; as a result, biological observation has at times taken the form of a devotional practice, bearing witness to an alleged teleology evidenced in the intricacies of individual organisms and their interrelations. But even without such explicitly theological intentions, the presupposition that animal species are defined by essential natures that clearly distinguish them from each other—and humans—has had a powerful hold on the thinking of both biologists and laypersons alike. In nineteenth- and twentieth-century thought, when divorced from the metaphysics of ensoulment, such species essentialism may be seen as the attempt to take up the task of ontologically distinguishing humans from animals on naturalistic, rather than theological, grounds.

To maintain such a position, one must rebut what some have discerned to be the most important implications of Darwinian evolutionary theory. In the nineteenth century, the Platonic notion that there are a priori distinctions between species and varieties was challenged by

Darwin's contention that the very concept of "species" is imprecise and to some degree discretionary. Darwin sought to establish that the mechanism of natural selection could produce new populations at any taxonomic level, and that if so, there is no essential difference between the features taken to define each level. Thus, some have concluded that within a pure Darwinian model there can be no categorical separation of human and other "species," because any proposed boundary will be too blurry to justify it. For example, philosopher James Rachels argues:

> If Darwin is correct, there are no absolute differences between humans and the members of all other species—in fact, there are no absolute differences between the members of *any* species and all others. Rather than sharp breaks between species, we find instead a profusion of similarities and differences between particular animals, with the characteristics typical of one species shading over into the characteristics typical of another. As Darwin puts it, there are only differences of degree—a complex pattern of similarities and differences that reflect common ancestry, as well as chance variations among individuals within a single species. Therefore, the fundamental reality is best represented by saying that the earth is populated by individuals who resemble one another, and who differ from one another, in myriad ways, rather than by saying that the earth is populated by different *kinds* of beings.[10]

However, Rachels almost certainly overstates the case, for while the differences among species may not be radical, neither are they negligible. To describe the biological world as "populated by individuals" alone is to imply that continuity functions seamlessly throughout the natural world, which flies in the face of the real gaps that separate specific populations. The recognition of these populations as *kinds* does not depend upon purely artificial classifications, inasmuch as post-Darwinian biology acknowledges their natural genealogy through genetic isolation. Thus, even if the boundaries between different species and varieties are less than absolute, Darwin himself misrepresents the biological reality when he describes these terms as "applied arbitrarily, and for mere convenience sake."[11] As a result, the species essentialist can still maintain in the post-Darwinian world that humans are fundamentally different from other animals by highlighting the objective reality of the superficial differences among species, and arguing that there are enough of them to make a fundamental, qualitative difference.

Nonetheless, the essentialist position is complicated by the basic point of evolutionary science that no single or simple biological criterion grounds distinctions between species; even interbreeding is a more ambiguous test than is generally thought.[12] If so, one must stipulate at

what point a number of more subtle differences between species is sufficient to justify their categorical separation. Even if this can be accomplished with sufficient clarity for the purposes of biological taxonomy, it
is unclear that this is adequate for the ethical point the species essentialist is trying to make. At what point is a sufficient threshold of difference
met to distinguish the human categorically from the nonhuman animal,
such that the latter is justifiably excluded from moral concern? The challenge is to identify a point that is neither arbitrary nor question begging,
and this seems to be a challenge the species essentialists have failed to
meet. Consider, for example, Tibor Machan's argument on this point:

> Quite independently of the implicit acknowledgment by animal rights
> advocates of the hierarchy of nature, there simply is evidence through
> the natural world of the existence of beings of greater complexity and of
> higher value. For example, while it makes no sense to evaluate as good
> or bad such things as planets or rocks or pebbles—except as they may
> relate to human purposes—when it comes to plants and animals the
> process of evaluation commences very naturally indeed. We can speak
> of better or worse trees, oaks, redwoods, or zebras, foxes or chimps.
> While at this point we confine our evaluation to the condition or behav-
> ior of such beings without any intimation of their responsibility for
> being better or worse, when we start discussing human beings our eval-
> uation takes on a moral component. Indeed, none are more ready to tes-
> tify to this than animal rights advocates who, after all, do not demand
> any change of behavior on the part of non-human animals and yet insist
> that human beings conform to certain moral edicts as a matter of their
> own choice. This means that even animal rights advocates admit out-
> right that to the best of our knowledge it is with human beings that the
> idea of moral goodness and moral responsibility enters the universe . . .
> Normal human life involves moral tasks, and that is why we are more
> important than other beings in nature.[13]

When used as part of a justification for excluding a moral standing for
nonhuman animals, such reasoning runs the risk of circularity: Why
may we exclude the animal from moral consideration? Because there is
an ontological distinction between humans and other animals. On what
do we base this distinction? The fact that only humans are moral beings.

There are two ways out of this vicious circle. First, we may add to
the argument (as Machan and others do) the premise that only moral
agents can possess morally significant attributes such as rights and interests. As discussed further in Chapter 4, the class of moral agents is not
strictly congruent with the species *Homo sapiens*, and so this amendment only taints the argument with arbitrariness. The second way is to
interpret the argument as alerting us to the possibility that traditional

moral categories may not be *adequate* for dealing with the animal because they were constructed by and for human beings conceived as rational moral agents. This is a position shared by various thinkers discussed in Parts III and IV, but it clearly is not endorsed by species essentialists, since it would not entail their conclusion that our treatment of other species requires no fundamental revaluation.

It therefore seems that there is no way of finessing the powerful impact that evolutionary biology must have on humanity's self-concept. Not only does it strike a serious—perhaps the fatal—blow against anthropological dualism, but it also undermines biological accounts of human uniqueness and priority in the natural world.[14] However, to see evolutionary theory only in the light of its potential affront to our dignity is to remain captive to the pre-Darwinian understanding of the animal as ontologically inferior to the human. On the contrary, as philosopher Hans Jonas argues, "If man is related to the animals, then the animals are also related to man and therefore, in degrees, possess that inwardness which man, their most highly advanced relative, is aware of in himself."[15] What has been scorned in philosophy and science as the anthropomorphizing of nonhumans becomes necessary in the post-Darwinian world to explain our own humanity. Our prized human features may still be prized, as long as we acknowledge their continuity with valuable presences throughout the natural world. Of most relevance to the present work, the untenability of species essentialism has a profound implication for ethics: as Scholtmeijer writes, "if the human person is to preserve his or her claim to moral consideration under the authority of the idea of continuity, then the individual animal attains moral status of a greater than sentimental variety."[16]

## Qualified Speciesism

Aside from the more abstract metaphysical and anthropological arguments discussed so far, the recent debate over animals is populated with arguments that the traditional understanding of animals is justified because there are morally relevant features that humans possess but animals lack—whether or not these features signal a fundamental ontological difference. Rachels labels such arguments with the useful term *qualified speciesism*,[17] which describes the logical space for more subtle discrimination against animals that remains after the rejection of species essentialism. Biological space is created for this possibility by the fact that higher-order functions such as sentience do not correspond in a simple way to underlying physiological mechanisms, and therefore biological continuity does not guarantee continuity of morally relevant properties of consciousness. The various contenders for the morally relevant attribute that nonhumans lack are surveyed below. They all, however, are subject to the same general grounds for rebuttal: (1) there is mounting evidence that human possession of each of these attributes is a difference of degree, rather than kind; (2) none of these attributes is possessed by all who are genetically human and, therefore, endowing them with decisive importance threatens the moral equality of human beings; (3) this way of assessing the moral worth of animals is question begging because it presupposes that humanity is the standard of value and nonhumans can be worthy of moral consideration only to the extent that they are like us.

*Rationality* On the question of whether any animals possess a rational capacity, David Hume argued that the answer is obvious: "Next to the ridicule of denying an evident truth, is that of taking much pains to defend it; and no truth appears to me more evident, than that beasts are endow'd with thought and reason as well as men. The arguments are in this case so obvious, that they never escape the most stupid and ignorant."[18] Despite the appeal of this commonsense position, the assertion that humans are essentially and uniquely rational beings is arguably the central idea of the Western philosophical tradition. This anthropological idea reflects the tradition's metaphysical separation of humanity from the world, and also poses a formidable challenge to evolutionary biology. For example, Alfred Wallace—Darwin's contemporary and co-defender of natural selection—argued that human evolution must have been divinely guided, since it was not clear to him how preliminary stages of human speculative systems would have bestowed any survival advantage upon early hominids. Darwin, of course, disagreed, but among subsequent investigators how and why rational human consciousness evolved has been the subject of much fascinating speculation, but little consensus. Such considerations aside, how are we to respond to those who would argue that categorizing humans as rational and animals as non-rational—whatever the origin or metaphysical implications of this difference—is sufficient to deny the extension of moral categories to the animal?

The first two general criticisms listed above will apply here: whatever behaviors are taken to indicate rational mentation in humans are known to be present to some extent in the animal world (most obviously among other primates, more dimly in our more distant relatives), and there are many humans who will not be capable of them at all (yet we do not deem them fit to be consumed as food or used to test the toxicity of household products). The third criticism is perhaps the most interesting one here, since it points to a broader problem of subjectivity in this discussion. Before we can meaningfully address the moral relevance of either possessing or lacking rationality, we need to be clear about what constitutes "rationality," and here precision is lacking. Owing at least in part to what Griffin calls "the heterogeneity of human consciousness," there is little agreement among philosophers on what defines rational thought, or on what the most important attributes of our conscious thinking are.[19] In addition to philosophical differences (such as the different roles reason plays in Plato's system versus Kant's system, for example), there is too much room here for subjective disagreement among individual thinkers, and the problem will only be exacerbated when trying to determine whether and to what extent nonhumans lack rationality. Whatever types of "thinking" or "reasoning" animals are capable of will be relevant to their own situations, whereas we are likely to define "rational" and "non-rational" in terms exclusively meaningful to humans—and philosophers, who allegedly are in the business of being "rational," are likely to do so in terms that serve their sense of self-importance.[20]

One might respond that this is all beside the essential point, in that it is possible to stipulate to an elementary definition of rationality (e.g., the ability to seek and offer objective grounds for one's actions and beliefs) such that most humans possess it while it is doubtful that any animals do. If so, the question then becomes to what degree a being's cognitive attributes are morally relevant. They obviously are relevant to moral agency: if one can reason, one ostensibly can explore alternatives, and thereby one becomes accountable for the paths one chooses. In turn, we evaluate the moral worth of one's actions based on the quality of reasons offered—or not offered—by way of justification. However, if we premise that this description does not apply to the nonhuman animal, would it follow from that ground that the cruelty or kindness of a human agent's actions toward them would be irrelevant? Would more substantive moral categories such as "animal rights" or the consideration of animal interests thereby be nullified?

Richard Sorabji makes clear why this immediate inference fails: even if we deny rational consciousness to animals, we still have to account for how they behave and what they experience. Doing so without resort to a rational faculty requires us to reevaluate the animal's faculties of perceptual consciousness, memory, and emotion; as a result, the operation of these faculties in animals may hold more moral significance than does their operation in humans.[21] Moreover, the prejudices of philosophers to the contrary, rational consciousness may not be inherently more valuable than our other organic capacities. This is a theme developed by Friedrich Nietzsche throughout his work; for example:

> In the tremendous multiplicity of events within an organism, the part which becomes conscious to us is a mere means: and the little bit of "virtue," "selflessness," and similar fictions are refuted radically by the total balance of events. We should study our organism in all its immorality—
>
> The animal functions are, as a matter of principle, a million times more important than all our beautiful moods and heights of consciousness: the latter are a surplus, except when they have to serve as tools of those animal functions. The entire conscious life, the spirit along with the soul, the heart, goodness, and virtue—in whose service do they labor? In the service of the greatest possible perfection of the means (means of nourishment, means of enhancement) of the basic animal functions: above all, the enhancement of life.[22]

Some important counterarguments to these considerations deserve attention. First, it seems reasonable that the moral significance of our actions' effects on nonhuman animals is in some way proportional to the degree to which they *matter* to the animal. For an experience to matter to a being in a morally significant way, it would seem to be necessary that the being can reflect on the experience and form beliefs about it; doing so requires cognitive and conscious abilities that are not obviously discernible in other animals. With these considerations in mind, Peter Carruthers asserts that animal experiences are as a category "nonconscious," and lacking the "distinctive phenomenology" of conscious human experiences. Consequently, he argues, any injuries we might inflict upon animals "are lacking even in indirect moral concern"; in turn, efforts to liberate animals from human oppression "are not only morally unsupportable but morally objectionable . . . Since [animals'] pains are nonconscious ones (as are all their mental states), they ought not be allowed to get in the way of any morally serious objective."[23]

Carruthers's inference may be valid, but his premise that animals are categorically non-conscious is questionable. In addition to the testimony of common sense, there are sound biological reasons to believe that a being that lacked basic powers of conceptualizing could neither learn nor survive in the ways that many animals clearly do. Griffin, for example, has argued extensively that with the attribution of conscious thoughts "a great deal of animal behavior can be understood as a consistent adaptive pattern."[24] Far from infusing metaphysical whims into science, this hypothesis can often provide the most parsimonious explanation for animal behaviors involved with food finding, predation, tool use, and communication. Where animals act as if they remember, hope, plan, and the like, the most reasonable explanation may be that they actually do.[25] Furthermore, since the optimal behavior in all possible situations cannot be preprogrammed, an animal's putative ability to deliberate consciously in the face of new challenges may satisfy adaptive economy;[26] yet, animal behavior that is instinctive is not necessarily therefore unconscious.[27] The case for animal consciousness and mentation is not ironclad, but the examples Griffin and other ethologists cite—including the versatile adaptability of many animals, their communicative behavior, and the neurophysiological analogies between humans and other animals—argue against a strict categorical denial of animal minds.

Nonetheless, one might grant the reality of perceptual consciousness in animals but still argue that any morally relevant experiences of which they are capable will be inconsequential without the amplification provided by the type of higher mental faculties humans possess. In response, we may note that while there is clearly a link between reason and experience, the moral implications of this connection are ambiguous. Rational humans are capable of appreciating a greater range of experience than other animals, and we may say that our greater capacity for anticipation and recollection would make a painful experience more intense for us than, say, a rat. But we can also rationalize our experience, divert our attention through fantasy, or even revel in the glow of martyrdom, whereas the rat, lacking these capacities, is more likely to have its whole capacity for experience consumed by a painful sensation.[28] As philosopher Steve Sapontzis—borrowing the language of Bentham's calculus—argues, "even if intellectually more sophisticated beings can enjoy a wider variety of feelings, those who are intellectually less sophisticated can compensate for and even overcome this deficit through greater intensity, duration, purity, extent, etc., of their feelings."[29] If so, then even if all nonhuman animals were categorized as non-rational, that would not justify our categorically banishing all their experiences to moral insignificance. As Leonard Nelson argues, to deny this carries difficult implications for our understanding of ourselves:

> To be able to lead a rational life, it is necessary, of course, for man to live. But whoever cites this to justify his right always to give preference to his own life over the conflicting interest of an animal, without weighing the particular interests in each given case, should consider the full implications of such a view. It requires him to be consistent in sub-

ordinating sensory to rational interests even when his own interests alone are in question, and consequently denies him the right to injure his true interest in favour of his sensory interest. He thus forfeits any claim to have those interests of his respected, which are not subordinated to the interest in a rational life. How many men are prepared to accept such a conclusion without deceiving themselves?[30]

*Language* Closely related to the issue of rationality—but deserving of separate mention—is the question of the moral relevance of language. Traditionally, one of the strongest reasons for denying any meaningful sense of consciousness or rationality to nonhuman animals is their lack of proper linguistic ability. For example, it is on this point that Descartes hinges his argument that while humans are thinking things, animals are best thought of as machines: while he could imagine a machine capable of mimicking the behavior of animals, not being privy to twenty-first-century technology he could not envisage one that could carry on a spontaneous conversation in the way that even feeble humans can.[31] While this argument may seem anachronistic today, the moral significance of language ought not to be underestimated. As James Rachels argues, even animal advocates must admit that language clearly "enriches almost all of one's psychological capacities; . . . that this has consequences that ramify throughout one's life; and that this is a fact that our moral outlook should accommodate."[32] It is, after all, language use on the part of our fellow humans that most clearly indicates their beliefs and desires; in turn, language is linked to self-consciousness in that the speaker usually intends to be recognized as a subject. More fundamentally, the word— justly sanctified in poetry and theology—accomplishes the conceptualizing that can take us out of the particular, and elevate mere sensation and feeling to the level of meaningful experience. Woven together by the narrative power of language, experiences become the fabric of our selves; language thereby binds our interiority, while it forms the bridge to the interior of the other. But this bridge cannot cross to the non-linguistic animal, whose inwardness, as a result, will seem so distant that we may question whether it exists at all.

Is this sufficient to deny moral concern for the animal? It seems quite plausible to argue that the life of a human is more valuable than the life of an animal because of the richness that language provides, because the narrative that is his or her life will be more substantially altered by premature death than can be claimed in the case of an animal. Thus, in those mostly hypothetical cases where a choice must be made between the life of a human and the life of an animal, language capacity may be a decisive factor.[33] Nonetheless, unless one is prepared to argue that language is a necessary condition for having morally relevant experiences or existence, it will seem to be less decisive in the more ordinary situations in which we use other animals, and clearly irrelevant to matters of cruelty or torture. To those who are so prepared, our three criticisms will apply.

First, there is evidence to suggest that some nonhumans may possess genuine, albeit rudimentary, linguistic ability—that is, the ability to use words or signs referentially. The most famous examples involve captive great apes such as pygmy chimpanzees and gorillas, but cetaceans and other non-primate species also have demonstrated possible language behavior. Ethological evidence indicates that even the communicative behavior of insects such as honeybees and wasps exhibits a kind of flexibility suggestive of contextual language use. Such claims are controversial, and behaviorists will argue that such phenomena can be explained without attributing mentation to the animal. Still, while human dependence on language is quantitatively and qualitatively unique, it should not surprise us to find elements of our linguistic capacity to be continuous with the proto-linguistic powers of animals. Moreover, whether or not we are correct in defining some animal behaviors as genuinely linguistic, the abilities to generalize and conceptualize—which in our case seems to depend upon language—must almost certainly have analogs in other animate species. As Bernard Rollin argues, "an organism with no power of generalization and abstraction, which could experience only particulars, could neither learn nor survive."[34] The animal learns its concepts "from the language of nature," the ability to synthesize experience being a necessary ingredient for animate life, irrespective of its formal linguistic capabilities.[35]

Second, there are of course human beings whose linguistic capacities are missing or defective, but we do not for that reason alone ignore their interests. The aphasiac is an object of compassion, not the whims of the verbal majority. Once we acknowledge that the type of enrichment language brings to existence does not follow strict, specific lines, we will be forced to recognize that some animals may have richer lives than some humans, and so these lines cannot demarcate moral boundaries.[36] Conversely, and relative to the third point of criticism, the argument can be made that the "richness" of language so separates us from the world that we may be unable to comprehend animal reality adequately. As Marian Scholtmeijer writes, "We have believed that language separates humankind from the rest of the animals. Language shapes thought and presents the human mind with a world quite different from that which animals occupy. Now that animals have assumed importance in our ways of knowing the world, doubts arise as to the power of language to escape culture and address nature."[37] Thus, while language admittedly enhances the moral worth of our own lives, it may also make us deaf to the value of the voiceless.[38]

*Personhood* Another way of capturing the type of morally relevant consciousness that rationality and language produce in human beings is with the concept of personhood. The term *person* is helpful here because its two broad senses bridge the psychological and ethical issues discussed in this section of the chapter. In the prescriptive sense of the term, persons are, as Sapontzis puts it, "beings whose interests are morally or legally protected against routine exploitation by those whose actions can be directly influenced by moral or legal concepts. Persons are those whom morality or the law indicates we . . . must not, as Kant would say, treat as mere means to the satisfaction of our interests."[39] Alternatively, as a description, "persons" may refer to beings who are self-aware, and who accordingly possess a consciousness—such as that of rational, language-using human beings—sufficiently sophisticated to qualify them for prescriptive personhood. If the case can be made that descriptive personhood is not only a sufficient but also a necessary condition for prescriptive personhood, then those nonhumans that fail to fulfill the psychological criteria for descriptive personhood may be denied the protection of prescriptive personhood.

However, among those who have explored this avenue to understanding the moral status of animals, there is no consensus about what the exact criteria for descriptive personhood are, or whether any nonhumans can fulfill them. For example, Gary Francione cites bioethicist Joseph Fletcher's fifteen positive criteria of personhood and concludes that "we are no longer able to doubt that *all* great apes . . . possess these characteristics," and that they—and perhaps other nonhuman animals—therefore merit moral and legal protection.[40] But animal psychologist Robert W. Mitchell, after reviewing a similarly extensive list of possible criteria, asserts: "it is clear that nonhuman beings, including the great apes, are not persons, in that they lack full self-consciousness." According to Mitchell, what is missing from the consciousness of nonhuman animals is "reflective self-awareness": the ability to incorporate "awareness of another's awareness of oneself into one's awareness of self."[41] While granting that other animals are capable of demonstrating degrees of self-consciousness, Mitchell believes that this kind of "triple reflection" (as the phenomenologist Maurice Merleau-Ponty termed it) is convincingly evidenced only by humans.

Clearly, reflective self-awareness is related to the rational and linguistic abilities discussed above: to recognize another as aware and as aware of oneself will require highly evolved cognitive powers, and the knitting together of another's awareness with one's own will be facilitated by (if not entirely dependent upon) the integrative power of language. Moreover, it is in this connection that these powers reach their peak of moral significance. As Mitchell writes: "Because of reflective self-awareness, the ideals of morality are possible. But along with such reflective self-awareness comes the ability to make a deliberate argument in support of one's moral vision . . . It would appear that humans, but not apes, because of reflective self-awareness . . . can ponder past and future and weigh alternative courses of action in the light of some vision of a whole life well lived."[42] If we accept the proposition that such full self-consciousness is a necessary condition of personhood in the descriptive sense, this adds up to a compelling case that only such persons can act meaningfully as moral and political beings. Without the ability to project into social space an understanding of myself as one agent in a community of others who see me as such, any prescriptive judgments I put into language and rationalize would be entirely academic—if it would be possible for me to form them at all.

Still, this falls short of establishing that we ought to withhold the protection of moral and legal personhood from all nonhumans. First, as I stated above, to limit the sphere of moral concern to our fellow moral agents is not the same as limiting this concern to our conspecifics, as some members of *Homo sapiens* are not reflectively self-aware. If, from the point of view of ethics, they are not to sink to the level of mere things, they—and possibly, in turn, nonhuman animals—must occupy a moral standing that rests on something other than moral agency. Second, Mitchell himself acknowledges that the self-consciousness of nonhumans seems to differ from human reflective self-awareness in degree rather than in kind. As Griffin argues, it is unwarranted to separate self-consciousness radically from the type of perceptual consciousness it is generally accepted that animals possess:

> Those who hold that self-awareness is a unique human attribute often fall back to an insistence that although animals may be perceptually conscious of their own bodies, they nevertheless cannot think such thoughts as "It is I who am running, or climbing this tree, or chasing that moth." Yet when an animal consciously perceives the running, climbing, or moth chasing of another animal, it must also be aware of who is doing these things. And if the animal is perceptually conscious of its own body, it is difficult to rule out similar recognition that it, itself, is doing the running, climbing, or chasing. If we grant that animals are capable of perceptual awareness, denying them some level of self-awareness would seem to be an arbitrary and unjustified restriction.[43]

That such self-awareness is on a continuum with human reflectivity is indicated by the many examples of *deceptive* behaviors in the animal world. For example, the mother plover that feigns an injury at the approach of a predator in an effort to distract it from her nest would seem to be aware that she will be perceived by others in certain ways, and can adjust her behavior accordingly.[44] Such examples open a window on a world of animal inter-subjectivity, in which the deceptive animal is able to recognize that "the other individual's and its own signals are only signals, which can be trusted, distrusted, falsified, denied, amplified, corrected, and so forth."[45]

It is not surprising that such a description of animal communication will have its detractors; but whether the use of such terms is unduly anthropomorphic is not decisive here. As Sapontzis notes, even if one is correct in denying that nonhumans can possess descriptive personhood, there remains plenty of logical space for the moral consideration of sentient animals.[46] Those who overlook this space and tend to equate descriptive and prescriptive personhood are not only guilty of the logical error of inferring an *ought* from an *is*, but also of question-begging anthropocentrism. It is noteworthy that the consideration of personhood occurs most often in reflection on the moral standing of the great apes and our other primate relatives. To explore the prospects for the moral revaluation of the animal in a serious manner, we need to do more than focus on attributes that might be shared only by those animals that are most humanlike, thereby ignoring over 99 percent of the planet's animate species. John Rodman's reflection on this point makes a fitting conclusion to this section:

> If it would seem arbitrary to a visitor from Mars to find one species claiming a monopoly of intrinsic value by virtue of its allegedly exclusive possession of reason, free will, soul or some other occult quality, would it not seem almost as arbitrary to find that same species claiming a monopoly of intrinsic value for itself and those species most resembling it (e.g. in type of nervous system and behaviour) by virtue of their common and allegedly exclusive possession of sentience? And would not the arbitrariness seem overwhelming if it were then discovered that the populations of nonhuman species who were most prominent in this "humane" coalition were what Darwin aptly called "domestic productions," that is, beings produced by the human manipulation of nonhuman animal gene pools for human purposes?[47]

## Species Solipsism

One final category of obstacles to the moral consideration of other animals is epistemological, rather than metaphysical or psychological, in nature. Let us grant, following from the analysis thus far, that the nature and consciousness of humans cannot be categorically separate from that of animals, and that this places animal reality on a continuum with our own world of morally relevant attributes and experiences. Still, it might be argued that we can never understand the consciousness of other animals with sufficient clarity for it to affect our moral deliberations. The conviction with which we hold our moral judgments depends in part upon the certainty with which we know all the relevant facts, and our knowledge of other animals' minds and experiences may never meet the threshold of sufficient certainty because—despite the arguments for continuity—they will always be alien from us in fundamental ways. Thus, the argument concludes, since our own clearly known interests and desires will always trump the putative, vaguely perceived concerns of other species, the animal is rightly excluded from the scope of ethics. Such reasoning takes the perennial philosophical problem of other minds and gives it an inter-specific twist, leading Griffin to coin the term *species solipsism* to describe this position.[48]

The traditional problem of solipsism, of course, concerns the possibility of humans knowing one another's minds, and while its significance is often exaggerated, trying to resolve it to the satisfaction of polemicists can prove maddening. It seems that I cannot know with absolute certainty that my experience of the world in general, or even of particular sensations, is the same as that of another person. Since I cannot have *direct* acquaintance with the consciousness of other persons, there is always an element of inference—which, however strong, could be incorrect—in the judgment that they experience the same feelings and sensations as I would under similar circumstances, or—taken to its extreme—that they experience anything at all. While this epistemological gap is real, it is rarely wide enough to hinder our dealings with each other. The case may well be different, however, when we consider the experience of beings that are radically different from us.

For example, in his famous essay, Thomas Nagel asks "What Is It Like to Be a Bat?" and answers that there is no way for us genuinely to appreciate the subjective consciousness of a flying, sonar-guided, insect-eating mammal. Our imaginative abilities have been formed by our own human situation; extrapolating to the bat's situation must therefore always be an incomplete project. Nagel does not go so far as to deny that the bat *has* a subjective consciousness, but instead his concern is that there is no way for us to comprehend it adequately.[49] The obstacles to this comprehension are, of course, not unique to the case of bats. One could as well ask, What is it like to be a chimpanzee? A cow? A crow? A clam? Can such beings be happy or sad? Do they enjoy their lives? Do they experience anything like the sensations or emotions I would when subjected to comparable circumstances? Answering such questions with precision is clearly impossible, and becomes more difficult the greater the cultural and physiological distance between ourselves and the animal in question.[50]

What exactly are the obstacles? In the case of the bat's use of sonar (or, the ability of some fish to sense electrical fields, or the conjectured ability of migrating birds to perceive the earth's magnet fields or the polarization of light), we encounter means of perception that are not obviously analogous to our own. Those that are analogous—such as another animal's ability to see a different range of the light spectrum— may be difficult enough to assimilate. Further, as psychiatric evidence suggests that the nature of our human consciousness is intimately connected with the body-image produced by the brain,[51] it is reasonable to believe that the various body-types of other animals would give them fundamentally different types of consciousness. It might take a Herculean act of imagination to envision the ways of being in the world occupied by the winged, the hoofed, the gilled, or the eight-legged with sufficient clarity that their experiences could be adequately compared with our own.[52] Finally, and echoing our discussion above about the nature of language, there is the Wittgensteinian argument that our mental lives are not strings of private events, but are constituted in social space through systems of conventional signs; if so, it will not be possible to compare our experiences with those of animals whose "form of life" is not similarly constructed in and by language. Thus, "If a lion could talk, we could not understand him"[53]—that is, even if the gift of speech were bestowed on an animal, its mind and way of life would still be so alien that they would not be translatable into human terms.

It seems, then, that Nagel is correct in exposing an unavoidable incompleteness in our understanding of the animal mind. Yet, while this lack of precision will affect some moral arguments (as we will see in the following chapter), it is not sufficient to rule out the possibility of making informed inferences that at least some nonhuman animals can have morally relevant experiences, and that we can at times understand them clearly enough to influence our actions. As I argued above in the discussion of rationality, if the Cartesian position that animals are mere automata cannot be conclusively refuted, enough is known about animal and human biology, physiology, and psychology to come very close. The physiological similarities between the nervous systems of humans and other mammals and birds, the analogies that can be drawn between many forms of human and nonhuman behavior, and the common evolutionary history shared by all life forms on the planet make a compelling case that some animals are conscious, some can experience pleasure and pain, and some even have emotionally and cognitively complex lives. It would be as unreasonable for the species solipsist to deny these judgments as it is for the classic solipsist to question the reality of other human beings' minds.

Further, once we acknowledge the biological continuity of body-types and the anatomical analogies between humans and other animals, we hit upon the foundation for inferring a continuity of consciousness as well. It is therefore reasonable to conclude that the mental lives of our closest relatives—the great apes—may be quite comparable to our own,[54] and that moral deliberation about actions and policies that affect gorillas and chimpanzees may readily approach sufficient certainty. The issue becomes grayer with animals whose posture and bearing are farther removed from our own, but in their case imaginative sympathy—and what some have termed "kinesthetic phenomenology"—may bring us a close enough understanding of their experience to afford them moral consideration.[55] As Rollin argues, this process may be simpler than we at first imagine: "We can understand the wants, needs, desires, and interests of other creatures. Perhaps in a deep sense we can understand these better than we can understand the needs of other humans despite language, because there are apparently so few layers of deception in animals. Perhaps we can understand them even better than we can understand our own everchanging needs. Human needs, after all, are socially, culturally, and historically determined and thus subject to far greater variation than those of animals."[56]

But, there is another possible link to the animal mind in the form of *object consciousness*.[57] If, like humans, other animals do not simply perceive sensory data, but are aware foremost of meaningful objects in their environment, the more subtle differences between human and animal perceptual consciousness—such as the bat's use of echolocation versus our own reliance on vision and hearing—may be less significant.[58] As Adriaan Kortlandt argues, the intentionality of our consciousness locates the mind not in the brain but in the world, situating the path to interspecies inter-subjectivity in the fabric of meaningful objects of which we can be conscious, rather than in neurological and skeletal analogies.[59] If Griffin is correct, "there is abundant evidence that many animals react not to stereotyped patterns of stimulation but to *objects* that they recognize, despite wide variations in the detailed sensations presented to the animal's central nervous system."[60] If so, then despite the obvious and important differences among various animal worlds, there is obviously important common ground in the world of objects feared, admired, avoided, and sought.

If evidence of a more precise type is demanded, recent science may be helpful. The new science of animal welfare, borrowing techniques from infant psychology, is learning to make use of preference testing and observation of physical expression as the "phenomenological starting point" in understanding the lives and desires of other animals.[61] The promise of a more direct understanding is offered by recent experiments in neuroscience in which electrodes are implanted in the relevant sensory centers of an animal's brain, and the data of electrical activity are analyzed and reintegrated to produce a facsimile of what the animal sees or hears. Of course, such devices only go so far in bridging the gap between us and the animal, which will likely never be completely closed. Yet, from the standpoint of biological science, we should not allow a "paralytic perfectionism" to block further investigation, when the possibility remains that substantial progress in understanding the subjective consciousness of other animals can still be made.[62] Moreover, from the standpoint of ethics, it is not clear whether any additional clarity is necessary to permit the animal to count in our moral deliberations. One need not know with absolute precision what it is like to be a laboratory rabbit in order to surmise that it very likely will suffer when caustic chemicals are placed in its eyes during a Draize test—and this awareness is sufficient to animate the machinery of moral concern.

## Conclusion

If nothing else, the cursory survey conducted in this chapter reinforces the theme advanced in the Introduction: that the animal is of fundamental philosophical importance. A clearer understanding of the animal would shed light on many metaphysical, anthropological, and epistemological problems; a philosophical system that ignores the problems raised by the animal's ethical status is thus robbed of a profound source of insight. However, pondering these problems reveals that there is no simple, single factor that distinguishes the human from the animal. A growing body of ethological evidence indicates that there are exceptions to all the traditional criteria—reasoning and language, as well as the development of culture and tradition and ritual, the creation of tools and structures and art, an awareness of individuality and death, even the capacity for altruism—in the nonhuman world. As Dorothy Yamamoto writes, the search for a clear demarcation "is starting to look futile— like the mediaeval quest to find the philosophers' stone, or, perhaps, like attempts to pinpoint the moment when an unborn baby acquires a 'soul.'"[63] Of course, in a climate in which behaviorist theorists question the meaningfulness of speaking about *human* consciousness, it will not be possible to establish to everyone's satisfaction the existence of animal minds. Still, those philosophers and scientists who view a more generous understanding of other species as unduly anthropomorphic seem, upon analysis, to be captive to the anthropocentric *prejudice* that our most valued attributes are uniquely human.[64]

Whatever the ultimate understanding of the animal might be, it is clear from all this that there is nothing *mere* about the animal. Animals are, as Griffin writes, "clearly more than mobile metabolisms. They appear to act, that is, to do things spontaneously, on their own . . . The complexity and the remoteness of animal actions from whatever external causes may be at work distinguishes them in an important fashion from microorganisms, plants, or physical systems. Most of these spontaneous activities are regulated by central nervous systems, and such systems, together with the adaptable behavior they make possible, are a special feature of living animals not found elsewhere in the known universe."[65] This insight places the animal squarely in the sights of ethical concern. Non-human animals may not be morally responsible agents, but to confine them therefore to the same status as inanimate things is to fall victim to a false dilemma. The evolutionary principle of continuity brings vitality *and* moral attention to the area between these extremes: the biological continuum argues for some type of moral continuum as well.[66] As a result, animals, since Darwin, "are demanding their place in the story of what is right and wrong, true or untrue, in life."[67]

---

Let us turn now to the question of how well this call has been answered. If it seems that the animal must have a moral standing greater than that afforded by the tradition, what path will lead to its discovery? Those thinkers who have formed the core of the recent debate have started the hunt in familiar territory, by looking at traditional ethical concepts and exploring whether they may be extended to produce an enhanced moral standing for animals. In Part II, I survey a variety of such extensionist arguments. My purpose in the following chapters is not to produce an exhaustive analysis of these arguments, but rather to assess whether the ethical theories they employ can accommodate an appropriate valuation of the animal. I address these arguments in descending order of the ostensible likelihood of their succeeding at this goal, beginning with utilitarian arguments and concluding with contractarian arguments. I proceed dialectically, demonstrating how each successive argument form addresses the shortcoming of the preceding.

## PART II

*Survey of*
*Extensionist Arguments*

# 3 Utilitarian Arguments:
# The Value of Animal Experience

## Early Utilitarians

Notwithstanding the protests of vegetarians, few of us will deny that a well-prepared piece of meat offers an abundance of sensory pleasures. The mere thought of the aroma of a seared steak can excite the appetite. The chewy texture of animal flesh offers a resistance that our teeth seem to have been designed to overcome, and the jaw muscles relish the triumph of every bite. And, of course, there is the simple pleasure of taste, and the sensuous flood of organic juices that overwhelms the mouth as it chews an excellent piece of meat. Still, the human carnivore may be made to pause in mid-bite by the knowledge that at the other end of the food chain now terminating in his or her mouth lie the factory farm and the slaughterhouse. Hidden from the view of modern consumers by a thin veil of civility—from the tidy cellophane and Styrofoam packages in the supermarket's meat section to the elegant table setting at the restaurant— is the reality of sentient creatures whose every biological function is monitored and controlled with a view to hastening the day when they can be killed and consumed. Common sense tells us that this reality contains some very real suffering, be it the psychological suffering of confinement or the physical suffering of branding and prodding. Do the sensual pleasures that attend consuming animal products justify this suffering? Does it matter whether the pleasures are those offered by a fine steak rather than a fast food burger? Does it matter whether humane steps are taken to minimize the suffering of farm animals? If their suffering is indeed real, can *any* amount of pleasure on the part of human consumers "cancel it out"?

To give prominence in our moral deliberations to such questions as these has been the hallmark of utilitarian ethical theory, which holds—at least in its classical formulation—that the moral worth of our actions is a function of the net pleasure or happiness they produce when taking into account all parties that are affected. The application of this theory to the question of the moral standing of animals is a natural starting point here, for in the modern West the first sustained philosophical efforts to rethink the traditional status of animals are discernible within the work of the English utilitarians of the eighteenth and nineteenth centuries. That these thinkers should have challenged the animal's exclusion from moral consideration is not surprising for two reasons. First, as I discussed in Chapter 1, various cultural factors at work in English society of the eighteenth and nineteenth centuries converged to make the morality of our treatment of animals an inevasible issue. Second, and more fundamentally, the core principles of utilitarianism make it more conducive than other ethical models to entertaining the moral consideration of animals. Jeremy Bentham opens his discussion of the principle of utility with the famous words: "Nature has placed mankind under the governance of two sovereign masters, *pain* and *pleasure*,"[1] but the domain of these masters clearly includes animals as well as humans. So, unlike other ethical theories that link moral categories with the type of cognitive abilities that can be unequivocally attributed only to humans, the classical utilitarian identification of the good with pleasure seamlessly invites the moral evaluation of those actions that affect other sentient animals.

While this much is generally recognized, one must not fail to see the marked dominionism that characterizes the early utilitarians. For example, Bentham's words from *An Introduction to the Principles of Morals and Legislation* are often cited in the debate over animals as sounding the call for the liberation of the animal:

> The day *may* come, when the rest of the animal creation may acquire those rights which never could have been withholden from them but by the hand of tyranny. The French have already discovered that the blackness of the skin is no reason why a human being should be abandoned without redress to the caprice of a tormentor (see Lewis XIV's Code Noir). It may come one day to be recognized, that the number of the legs, the villosity of the skin, or the termination of the *os sacrum*, are reasons equally insufficient for abandoning a sensitive being to the same fate. What else is it that should trace the insuperable line? Is it the faculty of reason, or, perhaps, the faculty of discourse? But a full-grown horse or dog is beyond comparison a more rational, as well as a more conversable animal, than an infant of a day, or a week, or even a month,

old. But suppose the case were otherwise, what would it avail? the question is not, Can they *reason?* nor, Can they *talk?* but, Can they *suffer?*[2]

What should not be overlooked, however, is that this bold statement is buried in a footnote of the final chapter of the work—its content barely broached in the body of the text—and that earlier in the same footnote Bentham writes:

> If the being eaten were all, there is very good reason why we should be suffered to eat such [animals] as we like to eat: we are the better for it, and they are never the worse. They have none of those long-protracted anticipations of future misery which we have. The death they suffer in our hands commonly is, and always may be, a speedier, and by that means a less painful one, than that which would await them in the inevitable course of nature. If the being killed were all, there is very good reason why we should be suffered to kill such as molest us: we should be the worse for their living, and they are never the worse for being dead.

From this we see that while Bentham's view may have been progressive, he does not question human beings' fundamental right to use animals for what he deemed legitimate purposes. Unopposed to meat eating or vivisection, Bentham is concerned with the overt and unnecessary cruelty of sport hunting, bear baiting, and the like.[3] Likewise, his godson John Stuart Mill did not oppose the use of animals for food or science, yet allied himself with the anticruelty movement, and made clear that the utilitarians' concept of the ultimate end—"an existence exempt as far as possible from pain, and as rich as possible in enjoyments, both in point of quantity and quality"—ought to be secured not only to humanity, "but, so far as the nature of things admits, to the whole sentient creation."[4] Mill's famous discussion of a dissatisfied Socrates and a satisfied pig makes clear that his version of utilitarianism leaves ample room for human interests to trump those of other sentient animals. The nineteenth-century reformer Henry Salt, who was influenced by the utilitarianism of Herbert Spencer, was perhaps more consistent in calling into question the legitimacy not only of blood sports, but also of the rearing of animals for food and research. Yet he, too, cannot completely escape the grip of traditional dominionism: "While admitting that man is justified, by the exigencies of his own destiny, in asserting his supremacy over the wild animals, we must deny him any right to turn his protectorate into a tyranny."[5]

Thus, while the early utilitarians provide a possible ground for the rational, ethical analysis of our treatment of other animals, their con-

clusions are only reformist in nature, and do not scrutinize the funda-
mentals of humanity's relationships to other animals. In this regard,
Bentham and Mill may be viewed as reflecting intuitions that are widely
held today: we are more important than animals, but overt cruelty
toward them is wrong. Beginning from this foundation, more recent
utilitarian attempts at animal advocacy have gone on to question
whether the uses of animals traditionally deemed "legitimate" meet the
standard of utility, and have proposed stricter limits on the extent to
which other species' interests may be justifiably compromised.

### Animal Liberation

The most noteworthy example of these recent efforts is to be found in
the work of the Oxford-educated Australian philosopher Peter Singer,
whose *Animal Liberation* (first published in 1975) is often credited with
sparking the recent debate over animals. Although Singer was one of
many like-minded Oxford thinkers (including Richard Ryder, Ruth Harris, Andrew Linzey, and Stephen Clark) of the 1960s and 1970s who
shared his philosophical and moral concern for animals, there is little
question that *Animal Liberation* was a singularly powerful force in
pointing both the moral compass of many laypersons and the curiosity
of many applied ethicists toward the treatment of other species. Because
of the power and popularity of the work, it has drawn an enormous
amount of commentary and criticism to which little if anything new
will be added here. However, some discussion of Singer's argument is
useful for our present purposes because it so clearly illustrates the challenges of extensionism. A student of R. M. Hare, Singer is an adherent of
"preference" utilitarianism—which holds that the good to be maximized by our actions is not a net gain in pleasure or happiness, but
instead a net gain in preferences fulfilled—rather than the classical
"hedonic" utilitarianism of Bentham and Mill.[6] Nonetheless, as we will
see subsequently, it is striking how far Singer must stray from the usual
territory of utilitarian calculation in order to reach his conclusions
about the moral standing of animals.[7]

The power of *Animal Liberation* lies in part with the strong emotions its discussion evokes: like Bentham, Singer highlights the moral
importance of our treatment of other animals by analogizing their plight
to the oppression of women and persons of color—thus aligning the call
for animal "liberation" with the various human liberation movements
of the nineteenth and twentieth centuries—and he embellishes the text
with graphic images of the treatment of animals in agriculture and sci-

ence. But beneath its provocative skin, there is an impressive parsimony to his argument proper; drawing from various utilitarian thinkers, he attempts to come to some very broad and unsettling conclusions about our treatment of animals from a small set of simple premises.

The bedrock of Singer's argument is the innocuous premise that if a being possesses *interests*, then non-arbitrary reasons must be given to justify those actions that adversely affect its interests. Singer reasons that all *sentient* beings—including all human and nonhuman animals that are capable of experiencing pain—have at least one clear interest, namely, avoiding painful experience.[8] While the issue of animal sentience is metaphysically and epistemologically more complex than Singer seems willing to acknowledge, in light of the evidence reviewed in Part I his conclusion that at least mammals and birds can suffer painful experiences is a reasonable one. From this ground, Singer argues that for humans to ignore the effects of their actions on the interests of other animals simply because they are nonhuman interests is morally arbitrary. It is on this point that his analogy between animal and human oppression rests: just as racism and sexism are morally wrong because a human being's race or gender is generally irrelevant to whether we ought to consider the effects of our actions on him or her, so too is ignoring a being's interests solely because of its species, or *speciesism*, a term coined by Richard Ryder.[9] As Singer defines it, "Speciesism . . . is a prejudice or attitude of bias in favor of the interests of members of one's own species and against those of members of other species."[10]

Under the somewhat misleading rubric "All Animals Are Equal," Singer argues that moral consistency requires the *equal consideration of interests*, irrespective of the nature of the beings that hold them. Of course, other animals are not our equals in fact: they lack, either in degree or in kind, the intellectual, linguistic, and moral attributes that characterize our humanness. However, the same is true of some human beings as well, and that by itself is not a sufficient justification for flouting their interests: "Equality is a moral idea, not an assertion of fact. There is no logically compelling reason for assuming that a factual difference in ability between two people justifies any difference in the amount of consideration we give to their needs and interests. *The principle of equality of human beings is not a description of an alleged actual equality among humans: it is a prescription of how we should treat human beings.*"[11] Invoking Bentham's claim (quoted at the beginning of this chapter) that the capacity for suffering trumps the moral relevance of rational or verbal ability, Singer argues that the scope of this prescriptive principle cannot end with our own species: "If a being can suffer there can be no moral justification for refusing to take that suffering into consideration. No matter what the nature of the being, the principle of equality requires that its suffering be counted equally with the like suffering—insofar as rough comparisons can be made—of any other being."[12] If so, Singer concludes, it follows that the various forms of animal exploitation that ignore animal suffering (e.g., intensive "factory" farming and scientific experiments that inflict pain on laboratory animals) must be viewed as seriously immoral.[13]

However, this analogy between human oppression and animal exploitation has drawn criticism on several fronts. First, the comparison has been challenged for amplifying the moral problem of animal exploitation at the expense of trivializing the evils of racial and sexual discrimination. Some who have fought for human rights find it offensive that the treatment of farm animals would be analogized to the rape, enslavement, and genocide of human beings.[14] Second, while sociobiological explanations of racism or misogyny have been ventured, the possibility that our discrimination against other species has a biological as well as a cultural component seems to be on surer ground. As Mary Midgley argues, species loyalty appears to be innate within all social animals, a natural emotional bond that reflects, among other things, the adaptive value of kin altruism.[15] If so, species discrimination on the part of human beings need not always be an irrational and immoral prejudice, but may reflect the need to apportion our obligations to others on the basis of emotional and social distance.[16] Third, while race and gender may be considered inessential when considering a human being's humanness, one obviously cannot know how to accommodate an animal's fundamental needs and interests if one ignores its species; thus, no one concerned with animal welfare could seriously advocate species blindness in the way that someone concerned with human equality would implore us to overcome racism and sexism.[17]

In spite of these concerns, the charge that speciesism is a morally arbitrary and malignant presence in Western culture still merits consideration. If we accept the consequentialist argument that the moral worth of an action is a function of the effects it produces, we are obliged to consider *all* the morally relevant effects of our actions, not just the ones that are convenient for our purposes. Further, if we accept the classical utilitarian argument that the only morally relevant effect of our actions is the total happiness (pleasure) and suffering (pain) they produce for *all* parties whose interests are at stake, the mere difference of species provides no clear justification for excluding animal pleasures and pains from the utilitarian calculus.[18] In light of such considerations, philosopher Colin McGinn calls the judgment that speciesism is morally arbitrary a "won argument."[19]

## The Animal Calculus

However, even if we accept McGinn's assessment, it is not clear that the equal consideration of animal interests can establish as much as Singer purports, which is a near total ban on agricultural, scientific, and commercial uses of animals. Granting that the effects of our actions on sentient animals should count in our moral deliberations, they, like the effects on our fellow humans, must still be subject to quantitative and qualitative evaluation. This kind of evaluation, which is unavoidable for the utilitarian who views the ends of actions as morally more significant than the actions themselves, opens up the prospect that at least some of the harm of ostensibly speciesist practices can be morally justified by appeal to the qualitatively and quantitatively greater human interests that they serve. Granting that other animals can suffer, it does not follow that there are no human goods that can supersede animal suffering; if Singer is correct in asserting that sentient animals have interests to be considered, that would not preclude humans having other interests that are more valuable.

Singer is, of course, aware of this, but he maintains that it does not affect the core of his argument. For example, in regard to using animals for medical research, he acknowledges that "some individual experiments—those that do not involve any or very much suffering for the animals, and promise major benefits for humans or animals—may be defensible on utilitarian grounds," but argues that few if any common research practices would meet this criterion.[20] Additionally, he argues that once human and animal interests are given equal consideration in our deliberations, even their qualitative evaluation will lead to unhappy conclusions for those who would limit moral concern to their fellow humans. He makes the case that if we believe the suffering imposed on a healthy adult mammal, such as a chimpanzee, during a medical experiment is justified by the alleviation of human suffering the experiment can eventually make possible, then we should also be prepared to perform similar experiments on human beings of comparable sentience to the chimp, say, severely retarded children. If we are not, he claims, our unwillingness merely reflects a morally arbitrary preference for our own species, and not a concern for maximizing utility.[21]

One can respond to such arguments singly;[22] however, even if we grant that these points are reasonable, the whole line of discussion raises a more fundamental problem. The utilitarian requirement that the net effect of our actions be calculated in order to determine their moral worth poses an unavoidable obstacle to Singer's goal of liberating the animal from human "tyranny." As Ingmar Persson has argued—reflecting broader criticisms that have been leveled against utilitarianism—at the heart of Singer's type of argument is a critical tension between the utilitarian goal of maximizing total fulfillment and the liberationist goal of equality. This tension is clear even when only human interests are under consideration: if it can be shown that those who are materially well off value their own lives, preferences, and pleasures more than do the poor, utility would not require sacrifice in the name of economic justice; likewise, since our value to each other varies, an equitable distribution of rewards and punishments likely will result in less than maximal utility within a society.[23] When such considerations are extended to the comparison of human and animal interests, the prospect of reaching consensus on something that might reasonably be termed "animal equality" seems very dim.

This problem dovetails with a larger epistemological one that haunts all utilitarian arguments concerning animals: How are we to calculate all the harm and benefit that our exploitation of other animals produces? There will be clear cases at the extremes, but the conclusions to be reached about common institutionalized practices are less obvious. Let us first consider the issue of using animals for food. The question of whether and to what extent this practice is morally justified is clearly an essential one. Given the spiritual, emotional, and even sexual significance that food holds for human beings cross-culturally, the possibility that prevalent eating habits might be seriously immoral has enormous implications. Indeed, the ubiquity of consuming meat and other animal products—and the sheer number of animals involved—makes the moral proscription of the practice almost unfathomable. As Marian Scholtmeijer writes, "farm animals are so profoundly entrenched in society as economic units that the attempt to find moral significance in their situation seems foolish. If farm animals do not merit activation of conscience, then why should any other animal?"[24] The domestication of animals for food is such a central institution in the history of human civilization that the practice is readily declared "natural" and "necessary," with the implication that it is thereby exempt from moral evaluation—a conclusion that bolsters the case against rethinking the moral standing of animals in general.[25] One of Singer's explicit intentions is to provoke a revaluation of such ideas, and defend the conclusion that vegetarianism is morally obligatory. Does he succeed?

For utilitarians—including Singer[26]—who do not hold that life is "sacred" or of inherent, absolute worth, the judgment that eating animal flesh is wrong cannot rest on an absolute proscription against killing, but rather on the calculation that utility is better served by abstaining.[27] Some calculations may be non-controversial: it seems clear (even to many non-vegetarians) that the additional suffering imposed on a confined veal calf cannot be justified by the additional pleasure experienced by those who prefer its tender flesh to ordinary beef;[28] likewise, it seems clear (except to extreme pacifists, such as Jains) that subsistence hunters inflict justifiable suffering on their prey when the alternative is a sacrifice of their own well-being. But between these extremes, would utility be better served by continuing to consume animal products while adopting "humane" husbandry practices, or by eliminating them entirely from our diets? As Singer and others have documented, in modern confinement agriculture (also known as "intensive" or "factory" farming, or "animal feeding operations"), domesticated animals are managed under conditions for which they are not evolutionarily adapted, and as a result their needs and interests are systematically violated.[29] Might a return to traditional extensive farming techniques—which would allow for a higher quality of life for the animals, *and* for humans to continue to enjoy consuming them—maximize utility better than either modern methods or forgoing animal husbandry altogether?

Even in the light of this possibility, Singer responds that vegetarianism is nonetheless obligatory. Yet, it is interesting how far he must step outside of purely utilitarian considerations to make the case:

> As a matter of strict logic, perhaps, there is no contradiction in taking an interest in animals on both compassionate and gastronomic grounds. If one is opposed to inflicting suffering on animals, but not to the painless killing of animals, one could consistently eat animals who had lived free of all suffering and been instantly, painlessly slaughtered. Yet practically and psychologically it is impossible to be consistent in one's concern for nonhuman animals while continuing to dine on them. If we are prepared to take the life of another being merely in order to satisfy our taste for a particular type of food, then that being is no more than a means to our end.[30]

This last sentence is especially telling, considering that a utilitarian purist would be committed to viewing everything as means to maximal utility. As Singer admits later in *Animal Liberation*,[31] his argument here is fundamentally a psychological prediction, rather than an estimate of utility. Similarly, Andrew Linzey argues not that it is impossible that utility might be served by eating other animals, but rather that "the current failure to secure humane farm management and slaughter renders 'moderate' meat eating ethically problematic . . . It is difficult to envisage a time when conditions will universally prevail so as to preclude animal suffering in agriculture."[32]

Bart Gruzalski has attempted a purer utilitarian argument prescribing vegetarianism, yet in outlining all of the relevant pleasures and pains to be taken into account, he only seems to underscore the futility of the attempt.[33] To reach a firm conclusion on a rule proscribing or advocating the raising of domesticated animals for food, one would have to take account of all the pleasures and pains experienced by farm animals under various conditions of treatment—and the loss of these experiences if domesticated animals were not to be bred for food; the pleasures and pains experienced by those humans who raise and consume farm animals; the pleasures and pains to be experienced by the wild animals that could occupy what is now farmland; and all the long-term economic, health-related, and environmental effects of each option (the implications for world hunger and social justice, the cultural value of farming as a way of life, nutritional arguments for and against a vegetarian diet, etc.). Clearly and objectively identifying, quantifying, and qualitatively evaluating all the relevant experiences of all species affected by these alternatives does not even seem possible in theory;[34] the utilitarian calculus simply cannot handle such complexity. Even if it could, it might well turn out, as Jan Narveson argues, that utility is best served by the "carnivorous regime" now in place.[35]

Similar complexity also confronts us when we examine other forms of animal exploitation, such as the use of animals in scientific research. Like the use of animals for food, the question of whether we are justified in experimenting upon other animals' living systems in the name of medical and other scientific progress is fundamental to clarifying the moral status of the animal. There is in the popular mind a sanctity to scientific research that other forms of exploitation no longer enjoy;[36] while the hunter's pursuit of game is commonly stereotyped as atavistic and cruel, the scientist's pursuit of knowledge is cloaked in nobility. As the one form of animal exploitation practiced exclusively by the learned elite, the scientific use of the animal has long been an important target of the animal welfare movement; if attitudes of the most educated cannot be changed, there would seem to be little hope of effecting other reforms.[37]

A classical utilitarian approach to the issue of whether this practice is morally justifiable will have to take into account the amount of harm inflicted on the animals used, the amount of benefit humans hope to gain as a result, and the qualitative value and relative certainty of each. As Hugh LaFollette and Niall Shanks have demonstrated, the possibility of producing an accurate calculation of all these factors is slim.[38] Here we have not only the difficulty of estimating and evaluating the physical and psychological suffering that laboratory conditions and experimental procedures will impose upon various other animals—from mice to our closest primate relatives—but also the problem of how to assess the benefits such research provides humans. Singer, for example, cites evidence suggesting that modern medical intervention has had only a marginal effect on human longevity and well-being, and that therefore the animal suffering required by medical research is not justified.[39] However, Carl Cohen, a staunch supporter of the continuing use of animals in research, counters: "The elimination of horrible disease, the increase of longevity, the avoidance of great pain, the saving of lives, and the improvement of the quality of lives . . . achieved through research using animals is so incalculably great that the argument of [utilitarian] critics . . . establishes not their conclusion but the reverse."[40] Determining whose calculation is correct seems a daunting, if not impossible, task. Add to the mix all other relevant factors (assessing the epistemological value of animal models, the relative merits of preventative and curative medicine, etc.) and the problem soon becomes ungainly.

That Singer and Cohen can reach such divergent conclusions about research, as Gruzalski and Narveson do about agriculture—while aware of the same basic facts relevant to the issues, and attempting to analyze them within the same ethical framework—reveals a serious limitation in the utilitarian approach: it is too vulnerable to factual disagreements about future consequences of actions and evaluative disagreements over the import of these consequences to provide sufficient certainty for our moral evaluation of such large-scale practices as institutionalized animal exploitation. As Steven R. L. Clark writes:

> Some recent philosophers have attempted to argue from utilitarian principle to the conclusion that we . . . should cease torturing and killing animals. They write in Mill's and Bentham's spirit. But the very fact that other philosophers have defended the status quo on just the same principles (for any alteration in the way we live will have unpleasant consequences for those currently employed in farms, laboratories and zoos) reveals that the calculation is . . . incalculable. Professed utilitarians only think they reason to their conclusions by the calculus: in fact they choose their goals by other means. Utilitarianism is always and entirely an excuse.[41]

## Other Problems

Singer's argument assimilates in a simple and powerful way the conclusion that emerged from the previous two chapters: the animal must be taken seriously in our moral thinking. Many—including myself—have found his reasoning sufficiently strong to induce them to reevaluate their use of animal products. Yet, on the level of moral theory, Clark's response, which echoes the broader theoretical criticisms that have been leveled against utilitarianism, is sufficient, I think, to render unsatisfying the utilitarian approach to the moral standing of animals. To those who would remain committed to utilitarian extensionism, further difficulties can be raised.

### SPECIES SOLIPSISM REVISITED

In Chapter 2, I discussed the problem that Griffin dubs "species solipsism": the impossibility of our having precise knowledge of other animals' mental lives. I argued there that the problem was real but insufficient to deny animals as a category any moral standing. However, the extent to which there are barriers to our assessment of other animals' experiences poses a real difficulty for the utilitarian. Even Griffin, who argues so strenuously that species solipsism should not be viewed as an insurmountable obstacle to the understanding of animal minds, asks, "how do we know whether some species suffer more than others? We have . . . very little firm knowledge on which to base decisions and trade-offs concerning animal welfare." He adds: "We are at present so extremely ignorant about the conscious mental experiences of animals that it will be a long time before scientific methods can be developed to measure just how much a given animal suffers under particular conditions."[42] Philosopher Gary Varner cites this problem as illustrating "how the dynamic state of relevant scientific research puts certain humanities scholars in a difficult position. What answers our theories give to hot-button social issues can depend critically on the resolution of empirical questions, some of which scientists have barely started to formulate, but which conscientious humanities scholars cannot ignore."[43]

Griffin attributes our ignorance of these empirical questions to the lack of attention on the part of scientists. The more fundamental causes have been reviewed in Chapter 2: the neurological analogies between humans and other animals make a reasonable case that they can suffer, but the differences alert us that qualitative and quantitative comparisons will be difficult; and the different body-types and cognitive structures other animals possess make it difficult to assay how these beings assimilate their painful experiences into their mental lives. As I reviewed, the Darwinian principle of species continuity tells us that the mental lives of our closest relatives—the great apes—may be comparable to our own, and therefore utilitarian conclusions about actions and policies that affect gorillas and chimpanzees may approach sufficient certainty. But a precise understanding of our more distant relatives' sentient lives seems out of reach.

The utilitarian cannot ignore this lack of precision, inasmuch as the certainty with which we can foresee an action's consequences is a relevant part of the calculus. Yet Singer, for example, fails to appreciate its impact on his argument. First, he underestimates the severity of the gap between human and animal minds, as when he states: "I do not think the problem is different in kind from the problem of comparing the subjective experiences of two members of our own species."[44] On the contrary, the factors discussed above argue that real quantitative and qualitative differences distinguish the assessment of human and animal experience. Second, even when acknowledging the problem, he discounts its importance by repeatedly arguing that there is nonetheless a sufficient number of clear cases to require the radical revaluation of our treatment of animals.[45] However, Singer's examples may be more controversial than they at first appear: "It seems undeniable that to put into the eye of a rabbit a chemical that causes the eye to blister or become ulcerated is to do more harm to the rabbit than we would do to any number of human beings by denying them the possibility of choosing a new type of shampoo that can be marketed only if the chemical is tested in this way. When such rough comparisons can be made, the mere fact that rabbits are 'lower animals' is no reason to give less weight to their suffering."[46] While most will agree with Singer's conclusion, it is not inarguable. If a human being's eyes were sprayed with caustic chemicals by a crazed attacker, the judgment that utility was served by the attacker's action would clearly be irrational, given the intensity of pain and suffering the victim would experience and the lack of fecundity that would attend any sadistic pleasure the attacker would feel. However, a similar judgment in the rabbit's case, while questionable, does not appear so obviously irrational. Recently, during a class discussion of this example, a student of mine steadfastly maintained that the confidence and self-esteem a human being might receive from an effective consumer product qualitatively outweighs the purely somatic suffering of the rabbit. One certainly may question the priorities of those who would experience genuine pleasure from a shampoo and rely on such pleasures to enhance their sense of self; yet, there is no clear error in maintaining that such human pleasures are indeed real and may outweigh—in either degree or significance—a "lower animal's" capacity to experience pain.

## PAIN, WELL-BEING, AND INTERESTS

Even where utilitarian calculations can be made with sufficient objectivity and clarity, we may still question whether it is morally acceptable to have one being's pleasure offset another being's suffering. This concern underlies the amendment to utilitarianism that Richard Ryder terms *painism*: the position that the main objective of morality is to reduce the amount of suffering experienced in the world—rather than to maximize pleasure—because pain is the only intrinsic evil.[47] If reducing pain has a higher obligatory force than producing pleasure, then the infliction of suffering—on either our fellow humans or other animals—cannot be compensated for by an equivalent gain of pleasure. According to this model, animal exploitation is only justified when it can be established that it will result in an overall reduction of suffering. Even with the complications of species solipsism, this approach would seem to offer a more manageable means of evaluating our uses of animals than does the traditional calculus.

The difficulties with this approach have been detailed by R. G. Frey, who argues, first, that the evaluative judgment "Pain is intrinsically evil" is not a tautology, and so painism will hold no weight with those—for example, adherents of various ascetic and religious ethics—who do not share this intuition.[48] Second, echoing Clark's concern about the ad hoc nature of utilitarian thinking, Frey asserts that animal advocates have an incentive to make pain the most important feature of sentience—and, in turn, moral status—because any more sophisticated candidate threatens to exclude the animal;[49] however, highlighting pain at the expense of other aspects of consciousness is not otherwise necessary: "Why, then, if one is determined to adopt a sentiency criterion, should it be formulated around experiences of pain and so be animal-including instead of being formulated around [for example] experiences of beauty and so be animal-excluding?"[50] Further, Frey challenges Singer's position that the capacity to feel pain is a prerequisite for having morally relevant interests, arguing that this leads to the counterintuitive conclusion that animals have interests, whereas some humans—such as someone rendered unable to feel pain by an injury—do not. On the contrary, we readily think of these latter as having interests, say, in receiving proper treatment, maintaining their good name, and the like.[51]

The larger problem here concerns the morally charged concept of *interests* itself. Human interests can be defined generally as the stake we hold in those things typically desired for our general well-being; such desiderata—which we understand only by virtue of being human—clearly include more than freedom from pain.[52] As David Degrazia argues,[53] trying to determine whether the well-being of nonhumans has similarly complex requirements raises perplexing but fundamental questions: Do other animals have an interest in life itself, irrespective of the value of their experiences?[54] Is the confinement that characterizes domestication a form of harm, even if it does not produce suffering? Do other animals have a stake in their natural functioning: Would cutting a dog's intelligence in half harm its well-being? Does its lack of ability to fulfill its "dog-ness" matter? These fascinating questions are clearly relevant to the moral assessment of our treatment of other animals; however, by introducing the possibility that there are morally relevant goods that cannot be reduced to the obvious goods of sentient consciousness, they also undermine the original appeal of the utilitarian approach to the animal.

## SENTIENTISM AND THE "LIBERATION OF NATURE"

One final difficulty with the utilitarian approach to the animal has been voiced by environmental ethicists—perhaps an unexpected source of criticism, given that they, like animal advocates, are committed to the objective of expanding the moral community beyond the human species. It has been questioned whether Singer's identification of sentience as a necessary condition for holding moral status represents merely another form of chauvinism—termed *sentientism*, after *speciesism* and the rest. As John Rodman puts it, Singer's focus on sentient animals condemns the vast majority of the planet's inhabitants to "a state of thinghood, having no intrinsic worth, acquiring instrumental value only as resources for the well-being of an elite of sentient beings."[55] (The spider whose web we were considering destroying in the Introduction would lack direct moral status under Singer's model, because its claim to humanlike sentience is dubious.[56]) Utilitarianism commits us to viewing all reality as means to states of feeling,[57] a way of valuing the world that Nietzsche diagnoses as a mad "extravagance of vanity."[58] Thus, in spite of the animal liberationist's claim to inclusiveness, it may be argued that the utilitarian approach only serves to secure humanity's moral priority, providing an extension of concern only to our nearest relatives.[59]

This point is important within a larger debate that occupies environmental ethics. Assuming that as moral agents we ought to be concerned about the fate of the nonhuman natural world, exactly what should be the object of our concern: individual sentient animals, non-sentient entities such as entire species and ecosystems, or perhaps (as popularized by the Gaian movement) the earth as a whole? There clearly will be cases where concerns will conflict (e.g., culling a herd may serve its long-term sustainability, but only at the expense of the individual animals sacrificed), and it is not obvious that the interests of individual sentient beings—even when sufficiently clear—should always prevail. Furthermore, it may be argued that utilitarianism commits humans to micromanaging the nonhuman world in order to maximize utility: for example, treating disease in wildlife, minimizing predator species, and so on.[60] If so, it would seem that the dominionism of Bentham and Mill still echoes through later utilitarian extensionism.

## Conclusion

Reflecting on the utilitarian approach to animals, we may find ourselves in agreement with James Gaffney: "Weighing suffering against benefit on a moral scale is not, of course, an exact science, and honest differences of estimate must be respected and may demand compromises. It is an effort to make such estimates carefully, in the light of all relevant data, that demonstrates the inclusion of animals within a civilized ethic."[61] Perhaps, but this hardly improves on the pre-reflective intuitions many hold toward animals without explicitly embracing utilitarian theory: animal suffering counts for something, but for how much? It may well be that a "civilized ethic" must afford some moral status to nonhuman animals, but as Narveson states bluntly, what that status should be "is not entirely clear if we opt for utilitarianism."[62] Hedonic utilitarianism's focus on the net result of pleasure and pain produced by our actions commits us to comparisons of human and animal mental states that may only rarely approach sufficient clarity to inform our moral decision making, and fails to address some of the fundamental aspects of human and animal well-being. Other forms of utilitarianism, which address other morally relevant interests besides maximizing pleasure and avoiding pain, likewise require unmanageably complex deliberations. As a result, the principle of utility will not deliver clear moral assessments of many forms of animal exploitation, including the institutionalized practices of using animals for food and research. We must look elsewhere, then, at other ethical models, to see whether they can produce a more workable understanding of the moral status of nonhumans.

# 4 Deontological Arguments: Do Animals Have Natural Rights?

## The Deontological Alternative

The difficulties attending the utilitarian analysis of our treatment of nonhumans do not by themselves preclude the development of a workable animal ethic. Those who are persuaded by the critique of consequentialist ethics outlined in the previous chapter have various non-consequentialist or deontological models to explore. These alternatives are attractive, for if the deontologist can establish that the moral worth of human actions rests with a duty other than to maximize the goods of consciousness, then moral deliberation may be a much simpler matter than it is under utilitarianism. If consequentialist calculations are not necessary to know what is right, then we may avoid the epistemological problems that plague nebulous comparisons of mental states and predictions about the future results of our actions. Moreover, as Marian Scholtmeijer argues, a deontological approach is a better fit with the non-teleological understanding of animal life that emerges from modern evolutionary biology: the two converge to acknowledge a value to individual animal lives that is independent of their usefulness to other agents or their place in some cosmic teleological process.[1] However, the ultimate foundation of deontological categories is controversial, and it is not obvious that these categories are applicable to animals.

In the tradition, the foremost figure to defend an uncompromising non-consequentialist approach to ethics is Immanuel Kant. Fundamental to his argument is the judgment that it cannot be the properly moral function of human practical reason to calculate which actions will effect the most advantageous consequences. It is noteworthy for the present discussion that in defending this judgment Kant draws upon an apparent distinction between humans and other animals: "In a being which has reason and a will, if the proper object of nature were its conservation, its welfare, in a word, its happiness, then nature would have hit upon a very bad arrangement in selecting the reason of the creature to carry out this purpose. For all the actions which the creature has to perform with a view to this purpose, and the whole rule of its conduct, would be far more surely prescribed to it by instinct, and that end would have been attained thereby much more certainly than it ever can be by reason."[2]

Kant's point seems to be that while those behaviors of non-rational animals that will produce the most agreeable effects are efficiently governed by non-conscious instincts, the human being's reliance on reason—which, he argues, is inept at such calculations[3]—must have a moral purpose other than maximizing utility. As he writes, "all these effects—agreeableness of one's condition and even the promotion of the happiness of others—could have been also brought about by other causes, so that for this there would have been no need of the will of a rational being; whereas it is in this alone that the supreme and unconditional good can be found."[4] From this foundation, Kant proceeds to develop the famous principles of his ethical system: that the moral worth of an action lies not with its expected effect, but with whether it has been willed for the sake of *duty*; that duty is respect for those moral *laws* that can function universally for all rational beings; and that the source of these laws is the unconditional worth of rational beings existing as *ends in themselves*.

While Kant takes pains to emphasize that the principles of ethics do not derive from the empirical details of "anthropology," but instead must hold for *any* rational being,[5] his concern is with the purity and necessity of moral laws, and there is no indication that he is entertaining the prospect that other animals might also qualify as rational beings. On the contrary, Kant is explicit in categorizing nonhuman animals as *things*, which may evoke love or fear or admiration, but never the moral respect reserved for rational persons.[6] So, while the classical utilitarian conception of the good as pleasure is prima facie animal-inclusive, Kant's declaration that the only intrinsic good is a good will—that is, a will informed by a rational being's respect for universal and necessary laws—precludes a direct moral status for nonhuman animals: "Animals are not self-conscious and are there merely as a means to an end. That end is man . . . Our duties toward animals are merely indirect duties toward humanity."[7] As Schopenhauer—who articulated an animal-inclusive ethic grounded on *compassion* rather than rationality—would later characterize the Kantian model, "only for practice are we to have sympathy for animals, and they are, so to speak, the pathological phantom for the purpose of practicing sympathy for human beings."[8]

Some more recent deontological thinkers have been more accepting of a direct moral status for animals.[9] In particular, those who have sought to clarify the moral status of animals by viewing them as bearers of *rights* may be seen in this light: as attempting to expand the Kantian principle of respect for persons to include more than rational human agents. The general concept of rights—so powerful in the past three centuries of human social history—is at first glance a welcome corrective to the utilitarian calculus. Brigid Brophy, in preparing her argument for animal rights, first makes the point convincingly with respect to human beings:

> The Declaration of Independence converts a perception of the *facts* about being alive and sentient into a declaration of the *right* to continue alive and obey the pleasure-pain principle—because, as a social document, it has to cope with the possibility that one person's necessity to live may conflict with another's. Reason makes that a matter of rights, because it sees there is no reasonable judging or measuring between two such necessities. Your need to live *may* be more needful, more valid, than mine. Your pleasure may be more pleasurable than my pain is painful. You may have received a special revelation to that effect, and your special revelation might be correct. But as neither you nor I can enter into the other's being or sentiency, we shan't convince one another; and an impartial, reasonable third person, who can't enter into either of us, possesses no reasonable scale for judging between us.[10]

By extension, those animal advocates who are aware of the difficulties in comparing animal and human sentient experience will find in the prospect of *animal* rights a more stable platform for the moral standing of nonhumans than the utilitarian's recognition of animal suffering can provide. As Paul Brett argues:

> To have compassion is to recognize a continuity of existence with the other. It is to suffer, to feel with—not just for—other creatures. It is to recognize with the heart and with the head that human and animal are made of the same stuff and that moral obligations arise from this . . . But there is a point beyond compassion to which the argument seems irresistibly to lead. To recognize the otherness of animals, and their place alongside human beings, is to recognize that they belong here as of right, no less than we do. It is to begin to see our relationship with animals as a question of justice. It is only with the attribution of rights to

animals that a secure basis can be found on which to work out our detailed ethical obligations.[11]

As a purely practical matter, to conceive of animals as the bearers of rights "is to institutionalize their claim to moral concern, to recognize this status in a way that is writ large."[12] Given the political power rights claims can wield, couching one's moral position in the language of rights can often be the most effective means of advocating it, especially in a social context where moral discourse is usually ideologically and politically combative.[13] As a result, in much of our colloquial moral and political discourse (and, I should add, the subtitle of the present work) we find a broad range of evaluative claims are expressed in terms of rights. Such imprecision is not unproblematic; as Steve Sapontzis contends, it is "simplistic to infer that because something has an impact on the basic interests of members of a group, and those interests should be protected, we must conclude that members of that group have a right to (or against) that something."[14] Nonetheless, even those who are otherwise unsympathetic to deontology may feel compelled to employ terms like *rights* because they are so expedient. For example, Peter Singer concedes on behalf of utilitarians: "The language of rights is a convenient political shorthand. It is even more valuable in the era of thirty-second TV news clips than it was in Bentham's day."[15] We find, therefore, that those who feel that speciesism is wrong, but are untroubled by—or unaware of—the theoretical difficulties in defining the moral status of nonhumans, have in the term *animal rights* an effective credo.

## The General Nature of Rights

Of course, the assertion that animals have rights can hardly go unchallenged when the existence and meaningfulness of *human* rights is a matter of considerable philosophical controversy. The literature on the general nature of rights is too vast to do it justice here, but some analysis of the foundation of supposed human rights is necessary. Such analysis reveals the obstacles that will confront those who would hope to find in the concept "animal rights" the means to clarifying the animal's moral status.

The clearest sense of normative rights is *contractual*, referring to the just claims one party has against others that they fulfill their expressed commitments; the meaning of such claims can be discerned by analysis of the details of the agreements that ground them. Other conceptions of rights may be viewed as extensions of this notion that attempt to define the just claims one holds against others even in the absence of explicit contractual agreements. Since it is untenable to conceive of nonhuman animals as informed parties to contracts, the possibility of non-contractual rights is a prerequisite to bringing the animal under the umbrella of rights theory. However, there are difficult questions about the meaningfulness and normative force of rights claims that are unsupported by explicit agreements. For example, must rights always take the form of actual claims that are made verbally, or can they also be less explicitly performative (as when we speak of *having* a claim versus *making* a claim)? How exactly are non-contractual rights correlative with duties? Can they ground positive obligations (e.g., of benevolence), or only negative duties of noninterference?

Least problematic among non-contractual rights will be those that are overtly legal or political in nature. *Legal* rights may be described as codifying the enforceable claims one party has against others irrespective of whether they are aware of or explicitly agree to the terms, the meaningfulness of these rights being dependent on the rules of the particular legal system. Likewise, in liberal democracies, general *political* rights—such as those articulated in the U.S. Bill of Rights—reflect the respect one can claim for general autonomy interests, regardless of whether that respect has been or can be explicitly codified in specific laws. There are no inevasible logical obstacles to the stipulation of legal or political rights for animals, and some have made strong cases for doing so.[16] Indeed, as a purely *practical* matter, the recognition of such rights may be the only efficacious means of preventing human harm to animals. However, as ecologist John Livingston argues, human legalistic concepts are a rough fit with the apolitical reality of nonhumans; thus, on the level of *theory*, to understand animals as bearers of rights is to conceptualize them in an alien environment: "The fundamental concept of rights seems itself to be incongruous and inappropriate in the non-human context. At its very simplest level, if the function of rights is political (to protect the interest of the individual against the interest of the collective), in . . . Nature the notion is without meaning . . . If, however, the function of rights is to protect Nature from humans, then that is to politicize Nature."[17]

As John Berger notes with respect to the "Disneyfication" of animals in modern popular culture, "the pettiness of current social practices is *universalized* by being projected onto the animal kingdom";[18] when we see Mickey Mouse and Donald Duck behaving like middle-class, white Americans the effect is to make such behavior appear to be part of the fabric of objective reality rather than a particular cultural construction. In like manner, Livingston seems to suggest that the concept of animal rights—and the attending image of mice and ducks as political agents with rights claims to assert—represents an attempt to naturalize our own "petty" ethical practices, an effort that cannot adequately reflect animal reality. Of course, the argument can be made that *domesticated* animals are indeed a part of humanity's social fabric, and therefore their political protection is not only a practical necessity but also theoretically valid. This contention, however, begs the question of the moral legitimacy of animal domestication—a problem explored subsequently in Parts III and IV—and seems to herald the conceptual domestication of the entire nonhuman world should the concept of rights be extended to wild animals and other natural entities.

In any case, logical difficulties are minimized when rights are understood as political entities that exist for members of a community of individual agents and other responsible authorities. Rights claims are most easily conceived as part of a social and linguistic context in which other political concepts such as *duty, obligation, privilege*, and *power* are also at home.[19] Furthermore, the meaningfulness of rights depends on our understanding that disagreement over the equitable distribution of social goods and responsibilities (or, as Brophy puts it, "that one person's necessity to live may conflict with another's") is inevitable. This fact, Livingston continues, further alienates the concept of rights from animal reality: "Like so many of our aberrations, the problem of access to power is uniquely human . . . Power and privilege seen by those without them to be improperly or unfairly held or exercised invite a variety of responses ranging from criticism to violence. This creates the political and intellectual environment for a concept of 'rights.'"[20]

For those who would still find value in the prospect of animal rights, a proper response to Livingston lies in the possibility that in addition to the legal or political rights recognized—or fought for—within particular societies, the animal may possess *natural* rights that have normative value irrespective of the vagaries of human political life. Logical space is created for the possibility that *humans* possess natural rights by the recognition that even de jure legal and political rights are open to rational moral evaluation. The moral condemnation of, for example, institutionalized slavery, the Nuremberg laws, or the apartheid system can be grounded in the judgment that each human being has prima facie an unacquired and equal claim to free political participation and the means therefor.[21] The claim that human beings have a right to such goods means at very least that interference with life, liberty, or property requires a *justification:* for example, that it is done in the name of punishment, required for self-defense, or the means to other necessary goods. This requirement in part defines our moral personhood, establishing that humans are not instruments to be used by others.

The argument for such basic human rights can be consequentialist in nature; for example, the rule utilitarian can make the case that the recognition of these rights will maximize social utility. But deontological theorists have instead sought the source in our definitively human capacities: autonomy, moral agency, and the ability to reach rational agreements—all of which have a political dimension. Their arguments rest in part on the premise that the equality and dignity of free, rational beings require the recognition of certain basic, unacquired rights irrespective of the social utility of doing so. As Tibor Machan puts it, rights "are political concepts applicable to human beings because human beings are moral agents, in need of what . . . Robert Nozick calls 'moral space,' that is, a definite sphere of jurisdiction where their authority to act is respected and protected."[22]

Consequently, the difficulty in applying the standard deontological theory of rights to other animals is evident: since nonhumans are not generally understood to be responsible agents, they cannot meaningfully participate in political or moral space as either the bearers or recipients of rights claims. If responsible agency is a necessary condition for holding unacquired *moral* rights, then "animal rights" is a misnomer. In turn, any *legal* or *political* rights a society extends to animals will amount to human largesse, and are only meaningful to the extent that they are executed through a human proxy; as such, they are more likely to· serve human interests and desires than animal nature. Some have attempted to salvage the application of moral rights to animals by arguing for a continuity of moral and political agency in the animal world. The notion is reflected in the habit of characterizing animal behavior as virtuous or vicious: the loyal dog, the courageous lion, the sly fox, and the like. Darwin apparently believed that some animals are moral agents, and perhaps the case is strengthened by recent evidence of ostensibly altruistic behavior among nonhuman primates.[23] More often, however, appeal is made to anecdotal accounts of seemingly "moral" behavior among other mammals,[24] and where such claims are not weakly supported, blatant anthropomorphizing, or patently implausible, they would extend the moral community only modestly, to include our closest relatives.

## *"Marginal Cases"*

A more promising way to preserve the deontological approach to animal rights is to explore whether a more fundamental property or capacity than moral agency—that is, one not unique to human beings—can ground a meaningful sense of rights possession. Such a possibility is not only of interest to the animal advocate, but is raised by a troubling implication of the standard deontological theories of rights. If moral agency is a necessary condition for bearing rights, then what becomes of the moral status of so-called marginal cases—an unfortunate term[25] used to describe those individuals who are biologically human but not fully rational, language-using moral agents: human embryos and fetuses, infants and children, the mentally ill and retarded, the severely ill, and the comatose. If the standard rights argument excludes nonhuman animals from the class of rights holders for lacking moral agency, it would seem that it must also exclude these human beings. This problem is not exclusive to rights theory but, as we saw in Chapter 2, is raised by any attempt to draw strict moral lines between humans and other animals; as James Nelson puts it, "whatever morally important property only humans have will not be had by all humans, and whatever morally important property all humans have will not be had by only humans."[26]

This fact is often hit upon by proponents of animal rights with the expectation that it will be found counterintuitive or otherwise unacceptable that infants and the enfeebled do not have basic rights. The hope is that modifying the standard rights argument to extend rights to marginals cannot avoid extending them to nonhumans as well. However, as several parties to this debate have noted, alternative conclusions are possible. First, it is not obvious that marginals ought to be considered bearers of rights. The conclusion that these human beings do not have moral rights is emotionally awkward, especially for those whose lives are directly touched by them; however, it is not otherwise an obviously incoherent position. It would imply that their legal status would be contingent upon the benevolent commitments of the society in which they find themselves, and that their moral status may be circumscribed by the indirect duties owed to their parents, guardians, or other agents—a position analogous to what traditional deontology implies for animals. It follows that the mere assertion of the analogy between marginals and nonhumans can establish that marginals do not possess rights as easily as it establishes that animals do. As Ingmar Persson concludes, "For the champion of animal welfare, the drawback of the argument from marginal cases is that it is powerless against theorists who are prepared to tolerate discrimination against intellectually disabled humans" or other marginals.[27]

Second, those opposed to extending rights to animals can raise objections to the analogy to marginals. Although not moral agents, marginals—unlike other animals—have long been extended moral and legal courtesy status as "moral patients" or "quasipersons." As Harlan B. Miller explains: "'Quasiperson' is a neologism, of course, but it refers to a sort of moral and legal status that our conceptual system has recognized, in various ways, for millennia. Some classes of human beings have been accorded a standing different from, and generally lower than, that of fully fledged persons, but higher than that of any other animals or any inanimate objects . . . Infants and children are quasipersons everywhere, as, generally, are the severely mentally impaired of any age. A quasiperson lacks the full range of rights accorded to a person, but enjoys at least most of the protections of personhood."[28] Can "quasiperson" status coherently be granted to marginals but withheld from other animals? Those who argue yes point to the important differences between marginals and other animals: the fetus and the newborn are potential agents in a way that animals never can be; the senile, unlike the animal, once were agents; and most of us will feel an affinity for the disabled—"That *could* be me!"—that is distinct from the compassion we may feel for other animals. Whether or not these considerations succeed in identifying a coherent basis for the rights of children and the enfeebled, the results would seem to be the same for the defender of animal rights: either at least one of them is successful, and the animal is justly excluded from the category of rights bearers; or they all fail, and so the analogy between animals and marginal cases cannot be used to establish the concept of animal rights.[29] A remaining possibility is to locate the source of a direct moral standing for marginals in something outside rights theory, such as the utility of their experiences, or the virtue of empathizing with them. Whether or not this strategy can succeed and also support an enhanced moral standing for animals, resorting to this alternative simply undercuts the importance of rights claims in forming our moral judgments, and effectively voids the prospect of establishing "animal rights" by analogy to marginals.

A final consideration echoes Livingston's discussion of the distinctly political nature of rights. If he is correct in arguing that rights are political devices ill suited to the reality of nonhuman animals, the same case can be made concerning marginals. As the controversies over abortion, reproductive technology, and euthanasia demonstrate, attaching the language of rights to fetuses, embryos, and the comatose has coincided with an unproductive politicization of birth and death that has done little to clarify the moral issues involved. Likewise, while the assertion of children's rights reflects appropriate concern about those adults who would fail in their duty to love and nurture, it is a political response to the reality of child exploitation and commodification, not a model for ideal relations between adults and children. As Livingston writes, "One need not invoke rights . . . when a relationship rests on mutual trust, respect, and (especially) affection"[30]—the last being particularly apropos in the case of moral patients.

## The Case for Animal Rights

While some have pinned their attempts to establish our moral duties to animals on the analogy to marginal cases,[31] I think the issue is less decisive than it at first appears, inasmuch as coherent judgments that concede rights to neither animals nor marginals, or to marginals but not animals, are both supportable. Still, the hope of finding a ground other than moral agency for the possession of rights is not thereby closed. One of the most important of such efforts has been undertaken by Tom Regan in *The Case for Animal Rights*. This comprehensive work not only attempts what its title implies—to argue that nonhuman animals possess unacquired moral rights—but also, not unlike the present work, uses the issue of the moral standing of animals as the starting point for a broader exploration of ethical theory. Thus, we find Regan's thesis is not simply that some nonhumans are properly understood as bearers of rights, but that rights theory provides a superior account of our duties to animals *and* to human moral agents and patients.

Roughly Kantian in his approach, Regan develops the principle of respect for persons into a "more catholic" *right to respectful treatment* that cannot be claimed by moral agents alone. In making this argument, he takes pains to distinguish his position from the type of utilitarian strategy discussed in Chapter 3. He is especially concerned with the implication of both act utilitarianism and Singer's preference utilitarianism that individual humans and animals are *mere receptacles* of value—namely, the intrinsic value of their pleasurable or painful experiences—whose interests can be overridden by appeal to the greater interests of others.[32] Echoing Persson's argument discussed in Chapter 3, Regan claims that considerations of justice require that we reject Singer's principle of *equal consideration of interests* in favor of recognizing the *equality of individuals* as beings that are valuable in themselves.[33] Only by postulating that human beings possess in equal measure an *"inherent value"* that proscribes their being used as others' instruments—a value that is neither subject to utilitarian qualification nor contingent upon one's accomplishments or talents—can an egalitarian conception of justice be maintained.

But precisely who may be said to possess this inherent value? Regan argues that a sufficient condition is that a being "bring a unified psychological presence to the world"[34] and can therefore be described as the experiencing *subject of a life*.[35] As he summarizes: "Individuals are subjects of a life if they are able to perceive and remember; if they have beliefs, desires, and preferences; if they are able to act intentionally in pursuit of their desires or goals; if they are sentient and have an emotional life; if they have a sense of the future, including a sense of their own future; if they have a psychophysical identity over time; and if they have an individual experiential welfare that is logically independent of their utility for, and the interests of, others. This criterion is a sufficient condition for making attributions of inherent value intelligible and nonarbitrary."[36] Subjects of a life can be harmed or benefited in a morally significant sense, because their welfare and continued existence matter *to them*. If living such a life establishes a defensible claim to respect and freedom from unnecessary harm, then both human moral agents and some marginals (including children and the not severely enfeebled) will unequivocally occupy the category of rights bearers, justifying what Regan calls the "reflective intuitions" that they are the beneficiaries of direct moral duties, and that their lives and interests ought not to be trumped by the more powerful desires of others.

But *Homo sapiens* cannot be the only denizen of this moral territory. Regan concludes his analysis of animal psychology in Chapters 1 and 2 of *The Case for Animal Rights* with the following claims: "Perception, memory, desire, belief, self-consciousness, intention, a sense of the future—these are among the leading attributes of the mental life of normal mammalian animals aged one or more. Add to this list the not unimportant categories of emotion . . . and sentience . . . and we begin to approach a fair rendering of the mental life of these animals."[37] If these ascriptions are correct, then there are at least[38] some animals that "have a biography, not merely a biology,"[39] and so exist as the subjects of their own lives. Since neither membership in a particular species nor being a moral agent is directly relevant to this "psychological presence," these animals must also possess an equal measure of inherent value, and so their exclusion from the category of rights holders would be morally arbitrary. By thus attributing a non-instrumental value to animal subjectivity, Regan is able to reach unequivocal moral conclusions about our treatment of animals, including absolute proscriptions against using animals for food[40] and research.[41]

In sum, Regan's rights approach seems a philosophically more substantial account of the animal's moral significance than the utilitarian is

able to provide. Yet this fact has not immunized it against significant criticism. First, nothing in Regan's account allays Livingston's concern about
the politicization of the animal that rights arguments entail. Indeed, since
Regan's argument is indifferent to whether a mature mammal is domesticated or wild, it invites the propagation of rights concepts into the natural
world.[42] Furthermore, as Regan acknowledges, moral rights only establish prima facie duties; ultimate duties can only be determined when conflicting rights claims are hashed out. If we grant that animals possess
rights to respect and freedom from unnecessary harm, those rights will
inevitably conflict with purported human rights to protect property,
obtain food, maintain heritage, hold spiritual beliefs, and the like. The
process of adjudicating these conflicts is inherently political—and, we
may add, reveals an underlying complexity to the rights approach that
may rival the unmanageability of utilitarianism.[43]

Second, like many rights arguments concerning this and other
issues, one suspects that Regan is guilty of some degree of ad hoc reasoning. Despite beginning with an attempt to clarify the basis of our duties
toward human beings, his account of the foundation of moral rights
seems constructed with a view to the conclusions it will allow him to
reach about nonhuman animals.[44] Regan's own words seem to justify
the suspicion: "The rights view, I believe, is rationally the most satisfactory moral theory . . . Of course, if it were possible to show that only
human beings are included within its scope, then a person like myself,
who believes in animal rights, would be obliged to look elsewhere."[45]
Particularly troublesome is Regan's keystone concept of "inherent
value," invented to ward off the unsavory implications of utilitarianism. Sapontzis calls the concept "mystifying";[46] Mary Anne Warren
agrees, adding that we are not told by Regan exactly what it is, only
what it implies for the theory of rights: "Inherent value appears as a
mysterious non-natural property which we must take on faith."[47]

Regan responds to such criticisms by explaining the postulate of
inherent value as a logical extension of Kant's understanding of personhood:

> The notion of inherent value is no less "mystifying" than Kant's idea of
> the end in itself. As applied to human beings, Kant's idea of end in itself
> attempts to articulate the cherished belief that the value or worth of a
> human being is not reducible to instrumental value—not reducible,
> that is, to how useful a human being happens to be in forwarding the
> interests or purposes of other human beings . . . All that the rights view
> alleges, then, is that to be consistent, the same moral judgment must be

made in those cases where nonhuman animals that are subjects of a life are treated in a similar fashion.[48]

Of course, this analogy assumes the legitimacy of Kant's assertion that humans exist as ends in themselves, which is not a given. Even if Kant's position is granted, this defense fails on at least two grounds. First, Kant's postulate of the end in itself is grounded in his understanding of the principle of morality, which, as we saw above, holds only for rational beings. A rational human agent could not consistently will to be governed by a universal law under which rational beings were not to be treated as ends, but there is no obvious inconsistency in willing that other subjects of a life be excluded from the kingdom of ends. Second, if it is indeed Kant's intention to express a "cherished belief" about human beings, then Regan's postulate is clearly ad hoc, for there is as of yet no generally held intuition about the *equal* moral worth of humans and nonhuman animals for the postulate to secure, and the equality of human beings can be secured by means other than postulating the equal inherent value of all subjects of a life.

Finally, while there are merits to acknowledging an inherent value to individuals both human and animal, Regan's insistence that all who hold this value do so equally and unconditionally leads to counterintuitive results.[49] For example, Regan writes concerning human beings: "The inherent value of moral agents cannot be viewed as something they can earn by dint of their efforts or as something they can lose by what they do or fail to do. A criminal is no less inherently valuable than a saint, if both are moral agents and if moral agents have inherent value."[50] This principle is intended to protect the weak from exploitation, but it may also immunize the exploiters from their just deserts. Genocidal despots and serial killers may articulate meaningful rights claims, but it is difficult to view their existence to be as inherently valuable as that of their victims. Furthermore, if all human subjects of a life have an equal inherent value irrespective of responsible participation in social space, then punishment of the guilty—whether conceived on retributive or utilitarian models—might lose its ethical justification.[51]

The equality of inherent value implies further problems concerning nonhumans. Elements of nature that are not subjects—whether animals that lack a subjective consciousness; non-sentient individuals such as plants, rocks, or bodies of water; or entire species or ecosystems—cannot meaningfully be said to hold valid claims (rights) to certain treatment, yet may be viewed appropriately as valuable in their own right. By Regan's account, being a subject of a life is a *sufficient* condition for the possession of inherent value, but it is not a *necessary* one, and thus he leaves open the possibility of an environmental ethic that extends equal inherent value to more than mature mammals.[52] However, this would do more than establish a ground for our moral obligations to nature: it would risk making the world so sacrosanct that humanity's very presence in it cannot avoid being morally objectionable.[53]

## Moral Individualism and the Value of Rights

As we see, Regan's strong animal rights position creates difficult problems of demarcation. Even if moral agents, marginal cases, and nonhuman animals all ought to be considered valuable, it is nonetheless problematic to declare them equally and inherently so. And if we reject the conditions traditionally recognized as necessary for holding rights, a line still must be drawn somewhere to preserve the livability of our existence. These difficulties reflect the fact that value seems naturally and necessarily subject to some type of qualification and quantification. If utilitarian deliberations are too complex to bring the requisite conviction to our moral judgments, reality is too complex for such homogenizing concepts as inherent value.

In this regard, James Rachels's arguments for the recognition of animal rights deserve brief separate mention for his treatment of the connection between moral rights and the underlying properties that ground their possession.[54] As we saw in Chapter 2, Rachels interprets Darwinian biology as substituting "individual organisms, with their profusion of similarities and differences, for the old idea of determinate species"; he terms the corresponding ethical idea "moral individualism," which "substitutes the view that our treatment of those organisms must be sensitive to those similarities and differences, for the old view that what matters is the species to which the organism belongs."[55] Thus, he argues that other rights arguments fail, in part, because they rest on finding a *single* characteristic that justifies rights possession in general, instead of identifying the particular characteristics that are relevant to each particular right.[56] This amendment to rights theory will allow us to bring rational human agents, marginal cases, and nonhumans all under the umbrella of moral rights, while justifying distinctions in the rights they are due by appealing to their differing properties and capacities.

However, if moral rights are not to be assigned categorically but contextually, then their relevance to reaching moral judgments is thereby called into question. Consider one of Rachels's examples: "Torture is wrong because it hurts. It is the capacity for suffering, not the possession of sophisticated concepts, that underlies the wrongness of torture. This is true for both people and rabbits; in both cases torture is wrong because of the suffering that is caused. The characteristic of humans that qualifies them as bearers of a right not to be tortured is, therefore, a characteristic also possessed by rabbits, and many other animals as well. Thus, I believe that, if humans have a right not to be tortured, so do other animals."[57] Rachels's concern for moral consistency is clearly justified. What is not clear is how much the assertion "Individual $X$ has a right not to be tortured" adds to the judgment "It is wrong to torture individual $X$," especially if the ground for the latter is as clear as Rachels asserts. Indeed, since the attribution of a right not to be tortured might only establish a prima facie duty, whereas the judgment that torture is wrong seems like an ultima facie conclusion, it is unclear why the former should be the more important one to establish. Since Rachels's argument implies that the claim about possessing rights depends upon the *prior* judgment that an action is wrong, this understanding of rights will not by itself help us to identify the moral limits to our treatment of other animals.

This problem points toward a larger question about the ultimate usefulness of the language of rights in our moral deliberations. As R. G. Frey argues, since we can reason about the rightness or wrongness of particular actions, or the acceptability of moral principles, without any reference to the concept of moral rights, debates about rights may obscure more than they illuminate: "We come to focus upon the much less immediate, important, and easily resolvable because wholly speculative questions of whether there really is this or that moral right that some people but not others allege that there is and of what the criteria are—and of how we ought to decide what the criteria are—for the possession of this or that right."[58] The point seems especially relevant in the case of our treatment of nonhumans, where there is such considerable disagreement about where the moral limits are. Were there a consensus about what human moral agents owe to other animals, we might use the term *animal rights* as shorthand to convey it. But in the absence of a consensus, the debate over the philosophical scaffolding necessary to support the concept of natural animal rights seems only to divert us from the essential question of what duties we have to other animals.

## Conclusion

Frey recommends that we jettison the concept of moral rights altogether. Most ethicists will reject this as too extreme, and insist that "rights" have some place in our moral and political thinking. Yet most ethicists will also acknowledge that recognizing rights claims and the duties to honor them cannot be the sum of moral deliberation, inasmuch as some moral considerations cannot be expressed adequately in the language of rights. The analysis in this chapter indicates that we should count our relationship to the animal among those issues that should be thought about in a different moral vocabulary. While those who have tried to bring animals under the umbrella of rights have done so with a view to solidifying their claim to moral recognition, it remains unclear whether nonhumans can meaningfully claim to have rights (say, not to be raised for food or experimented upon), whether the philosophical foundation necessary to support such alleged rights can be asserted coherently, how such rights might square with conflicting human rights, and whether such rights presuppose rather than generate moral judgments about the exploitation of animals.

If rights do have a place in our dealings with each other, this may only be, as Livingston asserts, "one of the 'field marks' . . . of human social pathology," in which case their application to the nonhuman world will herald its contamination rather than its liberation.[59] In any case, that the language of rights is so prevalent in our moral discourse, while being unsuited to the interests of other animals, perhaps signals the inherent speciesism and, as Sapontzis argues, the "intellectual bias" of our ethical thinking: "Currently our most powerful moral and legal concept, 'rights,' is one which is suited to the capacities and conditions of intellectually sophisticated agents; in a liberated ethic, concepts suited to the capacities and conditions of feeling beings who are not intellectually sophisticated agents must enjoy equal status and power with the concept of rights."[60] While each has its strengths with respect to forming a "liberated" animal ethic, neither utilitarianism nor rights theory seems able to manage all the fundamental practical and theoretical difficulties raised by the issue of the moral status of animals. Let us explore whether other approaches in the tradition of Western ethical thought are better suited to the task.

# 5 Aristotelian Arguments: Animal Telos and Human Aretē

## The Appeal of the Premodern

Because utilitarianism and deontology form the core of modern Western ethical thought, many treatments of the recent debate over animals have proceeded as if Peter Singer's and Tom Regan's arguments frame the discussion in its entirety. However, other forms of moral argument have been introduced in the debate, and have delivered some of its more perceptive insights. In this chapter, I discuss arguments that have been inspired by Aristotelian ethics, an approach that at first glance has much to recommend it. First, frustration with modern ethics' quest for an elusive precision concerning the rightness or wrongness of specific *actions*—a somewhat quixotic characteristic of the argument forms reviewed in the previous two chapters—has generated nostalgia for ancient ethical models with their concern for the "art of life," and the more general question of *how we are to live*.[1] Aristotle's caution that as students we should seek only the degree of exactness that the subject matter allows[2] is a necessary one here, where our subject is as broad and complex as the moral standing of other animals. If we cannot hope to define with precision the morality of all our actions that affect members of other species, perhaps a more manageable goal for an animal ethic is to articulate the general principles of a *moral way of life* that includes the nonhuman animal.

Second, one might expect Aristotelian thought to be especially helpful in navigating our subject, given the amount of scientific and philosophical attention Aristotle pays to the animal, and the biological flavor that pervades his whole system. Indeed, it is likely that Aristotle's Aegean biological studies were the principal catalyst in the evolution of his thought away from its Platonic roots. The resulting system of the mature Aristotle stands in marked contrast to Kant's idealism discussed in the previous chapter. While Kant insulates philosophy within the rational constructions of the human mind, Aristotle grounds human reality squarely within *physis*, where the philosopher cannot avoid dealing with the animal. While human beings may be distinctly rational and political, we are nonetheless—in Aristotle's famous phrases—rational and political *animals* by nature. Thus, we find that Aristotle not only attends to the animal in his work in natural history (including *On the Parts of Animals* and *The History of Animals*), but his treatments of metaphysics, epistemology, anthropology, and ethics all refer to the nature of the animal and the relationship between humans and nonhumans. As Richard Sorabji points out, in Aristotle's work philosophical theory and animal reality are used to shed light upon each other.[3] As clearly as any other major figure in the Western tradition, Aristotle appropriates the conclusion argued for in Part I: that the animal is of fundamental philosophical importance.

## The Rational Animal

Among Aristotle's various discussions of nonhuman animals, of special relevance to the debate over their moral standing is his biological "gradualism"—a proto-Darwinian acknowledgment of the necessary fuzziness of taxonomic boundaries: "For nature passes from lifeless objects to animals in such unbroken sequence . . . that scarcely any difference seems to exist between two neighboring groups owing to their close proximity."[4] This ambiguity is not limited to such matters as whether the sponge is more plant than animal, but also threatens the boundary between humans and other animals, where Aristotle recognizes analogies between physical organs, as well as a type of psychological[5] continuity. In most other animals, he argues, there are "traces" of our psychological traits: it is only by degree that other animals differ from humans in possessing temperaments such as boldness, cowardice, and mischievousness; and some animals possess analogous (but different) capacities to human intellectual powers, such as *technē* and *sophia*.[6]

However, this is not enough to preclude a categorical separation of humans from other forms of animate life, because Aristotle steadfastly denies that any nonhuman animals actually possess those higher intellectual capacities that involve rational thought and understanding.[7] Furthermore, as Aristotle's *Politics* makes clear, the distinction between animals that are merely perceptual and humans who are rational is not simply a descriptive scientific classification, but one that is evaluative and hierarchical:

> Where then there is such a difference as that between soul and body, or between men and animals (as in the case of those whose business is to use their body, and who can do nothing better), the lower sort are by nature slaves, and it is better for them as for all inferiors that they should be under the rule of a master. For he who can be, and therefore is, another's and he who participates in rational principle enough to apprehend, but not to have, such a principle, is a slave by nature. Whereas the lower animals cannot even apprehend a principle; they obey their instincts. And indeed the use made of slaves and of tame animals is not very different; for both with their bodies minister to the needs of life.[8]

He later adds that hunting (and presumably domesticating) wild animals—and suppressing those humans "intended by nature to be governed"—amounts to waging a *just war*.[9] Thus, the juxtaposition of human and animal leads to a type of moral continuity in Aristotle's thought, but not one that today's defender of the animal—or of democracy—will appreciate: If some humans and animals share a comparable moral-political status it is only because Aristotle's thought does not reflect the modern ideal of *human* equality, on the grounds that those humans who cannot fully possess *logos* are, like nonhuman animals, inferior by nature.

The complete development of Aristotle's ethics also hinges on the distinction between rational and non-rational beings, which bodes further ill for the animal. In the famous arguments of the *Nicomachean Ethics*, the details of human happiness and virtue (aretē) are seen to derive from the life of rational excellence, a function that defines human beings in distinction from other living things.[10] As the rational life is one in which the animal has no share, "neither horse nor ox" can be termed "happy";[11] in turn, since irrational animals are the natural slaves and instruments of rational human beings, there can be "nothing in common" between us, and thus neither friendship nor justice can characterize our relations with them.[12] Therefore, despite his sophisticated and detailed understanding of animal behavior and psychology, and the degree of attention he devotes to the animal, we find in Aristotle's system the foundation of that dismissive position that would characterize most subsequent Western philosophy: that nonhuman animals—categorically defined as non-rational—cannot by nature be the objects of direct moral concern.

The reach of Aristotle's influence on this point is demonstrated by some striking similarities between his thought and Kant's, two thousand years later. Despite the very different foundations of their systems (discussed above), and their very different conceptions of the nature of moral deliberation,[13] Aristotle and Kant establish both the source of human ethics and the exclusion of direct moral concern for animals on precisely the same ground: the rational capacity that they take as the essential facet of our humanity, and as what defines us as the end for which non-rational animals exist.[14] Many thinkers between Aristotle and Kant shared this view of the relationship between human and animal, but perhaps the most important force in sustaining this position for two millennia was the home it found in Latin Christianity.[15] To cite only the most obvious examples, the Platonist Augustine uses language notably similar to Aristotle's when defending the killing of animals,[16] and the Aristotelian Aquinas makes good use of the Philosopher's arguments when discussing the animal, such as in this example from the *Summa Theologica:* "The love of charity extends to none but God and our neighbor. But the word 'neighbor' cannot be extended to irrational creatures, since they have no fellowship with man in the rational life. Therefore, charity does not extend to irrational creatures."[17]

## Teleology

It is ironic, then, that some in the recent debate would draw inspiration from Aristotle to create a fresh picture of the moral status of nonhuman animals when his hand is so evident in the old one. According to Bernard Rollin, the key to a revitalized Aristotelian view of the animal lies beyond the specifics of Aristotle's distinction between rational and non-rational animals, in the larger philosophical context where it becomes ethically significant: Aristotle's teleology. Aristotle makes the link between *goods* and *ends* explicit in the opening line of the *Nicomachean Ethics,* with the result that the good for which the virtuous person aims—to excel at activity that expresses the soul's capacity for reason—is none other than the final end of human action: the *telos* or final cause of the human substance. For Aristotle, having a natural end or purpose is not a unique property of human beings, but is one of the causes of substance per se—indeed, of the cosmos as a whole. Is it possible that the final causes of other animals can also have moral significance?

Rollin answers this question in the affirmative, and his work is an attempt to use the teleological features of Aristotle's thought as the fulcrum by which to move ethics to extend considerations of justice and morality beyond rational human beings. In doing so, Rollin makes an interesting attempt at identifying the animal-inclusive way of life mentioned above; furthermore, he incorporates some of the insights of both the utilitarian and rights approaches while avoiding some of their difficulties. The foundation of Rollin's moral philosophy is the assertion that our awareness of other beings' *interests* is what constitutes our behavior toward them as morally significant.[18] In the case of human beings, it is clear that the things in which we have an interest cover a broad range of desires, aspirations, and needs that have moral weight in our dealings with each other. Not all these interests are exclusive to rational human agents, nor are they all reducible to sentience of pleasure and pain. Thus, Rollin argues that the ground of morally relevant interests will not be found in either traditional reason-centered ethics or utilitarian models, but must be sought in a broader look at "the essential characteristics of conscious life itself."[19] It is in this search that Rollin looks beyond modern ethical models to Aristotelian teleology.

Rollin introduces his teleological approach to the moral status of animals with the example of the spider (which we first saw in the Introduction): "When the spider is alive, it has what Aristotle called a *telos*, a nature, a function, a set of activities intrinsic to it, evolutionarily determined and genetically imprinted, that constitute its 'living spiderness.' Furthermore, its life consists precisely in a struggle to perform these functions, to actualize this nature, to fulfill these needs, to maintain this life, what Hobbes and Spinoza referred to as the *conatus* or drive to preserve its integrity and unity."[20] Of course, it is problematic to invoke the Aristotelian *telos* today, given the non-teleological commitments of contemporary physics and biology. However, Rollin believes it can still be useful within the constraints of post-Darwinian thought:

> Whereas Aristotle sees species as fixed, immutable, eternal, and unchanging, and hence sees their essences as at least in principle fully graspable, we post-Darwinians see a world far more dynamic, with species being mere momentary stages along the ever-changing route taken by developing life . . . On the other hand, biology gives us a powerful incentive to accept the idea of a nature. The genetic code of a given species provides us with a clear, scientific, testable, physicalistic locus for *telos*. And it is clear that this code determines behavioral, psychological, and social aspects of a creature's nature as well as physical ones . . . To understand the nature of an animal in a way that is relevant to ethics is not a great or profound epistemological problem; it involves only sympathetic observations of the animal's life and activities.[21]

Even granting that an animal's genetic code and the goal-directed behaviors determined thereby constitute a suitable modern approximation of the Aristotelian final cause, more is needed to make these aspects of animal reality morally significant. Specifically, the animal's telic *needs* must attain the status of *interests*, which Rollin argues comes with the attribution of animal awareness: "Few of us humans can consciously articulate all of our needs, but we can certainly know when these needs are thwarted and met. Pain and pleasure are, of course, the obvious ways these facts come to consciousness, but they are not the only ones. Frustration, anxiety, malaise, listlessness, boredom, anger are among the multitude of indicators of unmet needs, needs that become interests in virtue of these states of consciousness. Thus, to say that a living thing has interests is to suggest that it has some sort of conscious awareness, however rudimentary."[22] By appealing to the arguments of Donald Griffin (as I did in Chapter 2), Rollin offers that we should not reject a priori the possibility of consciousness "at any level of the animal kingdom." Consequently, he argues for a position more radical (and more questionable) than either Singer's or Regan's understanding of animal consciousness: that the "presence of a nervous system, pain behavior and endorphins . . . would take us down . . . at least to insects, worms, and perhaps planaria as animals with interests."[23]

Echoing Singer's position discussed in Chapter 3, Rollin argues that once we recognize the reality of interests held by nonhumans, the animal comes within the scope of moral deliberations proper.[24] Further, this claim to moral recognition can be codified in Regan's language of *basic rights:* "namely, *the right to be dealt with or considered as moral objects by any person who has moral principles, regardless of what those moral principles may be!*"[25] This last phrase bears emphasizing. Although Rollin ultimately couches his conclusions in the language of rights and Kantian deontology, the overall thrust of his argument is that the telic nature of animals dictates their inclusion in the scope of any ethical theory that can be considered adequate.[26] Indeed, the animal *telos* can be used to justify the extension of either the utilitarian consideration of interests or the deontological concept of rights, and Rollin brings both of these ethical concepts to bear in the most concise statement of his conclusion: "The essence of our substantive moral obligations to animals is that any animal has a right to the kind of life that its nature dictates. In short, I am arguing that an animal has the right to have the unique interests that characterize it morally considered in our treatment of it."[27]

   This position has important advantages over those reviewed in the previous two chapters. First, if we accept Rollin's judgment that an animal's nature or *telos* has a "clear, scientific, testable, physicalistic locus" in its genetic code, such a ground is preferable to the elusive content of animal sentience to which utilitarians such as Singer appeal, and the abstruse notion of "inherent value" that Regan conjures to solidify his case for animal rights. While many will dismiss out of hand the assertion that animal sentience can compare with human pleasures and pains, or that rights can meaningfully be applied to animals, it seems undeniable that animals possess natures that they work to fulfill. Second, by making the concept of *telos* fundamental to moral thought, Rollin facilitates the extension of moral concern to the broad scope of animal reality. If we accept Rollin's liberal understanding of animal consciousness, the teleological approach extends that concern smoothly throughout the animal world, and not just to those animals with the most humanlike sentience or subjectivity.

   Furthermore, the usefulness of the concept of *telos* in reaching moral conclusions is indicated by the fact that Rollin's central point has been reflected in a wide variety of arguments in the debate. For example, Henry Salt's sensitive if philosophically unsophisticated argument from the nineteenth century concludes that the proper understanding of the animal's moral status lies with the recognition that "animals have rights, and these rights consist in the 'restricted freedom' to live a natural life—a life, that is, which permits of individual development—subject to the limitations imposed by the permanent needs and interests of the community."[28] More recently, Mary Anne Warren's position, which she terms the "weak animal rights theory"—grounded in her careful philosophical analysis of Regan's arguments—includes the claim that "any creature whose natural mode of life includes the pursuit of certain satisfactions has the right not to be forced to exist without the opportunity to pursue those satisfactions."[29] The concept also has its proponents among environmental ethicists: Paul Taylor argues that a being's teleological center *creates a point of view*—the world can be viewed from the perspective of what helps or hinders the fulfillment of its ends—that merits moral respect; Holmes Rolston III puts the point quite starkly when he writes that "every genetic set is . . . a normative set; there is some *ought to be* beyond the *is*."[30] Thus, the judgment that moral weight should be attached to the animal's drive to fulfill its nature seems as strong a candidate as any in the debate for a possible consensus position among those who seek to raise the animal's moral standing.

Unfortunately, Rollin's further development of this judgment is more problematic. Since he abjures a more firm commitment to particular ethical principles, his teleological approach does not offer clear guidelines as to how competing interests and rights claims are to be adjudicated. As Rollin acknowledges, any further rights we may try to deduce from the right to be considered an object of moral attention—such as the right to life—will not be absolute, but are subject to being overridden by other, more compelling claims. However, how the inevitable conflicts—such as when a choice must be made between taking an animal's life and thwarting our human interests—are to be resolved cannot be determined a priori: "Ultimately it appears that these cases must be decided dialectically, on a case-by-case basis."[31] Further, Rollin is reluctant to offer general principles to aid in the assessment of conflicting human and animal interests: "We cannot simply resolve conflicts by adding interests. It might be tempting to say that if we must choose between the lives of two creatures, one of whom has interests a,b,c,d, and the other of whom has interests a,b,c,d, and e we always favor the latter since, after all, our morally relevant swing point is interests. But this is too simple, for clearly we need to consider not only the number of interests, but also quality and intensity of their satisfaction and frustration. Here as elsewhere in ethics, moral problems do not admit of simple accounting solutions."[32]

Rollin's candid recognition of the complexity involved here is refreshing, especially when juxtaposed with Singer's treatment of these matters. Like Singer, however, he relies on the hope that even if unclear cases are conceded to the anthropocentrist, we will still be obligated to change our treatment of other animals in radical ways.[33] But as we saw in Chapter 3, the lack of a clear ground for the comparison of human and animal interests will leave us at an impasse concerning the moral worth of many institutionalized uses of nonhuman animals, such as we find in agriculture and research.[34] In Rollin's case, the difficulty is compounded by the complexity and malleability of *human* nature. If *telos* is "basic to morality," then those human needs that may require the use of animals have undeniable moral weight, providing ammunition for those who would maintain the traditional priority of human over animal interests. After all, Aristotle's moral anthropocentrism goes hand in hand with the moral weight he attaches to the fulfillment of our natural human ends. However, as Rollin acknowledges, today we view the human *telos* as something more variable than Aristotle's metaphysics could have allowed.[35] Unlike the animal's, it is not reducible to the verifiable facts of our specific genetics; "human nature" is not only conditioned biologically, but also historically, socially, and volitionally. The comparison of animal and human interests would therefore seem to require a *stipulation* as to the essential elements of the human *telos*. Any such stipulation is liable to suffer from either arbitrariness or question begging, inasmuch as any self-conscious attempt to define ourselves is certain to presuppose some evaluative understanding of the relationship between human and animal. Thus, the teleological approach cannot by itself provide all the answers we may expect from an animal ethic.

Rollin is untroubled by these complexities for two reasons. First, treading the line between ethical theory and applied ethics, he sees it as a fundamental task of moral philosophy to effect progressive "gestalt shifts" in our practical moral outlook—allowing us to view reality in a morally more enlightened way—rather than to develop a conceptual machine that will ease the burden of moral reasoning.[36] He maintains that the argument for the moral significance of the animal's *telos* is sufficient to effect such a shift in our attitudes toward animal reality. If he is correct, then even though that by itself is not sufficient to determine what the moral assessment of each form of animal exploitation should be, his ethic will have succeeded by establishing that our treatment of all animals with interests—even "lowly" insects and spiders—must be understood in properly moral terms. As he writes, "Admitting that animals have rights would simply extend [the familiar] dialectical activity [of moral reasoning] into an area from which it has been withheld, but no fundamental changes in our conceptual apparatus would be required."[37] This will be unsatisfying to those who seek more precision from an ethical theory, or those who believe that fundamental changes to our conceptual apparatus are needed in order to accommodate the animal. Nonetheless, it may be a strength of Rollin's teleological approach that his more modest goal of a gestalt shift is a possible way of thinking about the animal-inclusive way of life I mentioned in the introduction to this chapter.

Second, and more problematic, much of Rollin's discussion is dedicated to advancing the notion of *legal* rights for animals as a practical way of effecting this gestalt shift, and he believes his ethical analysis is sufficient to ground significant progress in this regard. Making use of philosopher of law Ronald Dworkin's analysis of the relationship between the legal and the moral, Rollin argues that "enjoying legal rights follows and is indeed inseparable from enjoying moral status. So it also follows that animals ought to be considered as recipients of legal rights. Furthermore, it will not do to cite utilitarian arguments against granting legal rights to animals, because the entire point of rights considered from a social point of view is anti-utilitarian. If rights are designed to protect objects of moral concern from the excesses of utilitarianism, it certainly won't do to launch utilitarian arguments against rights!"[38] This argument will appeal to those who follow Dworkin in rejecting legal positivism, and again reflects Rollin's effort to point toward a way of life that extends our familiar prescriptive categories to the nonhuman animal. However, Rollin's discussion fails to address Livingston's concerns—discussed in Chapter 4—about the conceptual politicization of the nonhuman world that the extension of legal rights to animals represents. Indeed, Rollin's focus on legal rights seems very much at odds with his use of a naturalistic concept like *telos*. In practice, legal protections of animal interests may be the indispensable means of preventing a great deal of harm. But on the level of theory, the conception of the animal as *legal ward* is a less than fitting ideal. In our efforts to think about the proper respect for animal nature, we should be concerned with liberating the animal not only from inhumane exploitation but also from such purely human artifacts as legalistic rights.

## Virtue

The search for a moral way of life that includes the animal seems to recommend another characteristic of Aristotelian ethics: its focus on determining the virtuous character of the agent, rather than the moral worth of particular actions in themselves. With the exceptions of such actions as murder and adultery, and indulging such emotions as spite—whose very names imply that they are intrinsically wrong[39]—Aristotle holds that the praise- or blameworthiness of an act can only be surmised when viewed through the lens of what it reveals about the moral characteristics of the agent.[40] The value of our choices lies not only with the actions we choose but more fundamentally with ourselves: "No choice will be right without practical wisdom and virtue. For virtue determines the end, and practical wisdom makes us do what is conducive to the end."[41] Therefore, relative to our topic, one may ask whether and how the animal will be included in the life of the good person, that is, whether moral attention to the animal will be part of what may be considered a virtuous human existence.

These considerations are relevant to the development of an animal ethic for two reasons. First, the proscription against *cruelty* to animals—perhaps the most widely accepted judgment in the recent debate over animals—condemns not just a type of action, but more fundamentally a despicable trait of *character*. While the entreaty to be kind to animals rather than cruel cannot by itself produce a complete account of our duties toward other animals,[42] the analysis of why animal cruelty is condemnable is a reasonable first step in clarifying the proper moral status for nonhuman animals. Second, in addition to attempting to clarify the rightness and wrongness of our actions and effecting the kind of gestalt shifts that Rollin emphasizes, it is simply a reasonable and desirable goal for ethics to comprehend what makes a person good. To do so one must examine considerations other than specific types of action and their moral worth. As Lawrence Becker writes: "Being a good person is not just acting on principle, or doing the right thing, for the right reasons, most of the time. To be a good person is to be someone for whom right conduct is 'in character.'"[43] Therefore, a complete animal ethic should speak to the issue of traits of character as they relate to the treatment of other animals.

While some within the recent debate over animals (e.g., Steven R. L. Clark and Mary Midgley) have attempted to bring considerations of virtue to bear, Becker himself has produced a more systematic virtue-based animal ethic,[44] the result of which is a guarded ranking of human interests above those of animals. He argues that when we shift the emphasis in the debate away from what the standard moral principles imply for our treatment of other animals and look instead at what character traits are essential to human virtue, we will find that some degree of speciesism is morally obligatory: "The fact that we can find no reason for speciesism when we consider the consequences, or the morally relevant characteristics of animals vis-à-vis some humans, is irrelevant. If we want people to *be* virtuous—not just to act on principle, but to have the traits characteristic of virtue—then we are going to get some version of speciesism in people's behavior."[45]

Becker arrives at this position by focusing on two important constituents of virtue of character: reciprocity ("the disposition to make a proportional return of good for good") and empathic identification ("the ability and propensity to see situations from other points of view, to understand and indeed share others' experience empathetically").[46] Becker argues that both of these traits are generally considered essential components of moral excellence, and can be considered morally valuable by the criteria of other major ethical theories: utilitarianism, deontology, and contractarianism. Further, he argues that these aspects of human virtue require that one form preferences according to *social distance*:[47] one typically does distribute goods to, for example, intimate friends and family before considering the comparable interests of strangers, and Becker argues that virtue dictates that this *ought* to be the case.[48]

If this much of Becker's argument is sound, it has obvious and important implications for our relationships with other animals because the social distance between humans and other animals is typically greater than that among humans. This is true not only for the obvious reason that the quantity and immediacy of social interactions are typically less in our dealings with animals; Becker also argues that social distance is inversely proportional to the degree of *dependence* that characterizes a relationship, and animals are typically less dependent upon humans than humans are upon each other.[49] This insight gives Becker's argument two interesting advantages over the others we have reviewed. First, giving moral weight to dependence as it relates to social distance provides a subtle way of handling the marginal cases problem. Those humans such as children and the enfeebled who may be of comparable sentience and intelligence to other animals are dependent on human moral agents in ways that other animals usually will not be. If Becker's argument is correct, these facts provide a non-arbitrary justification for the intuition that we ought to give greater moral weight to the interests of marginals than to those of other animals. Second, by implicitly defining relationships between humans and animals on the model of *independence*, Becker's approach—aimed at securing the priority of human interests—ironically may be grounded on the most fitting understanding of animal reality. While many other arguments in the debate focus on how humans treat dependent, *domesticated* animals, Becker's argument carries the interesting implication that animal dependence on humans is anomalous.

Still, applying the concept of social distance to the animal is not without its difficulties. It is complicated, first, by the many examples of inter-specific relationships that are closer than the typical social distance experienced between humans and other animals—frequently closer than that experienced among humans. Becker is of course aware of these facts, but analogizes them to cases of atypical social distance in human relationships, such as when friends are closer than family: "This is not indicative of an inconsistency of moral character, or of a problem that needs to be resolved. On the contrary, it is a perfectly consistent expression of the traits of reciprocity and empathy."[50]

Second, and more important, one can argue that Becker's approach essentially begs the question of what type of relationships we *ought* to have with other animals. One might grant Becker's point that "it is surely implausible to think that impartial conduct, contrary to feelings and preferences, is virtuous,"[51] but still argue for a revaluation of our feelings toward animals. Whether in fact we *do* feel anything for the animals whose interests we upset is logically independent of whether we *can*, and, if we can, whether we *should*. Consider how those thinkers who attach moral importance to social distance often take pains to deny that their position provides any moral legitimacy to racism and sexism;[52] it is assumed that the virtuous person will extend reciprocity and empathy across the gulfs of ethnicity and gender, which—while having some foundation in the biology of race and sex—are largely the products of cultural construction. If the social distance between humans and other species is more objective than that among humans, this does not mean it is not also partly conditioned by culture. There may be practical and psychological limits to how far humans can extend empathy to other animals, but history shows these limits to be flexible, rather than absolute, making the *moral* limits far from obvious. Rollin cites examples of scientists who find themselves empathizing with their animal study-subjects—even single-cell organisms—after intensive investigation, and he argues that the greater our knowledge of ethology the more gestalt shifts in our capacity for empathy can be expected.[53] If so, the virtue approach must necessarily be highly malleable with respect to the specific boundaries across which empathy and reciprocity ought to be extended.

In part because of these complications, Becker's overall argument cannot support an absolute form of speciesism that would categorically give priority to human interests over those of other animals: he states up front that his argument "is not a defense of the cruelty to animals found in factory farming and much scientific experimentation,"[54] and he concedes that "animal interests do, often, outweigh nontrivial human ones for people we believe to be virtuous."[55] Instead, he adopts a position he labels "weak speciesism." Since our relationships with other animals typically involve greater distance than do our relationships with other humans, Becker argues that it follows as a requirement of human virtue that "when human and animal interests are equivalent (in terms of significance level and number)" we have prima facie grounds for believing "the human interests are to prevail."[56] This position is not an unreasonable one, and undercuts in a significant way Singer's assertion that speciesism per se is morally arbitrary.[57]

However, the ultimate usefulness of Becker's position is questionable, given the small number of human-animal interactions that will involve a conflict of clearly *equivalent* interests, and—as we have seen in connection with other arguments in the debate—the difficulty in defining equivalence in these matters. Thus, while Becker leaves open the possibility that stronger forms of speciesism may also be compatible with his premises, he is forced to acknowledge that "it is hard to say just how much of a speciesist position is authorized by my arguments."[58] The virtue approach must be "indeterminate with regard to using some sorts of animals for food and for some experiments,"[59] and Becker describes the search for a precise answer as to how many animal interests may be sacrificed for the sake of humans as "ludicrous and offensive."[60] But if what his approach ultimately implies for specific uses of animals is less than clear, for this result Becker is unapologetic: in the absence of an unequivocal animal ethic based on moral principles such as utility or deontological duty, Becker recommends—in Aristotelian fashion—that we accept "*as morally right*, whatever virtuous people agree is right."[61] The obvious problem is that at present there is no such agreement about our treatment of other animals, and it seems unreasonable that either all meat-eaters or all vegetarians, all vivisectionists or all vegans, should be consigned to the category of the vicious.

## Conclusion

The Aristotelian arguments reviewed in this chapter make important contributions to the debate over animals. In praise of Becker's approach, we may agree with Annette Baier that a "moral theory that makes the admittedly fuzzy concepts of virtue and vice the central ones at least openly avows both the imprecision concerning the relation between individual interest and the interest of others . . . and also the imprecise guidance the theory yields . . . concerning the details of moral duties."[62] Rollin, too, confronts the imprecision inherent in ethical thought, while refusing to let it excuse ethics from attending to its charge. Further, by highlighting the difference between *being moral* and *calculating what is right*, both Rollin and Becker remind us that ethics must address the former even when it cannot accomplish the latter in a completely satisfying way. In this way, they open the prospect that ethics might outline an animal-inclusive way of life, even if it cannot offer a precise assessment of all forms of animal exploitation. Finally, Rollin's use of the animal *telos* and Becker's premise of animal independence show sensitivity to the need to develop an animal ethic that is true to the animal's nature. No matter how well intentioned, an extensionist argument that fails on this point cannot avoid echoing the anthropocentric logic that underlies animal exploitation.

Nonetheless, the specific conclusions advanced by Rollin and Becker would be more useful at the end of the debate over animals than in the midst of the dispute. If it could be established that the ethical concepts at the core of much of our ordinary moral dialectics—utility and rights—are adequate for the moral assessment of animal interests, then Rollin's teleology could provide a reasonable framework for extending these concepts to cover our treatment of other animals. However, as the survey in the previous two chapters indicates, neither utilitarianism nor deontological rights theory completely befits the reality occupied by nonhumans; thus, Rollin's exhortation that our consideration of other animals' interests be conceived in moral terms is by itself insufficient to indicate where that consideration ought to lead. Likewise, if there were a discernible consensus among persons of character as to how we ought to behave toward nonhumans, then Becker's appeal to "virtue rather than principle" might be viewed as a reasonable corrective to the bickering among academic ethicists. As of yet, there seems to be no such consensus, in part because the modern debate is so new, and the possibility of direct moral duties to animals has been obscured for so long—by none other than the legacy of Aristotle.

# 6 Contractarian Arguments: Animals outside the State of Nature

## The Creation of Morality

Annette Baier's praise of the virtue approach to ethics, cited at the conclusion of the previous chapter, is offered in her search for a complement to the final school of moral thought I will discuss: contractarianism. Such a search appears to be necessary for the would-be contractarian animal advocate, because this school is prima facie animal-exclusive. Contractarians hold that principles of justice and considerations of moral right and wrong are mechanisms that emerge from agreements reached among rational, self-interested agents, and animals—as was noted in Chapter 4—cannot be informed parties to such agreements. We may feel compassion for faithful family pets or service animals, but it is a stretch to describe our obligations to them as resulting from contractual arrangements between them and us. In some hunting cultures, the shaman is believed to negotiate mystically with leaders of prey species concerning the terms and conditions of the hunt, but such mythology will hardly satisfy the modern contractarian. Thus, it is not clear how contract theory by itself can establish a direct moral status for nonhuman animals. If under contract doctrine wrongs and injustices arise from a type of contractual breach, then any moral problems associated with exploiting animals will concern those contractually recognized human interests that may be affected thereby, and not those of the exploited animals themselves. In turning now to the contractarian approach to the animal, one should expect to gain little leverage against the Western tradition's unwillingness to acknowledge any but indirect duties to nonhumans.[1]

Given such a lack of promise, why would someone interested in developing a more positive animal ethic consider using a contractarian framework? In general terms, contractarianism offers two important advantages over other ethical theories. First, as Jan Narveson points out, contract doctrine explains in a non-mystical way why human beings have morality at all: given our diffidence in the face of our fellows who can do us real harm, we reach contractual agreements to limit our conduct because doing so ultimately serves our self-interests.[2] Put simply, the contractarian holds that we *create* morality because it fulfills human *needs*, and this position is metaphysically and epistemologically simpler than those that place morality in the service of more transcendent ends. As I argued in Chapter 1, it seems clear that human beings *need* the animal—on various levels, and as something more than an exploitable resource; perhaps this need can serve as a clear and simple ground for venturing to clarify the moral status of animals. Second, if morality is created, rather than something natural that must be discovered, then a greater degree of control and clarity should be possible in our moral thinking. As Baier puts the point, contractarianism offers "the availability to the moral philosopher of the formal techniques of game theory and the theory of rational choice. One can *calculate* what would be agreed on by one's hypothetical contractors, given their hypothetical preference-based interests. One thereby gets at least the appearance of greater precision in one's moral theory."[3] Whether contract doctrine can bring genuine precision to an animal ethic remains to be seen. The question to be explored in this chapter is whether an adequate moral standing can be created for the animal in a way consistent with the contractarian account of justice.

## Modern Contract Theory

The animal-exclusive nature of contract theory is seen clearly in the work of Thomas Hobbes, the most prominent contractarian thinker in the early modern era.[4] In the arguments of his *Leviathan*, Hobbes contends that principles of law and justice emerge only from the artificial political agreements human beings reach as the means of escaping the dangerous uncertainty of their "natural" condition—a state he describes as a "war of every man against every man." In this hypothetical[5] extra-political existence, individual human beings are radically equal, with equal desires for the earth's resources and equal rights to them, making conflict inevitable. However, living thus "without a common power to keep them all in awe," human beings have no natural principles of justice by which to adjudicate these conflicts:

> To this war of every man against every man, this also is consequent; that nothing can be unjust. The notions of right and wrong, justice and injustice, have there no place. Where there is no common power, there is no law; where no law, no injustice. Force and fraud are in war the two cardinal virtues. Justice and injustice are none of the faculties neither of the body nor mind. If they were, they might be in a man that were alone in the world, as well as his senses and passions. They are qualities that relate to men in society, not in solitude. It is consequent also to the same condition that there be no propriety, no dominion, no mine and thine distinct; but only that to be every man's that he can get, and for so long as he can keep it.[6]

While the premise of such a "natural" human state—one outside the constraints of culture—would seem to argue for a continuity between the social existences of humans and other animals, Hobbes is quick to separate the two. He claims that since other social animals lack, among other things, the linguistic and rational abilities to produce the types of squabbles that plague human social life, they find harmony in their natural state effortlessly; human beings, in contrast, must construct the means of escaping war.[7] And those means are inevitably sought, because those humans living in the natural state want to survive, and this self-interest begets what Hobbes identifies as *natural laws*, the precepts of human self-preservation.[8] The first such law, "*seek peace, and follow it*," dictates the second: that the conflicts among humans' equal claims to the world be abated by the "mutual transferring of right," that is, by contract.[9] Only thus do the concepts of right and wrong, just and unjust, begin to have a place, relative to the contractual agreements that are reached. However, "covenants without the sword are but words, and of no strength to secure a man at all"; thus the laws of nature must eventually yield to the laws of the body politic, enforced by the power of government, and reaching its highest form in the *commonwealth*: "This is more than consent, or concord; it is a real unity of them all in one and the same person, made by covenant of every man with every man, in such manner as if every man should say to every man: *I authorise and give up my right of governing myself to this man, or to this assembly of men, on this condition; that thou give up, thy right to him, and authorise all his actions in like manner*."[10]

Both within and without the commonwealth the animal is due no direct moral consideration, according to Hobbes. In the state of nature, humans have right of dominion over animals; like Aristotle—although on very different grounds[11]—Hobbes analogizes this power to the right of human masters over their human slaves:

> This right of conquest, as it maketh one man master over another, so also maketh it a man to be master of the irrational creatures. For if a man in the state of nature, be in hostility with men, and thereby have lawful title to subdue or kill, according as his own conscience and discretion shall suggest unto him for his safety and benefit; much more may he do the same to beasts; that is to say, save and preserve for his own service, according to his discretion, such as are of nature apt to obey, and commodious for use; and to kill and destroy, with perpetual war, all other, as fierce, and noisome to him. And this dominion is therefore of the law of nature, and not of the divine law positive. For if there had been no such right before the revealing of God's will in the Scripture, then should no man, to whom the Scripture hath not come, have right to make use of those creatures, either for his food or sustenance. And it were a hard condition of mankind, that a fierce and savage beast should with more right kill a man, than the man a beast.[12]

No contracts—the means to preventing "perpetual war" among human beings—can limit this natural dominion: "To make covenants with brute beasts is impossible, because not understanding our speech, they understand not, nor accept of any translation of right, nor can translate any right to another: and without mutual acceptation, there is no covenant."[13] In turn, within the commonwealth animal exploitation must be discretionary—or possibly stipulatory, relative to particular agreements reached among humans—because the animal cannot be subsumed directly under the commonwealth's laws:

> A command consisteth in declaration or manifestation of the will of him that commandeth, by voice, writing, or some other sufficient argument of the same, we may understand that the command of the Commonwealth is law only to those that have means to take notice of it. Over natural fools, children, or madmen there is no law, no more than over brute beasts; nor are they capable of the title of just or unjust, because they had never power to make any covenant or to understand the consequences thereof, and consequently never took upon them to authorize the actions of any sovereign, as they must do that make to themselves a Commonwealth.[14]

We find, therefore, in Hobbes's argument a feature analogous to the common ground we identified between Aristotle and Kant in the previous chapter: the exclusion of the animal from moral consideration and the separation of human from nonhuman are established on the same foundation. According to Hobbes, central to that foundation is the role of *language*. Hobbes's materialism commits him to an impoverished, Cartesian understanding of animate life,[15] yet he nonetheless grants that understanding,[16] deliberation,[17] and prudence[18] all are shared by humans with other animals. What separates human consciousness from that of animals is the kind of understanding that only language can make possible, allowing the human to understand "not only his will, but his conceptions and thoughts, by the sequel and contexture of the names of things into affirmations, negations, and other forms of speech."[19] Language thus allows for "the discourse of the mind," which uniquely structures human thinking as "a hunting out of the causes of some effect, present or past; or of the effects of some present or past cause."[20] But the importance of language is not limited to psychology and epistemology, for Hobbes makes linguistic ability a necessary condition for the contract—the foundation of all morally and politically significant categories. Thus, he praises speech as "the most noble and profitable invention of all . . . without which there had been amongst men neither Commonwealth, nor society, nor contract, nor peace, no more than amongst lions, bears, and wolves."[21]

## A Theory of Justice

While many aspects of Hobbes's system certainly are dated, some contributors to the more recent debate over animals have maintained that his arguments still are relevant to the consideration of other animals' moral standing. Bonnie Steinbock, for example, argues that the impossibility of reaching agreements with members of other species is by itself—irrespective of considerations of utility or rights—sufficient to curtail the weight they can have in our moral deliberations: "If rats invade our houses, carrying disease and biting our children, we cannot reason with them, hoping to persuade them of the injustice they do us. We can only attempt to get rid of them. And it is this that makes it reasonable for us to accord them a separate and not equal moral status."[22] Still, both within and without the debate over animals, few today will be willing to embrace a pure Hobbesian account of the nature and origin of our moral obligations. Most problematic for our moral sensibilities is the concern that a strictly contractual account of justice—much like a strictly utilitarian account, as discussed in Chapter 3—will conflict with our moral intuitions about equality and fairness. For example, it might serve the self-interests of a

majority of a society's population to agree to oppress an arbitrarily desig-
nated minority, and it might not be irrational for the minority to comply
with the oppression as a means of self-preservation—the arrangement
might serve utility as well—all this despite that such a contract will
result in a distribution of social goods that from an objective (i.e., extracontractual) point of view would not seem equitable.

Since it seems that some types of contracts ought to be proscribed,
most post-Hobbesian contractarians have attempted to articulate a meaningful way of evaluating the contracts that human beings reach. The most
expedient way of doing so is to step outside of contract doctrine proper
and introduce prescriptive moral concepts that are external to contractual
considerations. Jean-Jacques Rousseau, for example, accepted the value of
the social contract for legitimizing human political arrangements, but
also argued for the natural value of *compassion*; he was thereby able to
create space for the moral evaluation of both political agreements *and* our
treatment of animals.[23] In the twentieth century, the most important
attempt to find room for the moral value of fairness *within* a contractual
theory of justice is found in the work of John Rawls. Rawls, who locates
his work in the tradition of Locke, Rousseau, and Kant, begins this
attempt by eliminating the classical contractarian hypothesis of the
"state of nature," substituting in its place a purely hypothetical situation
he terms "the original position." The contractors in this situation are not
merely in a "natural" state, unconstrained by the social rules we know,
but are cloaked by a "veil of ignorance," intended to ensure that the principles of justice they draw up for the society they create will fulfill the
demands of fairness: "Among the essential features of this situation is
that no one knows his place in society, his class position or social status,
nor does anyone know his fortune in the distribution of natural assets and
abilities, his intelligence, strength, and the like. I shall even assume that
the parties do not know their conceptions of the good or their special psychological propensities."[24]

Given this revision to the traditional starting point of the contractarians, it would be irrational for a founding contractor to agree to a
social arrangement that strayed very far from egalitarian ideals, inasmuch as capricious rules of social distribution, or even more objective
utilitarian or meritocratic principles, might prove disadvantageous to
the contractor once the veil of ignorance is lifted. If this veil prevents
the parties from knowing their race or gender, it would be foolish of
them to sanction oppression along those lines; likewise, not knowing
their native talents, it would be risky to endorse a distribution of social
goods that disproportionately rewarded some talents over others. Thus,

Rawls argues, rational self-interest alone will force the contractors in the original position to conceive of justice *as fairness*. The institutions in the society they construct will therefore be designed to comply with two fundamental principles: that each person has "an equal right to the most extensive total system of equal basic liberties," and that whatever social inequalities are tolerated should be arranged "to the greatest benefit of the least advantaged."[25]

The concepts of the original position and the veil of ignorance were among the most fruitful ideas in twentieth-century moral and political thought, and the emendations they make to traditional contract theory bring it more into line with common moral intuitions. However, as Rawls readily acknowledges,[26] they fail to render contractarianism a complete ethical theory, in part because it still cannot address what if any duties we have to those beings that are not rational agents. If those in the original position are "moral persons, that is . . . rational beings with their own ends and capable . . . of a sense of justice,"[27] and thus of sufficient intellectual capacity to help design the fair social arrangements that will govern their political existence, then those who fail to meet these criteria— including nonhuman animals and marginal cases—cannot be covered directly by the principles of justice. However, as Baier emphasizes in her account of these matters,[28] Rawls does not therefore conclude that the animal can have no legitimate moral standing. As Rawls writes:

> While I have not maintained that the capacity for a sense of justice is necessary in order to be owed the duties of justice, it does seem that we are not required to give strict justice anyway to creatures lacking this capacity. But it does not follow that there are no requirements at all in regard to them, nor in our relations with the natural order. Certainly it is wrong to be cruel to animals and the destruction of a whole species can be a great evil. The capacity for feelings of pleasure and pain and for the forms of life of which animals are capable clearly imposes duties of compassion and humanity in their case. I shall not attempt to explain these considered beliefs. They are outside the scope of the theory of justice, and it does not seem possible to extend the contract doctrine so as to include them in a natural way. A correct conception of our relations to animals and to nature would seem to depend upon a theory of the natural order and our place in it . . . How far justice as fairness will have to be revised to fit into this larger theory it is impossible to say.[29]

But perhaps Rawls concedes too much when he states that contract doctrine cannot be extended in a "natural way" to include the animal.[30] Some of the most interesting speculation in the recent debate over animals has centered on whether the "larger theory" of which he writes can adequately take the animal into account while not straying very far from a contractarian framework. Three different strategies for developing a Rawlsian animal ethic have been attempted. First, Bernard Rollin argues that even within the framework of justice-as-fairness that Rawls constructs, nonhumans can be found proper accommodation. He envisions that just as we might expect the contractors in the original position to act upon strong moral intuitions toward marginal cases, "it is perfectly possible, and indeed plausible, that rational agents setting up moral rules would favor a society where these rules were applied to animals. It is also possible that such rational agents might choose to make animals party to the original position by proxy, where their interests are represented by rational agents. Rational agents might well want a society where non-rational beings are granted rights and protection just like those granted to rational beings."[31] However, it is questionable whether this assertion is consistent with the conditions Rawls premises, since—like Rousseau's discussion of the animal—it seems to presuppose that these agents will act upon a *pre-contractual* appreciation for compassionate benevolence. Rawls himself resists the introduction of any such values as unnecessary, arguing instead that *mutual disinterest* and the veil of ignorance will secure social goods more certainly than will altruistic calculations.[32]

A more pointed objection to the strategy Rollin suggests is raised by Jan Narveson, who makes a compelling case that since the human contractors "have nothing generally to gain by voluntarily refraining from . . . killing animals or 'treating them as a mere means,' "[33] a contractarian model cannot place moral limits on animal exploitation. Indeed, Narveson argues that Rawls's device of the veil of ignorance, far from salvaging the contractarian approach, actually robs it of its rational foundation, which is that the contractors "know who they are and what they want," the rules of justice and morality they draw up being designed to serve their specific needs. Narveson thus emphasizes the rational egoism of classical contract doctrine: that the parties to the contract must have something to gain by subscribing to it, which in turn requires that they be capable of entering into an agreement. He concludes that the animal must be denied contractual justice on both of these counts. First, while there may be spiritual or other benefits from abstaining from animal products, it seems clear to him that on balance humans have more to gain by exploiting animals; therefore, "if one of the main planks in a moral platform is refraining from killing merely for self-interest, then it is quite clear that such a plank, in the case of animals, would not be worth it from the point of view of most of us. Taking our chances in the state of nature would be preferable."[34] Second, while Narveson acknowledges the possibility of *tacit* agreements being reached between humans and sophisticated animals, he questions whether such "contracts" could ever rise to the level where principles of justice or fairness are meaningfully at stake.[35]

This second point would seem to commit Narveson to a denial of moral standing for marginal humans as well as animals. However, he justifies a distinction between the cases by noting that "marginal humans are invariably members of families, or of other groupings, which make them the object of love and interest on the part of other members of those groups";[36] therefore, their respectful treatment will serve the self-interests of non-marginal contractors in a way that such treatment of animals generally will not. As Baier notes, Rawls uses a similar device to secure moral concern for future generations of human beings.[37] Employing a second possible strategy for including the animal in contractual considerations, she offers that this device might be modified to extend moral concern further to nonhumans:

> Rawls makes his self-interested contractors heads of families, in part to ensure that there will be some self-anchored reason for each hypothetical contractor to care about some of those in the next generation, to let concern spread. To make the contractors heads of families, caring about the members of their families, is to modify the claim that it is *self-interest*, in the right conditions (the veil of ignorance), that generates agreement on moral principles. We could perhaps extend the same tactic and make the hypothetical contractors heads of households that include domestic and other animals tolerated in the household, a group of Noahs each with an ark of humans and animals in his or her care. The principles then agreed on would include ones that would accommodate Rawls's intuitions about duties to animals.[38]

While this modification of the self-interest criterion is intriguing, it raises clear problems concerning the moral and ontological appropriateness of *domestication* as the model for our treatment of the animal, and the fairness of extending justice only to those species that humans happen to "tolerate."[39] Further, since it is still fundamentally *human* self-interest that is at stake in Baier's proposal, the inclusion of animals by proxy may be viewed, as Livingston argues, as completing "the 'humanization' of the planet," making other animals "unwitting participants" in our artificial moral hierarchy. And what if the animal could choose whether to participate in our moral arrangements, to board the "arks" Baier envisions? Livingston responds: "I should think that any naturalist would feel that wild nonhuman beings would just as soon go their own way and take their chances. One cannot imagine them willingly casting their lot with the chronically stressed and impoverished community of domesticates for whom rights had to be conceived in the first place."[40]

## Species and the Veil of Ignorance

Livingston playfully entertains the prospect of the animal choosing whether to be protected by the umbrella of human moral arrangements with a view to exposing their hopeless anthropocentrism. Yet this type of thought experiment lies at the heart of the most ambitious attempt to salvage a Rawlsian account of the animal. The anthropocentrism of Hobbes's thought is overt; in Rawls's argument, it is introduced more subtly through the very means he devises to advance contract doctrine toward more progressive moral sensibilities: the veil of ignorance. For while this veil shields the contractors from other results of the "natural lottery"—including their race, social class, and talents—it does not extend to *species:* those in the original position know that they are *human beings.* Many in the recent debate over animals have questioned why this should be the case. For example, Tom Regan argues that "to allow those in the original position to know what *species* they will belong to is to allow them knowledge no different in kind from allowing them to know what race or sex they will be," and that this knowledge "prejudice[s] the case against recognizing duties of justice to animals from the start."[41] Donald VanDeVeer adds that "if Rawls's strategy in designing the original position is to have a veil of ignorance sufficient to preclude its participants from choosing principles arbitrarily favoring themselves, and hence preferential to some relevant group to which they might belong, why should the veil *include* knowledge of species membership (in Homo sapiens)—when it is unreasonable to claim that many nonhumans are incapable of satisfactions and dissatisfactions?"[42]

If these objections are sound, they suggest a third possible extension of contract doctrine to include the animal, a strategy developed by Van-DeVeer. He proposes that a "neutral basis for ascertaining what principles might be chosen to regulate inter-specific social interactions"[43] can be had by raising the veil of ignorance higher than Rawls does, in order to prevent the contractors from arbitrarily prejudicing the principles of justice in favor of human beings. He thus offers what he terms the "pre-original position": What if those contemplating the rules of the society they will live in knew only that they would be *sentient beings,* and thus might occupy the position of a normal or enfeebled human, *or* that of a cow or a pig or some other animal? Cloaked behind such a veil, the founding contractors would have a direct and pressing *self*-interest in establishing principles of justice that served the interests of *all* sentient life, not just human beings. Consequently, they would likely reason toward principles of justice significantly different from those Rawls articulates. Specifically, VanDeVeer argues that those in the pre-original position would not accept Rawls's second principle of justice—that the existence of inequalities grounds obligations to aid "the least advantaged"—since it would entail a radical inequality of sacrifices to be made: rational human beings would be saddled with positive duties to underwrite the well-being of many other sentient beings who would be unable to reciprocate, and who in any case could never be made to transcend the specific limitations on their quality of life.[44]

Instead, VanDeVeer argues that the contractors would embrace a different principle that generated only *negative* duties: the principle of "Life Preferability," which would impose on moral agents the obligation to refrain from forcing upon another sentient being conditions that make its life not worth living.[45] This principle has obvious implications for some intensive farming practices and scientific research: no life might well be preferable to the tormented existence of a veal calf or vivisection subject. However, VanDeVeer maintains that it is not sufficient to proscribe all forms of animal exploitation, even those that end in death: "For *some* of the burdens of domestication animals receive compensating benefits. When these securities are provided for animals, they go *some* distance toward making its life preferable to no life at all."[46] Thus, he concludes that "participants [in the pre-original position], accepting the inevitabilities of the genetic lottery, would, I think, simply accept their genetic lot and its limits on possible satisfactions,"[47] knowing that their possible lot might well include being farmed and slaughtered, or otherwise exploited by human beings.

This argument is impressive for the ease and clarity with which it can validate fundamental moral intuitions about the animal: that extreme cruelty to the animal is wrong, but human lives—with their greater breadth and depth of satisfactions—are ultimately more morally significant than animal lives. Yet, it is still open to fundamental objections. First, VanDeVeer's prediction that the contractors will be resigned to their specific fate, even in the face of possible exploitation, assumes that they will follow a strategy of *minimax* rather than *maximin*—that is, they would be more concerned about what they would stand to lose as humans morally obligated to other animals than about what they would stand to gain as nonhuman beneficiaries of such obligations.[48] However, the reasonableness of this tactic depends not only on the degree of sacrifice these obligations would require—VanDeVeer's focus—but is also proportional to the likelihood of the contractors finding themselves as members of *Homo sapiens* once the veil of ignorance is lifted. If this knowledge were not hidden by the veil, it would surely argue against the minimax strategy, given that nonhuman animals— even limiting our focus to domesticated animals—greatly outnumber human beings.[49] This additional factor still is not sufficient to justify the extension of Rawls's second principle to cover sentient nonhumans, but it might argue for something stronger than VanDeVeer's minimalist alternative of Life Preferability.

Second, like Baier's modification of Rawls's argument discussed above, VanDeVeer's argument is premised on the legitimacy of animal domestication per se. In his case, this premise is not unsupported, for he does make appeal, as we saw, to the "compensating benefits" of domestication arrangements.[50] Further, it is perhaps unfair to be too critical of VanDeVeer on this point, inasmuch as he states up front that his argument concerns the principles that would govern "inter-specific *social interactions*," thus limiting its scope to those nonhuman domesticates with which humans have contact in social space. Still, one wonders whether those in the pre-original position would not only consider how domesticated animals ought to be treated, but also whether animals ought to be domesticated at all. Perhaps some might be more willing to accept their "genetic lot," as VanDeVeer suggests, if their potential nonhuman fate was to live as *wild* animals—to, as Livingston phrases it, "go their own way and take their chances." Given the species solipsism problem discussed in Part I, it may not be possible to determine with any certainty whether, for example, the secure, dependent, and abruptly shortened lives of domestic cattle are preferable to the more challenging and uncertain existence of wild ruminants. Contra Livingston, it could be argued that a preference for the domestic life over the wild is not entirely irrational; from there the contractarian could further argue that if domestication would be the rational choice of the contractors in the pre-original position, it is therefore a just institution. However, this line of argument would only open the door to the kind of absurd obligations of humans vis-à-vis animals that VanDeVeer fears, for it might further imply that justice *requires* the domestication of the animal, and saddle humans with the duty to augment the quality of life of wild sentient beings.

Finally, VanDeVeer's device of raising the veil of ignorance to exclude knowledge of species signals an acknowledgment of the *arbitrariness* of our genetic lot, and this knowledge can be used to a much different effect than it achieves in his argument. Collin McGinn, for example, argues that if we inform our species morality with "the idea of biological luck," we must reckon with the real "contingency of our biological supremacy as a species."[51] This thought is often repressed, but finds sublimated expression in fictional accounts of humans being victimized at the hands of overpowering aliens or monsters. However, the foundation of such speculation is not entirely fantastical. There is, in the post-Darwinian world, no biological or historical necessity to the superiority of *Homo sapiens*; other hominids *could* have evolved differently than they have, and we *may* yet encounter superior life forms elsewhere in the universe. Would the pre-original contractors still embrace their "genetic lot" in the face of such prospects? In constructing our animal ethic, McGinn suggests "that we take seriously the notion that we might have been, or could be," in a position of inferiority relative to other species, "and ask ourselves what moral principles we would want to see observed if indeed we were the weaker species."[52] If this is a legitimate way of assimilating our genetic contingency into our moral thinking, it is not clear that the principle of Life Preferability passes this test.

## Conclusion

Although the contractarian approach seemed unpromising, we have found that twentieth-century contract doctrine adds at least one important dimension to the debate over animals, and to ethics generally. Rawls's device of the veil of ignorance, by forcing us to look past our facticity, brings the *contingency of human affairs* to bear on ethics in a powerful way. That things could have been other than they are—the "*What if . . .?*"—is not only an inescapable characteristic of the human circumstance, but a necessary condition for our *moral being*. As McGinn notes, "morality is founded in a sense of the contingency of the world, and it is powered by the ability to envisage alternatives. Imagination is central to its operations. The morally complacent person is the person who cannot conceive how things could have been different; he or she fails to appreciate the role of luck—itself a concept that relies on imaging alternatives . . . Morality is thus based on modality: that is, on a mastery of the concepts of necessity and possibility. To be able to think morally is to be able to think modally."[53] While Rawls uses this insight to establish the self-interest humans have in dealing with each other fairly, it can also shed fresh light on our relations with other species. The "what-ifs" that can be raised relative to the animal—culminating with the theme of VanDeVeer's argument: "What if we were they?"— may not be sufficient to ground all the details of a fair animal ethic, but in an effective and elegant way they undermine moral complacency about our treatment of nonhumans.

Nonetheless, the precision and control that we said contract doctrine attempts to bring to moral philosophy—the promise of controlling the "what-ifs" through the principles of game theory—seem in the end to be inappropriate to animal reality. The efforts reviewed in this chapter to bring the animal under contract doctrine can at best extend some moral consideration to domesticated animals—those that humans control—at the cost to the animal of advancing domestication as the paradigm for our moral thinking about nonhumans. Further, the contractarian approach also seems inappropriate to our moral being generally, inasmuch as ethics itself becomes too contingent if it can only take stock of those things that humans can control, while failing to reflect a wider reality. As Baier writes, the price we pay for reducing all moral considerations to the con-tractual context is "a false pretence that moral reasoning is just a special case of individualistic self-interested reasoning, a special case of a com-petitive game. It may be a hard historical fact that the developed formal techniques in decision theory are those developed to meet the needs of capitalists and heads of armies. But that is no good reason to make ethics the moral equivalent of war, or of business competition."[54] If we must assimilate animals to the terms of such uniquely human enterprises in order to extend them justice, then Livingston's contention that they are better off without our justice must be taken seriously.

––––––––––

The preceding survey of the debate over animals is hardly complete. The historical picture is no doubt more complex and ambiguous than this lim-ited presentation may suggest, and the recent literature is vast and grow-ing as thinkers from within and without professional philosophy join the debate, with many ingenious arguments no doubt forthcoming. Still, I think it is sufficient to permit some general assessment of the capacity of Western ethical models to deal adequately with the animal, and some analysis of what this implies for ethics as a whole. In Part III, I begin this analysis by identifying where there is consensus among the arguments we have reviewed, where they have succeeded in terms of clarifying the moral status of animals and capturing our fundamental moral intuitions, and where they have failed. Subsequently, I explore the grounds of the failures, linking them with other critiques that have been leveled against the central ideas in the tradition of Western ethical thought.

## PART III

# The Animal or the Good?

# 7  *Extensionism and Its Limits*

---

In Part I, I offered various reasons why we should expect an adequate moral theory to clarify the moral standing of animals. In sum, I argued that none of the traditional arguments for excluding the animal from direct moral concern is insurmountable, and that questions of the nature and extent of our moral duties to nonhumans raise pressing issues that ethics should address. In Part II, I explored how the four major ethical theories in the tradition of Western philosophy have been used in the recent debate to try to produce a new animal ethic. While utilitarianism, deontology, virtue ethics, and contractarianism do not exhaust the logical possibilities for ethical argument, they account for a clear majority of Western moral thought and for the most prominent arguments in current applied ethics. If the argument in Part I is sound and the survey in Part II is fair, then it is my contention that together they provide a reasonable ground for drawing some more general conclusions about these moral theories, and about the tradition of ethical thought of which they are a part. The vulnerability of the most important extensionist arguments and the absence of a clear consensus on many issues related to our treatment of other animals lead to the conclusion that core concepts in Western ethics fail the test with which the animal confronts them. But the picture is not entirely negative; before exploiting its failure to produce an adequate animal ethic, we should first acknowledge the progress and success the recent debate can claim.

## Success and Consensus in the Debate over Animals

I noted in Chapter 1 that the question of the moral status of nonhuman animals was an interesting one in part because of the powerful pre-reflective intuitions it raises; I quoted Annette Baier's argument that a fundamental job of moral philosophy is to evaluate the role such intuitions should have in our moral deliberations. Our survey in Part II suggests that the principal ethical theories succeed in assimilating some of the most common intuitions about animals. First, perhaps the most catholic moral intuition concerning animals—and the one that most strongly bolsters the judgment that an animal ethic is needed—is the pervasive sense that at least some nonhuman animals can suffer from cruel treatment, and that it is wrong for a moral agent to commit such cruelty without justification. It seems clear that all the argument forms we have reviewed provide adequate grounds for making sense of this moral intuition. Whether expressed in terms of the disutility of cruelty, a sentient being's right to be free of unnecessary suffering, the virtue of empathy, or the interest we all have in agreeing to a social contract that rejects brutality, Western ethical thought can readily accommodate a proscription against unnecessary animal cruelty. It may be argued that this belief is reflected widely in Western culture, but the elasticity of the concepts *unnecessary* and *cruel* will result in an array of assessments on this point. In any case, buttressed with the growing body of biological and ethological evidence for the reality of suffering on the part of many species of nonhuman animals, this intuition appears to be on solid footing. Thus, common sense, longstanding tradition, and recent moral philosophy are in accord on this basic point. Without this as a foundation, the search for a more substantial animal ethic would seem to be futile.

Second, I also noted the prevalence of an intuition that runs in another direction: the ultimate primacy of human interests over those of other animals. *Absolute speciesism* (or *dominionism*)—the belief that human interests should *always* prevail over animal interests—is not universal, and would contradict the intuition that animal cruelty carries a negative moral weight. However, a *weaker* form of speciesism, one that favors human beings at least in those cases where human interests conflict with the lesser or roughly equivalent interest of other animals, enjoys broader appeal. Again, the theories surveyed in Part II can accommodate this intuition without difficulty. As noted several times, the species solipsism problem makes precision in the comparison of human and animal interests difficult. Nonetheless, the available evidence supports the judgment that there are greater depth and breadth of subjective experience in typical humans than in typical members of other species. All the theories we have reviewed are able to exploit this judgment to confirm that, prima facie, a human life has greater value than an animal life, and greater moral attention is owed to human interests than to the comparable interests of other animals. While it may seem unnecessary to belabor the point, it is crucial that an ethical theory be able to establish it clearly; otherwise, it would be impossible to embark upon the moral consideration of other animals' interests without being drawn into absurd, polemical challenges, such as whether a spider's life is of equal value to that of a normal human being.

As with other philosophical debates, there is little unanimity in the debate over animals. But following from the recognition of the wrongness of animal cruelty, there does seem to be a consensus on a few fundamental points that deserve mention. The first confirms one of the themes explored in Part I: that consistency would seem to demand that we conceive of our treatment of animals in moral terms of some type. Some Wittgensteinians,[1] behaviorists who maintain a Cartesian denial of animal consciousness, and various die-hard anthropocentrists[2] will dissent, but today they constitute a minority. Even some of those we have seen argue against a radical revaluation of our traditional animal ethics are comfortable using moral language in discussing our treatment of nonhumans.[3] This is not to deny the problems that emerged in Part II (and will be analyzed subsequently): some fundamental concepts in Western ethical thought—such as *rights*—are clearly a rough fit with the animal, and none of the arguments surveyed produces a completely satisfactory animal ethic. At the same time, none of these efforts—all tributes to their authors' ingenuity—is obviously absurd either. That this much can be said about the recent debate is sufficient to establish that it is not only sentimentality or considerations of prudence that can give us pause in our treatment of animals, but also legitimate moral concern.

Second, there seems to be a consensus among moral philosophers—reflecting a growing trend in popular opinion—that we do have some clear moral duties to animals and that morality demands the correction of at least some common practices involving them. Utilitarians and deontologists will quarrel about the underlying justification for doing so, and animal welfarists and animal rightists will dispute the ultimate objectives of moral concern for the animal. Nonetheless, the most severe intensive farming practices and questionable research experiments are widely condemned among those who have undertaken the search for a new animal ethic. Most important, this condemnation is echoed by some of those who reject the call for a broader reassessment of the moral precedence humans have traditionally taken over animals. Recall that Lawrence Becker, in his argument to defend the priority of human interests, takes pains to condemn the "cruelty to animals found in factory farming and much scientific experimentation"; likewise, Donald VanDeVeer's defense of the institutionalized slaughter of animals concludes with the caution that his argument provides "little support for public complacency about much of our current dealings with other sentient creatures."[4] Whatever the underlying motives for the shift away from such complacency that has been evident in the past several years, the philosophical justification provided for this shift by the arguments in the recent debate confirms another line of argument from Part I: that the recent attention to the animal is not merely a "fashionable piety," but a substantive step in moral progress.

## Shortcomings of the Debate

The success and consensus that have emerged from the recent debate, and the impact they have had, are not insignificant accomplishments. As a colleague of mine recently remarked, it is startling that a philosopher like Peter Singer has *actually changed things*, affecting not only the ideas of other academics but the behavior of many non-philosophers as well. To the extent that the recent debate has highlighted real problems in our treatment of animals and inspired practical efforts to correct them, it is all for the good, and stands as a unique example of the power that philosophy can have in the contemporary world. But stopping our analysis at this point of self-congratulation would leave other instructive lessons of the debate unexplored. Despite the positive claims that may be made on behalf of the recent debate over animals, I believe that its shortcomings—which are perhaps of little consequence to those involved in the practice of animal protection—are ultimately of equal if not greater significance for philosophy.

And what exactly are the shortcomings? Beyond the clear cases where there is marked agreement—animal cruelty is wrong, and human interests ultimately have priority over animal interests—lie hazier questions concerning various forms of animal exploitation, and on these there is no clear consensus. This was manifested repeatedly in the survey in Part II: while all the ethical theories reviewed can ground clear condemnations of specific acts of animal cruelty, none is able to produce an unequivocal moral assessment of the more general practices of using other animals for food and scientific research. It became clear in those chapters that *the core concepts of each theory could be used to condemn or sanction such institutions with equal facility.* Perhaps this should not be surprising, since a survey of the major arguments in other prominent moral controversies would likely reveal similar ambiguity;[5] ethics by its nature is contentious, and were it not for such ambiguity there would be little space for controversy. If so, this shortcoming of the debate over animals might be better viewed as a reflection of the contingencies of human existence and the harsh reality of our moral being, rather than as a fundamental problem for which ethics must answer. Indeed, the fact that we are now confused about the moral status of animals is perhaps a clear signal that the issue is at last being taken seriously.

However, as we have seen, there are good reasons for believing that the ambiguity in the debate over animals is especially troubling. First, I argued in Chapter 1 that the ubiquity of animal exploitation makes its moral evaluation especially pressing. Today there is hardly a person whose life has not been affected directly by the exploitation of nonhumans, and more generally it has been argued that such exploitation is fundamental to human civilization per se. If it is a goal of ethics to address how human beings ought to live, it cannot meaningfully reach that goal while failing to evaluate the innumerable human acts and omissions that affect other animals. Second, in Chapter 3, I addressed why among the various possible uses of the animal—as a source of labor, entertainment, sport, companionship, and so on—it seems especially important to assess the uses of animals as a food source and as research subjects. With billions of animals used every year for food, much is at stake in the question of whether their sacrifice is justified, and so we should expect that ethics produce a clear assessment of the institution of animal husbandry; and while many fewer animals are used in the service of science, the high esteem in which the practice is held—in both our intellectual tradition and public opinion—ought to be either confirmed or soundly rejected by our ethical theories.

Moreover, there is a fundamental issue that the recent debate has failed to address sufficiently: the context of domestication in which much of our contact with—and exploitation of—animals occurs. In Chapter 1, we explored the ambiguous standing of the animal, a feature most prominent in the case of domesticates, which exist simultaneously as sentient beings and use-objects. This ambiguity makes uncertainty in the moral analysis of institutionalized animal exploitation all but inevitable. As I noted throughout Part II, making liberal use of John Livingston's criticism, many arguments in the debate fail to address whether the perpetuation of animal domestication is in itself morally problematic, irrespective of the specific uses to which domesticates are put. The conclusions of some arguments in the debate seem to presuppose the circumstance of domestication as the paradigm for an animal ethic;[6] thereby these arguments fail to address the most profound moral question raised by animal exploitation. Indeed, given that domesticated animals are an organic part of most post-Neolithic cultures, extending moral consideration to domesticates represents a less radical shift in the status that human civilization affords the animal than it may appear at first. As is argued over the following chapters, by conceiving of animals as part of the domesticated dominion of human morals, ethical extensionism reveals itself to be another symptom of anthropocentrism even as it tries to think beyond it.

That none of the major theories in our ethical tradition seems to provide the means of clarifying the moral status of animals leaves us in a quandary. Baier makes the point this way: "Should we, when faced with an array of moral theories *none* of which . . . provide a theoretical basis for worrying very much about the fate of animals, give up worrying? Or should we declare the theories all inadequate precisely because none of them *do* accommodate the belief that we are not morally free to torture, hunt, and kill animals as we please? If there were unanimity in moral belief—if everyone agreed . . . that there are wrongs to animals—then it would be very clear that the theories, not the intuitions, are what need revision. But there is no such agreement."[7] This certainly overstates the case: as I have just argued, the important moral theories *can* be extended to accommodate at least *some* moral concern for the animal (at very least by proscribing animal cruelty); conversely, it is unrealistic to expect *unanimity* of moral belief before judgment can be passed on moral theory. Nonetheless, something like the problem Baier identifies must be confronted: either the reasoning that calls upon ethics to resolve the status of animals is flawed, or those ethical theories that fail to produce an unequivocal account of the animal must be reevaluated. To determine which is the more reasonable conclusion, we first should explore in more detail what accounts for the failure of the extensionist arguments in the debate, and whether the causes are incidental or intrinsic to Western ethical theory.

## Anthropocentrism

As we explored in Part I, one factor that makes the moral consideration of the animal so difficult is that the very prospect of having positive and direct moral duties to other animals is profoundly unsettling. The use of the animal is deeply ingrained in human beings' psychological and cultural identities; as a result, the possibility that animal exploitation is morally suspect has extremely broad repercussions, both socially and philosophically. In light of this, Baier offers the interesting speculation that since all human beings have a stake in our species advantage, perhaps all arguments in the debate over animals are thereby disqualified as too interested.[8] Clearly—as she points out—those who call for the reevaluation of traditional positions are less suspect in this regard than those who defend the status quo.[9] Nonetheless, her observation alerts us to the fact that anthropocentrism can readily contaminate our thinking about animals, since our relationship to them is such a fundamental element in our understanding of ourselves as human beings.

Ethical theories cannot be immune from this problem, for—despite the philosopher's pretense to transcendence—they emerge from within cultural traditions. In the main, Western ethical thought reflects the pre-Darwinian view that human beings are shaped less by biology than by culture, with the result that radical distinctions between the human and nonhuman worlds have become etched into ethical theory. This fact emerged in Part II, where I noted that various thinkers in the tradition used the same ground to distinguish the human from the animal and to justify the exclusion of the animal from moral concern. It is no surprise, then, that the central concepts of our principal ethical theories reflect a bias toward human beings generally, and autonomous moral agents in particular. To summarize the results of Part II:

*Utilitarianism* presents moral agents with a duty to consider the effects of their actions on other beings' interests, especially the interests they have in experiencing pleasure and avoiding pain. But the further removed in kind those other beings are from the agent—that is, the more dissimilar their consciousness from that of a human being—the less certain the agent can be of their sentient experience, and consequently the less weight their interests can exercise in moral deliberation. Thus, while ostensibly inviting the moral consideration of the animal, the principle of utility blurs the edges of the moral divide between humans and the rest of the world but does not erase it.

*Deontological rights* are most clearly applicable to rational moral agents, although even when so applied their existence as something natural rather than stipulatory is controversial. At best, applying the concept of natural rights to other types of beings is a shorthand for moral conclusions reached by other means or supported by pre-reflective intuitions; otherwise, it is both metaphysically and ethically questionable, requiring the support of such problematic concepts as Regan's "inherent value." Stipulatory (for example, legal) rights for animals may have a valuable practical effect, but are problematic to the extent that they involve the theoretical submersion of the nonhuman world in human political culture.

*Virtue theory* commends that a moral agent's character be informed by empathetic identification. But our feelings of empathy are clear and pressing in inverse proportion to the social distance that separates us. Those who are socially and emotionally proximate to an agent will—usually—be most like the agent himself. Concerning the treatment of more distant—and more morally ambiguous—beings, such as nonhuman animals that exist independently of humans, the virtuous are apparently their own standard of right and wrong.

*Contractarianism*, from its inception, was intended as an explanation of how human agents arrive at moral rules and principles of justice; those who cannot meaningfully participate in social space are excluded from the essential scope of the theory. Novel attempts to expand the theory to include nonhumans can at best extend some concern to domestic animals, on the grounds that doing so serves the self-interests of human moral agents.

From these examples it becomes clear that the fundamental concepts in Western ethical thought will function best when our practical sphere is divided between two ontological categories: human *persons* (Kantian *ends in-themselves*) and inhuman *things* (the *means* to those ends). Thus, one must thrust either personhood or thinghood upon nonhuman *animals* in order for traditional models to accommodate them effectively. But neither of these categories is a proper fit.[10] The moral intuitions discussed above embody this knowledge: the intuition that we should not be cruel to animals implies they are not mere things that may be used in any way we wish, and the intuition of human priority implies that animals are not equivalent to persons. An awkward element in the English language bears further witness: because common nouns in English are not gender-inflected, applying personal pronouns to animals often sounds anthropomorphic or childlike, while the standard use of the pronoun *it* for an animal antecedent is overtly objectifying.[11]

Contemporary biology and psychology, with their increasing knowledge of the continuities and discontinuities between humans and animals, add further evidence of the ambiguous nature of the animal. But there is also a very longstanding basis for human beings to be aware of this ambiguity: humanity's historical experience of animals as *domesticable* and *socializable*. As we saw in Chapter 1, Mary Midgley argues that animals can only be domesticated to the extent that they are social beings, and those who undertake the work of taming an animal must understand and appreciate the "point of view" it occupies—usually understood as a privilege of persons—as the kind of animal it is.[12] Thus, even if we reserve the category of personhood for *Homo sapiens*, those who would subject animals to systematic exploitation in a context of domestication cannot consistently view them as mere things.[13] Conversely, as I explore further in Part IV, the pet owner who relates to animals as if they were full-fledged persons may be a victim of self-delusion, projecting thoroughly human emotions and beliefs onto the silent animal without fear of being contradicted.

Many in the debate have overlooked the ambiguity of the animal, perpetuating the longstanding person/thing dichotomy even as they attempt to forge a new animal ethic. This problem can be seen on both sides in the debate: the commodification of animals is justified by concentrating exclusively on their otherness, and the extension of moral protections to animals is justified by noting the similarities they share with human persons while whimsically ignoring the differences. In either case, the framework is anthropocentric because proximity to humanness is taken as the principal criterion for whether the animal merits moral concern. The inconsistency in using such a framework for an animal ethic is made plain by Raymond Corbey:

> Is the fact that another being has an emotional life and a subjectivity similar to our own a good reason for respect? Or does respecting what is similar to ourselves rather than different from ourselves imply that we once again take our own, human nature and our allegedly unique dignity as the pivotal point of reference, as an absolute standard against which to measure everything else? In that case we would only be defending a new form of anthropocentrism. How, for instance, should we behave towards squid living in the dark depths of the Pacific Ocean, towards lobsters, spiders, rats?[14]

The Protagoreanism Corbey suspects is confirmed by a fact mentioned above: the preponderance of arguments in the debate that are suited to dealing with domesticated animals—that is, animals that have proven assimilable to human society—rather than exploring the deeper question of the value of animality per se. As was noted in Chapter 2, further evidence is found in the many arguments in the debate that either explicitly focus on the possible moral standing of other primates, or offer conclusions that could approach sufficient clarity only in the case of our nearest relatives.[15] Thus, even while embracing the moral consideration of the nonhuman world, much of the recent debate over animals is often silent about the vast majority of life forms that are very much different from ourselves.[16]

The depth of the problem of anthropocentrism in the debate over animals is highlighted by a review of a point made in Chapter 4. Of the arguments surveyed in Part II that attempt to establish positive duties toward other animals, Regan's strong animal rights position offers the least equivocal conclusions about the institutionalized use of other animals: if sound, his argument would justify a clear prohibition against using those animals that meet the subject-of-a-life criterion in agriculture or research. As we saw, what makes this firmness possible is his invocation of the non-utilitarian concept of inherent value, which he proposes might be extended more broadly in the nonhuman world as the means of securing our moral duties to other kinds of animals, and even to inanimate elements of the environment. The more widely Regan's argument is cast, however, it becomes clear that it would require not just some rethinking about particular actions involving other animals, but would couch the entirety of our impact on the nonhuman world in the strongest moral terms. Thus, it seems that if we extend our most powerful moral concepts to those nonhuman entities that are morally valuable, we do not simply bridge the dichotomy between person and thing, but rather lay the ground for a radical reassessment of human culture, including its intellectual, political, and moral ideals. Thus, the anthropocentrism of Western ethics destines ethical extensionism to produce self-defeating results. Consistency demands that we produce an animal ethic more substantial than the tradition has articulated, but our anthropocentric ethical systems result in inadequate and ambiguous conclusions; stretching these systems to reduce the ambiguity ultimately requires that we rethink the larger cultural tradition of which these systems are a part. To develop a fitting theoretical framework for our treatment of nonhuman animals, a "larger theory" (to use Rawls's phrase) of our place in the world—one that takes us outside ethics proper to matters of metaphysics, anthropology, and ontology—must be developed.[17] Scholtmeijer asserts that "the ideal would be a conception of animals as animals which finds ethical significance in their own state of being."[18] Even granting that such an ideal can be conceived, the tenacity of anthropocentrism raises doubts about whether such a conception of the animal can be coherently incorporated with the existing ethical and intellectual structures of Western culture.

## Rationalism

That Western ethical thought is human-centered has been coextensive with its being reason-centered. As we saw in Chapter 5, the tradition of excluding animals from direct moral concern can be traced back at least to Aristotle, who justified this exclusion on the same ground he used to justify the categorical separation of humans from other animals: that humans are by nature rational in ways that no nonhuman animals can duplicate. The result has been a mutual implication of anthropocentric and logocentric bias in the debate over animals. As Steve Sapontzis notes, it is no surprise that the human intellectuals conducting the debate retain a bias not only in favor of humans, but also in favor of the intellectual.[19] Thus, we find that the authors of extensionist arguments typically take pains to emphasize that their conclusions are the products of *rational consistency*, rather than sentiment or pre-reflective intuition.[20] In turn, the insistence that above all our moral deliberations be "rational" has required, as Livingston argues, that "they must proceed from the starting-point of the established structure of Western ethical systems," which systems—as we have just reviewed—are anthropocentric.[21]

Many of the problematic results of this rationalism in the debate over animals are identical with the results of anthropocentrism: the tendency to favor those animals that are most like us finds expression in the moral weight given to animal analogs to human rational abilities, notably—as I reviewed in Chapter 2—forming beliefs and general ideas, using language, and developing a concept of self. An additional problem of reason-centeredness in ethics is that it implies that moral importance can only be given properly to what can be rationally calculated. While the hope for a complete rational accounting in our moral thinking is not necessarily misguided, it nonetheless serves the interests of polemicists and those who would seek to preserve the status quo. Henry Salt's vivid description relays how this is manifested in the debate over animals: "The perilous vagueness of the word 'necessary' must leave a convenient loop-hole of escape to anyone who wishes to justify his own treatment of animals, however unjustifiable that treatment may appear; the vivisector will assert that his practice is necessary in the interests of science, the flesh-eater that he cannot maintain his health without animal food, and so on through the whole category of systematic oppression. The difficulty is an inevitable one. No form of words can be devised for the expression of rights, human or animal, which is not liable to some sort of evasion."[22]

Moreover, as should be clear from our survey in Part II, the animal confronts the thinker with many additional issues that do not admit of an obvious rational resolution. In contemplating a question that is as wide-ranging as the moral status of the various species of nonhuman animals, we must identify and evaluate—qualitatively and quantitatively—the morally relevant characteristics these beings have, and bring those data to bear on the moral assessment of innumerable human actions and decisions. Irrespective of the moral theory one is using, its application to the animal requires some means of objectively and with a reasonable degree of certainty comparing the interests of humans and those of other animals. If the problem of anthropocentrism does not preclude methodological objectivity, the species solipsism problem can always be exploited to cast doubt upon the certainty of the comparison. Thus, one could perhaps make the case that in the debate over animals we run up against the limits to the degree of clarity that rational deliberation alone can bring to our moral decision making.[23]

The will to reason is in part the will to simplify, but when the objects of our rational reflection are the very actions by which we manifest ourselves in the world, there is a limit to the details that can be overlooked before something important is lost. Those arguments that parse all moral considerations in the grammar of a single ethical theory embody what Richard Sorabji terms an "artificial parsimony": "Moral theories may seek to make things manageable by reducing all considerations to one. Insofar as they do, this is so much the worse for them."[24] If oversimplification is unavoidable in moral theorizing, then—as Sorabji suggests, and as many animal activists claim—we may do well to forgo moral theory altogether.[25] This kind of moral skepticism cannot be entertained lightly, as it leaves the door open to the polemical charge that animal advocacy is simply one of the masks worn by moral relativism or nihilism. Still, it is difficult for those who have examined the arguments to be optimistic that all the ethical and metaethical issues the debate raises can be resolved satisfactorily, and made consonant with our scientific knowledge and metaphysical commitments.

These considerations provide an argument in favor of the virtue approach to ethics, which—more clearly than the other theories we have reviewed—renounces the demand for precision and absolute congruity in ethics, and incorporates the need to assimilate the contextual details of action into moral deliberation. As Baier writes:

> It is also intrinsic to any theory of virtues to include some, such as Aristotle's equity and practical wisdom, that discriminate among the relevant *differences* between cases, and are displayed in good judgment concerning how they should be treated. A theory of virtues must give an important place to such discrimination and . . . value as a special virtue that "delicacy" and judgment that is shown by a thoughtful appreciation of the difference between proper treatment of a child, an adult, an idiot, a mad person, an ape, a pet lamb, a spider (and the proper appreciation of the differences between eating human and other flesh).[26]

As was noted in Chapter 5, this delicacy of judgment is not readily quantified, and clinging to a singular criterion to determine what merits moral concern is no substitute. One effect of this is that thinking about animals in properly moral terms may of necessity be confined to the concrete relationships agents have with specific animals: the farmer's relationship to his stock, the hunter to his prey, the owner to his pet, and so on.[27] Perhaps only in such specific cases can the nuanced details and differences be perceived with sufficient clarity to inform moral judgment. If so, the larger question of how human beings ought to treat the animal per se, and what kinds of relationships humans *ought* to have with other species, must be left dangling, perhaps to be addressed only by a kind of thinking that lies outside the scope of traditional ethical thought.

## Individualism

A third attribute of modern Western ethical systems contributes to their inability to account for the animal adequately: the reservation of moral concern for individual conscious beings. The authors of many extensionist arguments make clear that their premises only allow for the moral consideration of individual animals. For example, Peter Singer's argument for the equal consideration of interests can only be extended meaningfully to individual sentient beings with an interest in fulfilling their preferences;[28] Tom Regan's rights argument only extends to those individual beings that possess equal inherent value, most clearly those that meet the subject-of-a-life criterion;[29] and Bernard Rollin decries the "poetic rhetoric" that would extend direct moral concern to anything but those individual beings that are aware of their own telic needs and desires.[30] In addition, the various extensions of contract doctrine reviewed in Chapter 6 all take as their standard of justice the self-interests of the individual contractors in the original position.

It is not on its face unreasonable to link moral value to those individual conscious beings that can experience it; goods or their privation cannot matter to inanimate beings or nonsentient life forms, and collectives of conscious individuals (such as species) can only be affected indirectly by the experiences of their individual members. Yet this individualism dovetails with and reinforces the anthropocentric and rationalistic features of Western ethics. Reflecting on this point, we might extend Baier's criticism of contract doctrine to cover the other ethical theories we have reviewed as well: in simplifying the moral universe to include only the interests of discrete individuals, these theories reduce our moral behavior to participation in a competitive game. Without having to endorse explicitly a contractarian account of justice, making the individual the exclusive object of moral concern implies that the circumstance characteristic of much human political life—self-interested agents struggling to protect their interests from the interference of others—is also the proper context for all moral deliberation.[31] Such a conception is unduly narrow even when the "field of play" is human political existence. If it can be extended to nonhumans at all, it will only accommodate those animals that exhibit human-like subjectivity or are otherwise assimilable to human political existence: other primates and domesticated animals.

One could also argue that the individualism of ethical theory conflicts with the widely held sense that at least some non-subjects possess morally relevant value. Such is reflected in the legal protections afforded inanimate things such as valuable aesthetic objects and collectives such as endangered species. However, the argument can always be made that any moral value attached to such beings is not intrinsic but instrumental: such things are to be valued only because of the effects their existence or nonexistence will have on individual subjects. The inadequacies of moral individualism are more clearly revealed through the moral consideration of the animal, which seems to require that a broader view of the totality of biological reality be embraced. From such a perspective, the concept of the autonomous human individual is revealed to be a political artifact. As Livingston writes:

> Naturalists have difficulty with this cultural preoccupation with the individual. In full awareness of the role of the individual animal as a vector of genetic material, and in full knowledge also of its several contributory activities within the natural multispecies community, naturalists perceive in the demeanour of a wild animal less a self-interested single entity, more a manifestation of whole *being*. The naturalist sees a wild animal as one among uncountable ephemeral corporeal emergences, one minor miracle to remind us of the ineffable whole. It may be that loners, such as bears and tigers, are more evocative in this respect than are more gregarious beings. But even these are not usually seen as mere self-serving individuals; they are seen as revelations of bearness, of tigerness, of wildness.[32]

He argues further that the individual self-consciousness prized by humans may not be the most developed, but in fact the most "primitive" type of consciousness;[33] he suggests that the consciousness of other wild animals—aided by a very different sensory attunement to the world—"rather than being centered on the individual self, may be transcendent and *participatory*,"[34] reflecting a more complex awareness of environmental and inter-specific factors than human beings are typically capable of.[35]

This kind of language seems to open the door to a type of mysticism. Livingston's speculation about wild animal consciousness recalls descriptions of fusional religious experience: an ineffable awareness of the whole, in which the individual self dissolves.[36] As noted in Chapter 1, the debate over animals frequently crosses the boundary of rational discourse, making incursions into the affective and spiritual. Contiguous with parts of the debate has been the exploration of alternative, "neo-pagan" forms of spirituality: the religions of native peoples, Wicca, goddess worship, and Gaianism. Philosophers may be duly skeptical of such matters, and I do not intend to endorse them here. Nonetheless, heeding the call of the animal and our continuity requires that serious attention be paid to the broader biological relationships that cannot be readily accommodated by the political. This need not take the form of overt mysticism or spiritualism, but it may require that direct, extra-political *experience* of the nonhuman world be given equal status with—if not priority over—those of its attributes that can be rationally calculated.

## Conclusion

It is ironic that while moral agents arguably require morality to place checks on the pursuit of their own interests, Western ethical models carry with them a bias in favor of the interests of rational, autonomous human individuals.[37] In light of this, Sapontzis suggests that "morally and legally protecting the basic interests of nonhuman animals may involve some ingenuity and thoughtful working with a variety of moral and legal categories."[38] But even such intellectual flexibility may be insufficient: the anthropocentrism, rationalism, and individualism that prevent extensionist arguments from developing into an adequate animal ethic are not incidental or superficial, but rather strike to the core of Western ethical thought. In regard to the problem Baier raises, this does not by itself establish that the call of the animal must be heeded and the ethical theories rejected, but it does raise the suspicion that if an adequate way of thinking about (and experiencing, and treating) other animals is to be found, it may have to be outside the scope of what traditionally has been conceived in ethical thought.

This possibility has been raised by others who have analyzed the debate over animals. For example, Scholtmeijer offers that "ethics which include animals have . . . a great weight of long-standing cultural resistance to dislodge. Indeed, ethical systems alone may not have sufficient force to counter human aggression."[39] Paul Shepard echoes the point, adding:

> Ethically, there have been discourses against the enslavement, torture, and killing of people since civilization began without ending war, tyranny, or cruelty. There is no evidence that crime, brutality, or murder have diminished at all. If human behavior is not improved by the incorporation of such ethics into the dominant religions, what reason is there to suppose that such a new ethic can save animals? The very ideology that raises the importance of every individual and seeks the nobility in our species can be used to support the need to exploit animals, if need be, for the benefit of the most noble species. The avoidance of *unnecessary* cruelty, insofar as that is done, will make the moralists feel better and reduce pain, but it will not save animals.[40]

It is noteworthy that this type of provocative analysis of the debate has come mostly from outside the circle of professional philosophers and bioethicists, from literary critics such as Scholtmeijer and Duffy, and ecologists like Shepard and Livingston. One suspects that even those philosophers who have sought to expand the moral standing of animals have too much invested in traditional ethical theories to recognize the limitations of those theories when faced with the animal.

But this still leaves us with the quandary that Baier brings to our attention. The case that it is traditional ethics and not the animal that must be forsaken is strengthened by a review of other criticisms that have been leveled against the tradition. As I explore over the following chapters, various critiques of Western ethics and culture dovetail with the analysis presented in this chapter, and further illuminate the problem of the animal. Indeed, as Scholtmeijer argues, the debate over animals and the penchant for self-criticism in twentieth-century culture and philosophy may be facets of the same phenomenon:

> Civilization may not seem to be as much of a blessing now as it once seemed, especially when theories like Freud's and Girard's speak of repression and victimization as generative drives. Modern culture is having doubts about itself . . . The demand upon modern culture to wrestle with the reality of the animal is a crucial aspect of its current self-doubt. If the products of culture are now beginning to express the feeling that culture itself is under attack and cannot stride confidently forward to expropriate every phenomenon in the natural world, it is largely because the lives of animals are threatening the authority of culture.[41]

If so, a striking possibility emerges from our analysis: that through the ambiguity of the animal—at once invitingly assimilable to human thought, yet ever out of its reach—a broad repercussion in our intellectual machinery is triggered. If so, our attempt to think about the animal in moral terms may force us to pass beyond traditional ethical thought, effecting an instance of what Nietzsche termed the "self-overcoming of morality."

# 8 The Call and the Circle: The Animal in Postmodern Thought

The uncertainty cast in the previous chapter upon the plausibility of traditional ethics is hardly novel. Whether it is possible for *any* ethical theory to provide adequate ground for our moral judgments is a perennial concern for ethicists and logicians, and whether human reason can indeed deliver the clarity and certainty we desire in our practical lives is a weight that all moral agents must bear. These concerns have been made especially pressing of late, following from the cultural self-doubt that Scholtmeijer describes as characterizing post-Freudian—we may add: post-Darwinian, post-Marxian, post-Nietzschean, post-Holocaust, post–Cold War—civilization. The effects of this self-doubt have been acute throughout recent philosophical thought, especially among European thinkers, much of whose work has amounted to a sustained critique of the Western philosophical tradition itself. With this self-consciousness has come a heightened sensitivity to limitations, and so one finds that even the most substantive of this philosophical work is peppered with melodramatic rhetoric about our having reached the *end* of philosophy (of metaphysics, of science, of history, etc.), proclamations that leave ethical thought searching for a new ground. The various forms of thought and cultural activity that fall under the amorphous umbrella of "postmodernism" bring this self-doubt to an extreme, at times finding expression as a free-flowing skepticism of all things Western, a festival in which the various "isms" that characterize the tradition—such as those discussed in the previous chapter—are sacrificed. At such events, the very attempt to present a problem in traditional ethical terms appears atavistic.

With this recent history in mind, one might view the debate over animals and the light it throws on the limitations of ethics as simply one part of a much larger wave of self-critical philosophical thought. However, it must be noted that a good deal of recent continental philosophy has remained anthropocentric, retaining a blind spot for the animal while its eyes are wide open to other shortcomings of modernism. As Raymond Corbey argues:

> While in the English-speaking world most philosophers would subscribe—or would at least be inclined to do so—to the idea of perhaps large, but ultimately gradual differences between humans and animals, most philosophers from the European continent would not underwrite the continuity of beasts and humans. A considerable number of continental philosophers operate in the wake of Aristotle or Descartes rather than that of Locke or Hume. They engage in Kantian criticism rather than evolutionary epistemology, in phenomenology or hermeneutics rather than naturalistic philosophy of mind. As different as these continental philosophical outlooks may be, they do have one thing in common: they all, in one way or another, draw a strict boundary line between animals and humans, and assume the gap between both is unbridgeably wide.[1]

In support of this broad claim, Corbey cites only two specific examples: Max Scheler—who argued that although some nonhumans may be intelligent, nonetheless animals as a category are determined by their instincts, and are therefore neither "open to the world" nor conscious of themselves in the way that human beings are[2]—and Emmanuel Levinas, who,

> reflecting upon the way we experience the other person's gaze, has criticized traditional Western philosophy for taking the subject, the I, as the absolute point of reference for all other beings. Could this view of Levinas be . . . another case of anthropocentrism . . . because, while the intention is to think the irreducibility of "other" to self, our animal "others" are disregarded once again? Is the gaze, which, according to Levinas, appeals directly, without any mediation, to our moral awareness, different when it is not that of a human child but that of a gorilla child or an orangutan child?[3]

To these examples we can add the twentieth-century existentialist philosophers, most notably Jean-Paul Sartre. One might expect to find common ground between existentialist thinkers and animal advocates, because the critique of modern rationalism and individualism—two obstacles to the accommodation of the animal—takes systematic philosophical form in existential analysis. While modern political individualism conceives of the human self as a simple, self-transparent atom, the existentialists—following on the insights of Freud, Nietzsche, and Kierkegaard—posit a living ambiguity or incompleteness that exists in the world, ever transcending the beings within it. Arguing that, unlike other kinds of being, human existence lacks a predefined essence or nature, the existentialists reject ethical rationalism; if there is no eternal concept of what a human being is, then it cannot be determined a priori what human beings ought to do in their lives. Likewise, the existentialists reject ethical individualism: lacking an essential predetermination, human beings have no choice but to make themselves in the world—a world that always includes other human beings from which the individual is never actually separable.

However, in emphasizing the uniqueness of the human circumstance and its transcendence of the natural world, the existentialists betray of themselves what Corbey suggests of continental thought generally: namely, their allegiance to the anthropocentrism of Descartes and Kant. Nowhere is this clearer than in the case of Sartre, whose distinction between the *pour-soi*—the free being for-itself of humans—and the *en-soi*—the determined being in-itself of nonhuman entities—loudly echoes the Kantian dichotomy of *person* and *thing*. In the popular lecture in which he declares "the humanism of existentialism," Sartre implies that all reality divides between manufactured things such as a paper-cutter (whose essence or design precedes its existence) and the human being (whose existence precedes essence). The category of *the animal* is left out.[4] Likewise, numerous examples he employs in *Being and Nothingness* fail to take account of the animal; it is only with the *Critique of Dialectical Reason* that Sartre comes to discuss "the organism," but by that point in his career he had abandoned the framework of existentialism.

Thus, despite the contiguity of the debate over animals and post-Nietzschean philosophy, the animal advocate likely will find the tacit anthropocentrism of the latter unfruitful. But perhaps even more problematic is the degree to which some continental thought overtly blocks potential avenues to overcoming anthropocentrism. By challenging traditional Western ideals of objectivity and rationality, the postmodernist thinker raises the prospect that philosophy can never provide proper accommodation to the animal because there simply is no such thing. As Steve Baker writes, "Post-modern skepticism about the operation of truth and knowledge has undoubtedly complicated any thinking about animals: about what counts as 'authentic' experience, about the experience of wonder or fear as antidotes to anthropocentrism, and about the extent to which it is possible to shed . . . the 'baggage' of . . . Western thought."[5] Although historically coincident and apparently akin in their criticism of traditional ethical concepts, postmodernism and the recent animal rights/welfare/liberation movements pull in very different directions. If the latter reads post-Darwinian biology as blurring the boundaries between human and animal, and thereby justifying the expansion of traditional ethical and political categories, the former approaches all boundaries as human constructions and seeks pleasure in their blurring as an end in itself, rejecting all—even reformist—categorizations as uninteresting.

Accordingly, Baker offers the distinction between "animal-endorsing" and "animal-skeptical" perspectives in recent thought, the latter intent on exposing the ways in which our conceptions of the animal—including those expounded by animal advocates—are unavoidably mediated by cultural history, reflecting classification systems that ultimately are dictated by human needs and desires.[6] But if the animal-skeptical perspective keeps a needed check on the temptation to indulge in simplistic animal-endorsing moralizing, it also poses a real danger. Indeed, it can be argued that postmodern skepticism at traditional thought comes at the price of a new type of anthropocentrism: if there can be no objective truth about the animal, if all zoological concepts are ultimately rhetorical constructions, then the animal is destined forever to be the victim of historical and cultural forces. Against the presumptuousness that the nonhuman can be reduced to a construction of human thought, Scholtmeijer argues that the autonomy of animal consciousness ought to "nudge the projections of culture back into the human mind."[7] If instead of positing this autonomy as something objectively real we allow the animal's fate to be decided by a battle among political discourses none of which can claim best to approach the truth about the animal, one can only predict that the animal's interests cannot be served.

The postmodernist posture of taking promiscuous pleasure in the heightened ambiguity of human-animal relations has provided interesting material for recent art and criticism, but from the standpoint of ethics it is a luxury the animal can ill afford. In the twenty-first century, the impact of human civilization on the nonhuman world augurs a rate of species extinction from which it could take literally millions of years for the planet's biodiversity to recover;[8] domestically, the awesome power of biotechnology promises to make other species pure products of human caprice—not just conceptually, but in fact.[9] If there is a value to the extra-cultural existence of nonhuman animals, it is soon to be irretrievably lost—a loss unhindered, if not actively promoted, by the tide of postmodernism. The result of the discussion in this and the preceding chapter is thus a fascinating but treacherous circle: *if the call of the animal challenges modern humanism, postmodernism perhaps signals the demise of the animal.*

However, it is inappropriate to tag all recent continental philosophy with the dismissive label of *postmodernism*. While the past century has produced much work that is intentionally ironic and perhaps indulgent, it has also produced some serious and substantive attempts to rethink, among other things, the animal and its relationship to philosophy. It is to these efforts that I now turn, with the hope that they can move us closer to resolving the dilemma that follows us from the previous chapter: whether, as a result of their apparent incompatibility, it is traditional ethical thought or the animal that must be sacrificed.

## Heidegger: The Animal as "Poor in World"

In previous chapters, we noted Rawls's contention that the problem of the moral status of the animal can only be solved in the context of a larger metaphysical theory that works out the details of our relations to the natural world. One of the most important attempts at such an ontology of life—and one that values the need to think about the animal on its own terms—was offered by Martin Heidegger. While the problem of the animal concerned Heidegger throughout his career, it receives his lengthiest treatment in his 1929–30 lecture course entitled *The Fundamental Concepts of Metaphysics*. Following upon his existential analysis of human existence in *Being and Time* (1927), this lecture course is dedicated to unfolding the question, What is world? In attempting to rethink how world has been understood within traditional Western metaphysics, Heidegger finds himself compelled to confront animal reality.

Heidegger proposes that the world question be approached through a comparative analysis of the different possible relations that beings can have to the world, and in doing so he—like other existentialists—articulates the uniqueness and transcendence of human existence. Since *Being and Time*, Heidegger had interpreted human existence as *Dasein*, the *there* of *being*, the very place where the being of beings is disclosed; thus, in the lecture course, he describes the human relation to the world as "world-forming." In contrast, an inanimate object, such as a stone, is entirely "worldless" in its being: while *Dasein*'s openness to beings *as such* actually makes world possible, the stone is "*without access* to those beings amongst which it is in its own way . . . and this belongs to its being."[10] Unlike Sartre, however, Heidegger does not ignore the category of the animal, and he clearly recognizes that the animal's relationship to the world is not reducible either to the stone's or to *Dasein*'s. Because the animal has some type of access to other beings, yet is not revelatory of their being as such, the animal is ambiguously "poor in world" (*weltarm*, world-poor):

> If by world we understand beings in their accessibility in each case, if such accessibility of beings is a fundamental character of the concept of world, and if being a living being means having access to other beings, then the animal stands on the side of man. Man and animals alike have world. On the other hand, if the intermediate thesis concerning the animal's poverty in world is justified and poverty represents deprivation and deprivation in turn means not having something, then the animal stands on the side of the stone. The animal thus reveals itself as a being which both has and does not have world.[11]

Heidegger illustrates this specific manner of animal being with the following examples:

> The lizard has its own relation to the rock, to the sun, and to a host of other things. One is tempted to suggest that what we identify as the rock and the sun are just lizard-things for the lizard, so to speak. When we say that the lizard is lying on the rock, we ought to cross out the word "rock" in order to indicate that whatever the lizard is lying on is certainly given in some way for the lizard, and yet is not known to the lizard as a rock. If we cross out the word we do not simply mean to imply that something else is in question here or is taken as something else. Rather we imply that whatever it is is not accessible to it as a being. The blade of grass that the beetle crawls up, for example, is not a blade of grass for it at all; it is not something possibly destined to become part of the bundle of hay with which the peasant will feed his cow. The blade of grass is simply a beetle-path on which the beetle specifically seeks beetle-nourishment, and not just any edible matter in general.[12]

In this way Heidegger establishes the categorical otherness of the animal's way of relating to the world: "For it is *not* simply a question of a *qualitative otherness* of the animal world as compared with the human world, and especially not a question of quantitative distinctions in range, depth, and breadth—not a question of whether or how the animal takes what is given to it in a different way, but rather of whether the animal can apprehend something *as* something, something *as* a being, at all."[13] The condition of this categorical difference is not simply that the animal lacks the intelligence to recognize beings as such, but more fundamentally that the animal's capabilities with respect to other beings are all *instinctual behaviors*, products of a drivenness in which the animal nonetheless "retains itself and is intrinsically absorbed in itself."[14] Thus, as opposed to *Dasein*'s openness to beings as such,

> we shall describe *the specific way in which the animal remains with itself*—which has nothing to do with the selfhood of the human being comporting him- or herself as a person—this way in which the animal is absorbed in itself, and which makes possible behaviour of any and every kind, as *captivation*. The animal can only behave insofar as it is essentially captivated. The possibility of behaving in the manner of animal being is grounded in this essential structure of the animal . . . Captivation is the condition of possibility for the fact that, in accordance with its essence, the animal *behaves within an environment but never within a world*.[15]

While Heidegger's language of "poverty" and "captivation" recalls the tradition's dismissive attitude toward animals, his account of animality nonetheless may be praised for the respect it shows to animal reality. Throughout, Heidegger deftly preserves the ambiguity of the animal: he maintains the animal's otherness by resisting the temptation to employ concepts of humanlike purposiveness, consciousness, or personhood to explain animal behavior;[16] yet in like manner, he refuses to resort to the language of physical thinghood.[17] His respect for this ambiguous territory is further reflected in the fact that while he attempts to approach the animal *metaphysically*—that is, to identify the essential nature of animal life itself—Heidegger, as he does nowhere else, allows his ontology of the animal to be informed by the results of *empirical* science, creating space for new biological data to work against old philosophical prejudices. Furthermore, in doing so Heidegger does not focus on the most obvious or appealing facts—namely, our knowledge of other primates and domestic animals; instead, his discussion is informed by examples of lizards and beetles, and experimental evidence involving honeybees, glow worms, and unicellular animals. As a result, Heidegger seems earnest in his desire to think the animal in itself, and not through the lens of what is most assimilable to human culture.

However, Heidegger's treatment of the animal becomes problematic when we consider whether and to what degree it can inform the discussion of our moral responsibilities to nonhumans. He makes clear early in his discussion that the distinction between the animal's world-poverty and *Dasein*'s world-formativeness is not intended either to imply or to ground any hierarchical evaluation. Still, as Heidegger seems aware, the relationship between descriptive ontology and evaluative thinking is complex, and they cannot be isolated from each other by fiat:

> However ready we are to rank man as a higher being with respect to the animal, such an assessment is deeply questionable, especially when we consider that man can sink lower than any animal. No animal can become depraved in the same way as man. Of course in the last analysis this consideration itself reveals the necessity of speaking of a "higher" in some sense. But we can already see from all this that the criterion according to which we talk of height and depth in this connection is obscure. May we talk of a "higher" and a "lower" at all in the realm of what is essential? Is the essence of man higher than the essence of the animal? All this is questionable even as a question.[18]

Such questions—and their questionableness—are not only material for metaphysical reflection, but have enormous practical and ethical implications that Heidegger does not pursue; hence, those in search of an animal ethic are left to draw their own inferences from Heidegger's discussion. On the one hand, if his ontology of life is indeed to be understood as value-neutral and not designed to inform a revitalized animal ethic, then his whole discussion—as he himself seems to suggest[19]—can only be seen as decidedly anthropocentric (or at least *Dasein*centric). Because animals presumably do not experience their relationship to the world as an impoverishment, the description of the animal as "poor in world" is meaningful only from the point of view of *Dasein*. Furthermore, Heidegger pursues the discussion only as a means for unfolding a metaphysical problem—a project that is of exclusive importance to *Dasein*—and not with an ultimate view to understanding the animal for its own sake. Only with this in mind can we understand why Heidegger would homogenize *all* animals—from amoebae to great apes—into the category of "poor in world," and declare *all* animal behavior to be instinctual.

On the other hand, if one were to try to draw ethical conclusions from Heidegger's discussion, there would seem to be little room for reevaluating the traditional rejection of animal interests. Not being *Dasein*, the animal "refuses any going along with" the human being;[20] thereby, what would seem to be a necessary ground for any properly moral consideration of the animal is precluded. Moreover, given our discussion of domestication in the previous chapter, it seems telling that Heidegger hits upon *captivation* as the essential condition of animal behavior. Heidegger's German does not directly translate to the language of domestication, but it is equally problematic, and has a certain violence to it. The noun McNeill and Walker translate as "captivation" is *Benommenheit*, which refers to a state of being "stunned" or "torpid"; the verbal infinitive that they translate "to captivate" is *benehmen,* which means "to take away." Thus, the Heideggerian discourse describes the essential condition of the animal as *being stunned* and then *taken away.* Granted, this is not an overt concession to Aristotle's concept of the "just war" to be waged against the animal, or to the Kantian claim that the animal exists for human ends. Nonetheless, it provides irresistible material for a deconstructionist reading of Heidegger's work.

## Derrida: Animals and Animots

In concluding his discussion of the animal in *The Fundamental Concepts of Metaphysics,* Heidegger concedes that his attempt to think the essence of life is incomplete, and that therefore the animal "must remain a problem for us."[21] And it certainly did remain a problem for him. He states earlier in the course that "the animal is separated from man by an abyss,"[22] and he would resign himself to a similar assessment nearly twenty years later in the "Letter on Humanism": "Of all the beings that are, presumably the most difficult to think about are living creatures, because on the one hand they are in a certain way most closely akin to us, and on the other are at the same time separated from our ek-sistent essence by an abyss. However, it might also seem as though the essence of divinity is closer to us than what is so alien in other living creatures, closer, namely, in an essential distance which, however distant, is nonetheless more familiar to our ek-sistent essence than is our scarcely conceivable, abysmal bodily kinship with the beast."[23] Reflecting on this abyss in the lecture course, Heidegger asserts that the distance of the animal from *Dasein* "forces us to claim that *the essence of life can become accessible only if we consider it in a deconstructive fashion.*"[24] Thus, the appearance of the animal in Heidegger's work serves to locate his thinking at a cusp: heavy with a tradition it is trying to think past, while pulled in the direction of the work that still needs to be done. This work has been taken up by, among others, Jacques Derrida, who offers some of the most instructive commentary on Heidegger's discussion of the animal, especially in a 1991 interview entitled "Eating Well."[25]

While Heidegger's overall project can be described as an attempt to chart areas of philosophical reflection that had been obscured by the history of metaphysics from Plato to Nietzsche, Derrida is intent on alerting us to the remnants of the "hegemonic discourse of Western metaphysics" that haunt Heidegger's thought. If Heidegger's allegiance to this discourse is unwitting, it is not a "mistake" but rather signals his presence in what

Derrida terms "an indispensable phase"[26]—a phase that also includes the work of other post-traditional thinkers from Freud to Levinas, and, more important for our discussion, a phase in which the animal apparently plays a crucial role. Thus, in deconstructing Heidegger's work, we can think of Derrida as unearthing the anthropocentrism of the discussion of the animal we have just reviewed, while trying to indicate the enormity of what remains to be thought or deconstructed in our thinking about the animal during the present phase in the history of philosophy.

To the first, Derrida asserts that "the distinction between the animal (which has no or is not a *Dasein*) and man has nowhere been more radical nor more rigorous than in Heidegger,"[27] and he describes the Heideggerian discourse on the animal as "violent and awkward, at times contradictory."[28] In choosing to think about human reality as *Dasein*, which "stands in opposition to every other form of self-relation," Heidegger is destined to produce an "anthropo-teleological interpretation" of the animal.[29] Therefore, and despite that *Dasein* is a more fundamental interpretation of human reality than the rational subject of modern ethics—an interpretation that indeed exposes the "ontological fragility" of our traditional ethical and political concepts[30]—it is impossible to use the Heideggerian discourse to ground a rethinking of our animal ethics:

> Let us venture . . . a few questions. For example, does the animal hear the call that originates responsibility? Does it question? Moreover, can the call heard by *Dasein* come originally to or from the animal? Is there an advent of the animal? Can the voice of the friend be that of an animal? Is friendship possible for the animal or between animals? Like Aristotle, Heidegger would say: no. Do we not have a responsibility toward the living in general? The answer is still "no," and this may be because the question is formed, asked in such a way that the answer must necessarily be "no" according to the whole canonized or hegemonic discourse of Western metaphysics or religions, including the most original forms that this discourse might assume today, for example, in Heidegger or Levinas.[31]

These discourses thus "remain profound humanisms *to the extent that they do not sacrifice sacrifice*"[32]—that is, to the extent that they stop the work of deconstruction at those foundations that ground the institutionalized exploitation of the animal other.

However, Derrida's positive discourse, which outlines the work to be done in deconstructing the "sacrificial" structures of the Western tradition, is marked by tensions of its own. On the one hand, Derrida appreciates—in a way that is not apparent in Heidegger's discussion—the pressing, practical dimensions to the philosophical analysis of the animal. For example, in connection with the question of language, he states:

> . The idea according to which man is the only speaking being, in its tradi-
> tional form or in its Heideggerian form, seems to me at once undisplace-
> able and highly problematic . . . It is not a question of covering up
> ruptures and heterogeneities. I would simply contest that they give rise
> to a single linear, indivisible, oppositional limit, to a binary opposition
> between the human and the infra-human. And what I am proposing
> here should allow us to take into account scientific knowledge about
> the complexity of "animal languages," genetic coding, all forms of
> marking within which so-called human language, as original as it might
> be, does not allow us to "cut" once and for all where we would in gen-
> eral like to cut. As you can see, in spite of appearances, I am speaking
> here of very "concrete" and very "current" problems: the ethics and the
> politics of the living.[33]

On the other hand, whether and how Derrida's overall deconstructive project can aid in addressing these problems is uncertain. To his
credit, Derrida appreciates the complexity of these matters, and that the
radicalness of the analysis they require must forestall any ready
answers.[34] More substantively, Derrida intuits that the possibility of
humans having duties to animals lies so far beyond the capabilities of
Western ethical structures that at present this possibility can only be
apprehended as *excessive* and *incalculable*. As he states concerning Heidegger and Levinas:

> I feel compelled to underscore the *sacrificial* structure of the discourses
> to which I am referring . . . It is a matter of discerning a place left open,
> in the very structure of these discourses (which are also "cultures") for a
> noncriminal putting to death. Such are the executions of ingestion,
> incorporation, or introjection of the corpse. An operation as real as it is
> symbolic *when* the corpse is "animal" (and who can be made to believe
> that our cultures are carnivorous because animal proteins are irreplace-
> able?), a symbolic operation when the corpse is "human." But the
> "symbolic" is very difficult, truly impossible to delimit in this case,
> hence the enormity of the task, its *essential excessiveness*, a certain
> unclassifiability or the monstrosity of *that for which* we have to answer
> here, or *before* which (whom? what?) we have to answer.[35]

Indeed, if the dominant culture in the West were to be called to
account for its exploitation of the animal (*"Billions served!"*) no conceivable moral scheme could set things aright. Still, one must face the question of what ought to be done, of how one ought to comport oneself
toward animals, and here Derrida seems unable to offer guidance. In an

often quoted line from "Eating Well," Derrida states: "I am not recalling this in order to start a support group for vegetarianism, ecologism, or for the societies for the protection of animals—*which is something I might also want to do*, and something which would lead us to the center of the subject."[36] "*Might*"—but when? It seems that the deconstructionist must remain forever reticent at articulating moral proscriptions—even "provisional" ones[37]—because once articulated, they limit the *excessive*, almost mystical responsibility with which the animal calls us: "Responsibility is *excessive* or it is not a *responsibility*. A limited, measured, calculable, rationally distributed responsibility is already the becoming-right of morality; it is at times also, in the best *hypothesis*, the dream of every good conscience, in the worst hypothesis, of the small or grand inquisitors."[38] Although in his late reflection on the animal Derrida seems more sympathetic to the prescriptions that have been offered in the recent debate over animals, it is not in the context of doing rational ethics, but instead what he terms "zoo-auto-bio-bibliography," an intensely personal discourse that makes no pretense to addressing *animaux* in themselves, but instead generates *animots*: animated word-things that are creatures of the language he—and we—must still use.[39]

If Derrida is unwilling to defend an ethical proscription against using other animals in agriculture or research, an imperative that he does not hesitate to voice is the *duty to deconstruct*, a calling that "leaves no respite, no rest":[40]

> It is thus not a matter of opposing another discourse on the same "things" to the enormous multiplicity of traditional *discourses* on man, animal, plant, or stone, but of *ceaselessly* analyzing the whole conceptual machinery, and its interestedness, which has allowed us to speak of the "subject" up to now. And the analysis produces always more and something other than an analysis. It transforms; it translates a transformation already in progress. Translation is transformative. This explains the nervous distrust of those who want to keep all these themes, all these "words" ("man," "subject," etc.), sheltered from all questioning, and who manipulate an ethico-political suspicion with regard to deconstruction.[41]

But as essential as this work may be, Derrida's hesitance to utter specific prescriptions vis-à-vis the animal ignores the practical urgency I discussed above. The vegetarian may indeed be seeking the consolation of a "good conscience," but this is certainly not the only possibility. If it is the animal that in part summons the deconstructive gesture,[42] it is reasonable to expect the philosopher to grapple with the means of protecting the source of that valuable call.

## Deleuze and Guattari: Becoming-animal

One possible mapping of what lies on the other side of the kind of radical deconstruction proposed by Derrida is offered by French philosopher Gilles Deleuze in collaboration with psychologist Félix Guattari. With an alternative system of writing and thinking that cannot be done justice in the type of synopsis that must be attempted here, the two explore the philosophical and political possibilities precluded by the canonized discourse of the tradition. While the animal plays a central role in their work, one of the most pervasive themes in their writing is inspired by *botany* rather than zoology. In *A Thousand Plateaus*, they contrast the nature of the *tree*—a rooted unity from which ordered, dichotomous divisions follow—and the *rhizome*—a subterranean multiplicity that subverts and erupts like a contagion—and they exploit these differences as the means of distinguishing very different systems of thought.

In describing the tradition that Derrida implores us to deconstruct, Deleuze and Guattari discern what they term pervasive *"arborescent"* structures, even in its relationship to the animal:

> It is odd how the tree has dominated Western reality and all of Western thought, from botany to biology and anatomy, but also gnosiology, theology, ontology, all of philosophy . . .: the root-foundation, *Grund, racine, fondement*. The West has a special relation to the forest, and deforestation; the fields carved from the forest are populated with seed plants produced by cultivation based on species lineages of the arborescent type; animal raising, carried out on fallow fields, selects lineages forming an entire animal arborescence . . . Here in the West, the tree has implanted itself in our bodies, rigidifying and stratifying even the sexes.[43]

Embodying the domination of the tree, the arborescent political systems that have defined the West—patriarchal families and nation-states—are accordingly hierarchical; the corresponding models of thought that have dominated the West are likewise "hierarchical systems with centers of significance and subjectification, central automata like organized memories."[44] In a way that echoes John Livingston's critique of rights theory, Deleuze and Guattari propose that *signification* and *subjectivity* per se are symptomatic of—and only meaningful within—systems of hierarchical domination.[45] If this is correct, then the problems we have identified heretofore appear to be inevitable: Western ontology—even of the radical type undertaken by Heidegger—must impoverish the animal, and Western ethical theories—with their focus on rational moral agents—will be inadequate to discussing the moral status of the animal outside the context of domestication.

In contrast to the hierarchical model of the tree, a rhizomatic system of thought provides no footing for the traditional dualisms of subject and object, signifier and signified, substance and attribute: "The rhizome is an acentered, nonhierarchical, nonsignifying system without a General and without an organizing memory or central automaton, defined solely by a circulation of states. What is at question in the rhizome is a relation to sexuality—but also to the animal, the vegetal, the world, politics, the book, things natural and artificial—that is totally different from the arborescent relation: all manner of 'becomings.'"[46] As to what the rhizomatic relation of "becoming" might be like, it is described negatively throughout *A Thousand Plateaus:* the rhizome is *asubjective* and *asignifying;* "an anti-genealogy,"[47] an antimemory;[48] it opposes the long-term, signifiant memory of arborescent families and societies with the creative "production of the unconscious";[49] and so on. Nonetheless, Deleuze and Guattari reject the suggestion that they have created an "ontological dualism" of their own between the rhizome and the tree;[50] indeed, the relationship they see between these different kinds of systems seems to border on the symbiotic: "To be rhizomorphous is to produce stems and filaments that seem to be roots, or better yet connect with them by penetrating the trunk, but put them to strange new uses."[51]

This complex relationship is expressed in terms of *deterritorialization* and *reterritorialization*, a process Deleuze and Guattari explain with the intriguing example of the wasp and the orchid:

> The orchid deterritorializes by forming an image, a tracing of a wasp; but the wasp reterritorializes on that image. The wasp is nevertheless deterritorialized, becoming a piece in the orchid's reproductive apparatus. But it reterritorializes the orchid by transporting its pollen. Wasp and orchid, as heterogeneous elements, form a rhizome. It could be said that the orchid imitates the wasp, reproducing its image in a signifying fashion (mimesis, mimicry, lure, etc.) . . . At the same time, something else entirely is going on: not imitation at all but a . . . veritable becoming, a becoming-wasp of the orchid and a becoming-orchid of the wasp. Each of these becomings brings about the deterritorialization of one term and the reterritorialization of the other; the two becomings interlink and form relays in a circulation of intensities pushing the deterritorialization ever further. There is neither imitation nor resemblance, only an exploding of two heterogeneous series on the line of flight composed by a common rhizome that can no longer be attributed to or subjugated by anything signifying.[52]

The prospect of such inter-specific "becomings" is of special importance to our discussion, for by extension they blur the traditional territories of "human" and "animal": "We believe in the existence of very special becomings-animal traversing human beings and sweeping them away, affecting the animal no less than the human."[53] In order to effect such a transformation, one would have to alter one's arborescent rootedness in culture, and form a common "rhizome" with animal reality.

Deleuze and Guattari find evidence of these becomings in diverse contexts: literature—not only the obvious cases of metamorphosis, but also more subtle examples such as Ahab's "becoming-whale" in his pursuit of Moby Dick;[54] legends of becomings-bat (vampires) and becomings-wolf (werewolves); case studies in the psychoanalytic literature, such as the becoming-horse of Freud's youngest patient, Little Hans;[55] and more commonplace surges of *power:* "Who has not known the violence of these animal sequences, which uproot one from humanity, if only for an instant, making one scrape at one's bread like a rodent or giving one the yellow eyes of a feline?"[56] While the temptation is strong to find symbolic meaning in such phenomena—What does Kafka's insect *stand for?* What does it *mean* when a child insists on behaving like a dog?—Deleuze and Guattari contend that becomings-animal are only understood correctly when they are appreciated in their distinct, asignifying type of reality: "Becomings-animal are basically of another power, since their reality resides not in an animal one imitates or to which one corresponds but in themselves, in that which suddenly sweeps us up and makes us become—a *proximity, an indiscernibility* that extracts a shared element from the animal far more effectively than any domestication, utilization, or imitation could: 'the Beast.'"[57] In their proximity to the beast, becomings-animal are "anomic" phenomena, "more secret, more subterranean" than the mythic and ritualistic structures of a society, "irreducible dynamisms drawing lines of flight" beyond those preestablished systems of meaning, the affair of *the sorcerer* who occupies the fringes of society.[58]

This interpretation implies specific understandings of the natures of *becoming* and *animality.* To the first, while it is obvious that Deleuze and Guattari are not proposing a literal transmutation of the human into animal form, neither are they willing to write off becomings to activities of imitation or the imagination—activities that presuppose the immutability of the traditional subject, and the essential separation of human and animal. Between the false alternatives of merely imitating animals and "really" becoming one, they propose another possibility in which "a becoming lacks a subject distinct from itself": "Becoming produces nothing other than itself . . . What is real is the becoming itself, the block of becoming, not the supposedly fixed terms through which that which becomes passes."[59] Thus, in becoming-animal, the human pursues no ulterior goal, embarking upon a creative evolution that is not guided by arborescent structures of hierarchy and meaning. Deleuze and Guattari coin the term *involution* for this "evolution between heterogeneous terms, . . . on the condition that involution is in no way confused with regression. Becoming is involutionary, involution is creative. To regress is to move in the direction of something less differentiated. But to involve is to form a block that runs its own line 'between' the terms in play and beneath assignable relations."[60]

In order to effect such a line of flight between and beneath the assignable, the animality with which one becomes-animal cannot reflect the arborescent conceptions that have pervaded Western thought: individuated, "Oedipal" animals such as family pets; the animals of Western taxonomy defined by their characteristics and attributes; the archetypal animals of mythology. To these, Deleuze and Guattari oppose the "more demonic animals" of the *pack*:[61] "We do not wish to say that certain animals live in packs . . . What we are saying is that every animal is fundamentally a band, a pack. That it has pack modes, rather than characteristics, even if further distinctions within these modes are called for. It is at this point that the human being encounters the animal. We do not become animal without a fascination for the pack, for multiplicity. A fascination for the outside? Or is the multiplicity that fascinates us already related to a multiplicity dwelling within us?"[62] The proximity of such a multiplicity obliterates the individual self of modern ethical and political theory, while simultaneously making it impossible to draw a distinct boundary between the human and the animal. So understood, the ever-present possibility of becoming-animal bears witness to "an inhuman connivance with the animal, rather than an Oedipal symbolic community."[63]

If becomings-animal provide an always-accessible *line of flight* from any concretized, institutionalized definition of humanity, they are not unique in this regard. Instead, they occupy a "median region" in the realm of becoming, a realm framed by the introductory transition of *becoming-woman*, and the ultimate dissolution of self in *becoming-molecular*.[64] The common ground to all these becomings is their *minoritarian* status:

> All becoming is a becoming-minoritarian. When we say majority, we are referring not to a greater relative quantity but to the determination of a state or standard in relation to which larger quantities, as well as the smallest, can be said to be minoritarian: white-man, adult-male, etc. Majority implies a state of domination, not the reverse. It is not a

question of knowing whether there are more mosquitoes or flies than men, but of knowing how "man" constituted a standard in the universe in relation to which men necessarily (analytically) form a majority . . . In this sense women, children, but also animals, plants, and molecules, are minoritarian.[65]

Thus, the prescriptive value of the animal in Deleuze and Guattari's account is to be found in the *micro-political activity* of becoming, and the disruption of hegemonic culture it can effect:

There is an entire politics of becomings-animal, as well as a politics of sorcery, which is elaborated in assemblages that are neither those of the family nor of religion nor of the State. Instead, they express minoritarian groups, or groups that are oppressed, prohibited, in revolt, or always on the fringe of recognized institutions, groups all the more secret for being extrinsic, in other words, anomic. If becoming-animal takes the form of a Temptation, and of monsters aroused in the imagination by the demon, it is because it is accompanied, at its origin as in its undertaking, by a rupture with the central institutions that have established themselves or seek to become established.[66]

However, this raises the question of whether the discourse of becoming-animal is relevant to clarifying the moral and political status of the "real" nonhuman animal, or instead renders these matters meaningless. If the micro-political activity of becoming must ever operate on the fringe of what has been institutionalized, its mission cannot be to institutionalize new concepts of "animal rights" or any other model of inter-specific duty: once institutionalized, such concepts—no matter how reformist—would become *rooted*, part of the majoritarian, arborescent systems that becomings-animal must continually "work from within" and "trouble from without."[67] One might infer from their account of the line of *flight* an argument against the institutions of animal domestication; however, like Derrida's *excessive responsibility*, the unique value Deleuze and Guattari discern in the animal will be destroyed by any effort to tame it by means of institutionalized moral reasoning.

By linking the animal with the *demonic, bestial pack*, Deleuze and Guattari echo the misothery of traditional culture, which places the animal ever outside the boundaries of civilized life. The effect of this is muted by their attempt to chart the *proximity* of the beast to the human—to locate the pack that dwells within—but this move works against any imperative to protect the interests of nonhumans. If the inhuman multiplicity of the pack is something that dwells within us, then becomings-animal can be effectuated even in the absence of "real" animals: "Becoming can and should be qualified as becoming-animal even in the absence of a term that would be the animal become. The becoming-animal of the human being is real, even if the animal the human being becomes is not; and the becoming-other of the animal is real, even if that something other it becomes is not."[68] Thus, whatever political value can be attached to the processes of becoming-animal must be logically and ontologically distinct from any moral value that one would attach to the lives of other animals. If it is the eruption of the animal-within that makes becoming possible, the resulting rhizome—while certainly not anthropocentric in any usual sense—can thrive with or without the animal other.

## Conclusion

Heidegger's *abyss*, Derrida's *excessive* and *incalculable responsibility*, Deleuze and Guattari's *asignifying becoming*—these eruptions within twentieth-century thought embody the enigma that the animal presents to philosophy. They speak to the call of the animal—the demand that the animal be thought—and in the same breath they reveal the impotence of our canon to answer this call. Of course, these are not two separate events, but rather facets of the same phenomenon: in post-Nietzschean thought, the animal is appealing precisely because it marks a *line of flight* toward what has not and could not have been thought heretofore. To those willing to embrace this challenge to philosophy, the answer to Baier's dilemma presented in the previous chapter seems clear: it is the animal that must be heeded, and new forms of ethical—perhaps *post-ethical*—thinking must be found to accommodate the different type of responsibility the animal imposes upon us. But if the trajectory of recent continental thought leads to the resolution of our dilemma, it nonetheless provides little occasion for comfort. For if there is an imperative that this thinking can ground, it is that we must, as Derrida puts it, "go through the experience of a deconstruction . . . A concept (that is to say also an experience) of *responsibility* comes at this price. We have not finished paying for it."[69]

By throwing up to investigation the "fragility of human meaning and control," the line of flight blazed by the animal is a very rough path:[70] a deconstruction or dismemberment of human self-concepts awaits those who would embark upon it. With this said, the emerging biotechnologies cautioned against in the beginning of this chapter seem in their essence to be compatible with this deconstructive imperative. Just as the "cybernetic project" of recent information technologies embodies the reality of *différance*—the endless deferment of meaning among signifiers with no ultimate signified[71]—with the advent of genomics the traditional human self is shattered in a "becoming-animal"—indeed, a "becoming-molecular"—that substitutes thousands of manipulable segments of DNA for the immortal soul.[72] As laypersons and theologians alike have intuited, our traditional ethical categories cannot hold together where such a radical fracturing takes place.

But as we noted, the threat of nihilism comes with the fact that this technology proposes a similar fracturing and manipulation of the animal. Where animals cannot stand independent of culture, they—like ourselves—become, in Donna Haraway's phrase, *cyborgs:* "theorized and fabricated hybrids of machine and organism," compounds of the "organic, technical, textual, and political."[73] If the nonhuman is not only thought of as, but also reduced to, a socio-technological construction, then any line of flight the animal might offer would ostensibly be closed. Derrida proposes that "the animal looks at us, and we are naked before it. And thinking perhaps begins here."[74] Is it conceivable that we could feel similarly naked, provoked to a thought as deep, when we stand before a *cyborg?* That futuristic science fiction has explored this possibility perhaps reflects an intuition that the animal is on the way out, leaving us to search for related others among creatures of our own design.

The postmodernist analysis of the animal seems to leave us with a nihilistic circle: the animal calls our attention because of the intriguing way it countermands traditional culture, but post-traditional culture is too fractured to provide evaluative support for the animal. The way out of this circle may lie with the idea of *continuity* discussed in Part I. Scholtmeijer writes, "Culture may indeed represent an insuperable barrier to human understanding of the animal's reality. Yet the idea of continuity situates some of that extra-cultural reality inside of the human individual. The very least that can be said, then, is that culture has created a grave problem for itself in generating the idea of continuity. The possibly unreachable meaning of the animal has become integral to comprehension of the human being."[75] But if continuity locates an unreachable animality within the human being, it must likewise situate some degree of valuable otherness—such as culture has attempted to institutionalize in defining moral limits on our treatment of our fellows—within the animal world.[76] Today, the preservation of this value requires concrete social action on a large scale; this places upon the philosopher the duty to search for intellectual structures that not only preserve the conceptual otherness of the animal, but also render the practical protection of animals meaningful. This search will require the exploration of a possible alternative to the two problematic approaches we have analyzed thus far: the extension of traditional moral theories to cover the animal (domestication), and postmodernist skepticism at applying any normative categories to the animal (nihilism).

# 9 Ecophilosophy:
# Deep Ecology and Ecofeminism

The recent debate over animals—with its emphasis on extending traditional ethical models to include nonhumans—may serve to legitimize the animal's claim to moral attention; however, by translating the value of animal reality into terms assimilable to human culture, it also completes a form of intellectual domestication. Posttraditional thought locates the value of the animal in its extra-cultural objectivity, in that which evades domestication; however, such a segregation of animal and culture casts doubt on whether any viable cultural institutions can articulate a valuation of nonhuman life without humanizing it in the process. In this chapter, I explore the possibility of finding an alternative to these treatments of the animal among the various forms of recent environmental thought.

As one would expect, the literature that explores the nature and extent of our moral obligations to the nonhuman world in general is larger and more varied than that dedicated to the moral standing of animals alone. Its more complex subject matter seems to give rise to endless points of contention, with the frequent result that even thinkers in the same general school of environmental thought find themselves at serious odds. While some in the field have attempted to forge a unifying environmental ethic, an important strain of environmental thought openly rejects such efforts, opting instead to seek a direct transformation in the individual's way of experiencing the nonhuman world without relying on the mediation of universal philosophical schemes. Given this broad spectrum of environmental thought, I will not attempt a complete summary here. But a survey of its more provocative offerings is necessary, inasmuch as the attempt to inform Western culture with principles of respect for the natural world has been a cornerstone of modern environmental ethics in all its manifestations; it thereby holds out the prospect of a synthesis that recognizes the pressing need for a rethinking of the moral standing of nonhuman beings, while abjuring the traditional categories of Western ethics. Some of the themes developed by environmentalists are explored further in Part IV; the question to concern us here is whether recent ecophilosophy can provide a platform for the accommodation of the animal—one theoretically coherent enough to satisfy the demands of philosophy, and strong enough to produce practical protection of the animal. Any success in this direction will further reinforce the conclusion that the animal's demand for moral attention should be heeded, and any ethical or political structures that cannot respond adequately must be rethought.

In part because of their historical coincidence, the debate over animals and the search for an environmental ethic can be viewed as products of similar social forces outside academic philosophy. First, the political momentum of modern liberalism and the various human liberation movements that helped to provoke the moral revaluation of the animal also fueled the environmental movement. If industrialization and urbanization made the animal less of a threat and therefore a more sympathetic figure, the threat these human forces pose to the stability of the environment likewise helped to stir philosophical reflection on our duties to the rest of the nonhuman world. Furthermore, both animal advocacy and environmentalism owe a debt to modern biology: just as the science of ethology provided new empirical data for the debate over animals, the science of ecology—specifically systems ecology, which reached the level of science proper in the mid-twentieth century—did the same for environmental ethics by exposing the subtle interconnections among living organisms and their environments, and the depth of impact that human activity can have upon them. In sum, it is not difficult to see the recent debate over animals and the search for an environmental ethic as parts of the same historical moment.[1]

Nonetheless, although animal advocacy and environmentalism have contiguous concerns that would suggest these movements are closely allied, their philosophical commitments are not entirely congruent, for both cultural and theoretical reasons. To the first, while the debate over animals has clear English origins, and the critique of its modernist origins is associated with the European Continent, the philosophy of environmental ethics has had a distinctly North American influence. Of course, the significance of the natural environment is an old and worldwide concern, and recent environmental discourse has been enriched by many non-Western voices. But in the West, the frontier ethos that informed Euro-American culture from its inception, the influence of Native American cultures, and the pastoral tradition in American art combined to create an axiological space for the natural world that it has not generally had in Europe until recently: namely, as something to be valued in itself, and not only as the means to fulfilling human needs and desires, or as the counterpoint to human transcendence. Indeed, it would be difficult to imagine the tradition of Henry David Thoreau, George Perkins Marsh, John Muir, and Aldo Leopold— who continue to inspire more recent reflection on the environment— emerging in France or Germany rather than America.[2]

This cultural difference underscores the substantive philosophical difference between extensionist animal ethics and environmentalism, for the attempt to frame such non-conscious collectives as natural ecosystems as objects of moral concern presents even greater difficulties for traditional Western ethics than does the attempt to found a moral standing for animals. Consequently, pressure to look beyond traditional ethical categories has been a stronger force in shaping environmental thought. Those who have attempted to produce an environmental ethic while working *within* the confines of the tradition have produced two broad classes of arguments analogous to those found in the debate over animals. First, one finds defenses of classical humanism: the reduction of nature to a series of resources to be managed by and for human beings, unencumbered by any direct moral obligations to the nonhuman world. From this perspective, the goal of environmental action is to spare human beings from the effects of resource depletion and pollution. Environmental humanists argue that these negative practical consequences of environmental exploitation will encourage "wise use" of these resources, and that traditional moral concern for the interests of other human beings who may be negatively affected by environmental damage provides a sufficient ethical framework to prescribe it. This approach has been condemned by a number of environmental thinkers, most frequently because it is unrealistic about human and corporate behavior within modern economies; moreover, it ignores the possibility that those animals affected by environmental destruction have a legitimate claim to direct moral attention, and closes the door on the prospect that other elements of the nonhuman world may also. Thus, in response some have offered extensionist environmental arguments, that is, the use of traditional ethical categories to spell out positive moral duties to the nonhuman world. These arguments, as one might expect, tend to cover similar ground as the extensionist animal arguments we reviewed in Part II, inasmuch as most traditional ethical categories have possible meaning only in connection with sentient beings—a cactus cannot enter into a contract and a river cannot experience disutility. Therefore, for the sake of brevity, I simply will suggest here that such arguments are subject to the same types of criticism I offered in Chapter 7.

## Deep Ecology

A third option has emerged from the environmental debate, one that environmental philosopher J. Baird Callicott terms *ethical holism*.[3] From the holistic perspective, the traditional dualism of human and nature can be resolved by subordinating both the effects of human culture and the interests of individual nonhumans to a higher standard: an "ecocentric" or "biocentric" criterion. Holism is reflected in the work of many environmental thinkers, but nowhere is the principle of ecocentrism clearer than in the fundamental precept of naturalist Aldo Leopold's *land ethic*, a model for much subsequent environmental thought: "The 'key-log' which must be moved to release the evolutionary process for an [environmental] ethic is simply this: quit thinking about decent land-use as solely an economic problem. Examine each question in terms of what is ethically and esthetically right, as well as what is economically expedient. A thing is right when it tends to preserve the integrity, stability, and beauty of the biotic community. It is wrong when it tends otherwise."[4] Philosopher Arne Naess has described the environmental thought that adheres to this type of ecocentric criterion as "deep ecology" because it attempts to relocate the axiological context of human-nonhuman relations within the natural world itself.[5] The ecocentric deep ecologist opposes the "shallow" reformist ecologism of environmental humanism—which perpetuates the modern stereotypes of the natural world as "either natural resources or scenery"—and questions the ability of extensionist arguments to counter such stereotypes successfully.[6]

The philosophical justification for the ecocentric criterion lies ultimately with a reinterpretation of the relationship between the individual—whether human or not—and the natural world as a whole. While deep ecologists have appealed to various sources to ground this reinterpretation—both within and without the tradition, ranging from Plato and Spinoza in the West to Mahayana Buddhism and Mahatma Gandhi in the East—the most accessible starting point is to be found in modern biology. Just as animal advocates have developed the ethical implications of evolutionary biology and its blurring of species boundaries, deep

ecologists—by envisioning human beings and the other beings of the natural world as members of a biotic *community*—can be seen to elaborate
the ethical implications of ecosystemic biology. As some have argued, the
facts of our mutual evolution and environmental interdependence encourage us to extend morally relevant sentiments of kinship to *all* species on
the planet,[7] and moral respect to "the land" itself, the biotic context
within which we all emerge.[8] Thus, in opposition to anthropocentric
models of selfhood, which stress the discreteness of the human individual,
the deep ecologists offer the model of an "ecological self," an extension of
identity beyond human social structures to reflect the human being's
intrinsic relatedness to the natural world.[9]

Because they envision the elements of the natural world as *kin*, it is
clear that deep ecologists, like animal advocates, intend to establish
that beings other than humans can have an inherent moral worth that is
independent of their instrumental value as means to human ends. But in
assigning an imperative moral value to the integrity of the environment
as a whole, deep ecology exceeds animal advocacy by attempting to offer
what extensionism has failed to produce: an extra-cultural criterion
against which the morally relevant interests of humans and animals—
and conflicts between them—can be evaluated. Since the ecocentric criterion seems to afford no special consideration to the interests and lives
of rational, sentient, verbal *Homo sapiens*—which clearly would need
to be compromised in order to maximize ecocentric integrity—it represents an even stronger critique of traditional humanism than extensionist arguments in the debate over animals. (Indeed, reminiscent of
Nietzsche's famous diagnosis of man as a disease on the earth's skin,
there is a discernible strain of *misanthropy* within deep ecology and
environmental ethics generally, owing to the disruptions to the
integrity, stability, and beauty of the biotic community for which modern humans are responsible.[10]) Yet, because this criterion also implies
that there are situations in which the interests and lives of individual
animals may be sacrificed by humans—at times in ways that seem reminiscent of traditional humanism—many animal advocates have
rejected its role in nature ethics. As a result, while deep ecology clearly
shares with animal advocacy the general goal of undermining anthropocentrism, the two have clashed on a number of specific moral issues.

## Holistic versus Humane Ethics

The most frequently debated and pressing controversy concerns the
matters of biodiversity and species extinction, the planet's most urgent

ecological problems. Whereas the ecocentric criterion requires deep ecologists to place a prima facie higher value on the lives and interests of members of endangered species, animal advocates, while not insensitive to the issue of species extinction, generally have been hesitant to follow suit for fear of violating principles of moral equality. For example, as we saw in Part II, Peter Singer's principle of equal consideration of interests and Tom Regan's postulate of equal inherent worth allow no room for modifying an individual animal's moral value based on the abundance or scarcity of its species. Indeed, to do so would run contrary to the main thrust of many animal-advocating arguments: that in determining the moral consideration an *individual* being deserves, its species-member-ship is in itself morally irrelevant.

Moreover, while some ecocentrists argue that the role of species in "defending a form of life" within an ecosystem merits direct moral consideration,[11] the individualism and rationalism of traditional ethics make it difficult for extensionist arguments to conceive of the moral value of whole species as anything other than an aggregate of its individual members' interests. This tension is aggravated by the fact that the species that are ecologically most valuable and most frequently threatened with extinction at the hands of human activity are not sentient birds and mammals (although they, too, are at risk), but plants and invertebrate animals—the life forms least assimilable to traditional moral categories;[12] although it is difficult to isolate the effects of a single species, the more charismatic megafauna that are the focus of popular conservation efforts may at times be expendable from the point of view of ecosystemic health.[13] Thus, for example, the ecocentrist can coherently argue that an endangered plant species—both its members and the species as a whole—has a direct claim to moral attention, and that the culling of an overabundant mammalian species in the same ecosystem may not only be morally justifiable, but obligatory to the extent that it would serve the integrity of the biotic community. Extensionist animal arguments, however, can only afford direct moral status to the interests of individual animals with sufficient self-consciousness to be aware of those interests, and so can only allot an indirect, instrumental value for the non-sentient elements of the natural world; thus, in the example above, the extensionist would judge that the endangered plant species is to be valued only as a means to animal or human ends. As we saw in Chapter 3, this facet of animal advocacy has drawn the criticism of environmental thinkers like Callicott and John Rodman, who accuse extensionists like Singer of a sentientist chauvinism that echoes with the logic of traditional humanism.

The move of environmental ethics beyond the exclusive consideration of sentient life forms leads to more interesting differences between
deep ecologists and animal advocates concerning matters of *mortality*.
If from the point of view of modern human civilization pain and death
are intrinsic evils it is our moral obligation to combat, from an eco-
biological perspective they are value-neutral inevitabilities in the natural world. Thus, as Paul Shepard comments, the attempt on the part of
extensionists to export *humane* ethical categories into the wild nonhuman world "can only produce mischief, for it will see in the behaviors
and interrelationships among animals infinite cruelties and seek to prevent them. The sucking of the host's blood by the parasite, the competition among scavengers to eat a carcass, the exclusion of the weak and
sick, predation itself, the enormous mortality which removes the
majority of the newborn every year from nearly every species—all these
and more, humane action will try to prevent, just as it prevents dogs
from eating cats and men from eating dogs."[14] If civilized humans
understand suffering to be the paramount evil, transposing the human
quest for the good onto the natural world will impose upon moral agents
innumerable obligations that fly in the face of biological reality. Thus,
Callicott asserts—using Nietzschean rhetoric—that the extensionist
preoccupation with minimizing the pain and deaths of individual animals signals a "world-denying," "life-loathing" dimension to the theories they employ.[15] While philosophers of animal advocacy typically
have responded by denying that humans have a moral obligation to
interfere with such natural processes as predation, the denial is often
grounded in practical considerations or a general injunction against
humans "policing" nature, rather than upon the ethical theories at the
core of their extensionist arguments.

This dispute over applying humane ethics to nonhumans is reflective
of a wider axiological divergence concerning the value of *wildness*, both
human and nonhuman. As an example of the former, consider the question of whether hunting is morally justified. In its modern recreational
forms, hunting is condemned by animal advocates as a brutal trivializa-
tion of the prey animals' vital interests. Some deep ecologists, however,
not only justify the practice of selective hunting on ecocentric grounds,
but overtly endorse hunting activity as the means to reconnecting with
the natural order of the wilderness, and awakening what we saw Marian
Scholtmeijer describe as the "extra-cultural reality inside of the human
individual."[16] They frequently cite with approval the examples of various
Native American peoples, who incorporate the act of hunting within an
ethical and spiritual worldview of respectful use of nature.[17]

Of course, hunting has been a near-universal phenomenon in human cultures, but in discerning a positive moral value to the activity, the deep ecologists again locate themselves squarely within North American tradition. Thoreau, for example, advocated a simple vegetarian diet, yet praised hunting as essential to human development, and offered that "perhaps the hunter is the greatest friend of the animals hunted, not excepting the Humane Society."[18] In like vein, Leopold upheld the naturalness of the hunt: "The instinct that finds delight in the sight and pursuit of game is bred into the very fiber of the human race . . . A man may not care for gold and still be a man, but the man who does not like to see, hunt, photograph or otherwise outwit birds and animals is hardly normal. He is supercivilized, and I for one do not know how to deal with him."[19] Deep ecological thinkers such as Bill Devall and George Sessions, Paul Shepard, Holmes Rolston III, et al., incorporate similar ideas into their ecological ethics, presenting the stalking and killing of other animals as a powerful mechanism for producing an understanding of ourselves as embedded within the natural world, and for harvesting the values this embeddedness implies.[20] While none conceive of the hunt as a chaotic or barbaric indulgence of savagery, on their interpretation ecocentrism not only requires respect for the wildness of the world, but a corresponding rejection of human "super-civility" and an unleashing of the animality in ourselves.

Finally, the value ecocentrism ascribes to the wildness of nonhuman animals produces the most important difference between deep ecologists and animal advocates, in light of our analysis in Chapter 7. As I argued there, a fundamental source of extensionist arguments' inadequacies lies with their failure to address the institution of *domestication* per se. But the ecocentric criterion, purportedly grounded in concerns exterior to human civilization, provides a vantage point from which domesticity may be critiqued, over and above the evaluation of the interests or alleged rights of individual domestic animals. As Callicott summarizes:

> One of the more distressing aspects of the animal liberation movement is the failure of almost all its exponents to draw a sharp distinction between the very different plights (and rights) of wild and domestic animals. But this distinction lies at the very center of the land ethic. Domestic animals are creations of man. They are living artifacts, but artifacts nevertheless, and they constitute yet another mode of extension of the works of man into the ecosystem. From the perspective of the land ethic a herd of cattle, sheep, or pigs is as much or more a ruinous blight on the landscape as a fleet of four-wheel-drive off-road vehicles.[21]

On the level of theory, as I have indicated in previous chapters—making use of environmentalist John Livingston's analysis—extensionist arguments may be viewed as a similar blight, "another mode of extension of the works of man into the ecosystem." As to practice, the holistic ecologist argues that domestic animals be regarded as "a kind of human technology to be evaluated, like all other technologies, in terms of environmental impact,"[22] whereas wild animals and native plants have a particular place in nature that grounds their "evolutionary and ecological entitlement" to a more direct moral consideration.[23] An ecocentric condemnation of the factory farm need not rely on the utilitarian consideration of the suffering of pigs or veal calves, but can make use of broader criteria: the environmental impact such institutions inflict, and the intrusion of human technology into the natural processes of life that they represent. Likewise, the use of animals in research is condemnable not only because of the suffering of the vivisection subject, but also "the transmogrification of organic to mechanical processes" it effects.[24]

If these implications of ecocentric environmentalism signal that its concern for the morally relevant interests of individual sentient animals is less absolute than that prescribed by animal advocates, ironically this is a reflection of its more radical challenge to anthropocentric culture. First, deep ecology reflects a wider biological reality than the debate over animals has tended to appreciate: it positions human reality as a constituent of the biotic community to which we are related, rather than its *summum bonum*, and thereby abjures any hierarchical interpretation of evolution that would rank the moral priority of other animals based on their biological, psychological, or cultural proximity to human beings. Second, the deep ecologist therefore is able to conceive of human activity and culture—the peculiar forms human animality has taken—as manifestations of our eco-presence, to be evaluated according to their effects on the larger ecosystem rather than by the standards of humane ethics. This conception subverts the anthropocentric sense of entitlement to the unrestrained exploitation of the natural world, while simultaneously relieving us of the charge to disavow our own biological reality, our potential *wildness*, and the impact on other animals this may imply. The resulting ethical holism seems to undermine the separation of human and animal more constructively than extensionist arguments, by allowing for the critique of both animal exploitation *and* the context of domestication in which it occurs.[25]

The radicalness of ecocentrism is reflected further in the doubt it casts on some fundamental moral intuitions. In Chapter 7, I argued that it was to the credit of extensionist arguments that they could accommodate common judgments about animal cruelty and the priority of human interests, but deep ecology raises questions about both. By objecting to the export of humane ethics to the nonhuman world, the ecocentrist asks that we accept some of the cruelty of the natural world that we ostensibly could prevent. Likewise, by subordinating both human and animal to the ecocentric criterion, deep ecology contextualizes the question of priority of interests, allowing for the possibility that nonhuman interests ought to prevail for the sake of a given ecosystem's integrity. Moreover, to the extent that deep ecology argues for normative limits on our ability to affect elements of the natural world other than sentient animals, it offers what for many is the counterintuitive proposal that inanimate entities can have a direct moral standing.[26]

## *"Ecological Self" or "Competing Consciousness"?*

The deep ecological approach thus attempts to produce a biologically richer ethic than extensionist animal advocacy. However, its challenge to the tradition is so radical that some will question whether it is philosophically coherent, or sufficiently viable to produce appropriate protection of the animal's value. Concerning the first, some important philosophical challenges have been raised against ecocentric environmental ethics—often by animal advocates—the clearest of which is a charge of "is/ought" reasoning. Consider this statement by Rolston: "Life flows on. Life ought to flow on. Few can specify how we make that descriptive-prescriptive jump, but here, where biology and history draw so close to ethics, it is made easier than anywhere else. Fact and fact-to-be-desired join in 'the *ought*-ness is the *is*.'"[27] But does the ecocentric criterion, understood as a normative ethical principle, follow directly from the brute facts of ecological reality? The knowledge of our dependence upon ecosystemic forces external to human society will inform a *prudential*, self-interested concern for "the land," and our demonstrable relatedness to all forms of life may provide a *psychological* incentive to extend care and empathy to them. Nonetheless, the fact that humans are but a part of the larger natural world does not translate directly into the conclusion that inanimate beings, plants, entire species, and nature as a whole—entities that lack such morally relevant properties as sentience or interests—possess inherent worth with the power to support moral limits on human behavior.

A related difficulty concerns whether from within the ecological whole we can evaluate human behavior at all. Steven R. L. Clark addresses this point in a theological context:

If Nature's Way is to be our guide, it is pointless to complain of mass extinctions, or pollution. In a mechanistic universe terms like "pollution" (which implies that there are preferred states, or real goals) are out of place: there is only biochemical change. But "pollution" is also out of place in a pantheistic world: there are only openings up of new ecological niches, the testing of old-established kinds against new challenges. It is the office of each kind, each "separate" organism to maintain its own as best it may, so that the glory of the whole be made richer through the war of its parts. So the worship of Nature which has been so popular a response to environmental catastrophe bids fair to explain such things away. Think of it—and of genocide—as evolution in action, to no human end. Environmentally-minded theologians often suggest that it is "natural" (and so commendable) that gangs of dogs, for example, should pull down, kill, and disembowel their prey. Human predators are just as "natural," and it is quite unclear what limits they should put upon themselves, or what would count as an "unnatural" greed.[28]

If Clark is correct, there would seem to be no easy holistic solution to the problem of humanism in environmental ethics, since moral judgment apparently must proceed from a point—either psychological, cultural, or theological—that transcends the bare biological realities of the natural world.

With these difficulties in mind, some animal advocates have advanced what we might term a "nature-skeptical" perspective—analogous to the "animal-skeptical" perspective discussed in Chapter 8—which highlights the limits of our ability to capture the objective truth about the biotic community. Such a view is offered by Andrew Linzey, who writes, "what is 'given in nature' is as much a social construct as what may be presupposed in 'human nature.' No perception of nature is value-free. What we judge to be 'given in nature' often turns out to be what we ourselves judge on other criteria should be the case. In sum: There is no ecological shortcut to avoiding the question of whether the human killing of sentient animals is a moral issue."[29]

From this perspective, Leopold's ecocentric criteria appear unworkable. Even if we accept a duty to conserve and restore natural ecosystems—perhaps to sacrifice the interests of individual animals in the process—the practical implications of this duty are ambiguous. Given the rate at which the environment can transform in response to both human and natural forces, how are we to decide which of an ecosystem's various states are more "natural," more stable, more integrated, or more beautiful?[30] If all human influence on the environment is premised to be unnatural (or destabilizing, disintegrating, or ugly), then we face the impossible task of restoring the environment to a state not seen for millennia; if instead human activity is accepted as part of the course of nature, then there will be no clear criteria for answering these questions, and the direction that practical environmental action ought to take will seem to depend as much on human partiality as on ecological reality.

However, these criticisms presuppose a traditional dichotomy of subject and object, value and fact, that has itself been challenged by eco-centrism.[31] For example, Rolston, rejecting the dualism of Clark's type of analysis, proposes what he deems a more ecologically realistic account of how values emerge:

> We discover that decomposers and predators have value objectively in the ecosystem, and then realize that our own standing as subjective valuers atop the biotic pyramid is impossible except in consequence of decomposition and predation. An interlocking kinship suggests that values are not merely in the mind but at hand in the world. We start out valuing like land appraisers figuring out what it is worth to us, only to discover that we are part and parcel of this nature we appraise. The earthen landscape has upraised this landscape appraiser. We do not simply bestow value upon nature; nature also conveys value to us.[32]

Formal evaluative judgments may be the exclusive property of cultured human minds, yet cultured human minds are materially (and perhaps metaphysically) dependent on evolutionary processes in the natural world. Thus, value cannot be isolated to points of human consciousness but rather is "smeared" across all ecological categories that are responsible for the emergence of valuing consciousness.

On Rolston's model, value is not simply relative to a valuer, but is relational, with both valuer and valued interdependent facets of bio-functional processes. Thus, he concludes: "Seen in this way, it is not the objectivists but rather the thoroughgoing subjectivists who commit the naturalistic fallacy, for they must either derive value at a consummate stroke out of merely factual nature, getting it as it were *ex nihilo*, or out of something available but to no avail without us . . . But we do not commit this fallacy because we find fact and value inseparably co-evolve."[33] Because of this co-evolution, not just any cultural constructions may be projected onto the natural world; some will fit the biological reality better than others, and some will seem intuitively more attractive to us. Rolston argues that these alignments are not arbitrary or lucky coincidences, but a natural result of how values evolve.

The animal advocate may argue that this still falls short of a complete response to Clark and Linzey; to the extent that Rolston's account is reductive, it provides no clean way of separating human culture from natural evolution, and thus neither provides a clear perspective from which the other might be evaluated. However, Rolston's conclusion that human activity is "part and parcel" of the natural order does not imply that it is beyond judgment. Just as many purely biological emergences are abortive or disruptive, the same may be said of cultural products: even if human pollution and predation cannot be categorically defined as immoral on the ecocentric model, the cultural forces that fuel them may still be judged *pathological*. The ecocentric approach thus offers a more subtle paradigm of health and sickness—one that cannot exclude the difficulty of defining those terms, or navigating the murky gray area between them—in place of the standard ethical categories of moral rightness and wrongness. To the extent that this paradigm accurately reflects the complexity of our relationship to the nonhuman world, its inability to forestall the objections of nature-skeptics is not necessarily a failing.

However, there is another response to ecocentrism available to the animal advocate: namely, to emphasize the animal's role in our appreciation of this axiological complexity. Ecocentrism implies that there would be a normative value to nature even if humans or other highly conscious life forms were unable to appreciate that value.[34] But how likely is it that ecocentric values themselves would have evolved were it not for the mediating role that other animals play between humans and the rest of nature? To answer this, we might consider a variation on Dorothy Yamamoto's thought experiment, which was introduced in Chapter 1. Imagine that humans emerged on the planet much more quickly than was actually the case, and were preceded by very few sophisticated mammalian species, all of which had gone extinct. Would the humans in this strange world recognize the indebtedness of their valuing consciousness to the natural world if the only faces with which the world confronted them were those of insects, crustaceans, fish, and reptiles, adorned only with plants and inanimate matter? The axiological subjectivism that Rolston derides would be much more plausible were it not for the presence of our related others in the animal world. Only through the mirror that is the animal are we able to discover a ground to our valuing activity in the biotic community.

With this in mind, the animal advocate may develop a point introduced in Chapter 8: that while there may be no absolute checks on the human projection of meaning onto the natural world as a whole, the subjective point of view occupied by other sentient animals presents as an objective source of value that commands limits on human behavior. This argument is made eloquently by Scholtmeijer: "Confidence that human thought participates in the making of reality should receive a setback when a scan of the natural world encounters another animal.

Here, all of a sudden, is a being with a competing consciousness, whose own reality has an autonomy and holism that hinders the freeplay of human construction."[35] Similarly, Hans Jonas argues that while the unity we may perceive in other things in nature may well be a product of our own powers of perceptual construction, the self-unifying nature of the living organism presents us with something objectively substantial, and first supplies the human mind with "the ontological, as opposed to merely phenomenological, concept of the individual or subject."[36] This point has been mirrored by some contemporary artists who have made use of the enduring nature of the animal form—even including pre-served animal corpses or live animals in their works—for the access to objective, extra-cultural reality it offers.[37]

Thus, various thinkers have cast the individual animal as a defiant figure, ontologically better suited to resist the humanizing of the natural world than other nonhuman entities. While such a perspective may argue for an alliance between environmentalism and those who advance animal rights, it has also informed another charge animal advocates have leveled against ecocentrism: from the standpoint of modern ethical sensibilities, ecocentrism can only be viewed as fascistic because it subordinates the interests of individual humans and animals to the integrity of environ-mental collectives.[38] It is noteworthy that Callicott, for example, invokes the ancient, and undeniably totalitarian, political philosophy of Plato—which allows that the good of the community may mandate the suppres-sion of its individual members' nontrivial interests—as a precedent in the Western tradition for ethical holism.[39] This rejection of individualism is apparently embraced by those environmentalists who advocate strict measures to control the population of human beings, or other overabun-dant, destabilizing animal species. But the charge of environmental fas-cism must be tempered with the awareness that deep ecologists in general have argued that concern for wholes is not incompatible with respect for individuals. For example, Naess takes pains to emphasize the "biospheri-cal egalitarianism" of deep ecology, which he grounds on the "ontological democracy" of Spinoza's metaphysics.[40] From this understanding of deep ecology, the moral concern for natural wholes is correlative to an enlight-ened respect for the individual beings in the natural world. Indeed, Naess discusses the deep ecological concern for the "self-realization" of *all* beings—including animals and natural systems such as rivers, land-scapes, and ecosystems.[41]

But for many in the modern West, to come to identify with other natural beings to the point of appreciating them as capable of "self-realization" will require something on the order of a psychological or spiritual transformation—the actualization of what Naess terms an "ecological self"—rather than rational philosophical persuasion. The description of such an expansion of selfhood is not unique to the literature in deep ecology. Testimony from several quarters—spiritual, aesthetic, athletic, and pharmacological—indicates the possibility of subjective experiences in which the individual's sense of discrete selfhood is ecstatically enlarged, and correspondingly one perceives the world as a larger field or gestalt, rather than as a series of singular objects. Such are not the experiences of the rational agent for whom Western ethical models were constructed, and so it is no surprise that deep ecologists have identified overlapping concerns with gestalt psychology, Eastern spiritual philosophies such as Daoism and Zen Buddhism, Heideggerian phenomenology, and poetry, rather than with Bentham or Kant. It is enormously difficult—perhaps impossible—to work out a philosophically acceptable holistic ethic that grounds properly moral respect for individual humans and nonhuman animals, as well as for whole species of plants and insects, ecosystemic entities such as forests and rivers, and the earth as a whole. When confronted with this complexity, deep ecologists tend to retreat from theorizing, and advocate the allocation of cultural space to holistic *experiences* of the nonhuman world.[42] Thus, Naess defines deep ecology as a "*movement*," rather than a *philosophy*, grounded in its members' fragmentary *ecosophies*: "total views" of our relatedness to the environment that reflect the author's own personal experience and incomplete knowledge of the natural world.[43]

If the type of moral attention to the nonhuman world the deep ecologists seek cannot be neatly expressed though extensions of prevailing ethical concepts, and further seems to rely on personal, quasi-mystical experience of nature, then ecocentric environmentalism will seem to require a "bottom-up" approach to cultural transformation, that is, the nurturing of non-anthropocentric micro-cultures and direct political action by individuals as the means to dismantling the anthropocentric macro-culture. This is often advanced under the banner of "bioregionalism," the call for individuals to modify their personal and economic behavior to reflect the ecological needs of their immediate communities. It is interesting to note the emphasis several environmental ethicists place on the importance of *ritual* in reinforcing ecocentric attitudes;[44] to the extent that—unlike the Native American and Eastern cultures deep ecologists admire—the culture that dominates the contemporary West lacks or has corrupted any rituals surrounding mystical experience or our intrinsic relatedness to the natural world, new ones will have to be created out of the experiences of those in the ecological movement. In the place of environmental ethical theories, new myths will have to be woven in order to incorporate respect for the nonhuman world into culture.[45] There is nothing incoherent in such an approach, and it reinforces a conclusion offered in Chapter 8: that there is an inherent value to the direct experience of the nonhuman world for which culture ought to make room.

## The Feminine Voice

As valuable as our individually reconnecting with the natural world may be, and as much as such experiences should be encouraged, some have questioned whether this approach is sufficient, given the magnitude of the threat that human encroachment poses to the nonhuman world. With this in mind, the call has been made for a broader challenge to the dominant culture than deep ecological experience may offer. This call has come most forcefully from another school of environmental ethics: ecofeminism. While sharing with deep ecologists a general concern for biocentrism and an appreciation for personal interaction with nonhuman reality, ecofeminists have also offered some harsh criticism of Leopold, Callicott, and advocates of the deep ecological approach, as well as extensionists like Singer and Regan. Like deep ecology, ecofeminism is not a singular theory, and covers a broad range of thought; in rough terms, its criticism of other forms of nature ethics is grounded in an attempt to synthesize the insights of environmental ethics and animal advocacy with a feminist analysis of Western ethics and culture. The resulting attempt to rethink our relationship to the animal and nature casts speciesism and anthropocentrism as symptoms of a deeper patriarchy in the Western tradition that needs to be deconstructed before a successful animal ethic can be produced.

In previous chapters, we have touched upon the contiguity of feminist concerns and the moral consideration of nonhuman reality. I noted in Chapter 1 the historical proximity of modern animal advocacy and the various human liberation movements, and the connection seems especially strong in the case of the feminists of the nineteenth century. As Josephine Donovan details, there is evidence to suggest a strong emotional and philosophical affinity among Anglo-American anti-vivisectionists and suffragettes, who viewed their causes as common responses to Enlightenment rationalism and scientism, and jointly sought a "feminizing" of culture that would liberate human and animal alike.[46] Further, we saw in Chapter 3 that the first modern extensionists, the utilitarians, sought to ground the extension of moral concern to nonhumans by analogizing speciesism to the arbitrariness of racism and sexism, thereby joining the moral exclusion of the animal and the political exclusion of women in the same ethical problematic.

This link also has been explored by the post-traditional thinkers discussed in Chapter 8. Derrida, in outlining what he thinks has yet to be deconstructed in the tradition, coins the term *carno-phallogocentrism* to describe the unified schema constructed by the rationalism, humanism, and patriarchy of the Western tradition:

> Authority and autonomy . . . are, through this schema, attributed to the man (*homo* and *vir*) rather than to the woman, and to the woman rather than to the animal . . . The virile strength of the adult male, the father, husband, or brother . . . belongs to the schema that dominates the concept of subject. The subject does not want just to master and *possess* nature actively. In our cultures, he accepts sacrifice and eats flesh . . . In our countries, who would stand any chance of becoming a *chef d'Etat*, and of thereby acceding "to the head," by publicly, and therefore exemplarily, declaring him- or herself to be a vegetarian? . . . To say nothing of the celibate, of homosexuality, and even of femininity (which for the moment, and so rarely, is only admitted to the head of whatever it might be, especially the State, if it lets itself be translated into a virile and heroic schema).[47]

We saw a similar insight reflected in the work of Deleuze and Guattari, who unite the feminine and the animal in a common *minoritarian* status relative to the place of privilege the tradition affords the rational, adult, white male.[48] Because of the "special situation of women in relation to the man-standard," the lines of flight, the deterritorializations effected in *becomings*, "always pass through a becoming-woman."[49] Thus, one cannot shed one's major identity and undergo the experience of animal reality Deleuze and Guattari point toward—the *becoming-animal*—without assimilating to the political exclusion that has characterized the feminine in the West.

Additional indications that sexism and anthropocentrism are intrinsically related problems have come from various sources. For example, biologist Valerius Geist speculates that this relationship has informed human culture as early as the late Paleolithic age; the hunting males' interconnected anxieties concerning their dependence on animals (as prey) and women (as the producers of all other economic values) became institutionalized through their sublimation in man's earliest artwork and rituals.[50] This dovetails with the conclusions of some object-relations psychologists, who have situated anthropocentrism within a broader diagnosis of masculine psychology; cross-culturally, the male's dependence on both nature and women has been institutionally defined as a realm of contingency and vulnerability that must be transcended in order to develop a proper sense of masculine selfhood, as demonstrated in various rites of passage for boys.[51] In addition, a number of feminist critics have discerned the confluence of speciesism and sexism in a wide variety of practices institutionalized within both Western and non-Western cultures, involving sexuality, medicine and science, food, and politics.[52]

Feminist philosophers have argued that considerations such as these, which link a philosophical or ethical issue to its gender-political context, are essential for the correct understanding of the issue, and in turn for revising our culture. For unless one understands that the Western tradition is not only hierarchical but also *patriarchal*, not only anthropocentric but *androcentric*, then the social origins of philosophical problems will be overlooked. Consider, for example, the pervasive dualisms in Western thought—rational/emotional, objective/subjective, spiritual/corporeal, cultural/natural, and the like. As Marti Kheel points out, these distinctions are not simply descriptive, but have evaluative and gendered components as well, with the less valued member of each pair invariably aligned with *femininity*.[53] Thus, to think past simplistic dualistic categories successfully, one must not only make an epistemological readjustment to compensate for the deficiencies of binary logic, but also undertake the deconstruction of social power relations that are embedded in patriarchal culture. As Janis Birkeland offers, if a similar case can be made concerning the issue of our duties to animals and nature, then the ecofeminist challenge to both animal advocacy and deep ecology is clear: "The focus on changing our anthropocentric way of experiencing or perceiving nature is inadequate either as an analysis or a program of action. While human chauvinism must be overcome, it cannot be overcome without addressing male-centeredness and sexism."[54]

The feminist analysis of ethical theory is especially relevant to the issue of the moral standing of nonhumans, for by exposing the male-centeredness of Western ethical models, it links patriarchy to those elements of traditional ethical thought that complicate the accommodation of the animal and nature: anthropocentrism, individualism, and rationalism. A starting point for this feminist philosophical work has been Carol Gilligan's work in descriptive psychology, which argues that women and men have fundamentally different experiences of moral development, and correspondingly different understandings of the operation and goals of moral deliberation.[55] Her research suggests that while men tend to view ethical conduct and thought as a type of restraint, a limitation on desire and aggression, women tend to view them more positively, as encouraging cooperation and connectedness. As many feminists have argued, Western ethical theory—with its emphasis on *individual rights, a priori moral rules,* and the *rational calculation of moral value*—has advanced the more competitive, "masculine" understanding of morality, while denigrating the more "feminine" morality of *care, positive responsibility,* and *emotional involvement*.[56] To the extent that these masculinist aspects of traditional ethical theories are incompatible with the accommodation of the nonhuman world, the failure of extensionist arguments is inseparable from their roots in patriarchy.

As Birkeland argues, the exclusion of the alternative feminine voice in ethical thought has been a serious hindrance to cultural transformation generally: "Militarism, colonialism, racism, classism, sexism, capitalism, and other pathological 'isms' of modernity obtain legitimacy from the assumption that power relations and hierarchy are inevitably a part of human Society due to Man's 'inherent nature.' In other words, if Mankind is by nature autonomous, aggressive, and competitive (that is, 'masculine') then psychological and physical coercion or hierarchical structures are necessary to manage conflict and maintain social order."[57] This point is pertinent to the issue of our treatment of nonhumans, inasmuch as the argument that human exploitation of the animal and nature is "natural" or "inevitable" is frequently offered by defenders of traditional humanism.[58] But even more significantly, by failing to explore its connection to sexism and other "isms," those who would try to undermine human chauvinism risk overlooking its true etiology. As Linda Vance writes:

> Consider, for example, the separation of culture from nature. Radical environmentalists decry the fact that the scientific, intellectual, and industrial revolutions of the past three hundred years have corresponded to a devaluation and objectification of nature, a reduction of nature's role to that of something to be controlled and used by humans. But whose revolutions? For that matter, whose culture, whose nature, whose control and use? Women barely took part in the conceptualization of those revolutions, or, until recently, in the culture that emerged from them. Neither did the poor, or non-Europeans. We have been assigned much of the execution of the culture-building project, but we have had little say in its design. Thus, culture/nature dualism is hardly a shared experience. For privileged white men, the separation of culture and nature means a yearning for that which they have lost. For women and people of color, that same separation means a continual struggle for access to that which defines and controls us.[59]

If so, the anthropocentric drive toward unchecked exploitation of the nonhuman world emerges as a symptom of a particular androcentric, masculinist pathology that infects patriarchal culture—as much an effect of inequitable social power relations as of philosophical misjudgment.

However, if the feminist analysis of Western ethics is correct, then the attempt to remedy our treatment of animals and nature through extensionist reasoning is but another symptom of the disease, rather than a cure. As Kheel writes concerning this dilemma: "The founding of ethics on the twin pillars of human reason and human will is an act of violence in its own right. By denigrating instinctive and intuitive knowledge, it severs our ties to the natural world."[60] Thus, the feminist call for a moral revaluation of the animal is grounded less on concern with rational consistency in applying a favored ethical theory than on a desire to reintegrate into culture and politics what patriarchy has excluded from our moral lives. In this spirit, feminist ethicists have proposed an ethics based on a "unified sensibility": a synthesis of the political and the personal that provides space for both objective ratiocination and the traditionally excluded (traditionally characterized as feminine) emotion, "intuition," and "instinct."[61] The goal of such an ethic is emotional authenticity, opening our a priori moral reasoning to the advice of the agent's a posteriori affective involvement. This goal reflects the anthropological reality that human beings are not just thinking things, but feeling beings. Moreover, it informs ethical theory with the claim that it is with feelings—with the care we have about one another and things in the world—that our moral lives begin.[62]

In the place of the typical moral discourse about the rights of rational agents or the rational calculation of utility, feminists have proposed an ethics of *care, sympathy,* or *attentive love.*[63] But some advocates of these approaches take pains to emphasize that an ethic of care is not misologistic, for the emotions whose moral relevance they champion are not pure impulse, but a kind of rationality. For example, Donovan writes that sympathy "involves an exercise of the moral imagination, an intense attentiveness to another's reality, which requires strong powers of observation and concentration, as well as faculties of evaluation and judgment. It is a matter of trying to fairly see another's world, to understand what another's experience is. It is a cognitive as well as emotional exercise."[64] In making this case, feminist ethicists align themselves with an important minority school in the West. Its roots are as old as the tradition itself, for even a carno-phallogocentrist like Aristotle appreciated emotion's role in forming sound moral decisions. In the modern world, sympathy-based ethics have been advocated by various figures, many of whom have been especially sensitive to the moral standing of nonhumans: Rousseau, Hume, Schopenhauer, Buber, et al.[65] Nineteenth-century animal advocate Henry Salt made the link between respect for animals and respect for the emotions extremely clear; he argued that our isolation from nonhuman reality is a product of "our persistent culture of the ratiocinative faculty, and our persistent neglect of the instinctive," the correction of which rests with the recognition "that reason itself can never be at its best, can never be truly rational, except when it is in perfect harmony with the deep-seated emotional instincts and sympathies which underlie all thought."[66]

If the ground of the feminist ethic of care is not entirely alien to the tradition, neither are the results of its specific application to the treatment of other animals, which most closely resemble those of virtue ethics. Many feminists echo the arguments of Lawrence Becker and Mary Midgley, who call for moral attention to *relationships* and the details of the specific case. For example, Gruen characterizes the feminist search for an animal ethic in this way: "The beings we are considering are not always just animals; they are Lassie the dog and the family cat, bald eagles and bunnies, snakes and skunks. Similarly, humans are not just humans; they are friends and lovers, family and foe. The emotional force of kinship or closeness to another is a crucial element in thinking about moral deliberations. To ignore the reality of this influence in favor of some abstraction such as absolute equality may not only be impossible, but undesirable."[67] Kheel also makes the connection to virtue theory, by linking feminist ethics with a return to the ancient search for a *way of life*, and a rejection of the modern preoccupation with the rational apportionment of value.[68] As noted in Chapter 7, the virtue approach—which leaves ambiguous the broad question of how the animal per se ought to be treated—is attractive to those most skeptical of moral theory's ability to bring precision to our moral judgments. Thus, one finds that the feminist approach to animal advocacy generally has avoided committing to a specific practical ethic, or calling for the abolition of animal exploitation; instead, the focus has been to shift the ground of our moral thinking about animals away from theorizing, to what Donovan describes as "an emotional and spiritual conversation with nonhuman life-forms."[69] As an example of this approach, Kheel does not offer a theoretical argument for moral vegetarianism after the manner of Singer or Regan, but instead advocates that the meat-eater fully inform himself about the implications of his behavior by actually visiting a factory farm or a slaughterhouse.[70] The implication is that one's attitudes toward the animal-as-livestock can be altered radically by such an experience, whether or not the shift is supported by ethical theory.

Despite its rationale and its roots in the tradition, the feminist emphasis on emotional authenticity and personal experience has fueled the criticism—especially from extensionist animal advocates—that the ethic of care implies a degree of moral relativism that will preclude the practical protection of the animal. However much some individuals may claim to feel emotionally connected to the world around us, our emotional lives have an ineluctably subjective dimension. Gender-political analysis aside, it may be argued that the Western tradition grounded ethics on reason rather than emotion precisely to check the dangers of this subjectivity: to seek assurance that our practical judgments reflect objective reality, to bring solidity and confidence to our decisions and consistency to our characters.[71] Even some of those feminists who have called for a "unified sensibility" between reason and emotion have denigrated reason excessively,[72] or have allied feminism with an antiscientific embrace of "magic," holistic medicine, goddess worship, and the like. This type of skepticism concerning the objectivity of knowledge and moral judgment creates difficulties both within and without the feminist approach to nature ethics.

First, feminists and other thinkers who accept an imperative to establish a connection with the nonhuman world risk self-delusion if the connection is not informed by objective reason. The "emotional conversation" that Donovan calls for is inevitably one-sided, because of our limited access to the emotional lives of other animals. This problem has been developed clearly by Andrew Linzey in his analysis of the ethics of pet keeping, an issue too frequently left unexplored by animal advocates precisely because the emotional link some feel toward companion animals is so strong. Linzey makes the case that the practice of keeping pets may often involve "a selfish form of love which seeks to condition animal lives in accordance with our own human desires," a "false anthropomorphism" in which we humanize animals and "regard them as extensions of our own egos."[73] Thus, those who would ground moral obligations to other animals on alleged emotional connections need to beware of what Linzey terms a "self-deceiving tyranny."[74] Indeed, to the extent that feminists ignore this threat of emotional subjectivism, viewing the animal as an object of *care* may, rather than liberate the animal, effect a type of *emotional domestication* that destroys the animal's otherness.

Second, the relativity of human emotions makes them an obviously problematic foundation from which to persuade others—feminists and non-feminists alike—to transform their attitudes toward nonhumans. As

Carol Adams details, feminist concern for the autonomy of women's emotional lives and respect for pluralism have been serious obstacles to further strengthening the ties between feminism and animal advocacy; for example, some feminists have heard the call to moral vegetarianism as a patriarchal imposition upon the wills of individual women.[75] As for those outside the feminist school who do not already share a concern for nature ethics, it is not obvious that appeal to emotion would be any more effective than rational persuasion at transforming their attitudes. From those reared in anthropocentric culture, many elements of the nonhuman world may evoke either no emotional response, such negative responses as fear or disdain, or a humanistic urge to transform or despoil.[76] In sum, if feminist analysis finds extensionism an unlikely means of fostering respect for the animal, an ethic of care seems no less problematic.

## Ecofeminism: Holism without Hierarchy

The ecofeminist approach to nature ethics has tried to avoid these philosophical tangles by focusing on the criticism of the political and cultural forces that underlie them. Emphasizing the themes of community, holism, and integration, ecofeminists envision a synthesis of the concerns of environmentalism and feminism that compensates for their individual shortcomings. Gruen, for example, presents ecofeminism as a commitment to nonhierarchical thinking that overcomes the culture/nature dualism present in other schools of feminism. She argues that liberal and leftist feminists maintain this dualism to the extent that they define liberation as the full integration of women into masculinist culture, with all of its anthropocentric baggage. Likewise, she argues that radical feminism is not "fully liberatory," for it perpetuates the dichotomies of woman/man, emotion/reason, and nature/culture, only to reverse the evaluation these poles have in patriarchal culture.[77] Vance—invoking the thought of ecofeminist Ynestra King—echoes Gruen's analysis by proposing three options for modern feminists contemplating nature ethics: to reject the woman-nature connection and its relationship to patriarchal culture, to embrace this connection despite its ties to patriarchy, or—the ecofeminist approach—to "use the woman-nature connection as a starting point for the creation of a new politics and culture."[78]

In like manner, Birkeland identifies the androcentric concepts in various schools of environmental thought, and presents ecofeminism as a holistic alternative to the masculinist "power paradigm" to which other schools of environmentalism are captive. First, liberal ecologies—including deep ecology—focus on shifting the *individual's* experience of nature, and thereby ignore the gender political analysis feminists insist on. Because deep ecology fails to integrate such feminist analysis, the individual it encourages to reidentify with nature is implicitly the Rational Man of the patriarchal tradition; as a result, she argues, its analysis is colored by a "masculinist bias," and is "abstract, aloof, impersonal, gender-blind, and it ignores power."[79] Second, leftist ecologies such as eco-Marxism offer a critique of the role of institutionalized power in the environmental crisis, but still fail to address androcentrism. Inheriting from Marx the anthropocentric notion that human liberation is achieved through the transformation of nature, leftists maintain patriarchal ideas of rationality and power, and thus hold out environmental strategies that are "dictated by 'masculinist' terms (for example, control, choice, and change) rather than the 'feminist' concerns of relationship, communication, and caring that are requisite for living in harmony with nature."[80]

Ecofeminism thus purports to offer an integrated analysis of self-identity, culture, social power relations, and our relationship to nonhuman reality. In seeking this type of integration, ecofeminists—like animal advocates and deep ecologists—claim to adhere to a methodology that best fits the biological reality of their subject matter. As Vance writes, "Diversity of experience and expression, like diversity of life forms, is a necessary goal of ecofeminism. There can be no single set of answers, no one portal through which to enter. To insist on a single ideology, or a single praxis, is to deny the tremendous complexity of the problems that centuries of patriarchy have created. And it denies the dialectical realities of the complicated, interconnected life on this planet."[81]

Kheel contrasts the "heroic," "allopathic" nature of traditional ethical models—which attempt to resolve a moral problem by the imposition of a singular, simplistic rule or principle—with the holistic ecofeminist appreciation for the "ecology" of ethics: the attempt to identify the complete emotional and cultural context upon which our beliefs about nature depend, in the same way that systems ecology describes the interconnectedness of natural life forms.[82] Likewise, King argues: "Life on earth is an interconnected web, not a hierarchy. There is no natural hierarchy; human hierarchy is projected on to nature and then used to justify social domination. Therefore, ecofeminist theory seeks to show the connections between all forms of domination, including the domination of nonhuman nature, and ecofeminist practice is necessarily anti-hierarchical."[83]

King's last phrase is significant, because, as Kheel puts it, "the transformation that ecofeminists wish to bring about is . . . often *implicit in their critiques,*"[84] and as a result ecofeminism is often most powerful when it articulates what it is *against:* it is anti-hierarchy, anti-domination, anti-power.[85] An important way in which this is expressed is in ecofeminists' thoroughgoing skepticism at the categorical distinctions that have taken hold in other forms of nature ethics. Like the feminist analysts discussed above, ecofeminists reject the segregation of reason from emotion, political structure from personal experience that is apparent in much extensionist reasoning. In addition, their concern for nature as an "interconnected web" has allowed them—like deep ecologists—to voice ecocentric criticism of extensionist animal advocacy and its moral distinctions between types of natural beings: animate and inanimate, animal and plant, sentient and non-sentient. However, stressing that individuals of all these types have an inherent value, ecofeminists have in turn been critical of those environmentalists who would make moral distinctions between individuals and the species or ecosystem to which they belong, or between endangered and abundant life forms.[86] Moreover, in emphasizing personal experience and relationships as the ground for moral concern, ecofeminists have been loath to endorse the evaluative distinction—important to many deep ecologists—between domestic and wild animals; some feminists either explicitly or implicitly pose relationships with companion or farm animals as an essential link between humans and the natural world.[87]

Summarizing the extent to which ecofeminism seeks to overcome dualistic thought, Kheel speaks of the need for feminist nature ethics to reclaim the term *holism* from deep ecologists such as Callicott, who maintain hierarchical, and thus androcentric, frameworks.[88] However, in attempting to be *so* holistic as to reject nearly all evaluative categorizations, ecofeminism risks denying itself the conceptual framework necessary for constructing a coherent positive ethic. Yet this is a risk many ecofeminists openly embrace. Kheel writes that ecofeminism, like feminist animal advocacy, disavows the "hunt" for an ethic, opting instead to weave a number of "stories" into a critical "tapestry" that portrays the state of the world.[89] Likewise Vance, emphasizing ecofeminism's tolerance for pluralism, argues that each adherent's definition of ecofeminism will vary, reflecting "a particular intersection of race, class, geography, and conceptual orientation";[90] and Gruen speaks of a "methodological humility" that underlies ecofeminism's rejection of a single theoretical posture.

But if it is therefore the ecofeminist position that "the natural world will be 'saved' not by the sword of ethical theory, but rather through a transformed consciousness toward all of life,"[91] then in its practical results, ecofeminism comes to look much like deep ecology—despite the tensions between them. Reminiscent of Naess's advocacy of multiple "ecosophies," ecofeminism calls forth "multiple images of the Earth— fragmented, partial, and local representations," rather than a single conception or metaphor.[92] In turn, like the deep ecologists discussed above, ecofeminists have called for micro-political action that reflects bioregional concerns,[93] the creation of new rituals to reinforce identification with the nonhuman world, and the fostering of spiritualities that are earth-honoring.[94] If ecofeminism simply purports to offer the means to better understanding the problem of animals' moral status, rather than an unequivocal solution to that problem, then perhaps, like deep ecology, it is best understood as a *movement* rather than a philosophy.

## Conclusion

How then shall we situate deep ecology and ecofeminism in relation to extensionist animal advocacy and its poststructuralist critics? Unlike the thinkers reviewed in the previous chapter, ecophilosophers have placed a priority on the praxis needed to protect animal reality from ceaseless human manipulation. However, the deep ecologists' search for nontraditional—and therefore non-extensionist—normative theory to ground this praxis has taken them to territory replete with logical quagmires and steep metaphysical ascents. These difficulties reinforce the ecofeminists' skepticism at the value of theorizing for the protection of the nonhuman world, but this skepticism in turn leaves ecofeminist practice with no other foundation than the diligent criticism of other forms of nature ethics, and the unsteady ground of emotional subjectivism. The collective results of this ecophilosophical work thus include further support for the poststructuralist conclusion that there is no simple way to integrate the animal and its moral demands into existing cultural structures, and therefore further doubt about the legitimacy of extensionism.

Nonetheless, there is a confluence to the forms of thinking reviewed in the previous two chapters that allows us to draw some positive—and more fundamental—conclusions as well. First, the critique of extensionism forces us to readdress exactly where the value of the animal lies. In a way suggestive of Derrida's proposal that real thinking begins with the nakedness we feel before the animal's gaze, the ecophilosopher argues that there is value to an encounter with whole animal reality, and not just to those characteristics of certain types of animal that might be significant in our moral schemes. For example, while apparently reflecting incompatible nature ethics, the deep ecologist's romantic description of the hunt and the ecofeminist's hopeful call for a conversation with the nonhuman world both inform an imperative for us *to experience the animal directly*, and thereby to apprehend a type of responsibility that may be *incalculable* using the standard moral formulas. One suspects that such encounters will be more valuable outside the context of domestication in an extra-civilized setting, and should not have to end in the bloodshed of the hunt to prove enriching. In any case, poststructuralist thought and ecophilosophy both indicate that the value of the animal lies with something more fundamental and intimate than the aloof concern with moral consistency that defines extensionism. Authentic encounters with the animal force us to confront the larger reality that has been excluded from traditional Western thought.

Second, if poststructuralism and ecophilosophy are skeptical at the ability of ethical theory and ordinary political process to protect the animal, the implication is not quietism, but the subtly subversive practice of micro-politics. The ecophilosopher's focus on bioregionalism and individual social action perhaps marks radical environmentalism as *minoritarian* in something like the sense that Deleuze and Guattari intend.[95] For example, ecofeminist Deane Curtin argues that while no ethical theory can justify a universal proscription against eating meat, there is nonetheless a valuable political dimension to vegetarianism: "To *choose one's diet* in a patriarchal culture is one way of politicizing an ethic of care. It marks a daily, bodily commitment to resist ideological pressures to conform to patriarchal standards, and to establishing contexts in which caring for can be nonabusive."[96] Similarly, the deep ecologist who takes to the wild, who chooses to hunt rather than shop, embodies a micro-political challenge to the majoritarian ideology of super-civility. In these ways, adherents of ecophilosophy effect *deterritorializations*, cutting through major classifications of class, gender, and species, perhaps to embark upon the various becomings: -minoritarian, -woman, -animal. This dovetails with the description of both deep ecology and ecofeminism as pluralistic *movements* rather than systematic *philosophies*, and indicates that ecophilosophy is more akin to the *rhizome* than to the arboreal hierarchies of extensionist reasoning; it is noteworthy that Deleuze and Guattari speak of rhizomatic becoming as *asignifying*, while both deep ecologists and ecofeminists revel in the *uselessness* of wilderness.[97]

Finally, the ecophilosopher's call for the creation of new spirituality, new rituals, and new myths—rather than new prescriptive theories—

casts the ecological activist in the role of a modern-day *sorcerer:* one who moves along the fringes of society, conjuring strange alliances with the animal other. This spiritual dimension is quite essential to understanding where ecophilosophy and poststructuralism locate the animal. Throughout much of the Western tradition, the search for a limiting principle that could keep human avarice and hubris in check inevitably led to the religious realm; God—an incalculable value that transcends the social and conventional—filled just such a limiting role. Secular, post-Enlightenment critics of civilization have struggled to find a similarly authoritative ideal to demarcate the limits of human authority. The confluence of postmodern and ecophilosophical thought urges the animal to fill the vacancy, to embody that extra-cultural vantage point from which a critical view of culture may be had. As a result, these very recent movements are remarkably nostalgic, in that they serve to reinvest the animal with a sacredness it once held in ancient spiritual systems.

Yet, it must be acknowledged that such sorcery, while spiritually powerful for its practitioners, is relatively powerless against the forces of transnational capital that threaten the animal with further extinctions and commodification (which perhaps amount to the same thing). Furthermore, the attempt to slow the humanization of the wild animal's world by heralding that we, too, need to experience that world may ultimately be self-defeating if it bolsters an instrumental evaluation of nature, and thereby provokes the anthropocentrist's admonition not to ignore our other needs and desires that conflict with the animal's. The defender of extensionism may therefore reasonably assert that, for all their shortcomings, extensionist concepts are indispensable for securing the practical protection of the nonhuman world.[98] If the claims that wild animals have moral rights and trees deserve legal standing do not do full justice to the otherness of nonhuman reality, they nonetheless have a necessary place today. Still, they must be used with care: like all necessary evils, holy lies, and myths, they can conceal as much as they reveal. Extensionist concepts do not exhaust the ways in which concern for nonhumans may be expressed; indeed, these concepts must eventually be overcome in order that the full value of animals may be appreciated.

---

The limitations of extensionist arguments—in terms of their ability both to establish a moral standing befitting animal reality and to remedy the anthropocentrism of nature/culture dualism—are confirmed by several quarters: poststructuralist thought, environmentalism, and feminism. Collectively, these reflections on animal reality make the case that the tension between Part I and Part II should be resolved in favor of the animal—that is, if traditional ethical models cannot adequately extend moral concern to the nonhuman world, this should not lead us to doubt the importance of the animal's value, but should instead encourage us to work toward alternatives to traditional ethical thought that can accommodate that value. In Part IV, following the methodology outlined in Chapter 1, I reflect on what this conclusion means, for both philosophy and the animal.

# The Human Animals
## in the Menagerie

# 10  *Sacrifice and Self-Overcoming*

The present analysis of the moral status of animals might have ended with the conclusion of the previous chapter. The arguments reviewed up to that point lead toward some substantial and perhaps unexpected conclusions. While there are solid philosophical grounds for rethinking the animal's traditional exclusion from moral considerations, recent attempts to extend traditional ethical categories to include the animal have yielded incomplete results. The consideration of the moral status of animals seems to require not only the extension of traditional ethical categories to animals, but also a deeper reflection on those categories themselves. The animal embodies a reality that is not adequately reflected in our traditional thinking; the value of that reality, and the possibilities it holds for human culture to look critically at itself, are obscured if we stop our analysis with concepts like "animal rights" and the practical protections they imply. Serious reflection on the moral status of animals cannot end with opposition to eating meat or animal experimentation—however valid such concerns—but leads seamlessly to a broader cultural and political challenge and the invitation to experience in more direct ways the reality that animals occupy.

Yet, as valuable as these points may be, they fall short of reflecting everything the animal can teach us. In Chapter 1, I offered that one of the most telling dimensions to the human use of animals is *reflexivity:* with various intentions and outcomes, humans use their impressions of the animal to complete an understanding of themselves. The importance of this reflexivity has been explored in biophilic thought, which holds that we are compelled to turn our attention to the natural world because it was there—and not within the confines of civilization—that the essential path of human evolution was blazed. Especially interesting in this regard is Paul Shepard's fruitful speculation that it was by assimilating its relatedness to animal others that *Homo sapiens* evolved its unique and cherished form of self-consciousness, and that as a result the "ecology" of thought mirrors the natural ecology of the animal world. In the tradition of Western thought, however, the comparison of human and animal typically has been focused on the *otherness* of the animal in order to reinforce an understanding of humanity's uniqueness, to vindicate the superiority of culture over nature and the isolation of human reality from the larger ecology. But culturally constructed barriers to appreciating our *relatedness* to the animal cannot stand indefinitely. As the post-Darwinian world bears witness, when we gaze unflinchingly into the mirror of the animal, the products of human culture reflect back not as images of the transcendent, but rather as the peculiar physiognomy of our own animality. It is this confusing face—the face of an "ontological centaur, half immersed in nature, half transcending it"[1]— that the post-Darwinian thinker must confront, leading Scholtmeijer to quip: "The very least that can be said . . . is that culture has created a grave problem for itself in generating the idea of continuity."[2]

When viewed against this background, the product of culture that has been our focus here—the debate over the moral standing appropriate to animals—emerges as more than a stimulating exercise in casuistry. By casting our moral reasoning upon the extra-cultural reality of the nonhuman animal, the debate provides an occasion to glean insight about our ethical infrastructure, and we who depend upon it, from the images that are reflected back. The "grave problem" that this juxtaposition of animals and ethics forces us to address was expressed by Nietzsche—the first great post-Darwinian philosopher—in what he termed the "gravest question of all": "What, seen in the perspective of *life*, is the significance of morality?"[3] If moral thought and behavior are not purely products of culture, but instead are associable with our own animal lives, then "every table of values, every 'thou shalt' known to history or ethnology, requires first a *physiological* investigation and interpretation";[4] moral phenomena must be studied anew under the rubrics of the *typology*, *natural history*, and *genealogy* of morals. Absent the results of these more fundamental projects, Nietzsche argues that philosophy's traditional task in ethics—developing techniques for the rational justification of our moral judgments—is premature, if not altogether misguided, for it becomes unclear *what* about our moral judgments is to be justified, and whether as a category they are susceptible of justification at all. Thus, the grave problem that continuity creates for morality is that *morality itself becomes a problem*.[5]

One might at first suspect that what is fundamentally problematic about a biological interpretation of morality is the threat of nihilistic reductionism—something that Nietzsche's rhetoric seems to herald. Although Nietzsche explicitly and repeatedly rejected the efforts of his social-Darwinist contemporaries who sought to establish simplistic equations between the biologically useful and the good,[6] the biologistic language he employs in his nontraditional exploration of morality, especially in the *Genealogy of Morals*, is nonetheless suggestive of twentieth-century sociobiology (evolutionary psychology) and its attempt to reductively account for the vitality of moral principles by appeal to principles of evolutionary biology.[7] Yet Nietzsche himself offered clear repudiation of the most naïve of such attempts, arguing that the logical and teleological lines that connect a thing—whether physiological or cultural—with whatever original adaptive value it may have conferred are often circuitous, precluding any immediate inferences about a thing's *meaning* from its *origin*, or vice versa.[8] Subsequent philosophical and biological scrutiny of socio-biological explanations has made clear that there are logical and methodological impediments to applying strict adaptionism to the interpretation of particular—even ubiquitous—cultural phenomena (or biological phenomena, for that matter).[9] As a matter of both logic and biology, the existence of some ultimate biological foundation for the moral nature of human beings does not exclude space for ethical formations to operate at a cultural level that cannot be positivistically reduced to the function of genes.

If the threat of reductionism is less ominous than it at first appears, then what accounts for the air of gravity that surrounds the commingling of animality and ethics? The preceding analysis suggests that it is the impossibility of ever again neatly separating the two. If, as was noted in Part I, the debate over animals exploits a blurring of species boundaries that can be discerned in evolution science, the debate itself may be compromised by the blurring of biology and culture that erupts in the post-Darwinian world. Is the attempt to extend moral consideration to nonhuman animals simply a step in cultural evolution, to be evaluated on the merits of its rational grounds? Or does it signify something more fundamental: the need to grapple with the nature and extent of our own animality? The reflexive nature of our consciousness of the animal and the full import of the Darwinian revolution suggest the latter. In grappling with the morality of our treatment of the animal, we are forced to consider how our own animality is handled by our moral thinking. As

Raymond Corbey expresses the point, the debate over animals ultimately leaves us in the position of *"ambiguous apes"* because it prob-
lematizes and destabilizes our human identity.[10] Thus, the animal leads
us to very human existential dilemmas, for if the different postures
taken toward the moral standing of animals reflect different ways of
interpreting our own animality, we must inquire with which of these
interpretations we are to locate our humanity. Does our essential nature
lie with the products of culture, with our animality, or—as is likely—
with some combination of the two? Where reside human health and
sickness and what does this imply for ethics and our relationship with
other animals? If we are moral beings who should value animals, what
does it mean if the value of the animal cannot be successfully expressed
in moral terms? I now explore these questions, making use of the analysis in Parts II and III.

## The Moral Menagerie

Let us begin by identifying what insight Nietzsche's analysis can lend to
the questions he himself raises. While Nietzsche's explicit contribution
to the debate over our treatment of animals is confined to a handful of dis-
paraging remarks about vegetarians and antivivisectionists, his understanding of the "significance of morality" is nonetheless relevant to the
interpretation of the debate. Glossing over the subtle details of his
genealogical investigations and his discussion of the *various* possible uses
to which human beings have put their moral tablets, a broad conclusion
emerges from across his work: "the *meaning of all culture* is the reduction of the beast of prey 'man' to a tame and civilized animal, a *domestic
animal.*"[11] The model of *human domestication* is a fitting one for understanding the grave problem with which the post-Darwinian must deal,
because it expresses how inextricably our humanity is tied to both our
animality and our enculturation. It also provides an interesting means to
avoid a categorical dualism between culture and nature, inasmuch as
domestication signifies a *type of animality.* (Indeed, Nietzsche makes
explicit that human domestication likely serves certain interests of the
human species, and thus it would be "absurd" to assume that the rise of
civilization's values represents an "antibiological" phenomenon.[12])

Nietzsche offers numerous reinforcing images that reflect how the
dominant moral phenomena in the West have facilitated the process of
civilizing the human animal. We read in *The Gay Science* that the habil-
iments of the moral life—"duty, virtue, public sentiment, honorable-
ness, and disinterestedness"—constitute a *"disguise"* that masks the

"ignominious spectacle" of tame animals.[13] In *Beyond Good and Evil*, Nietzsche argues that, despite their apparent differences, the two principal doctrines of modern European ethics—the deontological theory of "equality of rights" and the utilitarian "sympathy for all that suffers"—are both symptomatic of a desire for "the universal green-pasture happiness of the herd."[14] In *The Genealogy of Morals*, the phenomenon of "bad conscience" is described as the product of millennia of *Selbst-tierquälerei*—self-inflicted cruelty to our animal nature.[15] As Nietzsche summarizes these points in a note for *The Will to Power*, if the cultured human being is a tamed animal, then "morality is a menagerie; its presupposition is that iron bars can be more profitable than freedom, even for the prisoners."[16]

One might be tempted to think that Nietzsche is simply being metaphorical in these texts, using animal imagery to capture how obedience to stale moral edicts can stifle the human spirit. But that would be to miss the depth of Nietzsche's struggle with the issue of human animality, a point he makes explicit in this important passage from *Beyond Good and Evil*:

> We know well enough how insulting it sounds when anybody counts man, unadorned and without metaphor, among the animals; but it will be charged against us as almost a *guilt* that precisely for the men of "modern ideas" we constantly employ such expressions as "herd," "herd instincts," and so forth. What can be done about it? We cannot do anything else for here exactly lies our novel insight. We have found that in all major moral judgments Europe is now of one mind, including even the countries dominated by the influence of Europe: plainly, one now *knows* in Europe what Socrates thought he did not know and what that famous old serpent once promised to teach—today one "knows" what is good and evil.
>
> Now it must sound harsh and cannot be heard easily when we keep insisting: that which here believes it knows, that which here glorifies itself with its praises and reproaches, calling itself good, that is the instinct of the herd animal, man, which has scored a breakthrough and attained prevalence and predominance over other instincts—and this development is continuing in accordance with the growing physiological approximation and assimilation of which it is the symptom. *Morality in Europe today is herd animal morality*—in other words, as we understand it, merely *one* type of human morality beside which, before which, and after which many other types, above all *higher* moralities, are, or ought to be, possible.[17]

This text makes clear that Nietzsche holds the moral ideals of the West to be literal symptoms of a degraded type of animality—that of a tame, domesticated, herd animal—and moreover that the effort to resist the problematizing of morality in this way is but another reflection of human domestication.

Nietzsche's account offers an interesting means of refuting socio-biological reductionism: if certain moral values are indeed products of human domestication, then their ubiquity may be explained by the hegemony of domesticated, agrarian culture, with no need to infer that these values have an adaptive foundation on the genetic level. More important for our purposes are the implications of Nietzsche's discussion of domestication for the debate over animals. What stands out immediately is the possible connection between his analysis and a problem with extensionist arguments that was broached in Part III. In Chapter 7, I noted with disappointment that the major extensionist arguments fail to produce unequivocal evaluations of institutionalized forms of animal exploitation, and that many arguments in the debate fail to address the context of domestication in which much of this exploitation occurs. Nietzsche's analysis provides an interesting explanation for this shortcoming: extensionist reasoning is incapable of critically assessing the domestication of other animals *because the theories employed therein are interwoven with the history of human self-domestication*. Indeed, the debate over animals provides reinforcement for Nietzsche's interpretation: *in the mirror of the animal, our moral principles are revealed as instruments of domestication*. The point dovetails with a less dramatic, sociological explanation of our cultural origins. It is widely accepted that the form of civilization that would ultimately dominate human culture begins with the development of agriculture, the domestication of animals and plants supplanting the cultures of hunting and gathering. If so, then the corresponding ethical models that civilization adopts will predictably reflect an agrarian bias in favor of sedentarization—and the taming of human animality this implies—and be blind to the moral problems of taming the nonhuman world.

This explanation also dovetails with John Livingston's criticism of extensionism, which was noted throughout Part II. To summarize, Livingston argues that to extend ethical concepts such as "rights" to non-humans "would be to 'humanize,' or domesticate the entire planet"; if extensionism were taken to its extreme, he argues, "all life would be a human farm."[18] The premise underlying these assertions is that our ethical models evolved within the unique political circumstances of human beings, and thus have no meaning when applied to the nonhuman world. Since the political circumstance of the Western tradition has been decidedly anthropocentric, extensionism thus subsumes nature under the same cultural rubric that allows for its exploitation—the essence of domestication. Moreover, it is striking that, like Nietzsche, Livingston diagnoses the cultural tradition that gives rise to our major ethical theories as symptomatic of a process of *human* domestication; his objection to extensionist reasoning thus does not rest on a generic dualism of culture and nature, but instead on the segregation of the domestic and the wild: "How could a domesticated human invention for domesticated human purposes be applied to the welfare of non-human beings?"[19]

Nietzsche implicitly defines domestication as a process of *taming*—the suppression and redirection of natural impulses, the internalization of drives that seek outward expression, the transmutation of the active into the reactive. But this will not do as a precise definition of the concept, inasmuch as many wild animals can be tamed and many domesticated ones can be quite ferocious. Livingston more accurately takes the hallmark of domestication to be *dependence*, which in the case of human beings is reflected in our dependence on the technological products of culture:

> All domesticated animals depend for their day-to-day survival upon their owners. The capacities of wild self-sufficiency having long since been subtracted from them, they must depend upon whatever prosthetic devices their owners see fit to provide. The human domesticate has become equally dependent, not upon a proprietor, but upon storable, retrievable, transmissable technique. Technology provides us with everything we require. Knowledge of how-to-do-it sustains us utterly. And since none of us knows how to do *everything*, we are further dependent upon the expertise of countless others to provide even the most basic of daily necessities. Like that of a race horse or a Pekinese, our dependence upon agents external to ourselves is total. Without knowledge of how-to-do-it, or access to someone else who does know how, we are irretrievably helpless.[20]

In this state of dependence, the various institutions of culture function as *prostheses*, "fabricated through accumulating tradition to stand in the place of natural, *biological*, inherent ways of being, those ways having been abrogated by the culturing process."[21] Echoing Nietzsche, Livingston argues that the history of human civilization is not one of progress but instead one of increasing dependence on the prosthetic devices of culture: "We are bound to technique, indentured to technique, and we grew naturally into that serfdom along our evolutionary way. The dependence into which we have grown has made us not merely the servants of how-to-do-it, but one of its very artifacts. The problem animal is its own creation, its own domesticate."[22]

Like Nietzsche, Livingston holds that morality plays an essential role in the process of self-domestication, for, like other techniques, ethical systems constitute domesticating prosthetic devices, "cultural surrogates for inherent (biological) ways of social and community organization."[23] When human societies reach a size and complexity that exceeds the capacity of our "genetic compulsion to comply," humans become dependent upon theoretical reflection on the distribution of power in order to maintain social order.[24] Most important is Livingston's description of the means by which this dependence is perpetuated. Human dependence upon cultural rather than biological modes of sociality leads to a "fanatical fixation on ideas"; as a result, rationality becomes not just another tool in the human toolbox, but instead our "hyperspecialization."[25] The uniqueness of this state of hyperspecialized dependence readily becomes the means to distinguish ourselves from the rest of the natural world: "Our hyperspecialization was deftly rationalized from unprecedented domesticated dependence into unprecedented species chauvinism. Crudely put: if you've got it, and you're stuck with it, flaunt it."[26] Finally, this chauvinism is reinforced by attributing to humans, but not to animals, the kind of identity that can best be handled by prosthetic moral theories: self-conscious individuality.[27] Thus, precisely those aspects of Western ethical models that hinder their smooth extension to the nonhuman animal—rationalism, anthropocentrism, and individualism, as we reviewed in Chapter 7—are explainable in Livingston's account by their emergence within a context of human domestication.

In the light of Nietzsche's and Livingston's analyses of the link between Western moral thought and the culture of domestication of which they are a product, the critical themes of Parts II and III—respectively, the limitations of extensionist arguments, and the obstacles to securing an alternative animal ethic that is culturally viable—come into greater focus. As Livingston concludes,

> nature does not appear to *need* an ethical prosthesis. Nature is whole . . . This is why, when we attempt to lay upon nature an ethical model, the overlay never quite *fits*. We always see something off-register . . . Nonhuman nature cannot fit *any* ethical model, because ethical models are human abstract constructions designed to serve the humans who constructed them. An ethical model arises out of the interest of the human society to which it is seen to be useful. Ethical models are tools of social management, part of the technological prosthesis. They are human-

specific, and society-specific. They are not designed to serve the inter-ests of other human societies, much less nonhuman societies.[28]

Thus, extensionism is doomed to fail because our exploitation of other animals and our dependence on rational ethical models are coextensive symptoms of our own domestication, our pathological hyperspecializa-tion. Moreover, if the dominant institutions of Western culture consti-tute a series of domesticating prostheses, the search for alternatives to extensionist models must take us far beyond what is ostensibly viable politically and socially.

Mary Midgley attempts to offer an extensionist ground for an animal ethic by identifying the "mixed community"—that is, the historical community of civilized human beings establishing morally significant relationships with other social, domesticated animals.[29] One cannot deny that such relationships exist, or that it is possible for humans to find meaning in their compassionate dealings with domesticates. How-ever, Nietzsche and Livingston make a compelling case that respect for the full breadth of animality ought also to lead us in a very different direction: if from the perch of our moral excellence we should extend rights and compassion to the animals in our homes and societies, we should also, in humility, allow the untamed animal to draw us past the confines of our own domestication and toward other cultural possibili-ties, other perspectives on the wider reality outside civilization. Indeed, on their analysis, the extensionist's creed—that subsuming the animal under the umbrella of our civility in a mixed community is the solution to the moral standing of animals—is in fact another symptom of the problem: a pathological, inter-specific fixation with domestication.

## Sacrificing the Sacrifice

Given that the process by which human beings came to surround them-selves with institutions of domestication—thereby obscuring other cul-tural possibilities—constitutes the most important transformation in the history of the species, it is startling that the etiology of this process is not entirely clear, the lack of unambiguous archeological evidence producing a wide range of speculation. Shepard argues there could have been no single or sudden cause, but instead a gradual, widespread giving way of late Paleolithic practices of hunting and gathering to Neolithic cultivation of grains and husbandry of goats and pigs, making possible sedentarization and the city-states that would become the platform for subsequent civilization.[30] Livingston, who ties domestication with reliance on technology, extends the process much farther, inasmuch as Paleolithic hunters' dependence on tools and fire preceded the development of agriculture by several millennia.[31] At the other extreme, Nietzsche describes man's self-domestication—an event "so new, profound, unheard of, enigmatic, contradictory, *and pregnant with a future* that the aspect of the earth was essentially altered"[32]—as a transformation that could not have happened gradually: it "did not represent an organic adaptation to new conditions but a break, a leap, a compulsion, an ineluctable disaster" that came about in response to the swift acts of intertribal violence and conquest that Nietzsche believed were necessary to form the first stable human civilizations.[33]

Scholars from various disciplines have attempted to solve this mystery.[34] But wherever the truth may lie, Shepard, Livingston, and Nietzsche seem to be correct in implying that there is no simple economic explanation for the hegemony of sedentary domestication over other cultural possibilities. Neither can the domestication of animals, which burgeoned roughly ten thousand years ago, be explained by economic considerations alone.[35] Stereotypical conceptions of "cave men" to the contrary, it has been argued by many students of the Mesolithic age that food was likely plentiful and attainable for most pre-agricultural hunter-gatherers; Neolithic population pressures on the food supply were more likely an effect of agricultural sedentariness, not its cause.[36] Successful hunters and gatherers must have a sophisticated understanding of ecology and biology, so the requisite knowledge of other animals' social and breeding behaviors must have been available long before the advent of Neolithic husbandry. Claims that climatic or other ecological events— such as the end of the Wurm glaciation and its effect on large prey animals—precipitated the need for the radical economic shift to domestic agriculture are only ambiguously supported by the archeological data. And finally, it can be argued that the more desirable agricultural properties of farm animals are relatively late *products* of generations of domestic breeding that could not have been anticipated at the inception of their domestication.[37]

These facts have led some cultural geographers and psychologists of religion to suggest that the domestication of other animals may have originated in a religious rather than an economic context, the earliest domesticates perhaps having been used for the purpose of *sacrifices*. While controversial,[38] the suggestion is potentially fruitful because the mythological structures surrounding early sacrificial rites evidence how ancient are the tensions between human culture and animality, and points toward a possible continuity between animal sacrifice and later ethical reasoning.

The Paleolithic hunt, rather than the ritualistic slaughter of domesticated animals in the Neolithic age, is arguably the earliest form of animal sacrifice. As Shepard writes:

> The variety of spiritual attention given by different tribes to all the steps of hunting in its many forms is immense. In all cases, however, men are engaged in more than a merely physical food-getting activity, for in hunting they are immersed in their most deeply held spiritual and aesthetic conceptions. Spiritual preparation for the hunt often takes several days; both ceremonial and practical details of daily life are prescribed. Exceptions to a formal style of hunting are found in areas of collision between hunting societies and civilized technology, where cultural deterioration has led to the breakdown of customs and to wanton killing.
>
> The magic and religion in primitive ritual reveal fundamental components of the hunter's attitude. The organized ceremony simultaneously serves not only a magic and a religious purpose, but ecological and social functions as well. It is aimed at maintaining equilibrium in the total situation. The whole of life, corporeal and spiritual, is to be affected.[39]

But while it seems obviously correct that hunting is likely to have had spiritual significance in early hunting cultures, as it does in those few that survive, two aspects of the ritual-mythological context surrounding the sacrament of the hunt indicate that its psychology is more ambivalent than Shepard indicates. First, one finds in the ancient myths of many hunting cultures that the details of the hunting ritual are relayed to humans as part of a pact reached between hunter and prey, or between a shaman and the "master of the animals"; prey species are thus not unwitting victims of human hunters, but are complicitous in the cycle of life and death, "willed gifts" to human hunters.[40] Second, several rituals surrounding the kill, such as the obligation that the hunters immediately consume certain vital organs and cover any blood or entrails that are spilled, suggest an almost childlike will to mask the full reality of the prey's death.[41] Thus despite the rosy picture Shepard paints of the hunter's mature attitudes toward the cycle of life,[42] these myths and rituals suggest that among our Paleolithic ancestors there were at least seeds of uneasiness with the reality of having to live by the death of other animals, and a corresponding *need* to turn the kill into a sacrifice.[43] If so, the obligation to conduct the hunt as a sacrament is correlative to the hunter's dependence on culture to relieve him of the guilt of the kill.

The transition from the sacrificial rites of hunting cultures to the institutionalized, ritualized sacrifice of domesticated animals is apparently accomplished by the enigmatic but universal phenomenon of totemism, an institution so profound that Sigmund Freud in his famous analysis saw its deciphering to be the key to understanding the origins of civilization. Among tribal societies, totemic institutions create a system of identification between social groups—families and clans—and animal species or other natural forms. A group's totem often functions as an object of ancestral reverence, thus engendering a proscription against the common exploitation of members of its species. It may seem understandable that the notion of *alliance* between human and animal that pervades early hunting cultures should evolve into a notion of *kinship* between a clan and its totem animal; but other aspects of the totem are perplexing. Especially mysterious is the exception to the general taboo against members of a clan harming or eating its totem animal: the *totem feast*, an obligatory, ritualized communal sacrifice in which the community as a whole mourns the totem while sharing in the guilt for the totem's death. As Freud makes clear, the more obvious sociological and economic interpretations of totemism will be at a loss to explain this phenomenon;[44] even those who have offered more philosophical accounts of totemic wisdom seem unable to account for the function of the totem's ritual sacrifice.[45] Thus, while Freud's own Oedipal interpretation of the totem may appear extravagant, some type of psychological explanation seems necessary.

One possible explanation—suggested by Freud's review of contemporary literature—is continuous with what hunting mythologies seem to reveal about pre-agricultural cultures, and with some interesting interpretations of later sacrificial rituals. Freud, drawing on the work of philologist and archeologist William Robertson Smith, summarizes the mechanics of the totem sacrifice in this way:

> The clan is celebrating the ceremonial occasion by the cruel slaughter of its totem animal and is devouring it raw—blood, flesh and bones. The clansmen are there, dressed in the likeness of the totem and imitating it in sound and movement, as though they are seeking to stress their identity with it. Each man is conscious that he is performing an act forbidden to the individual and justifiable only through the participation of the whole clan; nor may anyone absent himself from the killing and the meal. When the deed is done, the slaughtered animal is lamented and bewailed. The mourning is obligatory, imposed by dread of a threatened retribution . . . Its chief purpose is to disclaim responsibility for the killing. But the mourning is followed by demonstrations of festive rejoicing: every instinct is unfettered and there is license for every kind of gratification . . . What are we to make . . . of the prelude to this festive joy—the mourning over the death of the animal? If the clansmen rejoice over the killing of the totem—a normally forbidden act—why do they

mourn over it as well? . . . The clansmen acquire sanctity by consuming the totem: they reinforce their identification with it and one another.[46]

Robertson Smith emphasizes that it is through the ritual sacrifice and consumption of the totem that the community is bound together in its blood-guiltiness for the murder of the animal; but in the festive celebration of this rite, the individual is "sanctified," freed of the burden of guilt through ecstatic identification with the communal whole. Thus, in a way analogous to the psychological function of hunting mythology, the totem sacrifice is a mechanism for articulating the individual's dependence on culture as the means to relieve his guilt for the exploitation of the animal.[47]

As Marian Scholtmeijer argues, based on the work of René Girard, this same logic is revealed in the sacrifices of post-totemic, agricultural societies. The urgency and intensity of these sacrifices takes a quantum leap, however, with the *excessive anthropomorphism* that accompanies fully domesticated civilization:

> Clearly humankind cannot endlessly impose its own myths upon nature without cost. At some point in time or in the chain of reasoning, the difference of nature from human constructions asserts itself and generates fear and anger in the collective mind. The animal makes a perfect object for the need to sacrifice which arises from that fear and anger, for it represents that difference which has caused the fear and anger in the first place and, at the same time, it sustains the anthropomorphism which has become so excessive as to call attention to itself. Rather than assaulting nature wildly in an explosion of emotion, the community reinforces the sanctity of its myths through controlled sacrifice. Ritual anthropomorphizes killing, where killing is an act most hostile to culture. By means of animal sacrifice, the community can mollify nature without risking internal disintegration.[48]

Following this logic, the sacrificial rites in planting and agricultural cultures increase in violence—in the demand that violence be done, in attention to the details of the sacrificial victim's death—in proportion to those cultures' acquisitiveness vis-à-vis the natural world. The hunt and the totem sacrifice are tame fare when contrasted with the gory maiden sacrifices of early planting cultures. With the advent of sedentary civilization, culture comes to require a constant background of sacrificial violence; for example, Gunther Zuntz writes that the early Greek *polis* "in its continuous worship must have resounded with the shrieks of dying animals; its air reeking with the stench of blood and burning carcasses."[49]

The more powerful the sacrifice, the more indebted the individuals of the community become to the traditions of the ancestors; thus, psychological domestication through dependence upon culture escalates through the growth of the sacrifice.[50] Inevitably, however, under conditions of domestication, the notion of animal as *sacred* gives way to *misothery:* domesticated animals themselves become increasingly less noble—dumber, clumsier, less perceptually acute, more manipulable—after generations of breeding for tameness,[51] and their increasing value as use objects reduces them to a state of thinghood.[52] As F. B. Jevons writes, "the domestication to which totemism inevitably leads (when there are any animals capable of domestication) is fatal to totemism."[53] The death of totemism thus paves the way for more transcendent forms of religious ritual and abstract forms of ethical reasoning, once the ties that bind the community can no longer be reinvigorated through ritual consumption of the sacrificed animal.

Of course, all these issues are enormously complex, and I do not pretend to have given an account adequate to explain all the nuances of sacrificial rituals. If, however, the core contention of the theories just reviewed—that the ritualized sacrifice of the animal attests to human beings' struggle with their apprehension at exploiting the nonhuman world—has merit, then it will add insight to the Western philosophical tradition's difficulty in accommodating the animal. At first, the connection may seem tenuous, given how remote and bizarre the practice of animal sacrifice seems today. But as Scholtmeijer concludes, the supplantation of bloody rituals by rational systems does not signify a break in human attitudes toward the animal: "The disappearance of animal sacrifice speaks less of the kindness of culture and more of its imperialism. The actual domestication of animals, the expansion of humanity into wild regions of the earth, and the symbolic domestication of wild animals by means of empirical objectivity may well negate the need for sacrifice but only because these processes supersede the natural prohibition against appropriation."[54] Moreover, there are echoes of the practice of sacrifice throughout the Western tradition. As Zuntz's comment reminds us, religious sacrifice of animals was ubiquitous in pre-Christian Greece—the cradle of Western philosophical thought;[55] we should not ignore that Socrates' dying words concerned the rooster he owed to Asclepius. Christianity itself and other Western religions are laden with imagery that recalls earlier pagan rites: the second and third persons of Christianity's trinity are symbolically referenced by *the lamb* and *the dove*—two domesticated animals used in early sacrificial rituals. The mystery of the Eucharist takes the consumption of the sacrifice to a transcendent extreme. Furthermore, it is noteworthy that lab animals killed in the course of research are referred to as having been "sacrificed," evidence that the sanctifying power of ritualized killing can still hold, even in the realm of modern science.[56]

Most important for our analysis is what can be described as a *sacrificial dimension* to a fundamental feature of Western ethics that was noted in Part II. Recall in Chapter 5 the essential similarity observed in the ethical philosophies of Aristotle and Kant (and several figures in between): both assert that the possession of rationality is the defining attribute of human beings, and that non-rational beings—including non-human animals and the rest of the natural world—exist by nature *for the sake of* rational humans. We are now in a position to appreciate that in these ideas we find *the logic of sacrifice perfected: all rational humans exist in perpetual communion, freed of any possible guiltiness for their exploitation of the natural world because it exists for human ends.*[57] The modern West may have forsaken the knife and the altar, but only because this way of apprehending the relationship between the rational human agent and the nonhuman animal renders the bloody rituals of earlier civilization superfluous.

In Chapter 8, we saw that Derrida discerns a "sacrificial structure" in traditional ethical models, which leave open a place "for a noncriminal putting to death" of the animal; he notes that Heidegger and Levinas fail to transcend the humanism of the tradition "*to the extent that they do not sacrifice sacrifice.*" We can now reevaluate extensionist arguments for the abolition of animal exploitation as attempting what Heidegger and Levinas did not venture: by employing standard ethical theories to reproblematize what the sacrificial structures of traditional ethics rationalize, *extensionism amounts to the sacrifice sacrificing itself*—an instance of what Nietzsche termed "*the self-overcoming of morality.*"[58] And therein lies the real value of the recent extensionist debate over animals. If it is viewed as the end of the question of the moral status of animals, it cannot fail—as we saw in Chapter 7—to produce incomplete results; but when viewed instead as the beginning of the task of rethinking the animal, it can be appreciated as a necessary transitional stage that prepares the ground for critical reflection on the larger "sacrificial" context in which the very ethical models used by extensionists came into being.

## "Going Feral"

Although the image of domestication may be a fitting one to describe the effects of civilization upon our animality, its meaning when applied to human beings is somewhat imprecise. As Shepard reminds us, when applied to animals the term implies more than simply taming a wild being's impulses: it signifies an actual genetic modification of a species through generations of selective breeding. While there is some evidence to suggest that modern humans bear a biological relationship to our Paleolithic ancestors analogous to that borne by domesticated animals to their wild counterparts,[59] Shepard argues that modern humans' retention of intra-specific social and communication abilities—which are distorted and degraded in domesticates—proves that while we may be *civilized*, we are not truly domesticated.[60] Even those who have interpreted human civilization as a literal form of domestication seem hopeful that it does not represent an irreversible, constitutional change to the human species, but something more akin to an *illness*. For example, the language of "health" and "sickness" pervades Nietzsche's writing, and his affirmative philosophy is premised on the possibility of human convalescence: "The domestication (the 'culture') of man does not go deep . . . The 'savage' (or, in moral terms, the evil man) is a return to nature—and in a certain sense his recovery, his *cure* from 'culture.'"[61] And in a similar vein, Livingston writes, "'There is,' [Shepard] concludes, 'a secret person undamaged in every individual. We have not lost, and cannot lose, the genuine impulse. It awaits only an authentic expression.' I interpret this to mean that in our biology—our animalness—is the uncorrupted genuine impulse. All else is prosthetic overlay. We may *look* crippled, but we are not. The human domestication is culturally, not biologically induced. As sensate beings we remain intact."[62]

Whether nor not such optimism is warranted, and whether domestication is taken to be a literal or a metaphorical description of the human condition circumscribed by Western civilization, the invocation in these texts of a wild type of humanity—"our animalness," the "savage"—clearly signals a radical challenge to the status quo. Scholtmeijer notes that "because culture and domestication are deeply interlinked, the disruption caused by the legitimization of wildness is profound,"[63] and it is precisely this objective of "legitimizing wildness" that serves as a point of confluence for many of the forms of thinking we have reviewed. Post-traditional thinkers such as Nietzsche and some of his twentieth-century heirs, as well as Shepard, Livingston, and other ecophilosophical thinkers, raise the prospect that the consummate embodiments of humanity lie beyond what has been actualized within the history of civilization—not at the end of some civilizing teleology, but outside the process of civilization altogether. This challenge can be illuminated by noting its relationship to the debate over animals. Again using the animal as a mirror, we

can envision those who have confronted the limitations of extensionism—who recognize that the moral demands the animal evokes cannot
be addressed properly by the sacrificial structures of traditional thought—
as struggling against the chains of civility while trying to heed the summons of the wild. If these chains may be described as the confines of
domestication, then perhaps, as Brian Luke suggests, those who search for
a post-extensionist animal ethic are placed "in the position of *feral animals*, formerly domesticated but now occupying a semiwild state on the
boundaries of hierarchical civilization."[64]

The image of human ferality is intriguing, but certainly ambiguous—and as we shall see, fundamentally problematic. What exactly
would wild, extra-cultural, post-domesticated human reality look like,
and what does it imply for our relationship with other animals? Such
questions have long been a matter of considerable speculation, with the
possibilities seeming to run in opposing directions. First, if the sacrificial structures of domesticated civilization serve to mollify any guiltiness associated with the exploitation of the nonhuman world, thereby
facilitating the continuation of the exploitation, then post-sacrificial
ferality might conjure an Edenic vision in which animal exploitation is
forsaken, a state of innocent kinship with other animals, perhaps re-
creating something that anteceded humanity's fall into civility.[65] However, rejecting in this way what has been traditionally associated with
our humanity might also amount to rejecting an essential part of our
animality. Perhaps it is not the mollification of guilt but the guilt itself
that needs to be transcended. In that case, human ferality, while standing in opposition to the sacrificial prosthetics of civilization, might
guiltlessly embrace the violence toward other animals that our own animal nature requires, something more at home in mythological Arca-
dia—where Dionysus and the satyrs were known to romp—than Eden.

This second interpretation of human wildness is, of course, the
Nietzschean option. The theme of contrasting a more brutal depiction
of human ferality to both the constructs of culture and a more sedate,
pastoral interpretation of "natural" human existence appears early in
Nietzsche's work, as seen in this passage from *The Birth of Tragedy:*

> The satyr, like the idyllic shepherd of more recent times, is the offspring
> of a longing for the primitive and the natural; but how firmly and fear-
> lessly the Greek embraced the man of the woods, and how timorously
> and mawkishly modern man dallied with the flattering image of a senti-
> mental, flute-playing, tender shepherd! . . . The satyr chorus . . . repre-
> sents existence more truthfully, really, and completely than the man of
> culture does who ordinarily considers himself as the only reality . . . The

idyllic shepherd of modern man is merely a counterfeit of the sum of cultural illusions that are allegedly nature; the Dionysian Greek wants truth and nature in their most forceful form—and sees himself changed, as by magic, into a satyr.[66]

Nietzsche would go on to use the image of the Dionysian throughout his subsequent work as an icon for all that stands opposed to the domesticated moral ideals of the tradition, reflecting his commitment to, in the words of his Zarathustra, *remain true to the meaning of the earth*—an attempt to reaffirm the body, the "instincts," the animal within us, and nature itself in the face of the anti-natural forces of domesticating civilization.

While Nietzsche does not explicitly invoke the term *ferality*, his understanding of the relationship between civilized humans and the natural world seems to make the image of an animal turning feral an appropriate icon for his project of overcoming conventional morality: "There has never yet been a natural humanity. The scholasticism of un- and *anti*-natural value is the rule, is the beginning; man reaches nature only after a long struggle—he never 'returns'—Nature: i.e., daring to be immoral like nature."[67] In other words, if all that we have known as "humanity" has existed under conditions of civil domestication, then, like a loosed dog, to go wild is to experience something we have never known. However, this also implies that there is no actual model of extra-cultural humanity on which to base an understanding of human ferality, making the matter necessarily speculative and subject to cultural biases about the nature of animality in general.

If morality is a symptom of domestication, then satyric human ferality can only signify a state of being "immoral like nature," whether this implies innocent amorality, or a more mischievous anti-morality. In either case, the additional animal imagery that Nietzsche associates with human ferality conjures an image that is violent and disturbing: as we saw above, the human animal that is tamed by culture—or fights against the chains of culture to return to the wilderness—is depicted as *a beast of prey* (Nietzsche also uses the phrases "the blond beast," "the bird of prey," etc.). Again, any temptation to read Nietzsche's animalistic language metaphorically—that is, as not literally denoting the unconscionable violence of extra-cultural human existence—is squelched by his own elaboration on the term.[68] Of course, it has long been a subject of debate whether human beings are naturally violent and aggressive, whether in a "state of nature," as the contractarians put it, humans would be violent brutes or subjects of a peaceable kingdom—the former verdict likely to inform a defense of culture (for example, Hobbes), the latter, its critique (for example, Rousseau). Nietzsche, in his attempt to reinvigorate the tragic vision of the Dionysians, makes the courageous effort to fuse the acceptance of natural brutality with the renunciation of cultural taming.

However, because Nietzsche so vehemently segregates the moral ideals of the modern West from extra-cultural reality, he risks creating an image of nature that is as biologically unrealistic as the idyllic fantasy he opposes. There is certainly brutality and violence in the animal world and, as we saw in Chapter 9, ecophilosophers are correct to caution humane animal advocates against whitewashing this reality. But to define nature as a state of terrible brutality seems to echo the *anti-natural* projections of the anthropocentric tradition.[69] Moreover, Nietzsche's interpretation of life as essentially *will to power* seems to invite the charge that he is guilty of his own version of extensionism: while cautioning against projecting moral concepts and social "idiosyncrasies" (such as "guilt, punishment, justice, honesty, freedom, love, etc."[70]) onto existence, he shows little hesitation when projecting human political concepts (and pathologies)—the power-related concepts of *tyranny, aristocracy, slavery, ordering of rank*—to the realms of nature and biology.[71]

Of course, Nietzsche's understanding of power is more subtle and complex than is suggested prima facie. While there are several passages in which Nietzsche associates the will to power with political violence, it is clearly a much more generic principle that runs across physics, biology, and psychology, as well as human politics. All told, Nietzsche clearly is more interested in associating power with *affirmation* and *creation* than with the lust for *domination*. Perhaps his most interesting description is found in note 617 of *The Will to Power*: "To impose upon becoming the character of being—that is the supreme will to power"—a wonderfully generic description that applies even to the types of moral, religious, artistic, and scientific projects that Nietzsche rejects—indeed, to the whole range of human, and perhaps nonhuman, activity.[72] In fact, Nietzsche identifies the will to domesticated morality as a will to power,[73] and likewise the will to submit, obey, comply.[74]

Still, none of this nullifies Nietzsche's glorification of acquisition, becoming-more, goal-directedness, and his alacritous embrace of anti-moral, Dionysian terror, tyranny, and violence, and it remains questionable whether these aspects of his thought reflect nonhuman reality as accurately as he proposed.[75] Indeed, if they offer an accurate glimpse of what human ferality would be, then they might better serve to explain some of the damaging impact that humans have had on the environment than to indicate a model for our relationship to nature. As Livingston argues, there is an analogy to be drawn between the ecological effects of human migrations over the past several thousand years and the generally disruptive and destructive effects of feral domesticated animals, who have no natural niche in the ecosystems they invade.[76] Carnivorous *Homos*, more than a million years prior to the appearance of anatomically modern humans, made swift migrations across the planet, allowing them to inject themselves, like feral animals, into habitats in which they had no natural place. Mounting paleological evidence suggests that when the technologically superior *Homo sapiens* initiated such a diaspora (beginning some forty thousand years ago, well before the advent of agriculture or the Industrial Revolution) there occurred a series of rapid, large-scale megafauna extinctions—referred to by paleoecologists as *Blitzkrieg* extinctions—correlating with the arrival of these Paleolithic hunters at new hunting grounds.[77] Is this the will to power in action, an indication of how wild, nomadic humans would comport themselves toward other animals? If so, a turn to ferality today would totalize the ecological devastation wrought by domesticated civilization.

Some may object that the behavior of early humans is as "natural" as that of any other animal, and that one cannot consistently advocate wildness while condemning the inevitable impact of human wildness on other life forms. But while species extinctions are natural phenomena, none short of those resulting from catastrophic environmental events rival the scope and swiftness of those brought about by human territorialization. With this in mind, it can be argued that the political and ecological manifestations of human power and domination are quite alien to the nonhuman world, in all its amoral glory. This is Livingston's position, grounded not on an effort to project humane moral values onto the natural world, but rather on his resistance to those students of nature who employ competitive economic models to interpret the behavior of other animals. He questions the "Victorian chauvinism" of terms frequently applied to animal behavior by laypersons and biologists alike: aggression, competition, dominance and submission, hierarchy, territoriality; when such terms are appropriate, they describe behaviors that in general are pathological among wild social animals, often reactions to unusual stressors.[78] Alternatively, Livingston suggests that the language of *cooperation, reciprocity,* and *compliance* may constitute a biologically sounder framework for interpreting the wild animal: "I am satisfied that it is interspecies compliance that, in effect, maintains and sustains the complex interwoven fabric of natural communities and association, and the integrity of regions and biomes . . . Competition could never achieve results so ineffably perfect, because competition is about rivalry and striving. No horseshoe crab or bustard or buffalo of my acquaintance ever strove, so far as I can tell. But each complied, in living and dying, with the needs and requirements of its community, by the simplest and most beautiful of expedients—by being."[79]

There is a will to power at work in the integrity to which Livingston refers: an affirmation of biotic stability in the face of the disintegrating flux of other natural forces. Livingston names this will the *"compulsion to comply,"* and he asserts it as a trans-specific, inherent biological principle that underlies all forms of social order—including the ones striven for by human beings.[80] In addition to providing an interesting platform for recognizing the continuity of human moral behavior and animal reality, the notion that there lies beneath the surface of our moral constructs a biological compulsion to *comply* suggests the possibility of very different types of human ferality from the more brutal one implied by Nietzsche's analysis. Such a possibility is developed by Luke, who, as noted above, invokes the concept of ferality to describe the effort to move beyond extensionist animal advocacy.

Like Livingston and Nietzsche, Luke identifies Western ethical models as mechanisms of human self-domestication, patriarchal impositions of rational control upon our emotional selves. However, he asserts that within the feral alternative to these mechanisms it is not a lust for power and conquest that is unleashed, but instead "our officially circumscribed compassion for animals."[81] Rationalistic ethical systems are not needed to protect the animal, but are constructed precisely to subvert our natural emotional revulsion at the mutilation of other animals, and thereby pave the way for the praxis of institutionalized animal exploitation. Luke argues that extensionist arguments do not fail because they effect a humane domestication of the animal, but rather—echoing the point made above about the sacrificial nature of traditional ethical models—because they reinforce the structures of domination that tame our native sympathy to the human-animal connection: "So long as we remain committed to animal liberation, yet also see the direct sympathetic responsiveness of individual humans to animal suffering as undependable, we will be drawn toward authoritarian structures that promise this taming, through the domination of emotion by reason, selfishness by patriarchal ethics, and people by political authorities and their philosophical advisors."[82]

## Conclusion

So where does this leave us? Does the quest for a post-domesticated relationship with other animals—and our own animality—spell enhanced compassion, or the rejection of humaneness? José Ortega y Gasset asserts that the human being "combines the two extreme conditions of the mammal, and therefore he goes through life vacillating between being a sheep and being a tiger."[83] Toward which of these extremes would feral humans gravitate: the compassionate renunciation of animal exploitation that Luke defends, or the conscienceless amorality of the beast of prey that Nietzsche envisions? *Neither seems viable.* If, as was noted above, those feral animals that survive tend to overwhelm their environment, it must also be noted that the environment overwhelms the vast majority of them, who simply perish. Within the world of the wild animal both unchecked savagery and selfless pity are out of place—pathological extremes that are untrue to the nature of animality. That humans seem drawn to both when envisioning extra-cultural reality only underlines the real gap that separates us from the animal. Once again using the animal as a mirror, we are compelled to see that, alas, *we are not like them.* Just as subjecting the animal to our domesticated ethical models amounts to an abortive effort at anthropomorphizing, the naïve prospect of "zoomorphizing" ourselves—the daydream of returning to an idealized state of wildness—is not a realistic strategy.[84] While the post-Darwinian must acknowledge the influence of our biology on our morality, our dependence on culture of some type is not only undeniable, but necessary for our own survival and the preservation of the animal world. Writes Livingston: "The cultural prosthesis is not a mere whim, fancy, or conceit. It is necessary. Our physical and sociobehavioural evolution have brought us to a point at which we cannot do without it. We need it in order to function as social beings, in precisely the same way that animals we keep in domestication or captivity, for example, are dependent upon *us* . . . Our historic rejection of our own biology, which is commonly expressed as the human/Nature distinction, means that we require an artificial device to replace it."[85]

The form that animality has taken in *Homo sapiens* cannot neatly be fit into a simplistic dualism of domestication and wildness; thus, the human good cannot reside with either of these categories alone. The remaining question is whether there are viable cultural models that can allow domesticated human beings to maintain contact with those aspects of animality that civilization has marginalized.

# 11 *The Child, the Hunter,*
## *and the Artist*

In his search for an alternative to the prosthetics of domesticated civilization, Livingston argues that what is needed to ensure our healthy functioning is a model for reestablishing the "comfortably shifting experiential balance" between nature and nurture, biology and culture.[1] We might add: between the Dionysian and the Apollonian. In *The Birth of Tragedy*, Nietzsche interpreted the need for both of these principles in Greek tragic culture as arising out of an aesthetic urge, on the model of dissonance in music. Despite that so much of his subsequent rhetoric would focus on the creative will to destruction raised to the level of art in the Dionysian experience, it is clear that Nietzsche did not pose either his satyric or "beast of prey" representation of human animality as an ethical ideal for the human species. Given his cautions that power not be confused with being "unbridled," and that "natural" not be mistaken to imply an anarchic "letting go," his overall vision of human health may be more closely allied to the kind of balance Livingston describes.[2]

Apropos of our subject, consider the metaphors Nietzsche uses in "On the Three Metamorphoses," the first of his Zarathustra's speeches: "how the spirit becomes a camel; and the camel, a lion; and the lion, finally, a child." Here the emphasis is not a Manichean opposition between the domestic beast of burden and the wild beast of prey, but rather the distinctly human culmination: "The child is innocence and forgetting, a new beginning, a game, a self-propelled wheel, a first movement, a sacred 'Yes.'" For Nietzsche, the child represents the yea-sayer, who holds out the innocent affirmation of our existence in the treacherous world of becoming as the source of values. Livingston also uses the image of the child as a model for our relationship to nonhuman reality; he invites us to recover the "sweet bondage of wildness" that is captured in the child's free affective involvement with the natural world.[3] And, in a similar vein, Mary Midgley offers this: "When some portion of the biosphere is rather unpopular with the human race—a crocodile, a dandelion, a stony valley, a snowstorm, an odd-shaped flint—there are three sorts of human being who are particularly likely to still see a point in it and befriend it. They are poets, scientists and children. Inside each of us, I suggest, representatives of all these groups may be found. The decision whether to [curtail moral concern for the animal] is the decision whether to suppress them or take their advice."[4]

## "Going Paleolithic"

These uses of the image of the child offer an interesting model for the *individual's* reconnecting with the animal's world, traversing the boundary between civilization and nature. Midgley's statement together with the material surveyed in Part III suggests there is a range of other examples to be found among environmentalists, minoritarian political activists, and naturalists of various artistic and scientific stripes. But a philosophy of the animal must also explore whether there are broader *cultural* models that can institutionalize and foster their experiences, and counter the anthropocentric cultural forces that threaten the animal. Some have argued that an answer may lie in reviving possibilities from the collective "childhood" of humankind. Diverse thinkers have made a compelling case that a model for understanding our own animality and its relationship to the nonhuman animal may be found among the earliest discernible cultural constructions in our species' history, namely, the institutions of Paleolithic hunter-gatherers and those cultures that continue them—that is, the institutions that have been eclipsed by the hegemony of domestication. Such claims are sometimes heard from members of the so-called primitivist movement, and this may taint them with the suspicion that they constitute a knee-jerk reaction to the ills of modern civilization; as José Ortega y Gasset notes, it is a near-universal phenomenon that in times of cultural crisis there is likely to emerge a quixotic nostalgia for an imagined golden age at the beginning of time.[5] But as Ortega himself recognizes, a more substantive and philosophically significant possibility exists: the world of the hunter evokes "that early state in which, already human, [man] still lived within the orbit of animal existence,"[6] a state so elemental as to contain, at least in principle, *"permanent availabilities in man."*[7] If it is impossible to completely renounce our dependence on culture in favor of a never seen, extracultural human animality—if, indeed, cultured-ness is the form that human animality takes—then the products of that early state, if they indeed still are available to us, may hold the key to balancing culture and nature. In this vein, Shepard argues that hunting cultures, rather than representing just one possible interpretation of humanity, may instead embody those conditions needed to maximize personal, social, and ecological health: "In his relationship to other individuals, and in his ecological relationship to the whole of his environment, man the hunter and gatherer has a great advantage in that the social and environmental perceptions necessary for his way of life are similar to those in which man evolved, so that his life style is the normal expression of his psychology and physiology. His humanity is therefore more fully achieved, and his community more durable and beautiful."[8] Just as those who appeal to the image of the child attempt to extract from it a model of natural innocence, so too the appeal to the Paleolithic seems to carry with it the hope that there—as opposed to an illusory ferality—we will find the "natural" human condition: "'Natural' man is first 'prehistoric' man—the hunter."[9]

However, the underlying premise here must be scrutinized. Ortega asserts: "The true meaning of the term 'Paleolithic being' is 'hunter.' This was the essential fact of his condition—not that he hunted with more or less polished stones. Then, and only then, living was hunting. Later, innumerable men hunted, but none has been fundamentally—that is, exclusively—a hunter."[10] But, were early humans "essentially" hunters? Did the defining attributes of anatomically modern humans evolve within the context of a hunting mode of existence? While all paleoanthropological assertions are infused with some degree of conjecture, the theory that hunting played a defining role in the evolution of *Homo sapiens* enjoys wide support. The archeological evidence suggests that the definitively human dependence on tools can be correlated with the degree to which hunting played a role in the livelihood of Paleolithic humans; likewise, the complex planning and social organization that would be required for humans to stalk, kill, and butcher large animals could well explain our essential sociality and high intelligence. The brains and bodies of modern humans—much larger than those of earlier hominids—require a high-calorie, high-protein diet, which can be efficiently obtained from the consumption of meat. The nutrient density of animal flesh would have freed early humans from the constant gathering of other food sources, providing leisure for tool and skill development, and making possible other intellectual and social enrichment. In sum, a broad array of archeological fact and anthropological theory has been amassed in support of the conclusion that hunting made humans what we are. As biologist Valerius Geist summarizes the point: "Whether we love it or hate it, eulogize its blinding passion or condemn it, hunting was the force that shaped our bodies, molded our souls, and honed our minds."[11]

Of course, others have advanced competing theories of our evolution,[12] and the experts are far from consensus on a number of fundamental points. But one need not become embroiled in the controversies of paleo-archeology and evolutionary genetics in order to explore whether human health is better exemplified in hunting or agricultural society, where our definitively human attributes are maximized, and which attitudes toward the animal are ecologically sensitive and biologically realistic today. Geist's argument for the decisive importance of hunting culture draws on broad biological principles. He maintains that the upper Paleolithic hunter embodies the "dispersal phenotype"—that is the phenotype of an organism that is most adaptable to new and variable environments—of *Homo sapiens*.[13] Those early humans who first dispersed from Africa would be expected to exhibit the larger body and brain, vigorousness, and self-control that are typical of all species' dispersal phenotypes, and only beings with such strength and ingenuity could survive in the northern-most, periglacial regions of Paleolithic migration. There pre-agricultural *Homo sapiens* could survive only by hunting migratory ungulates, and thus, Geist concludes, we find in the Eurasian hunting culture of the upper Paleolithic institutions that reflect the maximized potential of the human genotype: activities that require and maintain great physical endurance; a relationship to the natural world that requires great intelligence, ingenuity, and planning; an economy that requires the individual to be competent at a variety of skills; and small, stable family units that require self-controlled and caring members.

Lest we suspect that the Paleolithic worldview was purely utilitarian, there is ample evidence to suggest that upper Paleolithic humans first experienced the type of sophisticated interiority that would be prized by later cultures as the life of the self-conscious mind. What remains of the art, ritual, and spirituality of these primitive hunters indicates the growth of emotional and intellectual concerns that transcend physical needs, and at a level of sophistication well beyond the fearful superstition one might associate with the primitive. Of special note are the Franco-Cantabrian cave temples, renowned for the detail and aesthetic sensibility of the paintings of animals and shamans that grace their walls, and for the sense that they offer a glimpse into the

Paleolithic soul. Consider the stirring interpretation of these artifacts offered by mythologist Joseph Campbell:

> What a coincidence of nature and the mind these caves reveal! And what an evocation it must have been that drew forth these images! Apparently the cave, as literal fact, evoked, in the way of a sign stimulus, the latent energies of that other cave, the unfathomed human heart, and what poured forth was the first creation of a temple in the history of the world . . . A temple is the projection into earthly space of a house of myth, and as far as history and archaeology have yet shown, these paleolithic temple-caves were the first realizations of this kind, the first manifestations of the fact that there is a readiness in man's heart for the supernormal image, and in his mind and hand the capacity to create it. Here, therefore, nature supplied the catalyst, a literal, actual presentation of the void. And when the sense of time and space was gone, the visionary journey of the seer began . . . The placement of the shaman in the crypt of Lascaux, the emphasized form of the dancing shaman of Trois Freres, and the plastic rendition of the bison pair of Tuc d'Audoubert speak volumes for the degree of esthetic sensibility of the artists of these caves, who were greater men by far than mere primitive magicians, conjuring animals. They were mystagogues, conjuring the minds of men.[14]

Other, more mundane, interpretations abound: perhaps these artifacts are more pragmatic than Campbell suggests, part of rituals to ensure successful hunts; others have reductively linked them to the evolution of semiotic structures in the human brain.[15] What is striking about Campbell's mythogenetic interpretation is how it dovetails with the argument of Shepard noted in Chapter 1: that through the agency of animal imagery human self-consciousness is first effected, and that the "coincidence of nature and the mind" is maintained only through the medium of the animal.

Shepard's analysis of human consciousness is but part of a larger theme that cuts across his work: his praise of hunting culture and his careful criticism of the values of agrarian and urban civilization. According to Shepard, the peasant and the city-dweller are forced to make virtues of their "stolid submission to drudgery," "competitive pride in family and possessions," "self-righteous manipulation of the environment," and "political sense of hierarchy and orientation to authority."[16] In contrast, hunting peoples

> are leisured, generous, hospitable. They do not stockpile possessions or children. Their only private property is personality. Among them, social reciprocity and sharing are normal events, not a charity. The aged are active, revered members of society. Their world philosophy is polemical, conservative, and normative, not opportunistic, progressive, or

existential. The men are deeply attached to place and home, yet are mobile and free of defensive boundary fixations. Among them leadership is advisory rather than executive. Action is taken by consent. Their populations are not expansive. Group aggression, plunder, slavery, do not exist. There is no political machinery, little feuding, and no war.

These are fully technological men, evolved and individually involved with the manufacture and use of tools. Tools and art came into existence with the emergence of human consciousness and are part of the rise to personal consciousness of each individual. Because he is a hunter, he is the most deeply loving and profoundly compassionate animal. Generally he is free of communicable disease and famine. The past and future are not sources of anxiety because of the stability of the natural environment and because the rate of cultural change is small. The concept of time is that of simultaneity, which engages every individual and all of the past in complete attention to the present.[17]

For Shepard, the contrast between hunters and the civilized descendents of planters ultimately signifies degrees of maturity. While the stress and superficiality of civilized life—isolated from the natural world in which the human mind has evolved to flourish—leave modern humans floundering in various stages of arrested immaturity and adolescence, the life of the hunter affords the individual the personal and ecological space needed for the human potential to evolve, free of existential crisis. Although the analogy between the child and the primitive hunter may have its place, for Shepard, venatic humans are anything but childish: instead, they embody the human potential at its most developed and mature.

Even if such high praise can stand up to scrutiny, the advocacy of hunting culture will amount to no more than a novel form of speciesism unless it can be demonstrated that, in addition to maximizing human interests, hunting culture bodes better for the animal than does domesticating civilization. As noted in Chapter 9, such claims abound in the literature of deep ecology, and they have been echoed by extensionists like Rollin, who writes that "few cultures have understood animals better or have more respect for them as ends in themselves than some hunting cultures, for whom the hunted animal is often an object of moral concern . . . and often even an object of reverence."[18] It may be argued that because of the hunter's need for detailed knowledge of the wild animal, hunting cultures afford epistemological space to the animal that is only being reintroduced to modern culture with the recent advent of ethology. More fundamentally, the successful hunter must occupy natural, extra-social space in the way that the wild animal does: by means of the hunt, a becoming-animal is effected.[19] As Ortega writes, "we will not understand hunting if we take it as a human fact and not as a zoological fact that man takes delight in producing."[20] The respect for the animal of which the hunter is alone capable comes from this intimate acquaintance with the nature of animality, something of a fundamentally different order from humane compassion for the prey.

The humane animal advocate no doubt will respond that it can only strike us as paradoxical that hunting—stalking, killing, dismembering, and consuming—should be the means to respecting animals. One must bear in mind the discussion of Paleolithic "Blitzkrieg" extinctions earlier in this chapter, and there is evidence to suggest that highly practical factors, rather than moral or spiritual concerns, mitigated comparable ecological impact on the part of later hunting peoples. For example, new paleoecological evidence shatters the idealized image of Native Americans as respectful users of the animal; it recently has been argued that it was only the existence of large "buffer zones" between warring pre-Columbian tribes—which provided safe haven for large prey like bison and elk—that prevented these megafauna from being hunted to extinction before the arrival of Europeans.[21] Likewise, in the modern world, many traditional peoples, having lived in apparent "harmony" with their environments for centuries, quickly decimate the wild animal species they depend upon once provided with the imported weaponry or economic incentives to do so.

Nonetheless, there is an enormous difference between the wild-animal-as-prey of hunting cultures and the wild-animal-as-enemy in agricultural societies—the object of Aristotle's "just war"—even if both constructions spell death for individual animals. As Geist writes concerning the ecological attitudes of agrarian cultures: "The agriculturist is . . . a victim of the weather, be it too much sun, wind, rain, or hail, as well as the depredation of wildlife. His view of nature changes. If he has milk, and therefore an assured protein supply, animals are no longer brothers, but enemies to be hunted and killed as an exercise for war . . . Only if wild animals continue to supply a significant amount of protein to the agriculturist do they not fall in contempt, as exemplified by the Zapotec, for instance."[22] Thus, the activity of hunting as institutionalized in agrarian culture is, like that culture's treatment of domesticated animals, human-centered: the civilized hunter is protecting territory, displaying social prestige, or seeking recreational escape from the stress of his own civility. However, as Ortega argues, hunting in its purest form actually "is a relationship that *certain animals impose on man*": "Before any particular hunter pursues them they feel themselves to be possible prey, and they model their whole existence in terms of this condition. Thus they automatically convert any normal man who comes upon them into a hunter.

*The only adequate response to a being that lives obsessed with avoiding capture is to try to catch it.*"[23] While domestication bastardizes animality, in the act of hunting—at least in the social and ecological context of hunting culture proper—the hunter does not subject the animal to a fate incompatible with its nature, and this fact renders the hunt a legitimate, if morally enigmatic, form of respect.[24]

Defenders of a humane animal ethic will not be the only ones to find something problematic in Geist's, Shepard's, and Ortega's nostalgia for the Paleolithic. If the logic of animal advocacy ultimately leads us back to prehistory, it might reasonably be objected that heeding the call of the animal signals not a liberal extension of moral sensitivity, but instead a very reactionary challenge to moral and social progress. Defenders of humanism might be eager to construct such a case; among nature ethicists, the ecofeminists have offered the strongest critique of the hunting ethic, presenting it as a violent and unnecessary product of patriarchal, androcentric mythology. For example, Lori Gruen offers this response to the anthropologist's account of hunting's role in human evolution:

> This Myth of Man the Hunter was created by mid-twentieth-century Western minds (influenced by post–World War II political hostilities; the creation, use, and continuing development of nuclear weapons; and increased consumption in "advanced" Western societies); it defined a biologically determined being whose "natural" behavior served as the foundation of culture. It is hardly a coincidence that the act of killing was what established the superiority of man over animal and that the value of such behavior was naturalized and exalted. The myth thus serves not only to posit an essential difference between man and animal but also to elevate man because of his ability to systematically destroy animals.
>
> Theoreticians, by creating a history in which man is separate from and superior to animals, establish a mechanism in which a separation from woman can be grounded. In this account of human social evolution, woman's body (being smaller, weaker, and reproductive) prevents her from participating in the hunt, and thus relegates her to the arena of non-culture. Woman's nonparticipation is conceived as naturally inferior . . . Constructed in this way, human social evolution establishes the subservient status of woman and animals.[25]

However, the target of this type of criticism is an understanding of gender power relations that is likely the historical product of agrarian cultures, and is not endorsed by the advocates of hunting culture just reviewed. Geist, for example, argues that the Paleolithic male was acutely aware of the value of women's cultural and economic contributions, and his dependence on them.[26] While acknowledging that a degraded status for women and animals can be tied to masculinist militarism, Geist argues that this way of institutionalizing male aggression is made possible by the domestication of animals for food and labor, and would be quite out of place in the world of the hunter.[27] Likewise, Shepard argues that while women are typically excluded from the hunt, the smaller size of families in hunting cultures liberates women from the lackey status they endure in agrarian societies; since the role of females is not defined as maximal reproduction, hunting cultures are more likely to afford matriarchal, "wise woman" roles for those beyond their child-bearing years.[28]

Recent feminist anthropological work seems to vindicate Geist's and Shepard's interpretations. For example, while the "Venus" figurines of the upper Paleolithic have traditionally been interpreted—mostly by male anthropologists—as fertility symbols or sexual icons, a plausible case has recently been made that they represent homage to the value and quality of the weaving and sewing mastered by the non-hunting females.[29] In a similar revaluation, primatologist Sarah Blafer Hrdy notes that as opposed to the aggressive, "alpha male" model of power that one might expect among hunter-gatherers, "quite a different style of leadership [is] admired there: the consensus-building, wise-man mode, with an aversion to discord and bullying."[30]

Hrdy's point reinforces another theme of the advocates of venatic culture: the emotional security found in the hunter. As Geist writes, "Hunters are not nearly as insecure as agriculturists and need not depend for their survival on the whims of weather, or the absence of agents detrimental to the crops. It is agriculturists, not hunters and gatherers, that consider themselves at the mercy of the supernatural. It is not surprising, therefore, that given the chronic insecurity of agriculturists, sorcery is well developed even in primitive agricultural societies."[31] It is the agriculturist who views nature and the animal as things that need to be controlled, defended against, overpowered. The power that the hunter exudes is not the obvious power that culminates with the domination of the prey, but instead the more subtle power to embrace animality as it is lived in the wild. In Ortega's words, "If we want to enjoy that intense and pure happiness which is a 'return to Nature,' we have to seek the company of the surly beast, descend to his level, feel emulation toward him, pursue him."[32] The will to power of the hunter is thus the will to comply with the larger reality of the animal's world.

## Sublimation and the Sublime: The Aesthetics of Mourning the Animal

While the arguments of Ortega, Geist, and Shepard—among many others—make a compelling case for the model of human-animal relations embodied in traditional hunting cultures, it would be quixotic in the twenty-first century to suppose that this model could be duplicated and put into practice on a scale sufficient to transform the preponderant cultural forces.[33] Indeed, these forces pull in the opposite direction to that pursued in the present work. While I have tried to demonstrate how essential the animal was to humanity's past and is to philosophy's present, no feasible vision of the future can omit the prediction that animals will continue to play a dwindling role in our lives. This verdict is already prevalent in popular science fiction. There it seems that in the coming centuries food, clothing, and other necessities will be synthetically "replicated," making both husbandry and hunting unnecessary, and other material uses of animals obsolete; our descendents will experience animals only virtually, by way of computer-generated, holographic projections; and, when the exploration of what lies beyond our solar system commences, the nonhuman species of animate life that human space travelers encounter in other parts of the universe will be remarkably humanoid in appearance and behavior. Alas, this fictional work also suggests that the debate over animals surveyed here will likely be eclipsed by the already active debate concerning the possible sentience, self-awareness, and moral standing of the artificial intelligences that human beings will create. Robbed of the animal-mirror as a source of self-understanding, humans will be forced to look at themselves through a darker glass: the technological creatures of their own design.

One need not rely on the intuitions of science fiction writers to conclude that the animal is on the way out. As John Berger notes, the sense that animality constitutes part of a receding past from which modern humans are increasingly estranged is already discernible in the science and art of the eighteenth and nineteenth centuries,[34] and more recent events have only served to intensify this feeling. Despite the vehement efforts of environmentalists and animal advocates, by some estimates wild animal and plant species presently are becoming extinct at hundreds of times the natural background rate as a result of human activities; it would require several million years for the planet's biodiversity to recover from the number of extinctions that humans have already caused. As the population of wild animals has declined in recent decades, the will to domesticate has taken new forms that further diminish the power of the animal to illuminate the extracultural. A growing number of bird and mammal species that in the past were exclusively wild are now commonly bred as domesticated livestock, and as wild fish populations become decimated by overfishing a growing portion of the seafood market must be supplied by farming domesticated varieties of sea life. The pet industry's efforts to maintain market interest have led, with increasing frequency, to the captive breeding of new animals from every family. The pressure to do so mounts with the intensifying competition presented by the toy industry, which presently produces a slew of robotic "pets" that mimic the behaviors of animals. This phenomenon, which so blatantly obscures the line between the technological and the biological, foreshadows the exacerbated commodification and transmogrification of animals certain to result from the technologies of genetic modification and cybernetics.[35]

All told, cultural anthropocentrism and the growing human population it serves presently threaten the independent existence of the non-human world so profoundly that it is not inconceivable that one day human experience of non-domesticated animals may be so rare as to be negligible. Efforts to forestall this conclusion to the story of animal life on earth are complicated by the fact that there is literally no place on the planet that has not been affected by human activity, confounding the very distinction between "natural" and "unnatural." Even among those who believe that animal reality possesses an inherent value and ought not to be subject to human manipulation, few will deny the need for unnatural intervention to preserve what is left of that reality. In Chapter 1, I described the term *wildlife management* as oxymoronic, the subordination of natural forces to human regulation embodying the essential spirit of domestication; yet, the near certainty that unregulated human interactions with wild animals end badly for the latter necessitates that nature be "managed" intelligently if it is to be preserved at all. Moreover, despite my arguments that extensionist reasoning is grounded firmly in the culture of domestication, and so is destined to produce an incomplete valuation of nonhumans, I also acknowledged that the extension of such concepts as moral and legal rights may be an unavoidable instrument for securing practical protection of animals.

The most impressive examples of such protection are our great parks and wildlife refuges. Yet one wonders how long they can stand given the economic and political forces mounting against them. Even as they do stand today, the experience of wilderness they offer is tinged with pathos, as the din of motor homes and snowmobiles competes with the song of the wild. Indeed, we face an inevitable dilemma: the more accessible we make the wilderness the more domesticated it appears. If we try to escape our super-civility by turning to those less fragile areas where hunting and other unmediated encounters with wildlife are ecologically feasible, our efforts are still unlikely today to afford anything resembling the experience of our Paleolithic ancestors. As wilderness and our access to it continue to shrink, we may have little choice but to rely on such impoverished and self-defeating devices as the "game farm" and the zoo to preserve the memory of the very existence of the animal's world. Whatever may be said about the merits of our modern menageries, it seems inarguable that their apparent necessity indicates the tenuousness of our connection to the animal's world.

Berger astutely describes the zoo as an *epitaph*, a monument to the animal's permanent marginalization.[36] Notwithstanding many recent efforts to make zoos more livable for animals and less artificial for their human spectators, and the now active debate over the function and ultimate purpose of zoos, their prominence in wildlife conservation is a concession that authentic encounters with animals are themselves an endangered species. Such realism ought not to be used as an excuse for abjuring the responsibility to strive toward a practical animal ethic; as I made clear in my critique of postmodernism, an adequate philosophy of the animal must attempt to ground the praxis needed to prevent the animal's world from being reduced to a mere extension of human culture. Likewise, excursions into the theoretical questions concerning how the animal ought to be valued have yielded an important critical perspective on culture, and we should implore philosophers and other thinkers to venture more such journeys. Nonetheless, we have good reason to suspect that neither our theoretical nor our practical efforts may succeed in preserving the independent reality of the animal's world. Thus, *how we are to mourn the resulting loss* becomes a question we are also obligated to ponder.

With those thinkers—reviewed in Parts III and IV—who locate the value of the animal in the challenge it poses to our canonical thought and the domesticated civilization it serves, this exploration has already begun. For while a successful mourning process obviously involves the catharsis of acute grief, more fundamentally it must also encourage a broader *taking account*: an attempt to come to grips with exactly what has been lost, and why. Indeed, the imperative to contemplate the possibility of a *post-zoic* world recasts the present analysis as preparation for the type of reflection that must attend the coming lamentation. However, such reflection cannot be a purely theoretical exercise; it requires a dimension of *atonement*, not only in the sense of acknowledging our complicity in the loss—which is certainly appropriate here—but also in the broader, literal sense of making ourselves *at one* with the loss, to make it ours, and to appreciate how deeply it affects us. As we saw in Chapter 8, Derrida appropriates this point clearly when—in trying to articulate what the revaluation of the tradition's "sacrificial" structures implies—he speaks of "the monstrosity of that for which we have to answer here." To think about the animal authentically requires more than the respect for logical and moral consistency that fuels ethical extensionism. Once we acknowledge that there may be something fundamentally problematic about domesticated civilization's relationship to the nonhuman world, we must be prepared to confront cultural and existential crises of perhaps incalculable magnitude. For Derrida, this confrontation takes the form of a rejuvenated philosophical activity; his attention to the animal is but a part of the deconstructive imperative to analyze our conceptual machinery: a ceaseless, excessive responsibility that refuses to yield the respite of a clear conscience.

This Derridian approach befits the problem of how to value the animal. By forgoing the hope of a happy resolution, it forces us to grapple with the conflicted history of human civilization, and both the benefits and costs of its alienation from the natural world. But, faced with the overwhelming responsibility Derrida embraces, atoning for the loss of the animal may easily devolve into brooding. Inasmuch as the mourning process is only complete when it allows us to work past the temptation to obsess morbidly over what has been lost, and to explore creative possibilities for reintegrating our lives,[37] we must ask in connection with our mourning the animal: If the animal is facing extinction, can a surrogate source of human self-understanding be found? If the hunt is no longer a viable option, can the drive to pursue the animal into extra-cultural space be sublimated without being perverted or destroyed? Pursuing these questions may not only prepare us for the possibility of an azoic doomsday, but also shed light on how animals should be valued in the present.

Unfortunately, the preceding analysis justifies a skeptical response to these questions. If ethical extensionism—captive as it is to the structures of domestication—cannot avoid producing an incomplete evaluation of animality, one should expect other attempts to sublimate the animal's perspective into existing institutions of domesticated civilization to be equally unsatisfactory. Yet there is one possibility I wish to explore briefly in closing. Nature ethics and poststructuralist thought have not been the only venues for renewed reflection on the borders between human and animal, civilization and the wild; various modes of *aesthetic experience and activity* speak to these issues, and they seem especially suited to the task. That there is an aesthetic dimension to our experience of animals is unmistakable. The elegance and sensual richness of many species is a profound source of aesthetic pleasure; as suggested by the discussion of Paleolithic art earlier in this chapter, animals were perhaps the archetypal aesthetic objects for human beings.[38] Since those earliest days of human culture, the animal form and perspective perennially have inspired profound works of plastic art, literature, and music. Today, in a strong parallel to the recent attention to the animal's moral standing, new uses of animals in art and new discoveries in animal psychology have forced reflection on a range of questions related to "animal aesthetics": Do other animals have an aesthetic sense and, if so, what is its relationship to that of humans? Can other animals appreciate or create anything legitimately termed "art"? What does our aesthetic appreciation of animals reveal about us?

The history of thought related to such inquiries is complex, and doing it justice would require a separate work of equal length to this one. Nonetheless, the prominence and meaningfulness of these questions today lead us to consider how important aesthetic considerations are and should be in our evaluation of animals. Several thinkers—including some extensionsists—have suggested that, quite apart from the question of the animal's proper moral standing, the aesthetic appreciation of animals is fundamental to their axiology.[39] Such appreciation extends not only to the distanced observation of animals and their depiction in art, but also to fiercer, more immediate encounters. Even the hunt—which was described above as the means of maintaining access to the animal's world that is institutionalized in non-agrarian cultures—invites aesthetic assessment because of its sensuousness[40] and narrative structure. Quite aside from its practical ends and moral difficulties, hunting may be performed and appreciated as a dramatic art. As Maureen Duffy writes, "all hunting . . . is allied to art forms like the happening and the drama or perhaps, in its extreme solitary and meditative Waltonesque manifestation, to novel reading." This alliance between venatic and aesthetic activity opens a possibility that should be explored: by means of aesthetic vehicles we may preserve the perspective on reality and culture that the animal embodies—a form of sublimation that allows us to, in Duffy's words, "identify and experience without needing to physically possess."[41]

The importance of this possibility is enhanced by the fact that aesthetic appreciation entails an alternative mode of evaluation to the moral respect due to persons and the usefulness of mere things—the dichotomy in Kantian ethics which, as was noted in Chapter 7, leaves little room for the appreciation of animal nature. Especially interesting in this regard is Kant's own famous description in the *Critique of Judgment* of how aesthetic satisfaction differs from these other modes of evaluation:

> That which *gratifies* a man is called *pleasant*; that which merely *pleases* him is *beautiful*; that which is *esteemed* . . . by him, i.e. that to which he accords an objective worth, is *good*. Pleasantness concerns

irrational animals also, but beauty only concerns men, i.e. animals, but still rational, beings—not merely *qua* rational . . . but *qua* animal also— and the good concerns every rational being in general . . . We may say that, of all these three kinds of satisfaction, that of *taste* in the beautiful is alone a disinterested and free satisfaction; for no interest either of sense or of reason, here forces our assent.[42]

While Kant reserves moral categories for rational persons, he seems to indicate here that the appreciation of beauty is grounded in the broader, more complex, and more ambiguous human reality that encompasses our animality as well. This claim, which has been developed by later thinkers,[43] points toward a theoretical possibility that must be pursued: that valuing the ambiguous animal—neither person nor thing—on the model of aesthetic appreciation, rather than moral deliberation, may be truer to both the animal's nature and our own.

In practice, however, the Western tradition's aesthetic considera- tion of the animal has been as problematic as ethical extensionism. The sublimation of the "need to possess" may indeed embody the ideal of humane culture; however, a humane animal aesthetic—much like a humane animal ethic—is unlikely to reflect the nature of wild animal- ity. While the use of animals in Western art is multifaceted, a conven- ient example of this problem is Edward Hicks's nineteenth-century work *The Peaceable Kingdom:* a meditation on the utopian prophecy of Isaiah 11:6–9,[44] the work is a series of oil paintings portraying soft-eyed children and domestic animals placidly coexisting with tame lions and other usually wild carnivores. Such depictions omit the wildness— indeed, *the animal*—of animals in favor of a more palatable aesthetic. Thereby, they mirror the implausibility of ethical extensionism: those aspects of animals that civilized humans find aesthetically pleasing will likely be those that are most assimilable to domestic culture.[45] As Baker notes, "No rethinking of human or animal identity is likely to emerge . . . if art and philosophy choose to present the animal primarily as mat- ter for human 'solace and pleasure,'" and thereby ignore what lies beyond domesticated existence.[46]

Baker's comment certainly addresses much of the Christian era, dur- ing which the less peaceable aspects of the nonhuman world were judged by most thinkers in the West to have only a negative value, both aestheti- cally and morally. In the modern age, however, the picture becomes more ambiguous. This is seen in the eighteenth-century aesthetic discourse of the *sublime* in nature—found in British and European literature and criti- cism—indicating an admixture of unease and awe with which the natural world comes to be beheld.[47] While such a view of nature creates a context for its more positive aesthetic evaluation, the ambiguity of the experience is nonetheless interpreted by many eighteenth-century thinkers as an indication of the extent to which human beings cannot be at home in the undomesticated world of the animal. Kant, for example, argued that when the human mind encounters nature's chaotically powerful manifestations ("threatening rocks, thunderclouds piled up the vault of heaven, borne along with flashes and peals, volcanos in all their violence of destruction, hurricanes leaving desolation in their track, the boundless ocean rising with rebellious force, the high waterfall of some mighty river") it will be moved to experience the sublime—*not* at these objects themselves, but at the corresponding apprehension of our own supremacy as rational beings, capable of apprehending the moral ideals of culture that no natural force can compel us to abandon.[48] As Marian Scholtmeijer details, early-nineteenth-century thinkers continued in this vein, conceiving extracultural nature as a morally objectionable enemy of culture that required the counteraction of human art. The resulting aesthetic is thus an extension of domestication: the world is a *garden* that human beings have a moral and aesthetic duty to tend.[49] From this perspective, the uncultivated world in which the wild animal is at home has no inherent value, and can at best serve as the counterpoint to the humanization of the world.

Later in the nineteenth century, Romanticism's open embrace of what is untidy in nature paved the way for a clearer break with the traditional assessment of the nonhuman world. The resulting revolution in aesthetics not only entailed a reassessment of the classical appreciation of proportion and symmetry—something brewing since at least the end of the eighteenth century—but also a rethinking of the nature of art. No longer just a skilled imitator of nature, the artist comes to be conceived as a shaper of reality; effective art no longer simply informs the viewer with a sensuous imitation of reality, but must have the power to transform those who experience it. Yet even in this postclassical aesthetic, traditional attitudes made it difficult to include the full extent of animal reality. For, whether conceived as peaceful beings worthy of human compassion or as part of an untame existence that humans must transcend and transform, both the art and ethics of the Western tradition have constituted the animal as passive object, and thus obscure the power of the animal *to act upon humans.* As noted in Chapter 4, the animal's lack of responsible agency leaves ethical extensionists little choice but to consider animals as "moral *patients*" or "moral *objects.*" To a similar effect, Berger notes the objectification of animals in nineteenth- and twentieth-century photographic art: "In the accompanying ideology, animals are always the observed. The fact that *they can observe us* has lost all significance. They are the objects of our ever-extending knowledge. What we know about them is an index of our power, and thus an index of what separates us from them. The more we know, the further away they are."[50] It is for such reasons that both Shepard and Ortega bemoan the inauthenticity of "photographic hunting," and insist that an authentic encounter with the wild animal must end with the kill; only thus, they claim, are we truly affected by the animal, drawn sufficiently beyond civility to taste that part of ourselves which is akin to the animal.[51]

Is it possible for art to reproduce this aspect of the hunt: the ability of the animal to impose upon the human being and to impel culture to reflect a broader reality? Is it possible today to cultivate a sense of the sublime that runs in the opposite direction of Kant's interpretation: a disquieting apprehension at the awesome power of domesticated culture and an attendant longing to engage the wider nonhuman world? Finding the answers to these questions will require an aesthetic analysis focused on the animal, rather than the broader aesthetics of nature that occupied the Romantics. For while the enormity of nature can alienate us by highlighting our insignificance, the face of the animal—at once different yet kin—can serve as the invitation for us to participate in the natural world. In some important recent artwork, we find artists exploring this aesthetic power of animals and, in turn, drawing our attention to the animal's marginalization and possible demise. This work includes late-twentieth-century attempts to use animal reality as an artistic medium in its own right, whether in the form of live animals, preserved animal corpses and body parts, or markings such as bite-marks or stains made by wild animals.[52] As Baker argues, these efforts reflect an appreciation of animal reality as something that must be experienced directly, without interpretation; here the animal is not used as a symbol of culturally inscribed meanings, but is instead to be confronted as "the face of the real."[53] Similarly, Scholtmeijer sees the use of animals in modern fiction functioning as a tool for grappling with the limitations of human language and conceptual schemes, and as the means for grasping extra-cultural nature: "Since fiction does not close off the world, it is in a unique position to give material representation to the inadequacies of language and thus to sustain without finality the multisided and conflicted being of the animal . . . Conscious of the estrangement of culture from nature, modern fiction restores value and meaning to the total animal which other modes of discourse disavow. Modern fiction works with the animal's resistance to assimilation into culture."[54]

If these characterizations by Baker and Scholtmeijer are correct, we may think of the aesthetic that emerges from the use of animals in contemporary art and literature on analogy with the rituals of hunting societies: both are cultural products that attempt to institutionalize our engagement with those aspects of animal reality that transcend culture. With this analogy in mind, we find that even outside the confines of formal art the model of aesthetic appreciation may offer insight as to how we should value living animals, both wild and domestic. Above, we saw this suggestion hinted at by Kant's description of aesthetic satisfaction. But we need not—and should not—remain captive to the details of Kant's analysis in order to pursue this possibility, inasmuch as his discussion is shaped by the technical role the aesthetic plays in his system, and would exclude much of what we today might consider relevant to developing an aesthetic of animality. For example, Kant's stipulation that judgments of taste be pure, "disinterested" judgments—that is, judgments that are not dependent on any practical objectives that would require the actual existence of the object—seems ill suited to our appreciation of animals or natural objects. Kant himself acknowledges as much: he argues that the lover of natural beauty is not merely pleased by natural forms, but has an immediate, intellectual interest in the existence of natural aesthetic objects; for example, one's aesthetic enjoyment of a flower or a birdsong would be radically altered were the object of enjoyment revealed to be a convincing artifact rather than a natural being.[55] However, he attempts to mask this tension with the implausible claim that the ground of our interest in natural beauty is not purely aesthetic, but rather is "akin" to the moral.

As the discussion in Part I highlighted, our experience of animals is complex and multilayered. Nonetheless, there are some aesthetic moments in which our perceptions of animals are unambiguously independent of moral and practical objectives yet dependent on the actual reality of the animal; for example, there is a delight that most persons experience upon unexpectedly encountering a wild animal, a satisfaction that is—at least initially—unmixed with inclination, yet only possible because of the concrete reality that is confronted.[56] As many writers and naturalists have reported, these experiences can be profound, and they demand an alternative to the Kantian analysis.[57] The comments of Baker and Scholtmeijer about animal-inclusive art provide a possible clue as to the direction this alternative might take. When we have an aesthetic intuition of a wild animal—whether in the guise of artistic expression or the layperson's intuitive experience—we apprehend a concrete living reality whose nature transcends the walls of culture. The satisfaction that attends these intuitions is not—as Kant implausibly claimed—a product of our moral sense finding a home in the orderliness of nature, but rather is only possible because initially they are not mediated by abstract moral or logical categories. In the Introduction, we saw Bernard Rollin describe extensionism as a product of memory, a Platonic recollection of what our standard moral reasoning has always implied for animals; perhaps in these aesthetic moments we are remembering something much older and deeper: our kinship to something that at first defies the conceptual categories of civilization.

Because domestication is just such a category, the case of domesticated animals is more complex. Practical interests in ownership, use value, and companionship are inseparable from the positive satisfaction we might feel in our perceptions of pets and farm animals. However, this does not mean that our aesthetic apprehension of domesticates cannot provide comparable insight to that afforded by wild animals. Regardless of what our moral deliberations determine about pet keeping or the use of animals in agriculture or research, our more immediate intuition of a coiffed show dog, a pig confined to a factory farm, or a genetically modified lab mouse presents us with a concrete, disquieting apprehension of the teleology of domestication. Such an intuition may—and should—inspire moral reflection on these practices, but more fundamentally it can embody a critical insight on the civilization of which both our exploitation of animals and our moral categories are a product. Both wild and domesticated animals are powerful mirrors: we discover something of ourselves in each.

These points deserve a more complete analysis, but even a minimal appreciation of this aesthetic dimension to animals is sufficient to show what it may contribute to the axiology of animals. Indeed, it will allow us to give a more forceful articulation of the conclusions reached in preceding chapters. While moral reasoning dresses the animal with our accoutrements of rights and duties, aesthetic intuition presents the naked reality of animals, and—unencumbered by the "sacrificial" structures of moral reasoning—is freer to offer a critical perspective on the civilized garb we don. Thus, when extensionist deliberation is used to draw our attention to the value of animals, it may obscure as much as it reveals. A philosophical argument that secured the rights of animals without acknowledging the insight that our more immediate intuition of animals can afford will have fallen far short of assessing the value of animals and how we ought to live with them. It may be argued, quite correctly, that producing such a total axiology is not the job of ethics; all the more reason for ethics to be set aside when we confront animal reality, so that the full power of that reality may act upon us.

That today this aesthetic power of animals is obscured, and that in the future it may only be available through the artificial medium of art, must strike us with a poignancy that ought to occasion the atonement discussed above. Yet this anguish itself has been captured in powerful ways by recent animal-inclusive art: who could miss the painful irony of a wild tiger shark preserved in a Plexiglas tank of formaldehyde? Indeed, successful works of art, which appeal simultaneously to multiple dimensions of our being, can be equal to the challenge of integrating the competing dimensions of mourning. When the need is felt to memorialize a great loss, we intuitively turn to art—whether great shrines or popular song. Many thinkers who have explored the subject suggest that a successful memorial does not sanitize history by trying to resurrect what has been lost, but rather preserves the complexity of what is to be remembered.[58] Thus, as the often-preferred means of expressing what cannot yield to simple analysis, art may not only be uniquely suited to explore our ambiguous and complex connection to the animal, but also to memorialize how much of that connection may be lost to us. Better epitaphs than the cages of zoos remain to be written.

## Conclusion

While extensionists make a reasonable case for extending moral concern to animals, those who would fully appropriate the value of animals will feel compelled to extend *themselves:* to "go Paleolithic" and embrace their full humanity by reconnecting with the animal's world in the way that traditional hunting cultures institutionalized. Yet, to see these cultures as a model that could be emulated in the developed West today can only be described as fanciful. With the continuing subsumption of the animal's world into human civilization—one face of which is, ironically, extensionist animal advocacy—we are forced to pursue sublimated forms of the Paleolithic drive. The prey may evoke the hunt from the hunter, but new institutions need to be built around this power of animals to impel us toward their world. For this process to begin, the preoccupation with rights and other ethical categories that has characterized so much recent thinking about animals must be set aside, and something more akin to the aesthetic must take its place. Such a move is discernible in various works of contemporary art, including fiction, sculpture, and installation pieces. There one finds an emerging animal aesthetic in which animality is not revealed as conforming to our standard evaluative categories, but is instead valued for the challenge it poses to them.

While this artistic sublimation of the animal is especially valuable because of the threats to the independent reality of animals, endorsing this aesthetic should not be confused with quietism. Indeed, the uniqueness of our aesthetic experience of animals is that it is not disinterested in the Kantian sense: it requires the foundation of animal reality, and thus can breathe life into the practical steps that will make encounters with real animals possible for as long as possible. Thus, over and above the plastic arts and literature, the animal today invites what may be described as a type of *performance art*. While there are still wild animals extant, we ought to encounter them in the flesh: we ought to seek them out and live with them, expose ourselves to their gaze and apprehend ourselves being apprehended by them. If today we are unwilling or unable to hunt, there is no surer way to appreciate the extent of our own domestication—and to instill a hunger for something more—than to feel ourselves vulnerable before a being that has no need for the devices of civilization. That such encounters are increasingly rare makes them more imperative, and their power to illuminate what must be atoned more profound. The time may well come when such experiences will have vanished entirely. While we grieve this possible loss, we must endeavor to re-create their effect through the critical vigor of our thinking and the aesthetic intensity of our art. In this way, the animal will continue to beckon us as it has since the days of the first human hunters.

# Conclusion

Having tracked the animal through the woods of philosophical ethics, we find that the spoor has led back to ourselves. The analysis of the debate over animals compels us to explore not only their nature but our own, and the various ways in which human cultures have interpreted our own animality. That projecting our models of rights and duties upon the animal illuminates the difficulties of those models and of our existence as moral beings—the reflexive dimension to our reflecting on the animal—is one of many finds we may not have anticipated when this journey began. Indeed, having joined the hunt for the proper moral standing of animals in the hopes of securing clarity, we have found instead that our prey is wily, able to divert us down unexpected and paradoxical paths. Perhaps the most unexpected paradox is to be found in the overarching theme that has emerged from the preceding analysis: while the debate taken as a whole makes a compelling case that the animal is to be valued, the extensionist arguments that comprise much of the debate may ultimately obscure, rather than clarify, the animal's fundamental value for us—namely, as a living bridge between our civilized world and the wider reality.

This theme emerged with the help of another unexpected discovery: the confluence of post-traditional and ecophilosophical thinking. Despite the clash between the technophilic amorality that characterizes much postmodern thought and the at times reactionary moralizing of ecological thought, these movements are allied in challenging the adequacy of traditional ethical models for evaluating our relationship to the animal, and in turn clarifying the good life for human beings. This alliance is clear in the works of Nietzsche and Livingston, both of whom interpret the principal ideas of Western ethics as symptomatic and per-petuative of an impoverished state of human domestication. By their reading of the biology of ethics, the rational agents for whom ethical theories have been calibrated—who pride themselves on their ability to make promises, respect each other's rights, and develop rational justifi-cations for their behavior—are tame creatures of culture whose degraded sensibility renders them utterly dependent upon their master. The institutions of civilization from which the anthropocentrist looks down on the animal take on a problematic appearance when viewed from the extra-cultural perspective of the nonhuman animal. Quips Nietzsche: "We do not regard the animals as moral beings. But do you suppose the animals regard us as moral beings?—An animal which could speak said: 'Humanity is a prejudice of which we animals at least are free.'"[1]

The confluence of non-extensionist thinking is also observed in its critique of human beings' relationship to the domesticated animal. As we saw in Chapter 11, Nietzsche's critique of the pastoral fantasy under-lines how far removed from nature is the patron of the domesticate. Shepard's analysis of pet keeping has a similar effect: "When children or adult neurotics make substitute people out of their animals they put demands on them that far exceed the animals' capabilities. The human authoritarian control exercised over pets creates an illusion of social adjustment. The animals are unconsciously expected to fulfill human roles; they are not thought of as species with their own purposes, differ-ent from men and deserving honor for their difference. Instead, they are pseudo-totemic fathers, mates, slaves, children, brothers, scapegoats, doormats, and sexual objects."[2] The spirit of these comments is notably similar to the analysis of Deleuze and Guattari, who describe pets as "Oedipal animals each with its own petty history, 'my' cat, 'my' dog. These animals invite us to regress, draw us into narcissistic contempla-tion . . .: *anyone who likes cats or dogs is a fool.*"[3] These comments ought not to be taken as justifying apathy at the real ills of systematic animal exploitation. But, at this point of convergence for those who are skeptical of extensionism, it becomes clear that if the animal summons us past the domesticating domain of ethics, it is because the complete picture of animality will not be found in the household, the cage, or the barnyard.

In Chapter 1, I noted that the roots of modern animal advocacy may be traced back to the advent of household pet keeping in eighteenth- and nineteenth-century England. But in Part IV we were led to the conclusion that the cat fancier who opposes vivisection and the dog lover who abstains from flesh—notwithstanding all their humane intentions, and the harm their convictions may prevent—stand in an incomplete relationship to animality. More incongruous still is the prospect that the model for authenticity is found in the world of the hunter, who does not content himself with fondling lap dogs but instead immerses himself in the stalking and slaughter of wild prey. The patron of the domesticate degrades animality by reducing it to what may be submersed in the psychological and social realm of human civilization, thereby robbing the animal of its power to illuminate a broader reality. In contrast, hunting culture institutionalizes the animal as a portal to the nonhuman world; if human "ferality" is a fantasy, the example of hunter-gatherers demonstrates that cultured humans need not sever their evolutionary bond to the wild. The yearning the hunter feels for the animal is not merely the desire to capture, but to *become*—to exploit one's full humanity by experiencing that part of it that is akin to the wild animal. (That this yearning for something beyond culture may eventually be expressible only through sublimated forms of art simply underscores the elusiveness of our prey.) None of this is to suggest that we should turn a blind eye to the mistreatment of pets and farm animals, or that we must take to the wilderness and shoot at whatever moves in order to appreciate animal reality. Still, it is telling that while the humane animal advocate feels compassion for the suffering animal, it may be the hunter who truly befriends the animal, and heeds its call.

What does this imply for that other type of *philia*, the love of wisdom, which I argued in Part I has so much at stake in the issues raised by the debate over animals? Is an ironic twist at hand: does admiring the hunter who heeds the call of the animal, and casting a critical eye at the super-civilized mode of domestication imply that one must reject philosophy? Ortega's answer to this question is heartening. He concludes his analysis of the hunt by describing the hunter as "the alert man": to succeed, the hunter must not fix his attention on sites he presumes will be visited by game, but must instead embody a "universal" attention that is unhindered by presumption. Thereby, the hunter imitates "the perpetual alertness of the wild animal."[4] However, Ortega goes on to assert that the extra-domestic consciousness the hunter achieves is not only essential for catching prey, but also for the invigoration of philosophy. In maintaining a critical stance with respect to the conventional and the comfortable, and tracking ideas to their most unforeseeable conclusions, the authentic thinker embodies the type of awareness that the animal elicits from the hunter: a being-open to the evasive and unpredictable realm of that which has not yet been assimilated by human civ-ilization. Ortega concludes: "Like the hunter in the absolute outside of the countryside, the philosopher is the alert man in the absolute inside of ideas, which are also an unconquerable and dangerous jungle. As problematic a task as hunting, meditation always runs the risk of returning empty-handed."[5]

If it was our hope in this meditation to capture the rights of animals, we may consider this risk to have been realized. But although we had no luck on the familiar paths of conventional moral thought, we remained alert, and our prey rewarded us by leading us through parts of the coun-tryside we might not have anticipated exploring. Therein lies the prize we were stalking all along. For both the hunter and the philosopher, the animal provides an enlivening chase.

# NOTES

## Introduction

1. Bernard Rollin, *Animal Rights and Human Morality*, rev. ed. (Buffalo: Prometheus Books, 1992), 75.

2. Ibid., 128. On recent attempts to make this a reality, see William Glaberson, "Redefining a Jury of Their Peers," *New York Times*, 22 August 1999, Week in Review, 1.

3. Tibor R. Machan, "Do Animals Have Rights?" *Public Affairs Quarterly* 5, no. 2 (April 1991): 163.

4. Bernard Rollin, "The Ascent of Apes—Broadening the Moral Community," in *The Great Ape Project: Equality Beyond Humanity*, ed. Paola Cavalieri and Peter Singer (New York: St. Martin's Press, 1993), 211.

5. I owe the use of the term *extensionism* to describe such arguments to environmental ethicist J. Baird Callicott, whose work is discussed in Chapter 9.

## Chapter 1: Why Care about Animals?

1. Dorothy Yamamoto, "Aquinas and Animals: Patrolling the Boundary?" in *Animals on the Agenda: Questions about Animals for Theology and Ethics*, ed. Andrew Linzey and Dorothy Yamamoto (Urbana and Chicago: University of Illinois Press, 1998), 89.

2. Marian Scholtmeijer, *Animal Victims in Modern Fiction: From Sanctity to Sacrifice* (Toronto: University of Toronto Press, 1993), 52.

3. Maureen Duffy, "Beasts for Pleasure," in *Animals, Men and Morals: An Enquiry into the Maltreatment of Non-humans*, ed. Stanley Godlovitch, Roslind Godlovitch, and John Harris (New York: Taplinger Publishing Company, 1972), 113 (italics added).

4. Mary Midgley, *Animals and Why They Matter* (Athens: University of Georgia Press, 1983), 112–14.

5. René Girard, *Things Hidden since the Foundation of the World*, discussed in Scholtmeijer, *Animal Victims*, 78–79. The topic of sacrifice is discussed further in Chapter 10.

6. Donald R. Griffin, *Animal Thinking* (Cambridge, Mass.: Harvard University Press, 1984), 16–17.

7. Scholtmeijer, *Animal Victims*, 84.

8. See Steve Baker, *The Postmodern Animal* (London: Reaktion Books, 1999), 96. On a related point, Baker (ibid., 16) quotes art critic Norman Bryson ("Mark

Dion and the Birds of Antwerp"), who describes the animal as "an excess lying beyond the scope of representation, as a reserve which the production of truth draws upon, but cannot exhaust or contain."

9. See John Berger, "Why Look at Animals?" in John Berger, *About Looking* (New York: Pantheon Books, 1980), 13.

10. J. E. Brown, *The Sacred Pipe* (Norman: University of Oklahoma Press, 1967), 95. As naturalist David Quammen has offered, such empathy can be cemented not only through the institutions of hunting, but also by the experience of *being hunted*. See his analysis of the role such "alpha predators" as lions, crocodiles, and sharks played in the formation of human cultures: *Monster of God: The Man-Eating Predator in the Jungles of History and the Mind* (New York: W. W. Norton and Company, 2003).

11. Clifford Geertz, *Local Knowledge: Further Essays in Interpretive Anthropology* (New York: Basic Books, 1983), 16.

12. See Marian Scholtmeijer, "Animal Presence, Metamorphosis," in *Encyclopedia of Animal Rights and Animal Welfare*, ed. Marc Bekoff and Carron A. Meaney (Westport, Conn.: Greenwood Press, 1998), 42; and Berger, "Why Look at Animals?" 16.

13. Giles Deleuze and Felix Guattari, *Kafka: Towards a Minor Literature*, quoted and discussed in Baker, *The Postmodern Animal*, 120. I discuss Deleuze and Guattari's analysis of becoming-animal further in Chapter 8.

14. The term *biophilia* was coined by biologist E. O. Wilson. See his *Biophilia* (Cambridge, Mass.: Harvard University Press, 1984); an anthology of biophilic thought can be found in *The Biophilia Hypothesis*, ed. Stephen R. Kellert and Edward O. Wilson (Washington, D.C.: Island Press, 1993).

15. Paul Shepard, *Thinking Animals: Animals and the Development of Human Intelligence* (New York: Viking Press, 1978), 1–2.

16. Evolutionary psychologist Nicholas Humphrey refers to these early hominids as "natural psychologists" whose understanding of the feelings and intentions of their peers was essential to their successful social functioning.

17. Shepard, *Thinking Animals*, 19–28. Berger makes a similar argument ("Why Look at Animals?" 2–3), noting that human encounters with animals who are "both alike and unalike" occasion self-awareness: "The eyes of an animal when they consider a man are attentive and wary. The same animal may well look at other species in the same way. He does not reserve a special look for man. But by no other species except man will the animal's look be recognized as familiar. Other animals are held by the look. Man becomes aware of himself returning the look."

18. Various other thinkers have offered compatible and complementary accounts of the origins of human consciousness. Shepard himself makes generous use of structuralist anthropologist Claude Lévi-Strauss's work, whose relevant arguments are encapsulated in his often quoted assertion that "animals are good to think." Berger makes similar use of Lévi-Strauss's work, arguing that animals are the original source of symbols and metaphors, without which many things might be indescribable by humans; see "Why Look at Animals?" 7–8. Griffin (*Animal Thinking*, 16) suggests that our concern for and curiosity about other animals are probably holdovers of early hunting cultures in which constant direct involvement with the animal world was essential to human life and

development. This theme is developed in detail by biologist Valerius Geist, whose arguments are discussed in Chapter 11.

19. José Ortega y Gasset, *Meditations on Hunting*, trans. Howard B. Wescott (New York: Charles Scribner's Sons, 1972), 98.

20. Scholtmeijer, *Animal Victims*, 3–5.

21. Ibid., 296.

22. Richard Sorabji, *Animal Minds and Human Morals: The Origin of the Western Debate* (Ithaca, N.Y.: Cornell University Press, 1993).

23. The details of Aristotle's position are discussed in Chapter 5.

24. This is the position of Immanuel Kant, who held that although we have no direct duties toward animals, their kind treatment is a moral good because "thus we cultivate the corresponding duties towards human beings." See "Duties to Animals and Spirits," trans. Louis Infield, in Regan and Singer, *Animal Rights*, 23–24. (Kant's arguments are discussed further in Chapter 4.) It is interesting to note that a correlation between empathy with animals and moral treatment of humans has been confirmed by modern psychology. See Elizabeth Paul, "Empathy for Animals," in Bekoff and Meaney, *Encyclopedia of Animal Rights*, 153–54; and Miriam Rothschild, *Animals and Man* (Oxford: Oxford University Press, 1986).

25. A possibility discussed in Scholtmeijer, *Animal Victims*, 52.

26. Marc Shell's position, discussed by Linzey in "Animal Welfare and Rights: Pet and Companion Animals," in *Encyclopedia of Bioethics*, vol. 1, rev. ed. (New York: Simon & Schuster Macmillan, 1995), 180.

27. Cavalieri and Singer, *Great Ape Project*, 3.

28. Martin Heidegger, *The Fundamental Concepts of Metaphysics: World, Finitude, Solitude*, trans. William McNeill and Nicholas Walker (Bloomington and Indianapolis: Indiana University Press, 1995), 189.

29. Morton O. Beckner, "Darwinism," in *Encyclopedia of Philosophy*, vol. 2 (New York: Macmillan, 1967), 296.

30. See the annotated bibliography to Henry S. Salt's 1892 *Animals' Rights Considered in Relation to Social Progress* (Reprint, Clarks Summit, Pa.: Society for Animal Rights, 1980), 136–66.

31. Ibid., 137 and 149.

32. See Alan Rudrum, "Ethical Vegetarianism in 17th Century Britain: Its Roots in 16th Century European Theological Debate," *The Seventeenth Century* 18, no. 1 (Spring 2003): 76–92.

33. See Marjorie Hope Nicolson, *Mountain Gloom and Mountain Glory: The Development of the Aesthetic of the Infinite* (Seattle: University of Washington Press, 1997).

34. Scholtmeijer, *Animal Victims*, 15–20.

35. Ortega, *Meditations on Hunting*, 108.

36. The first known animal welfare group was founded in England in 1824, the first antivivisection organization—also English—in 1875. This tradition continues today with some three thousand such organizations. These include not just the expected advocacy groups on behalf of pets and farm animals, but fringe groups dedicated to the preservation of bats, frogs, and insects, as well as hunt saboteurs and the terrorist Animal Liberation Front.

37. Salt (*Animals' Rights*, 4–5) cites Paine and Wollstonecraft as essential precursors to the concern for animals in the eighteenth and nineteenth centuries.

We should note that the political ramifications of Darwinism further advanced the process of liberalization: if, as Darwinism implies, human behavior is ultimately historically conditioned, then it is also malleable and therefore social progress can be made.

38. David Sztybel, "Distinguishing Animal Rights From Animal Welfare," in Bekoff and Meaney, *Encyclopedia of Animal Rights*, 44.

39. Harlan B. Miller, "'Platonists' and 'Aristotelians,'" in *Ethics and Animals*, ed. Harlan B. Miller and William H. Williams (Clifton, N.J.: Humana Press, 1983), 5–7.

40. Heidegger, *Fundamental Concepts of Metaphysics*, 188.

41. Such an understanding would seem to be precluded in a laboratory environment, inasmuch as most laboratory animals are "purpose bred" to be compliant with the needs of researchers, and so their behavior there reveals more about laboratory methodology than natural animality. See Griffin, *Animal Thinking*, 13.

42. Ibid., 14.

43. Paul Shepard, *The Tender Carnivore and the Sacred Game* (Athens: University of Georgia Press, 1973), 13.

44. Donald Griffin, *Animal Minds* (Chicago: University of Chicago Press, 1992), 5–6.

45. Ibid., 252–53. This point has been echoed by diverse thinkers. Consider Thoreau's comment (from a journal entry of 18 February 1860, quoted in Salt, *Animals' Rights*, 91–92): "I think that the most important requisite in describing an animal is to be sure that you give its character and spirit, for in that you have, without error, the sum and effect of all its parts known and unknown. Surely the most important part of an animal is its anima, its vital spirit, on which is based its character and all the particulars by which it most concerns us. Yet most scientific books which treat of animals leave this out altogether, and what they describe are, as it were, phenomena of dead matter." In a very different context, Giles Deleuze and Félix Guattari [*A Thousand Plateaus: Capitalism and Schizophrenia*, trans. Brian Massumi (Minneapolis: University of Minnesota Press, 1987), 257] argue: "A racehorse is more different from a workhorse than a workhorse is from an ox . . . We know nothing about a body until we know what it can do, in other words, what its affects are, how they can or cannot enter into composition with other affects, with the affects of another body, either to destroy that body or to be destroyed by it, either to exchange actions and passions with it or to join with it in composing a more powerful body." Rollin makes the point more simply (*Animal Rights and Human Morality*, 92–93): "we are too busy studying the creature's body to know the creature."

46. Of special note is the very recent revelation that the human genome may contain surprisingly few genes (closer to thirty thousand—or barely 50 percent more than a roundworm—than the once predicted hundred thousand plus), only a handful of which have been identified as having no correlates in other organisms, and some of which appear to have come to us laterally from bacterial life forms. These and other data have forced scientists to rethink the "tree of life" model that imagines evolution as a simplistic process of linear descent. It is now believed that the earliest stage of life on the planet was a chaotic period that involved a good deal of lateral transmission of genetic material among organ-

isms, a process that continues today through the mechanism of viruses. On this last point, see Deleuze and Guattari, *A Thousand Plateaus*, 10–11.

47. Rollin, *Animal Rights*, 94. See also Scholtmeijer's discussion of Schopenhauer on this point in *Animal Victims*, 35.

48. See Griffin, *Animal Thinking*, 35–36, 111–12, 116. See also Rollin, *Animal Rights*, 64, where he discusses the presence of pain-relieving endorphins in insects such as earthworms.

49. Because of his pioneering role in cognitive ethology, I focus here and in Chapter 2 on the arguments of Griffin. However, not all those thinkers who are sympathetic to the prospect of animal minds speak with one voice. For example, philosopher Colin Allen, environmental biologist Marc Bekoff, and ecological philosopher Dale Jamieson offer significantly different approaches to the question of animal mentation from that argued for by Griffin. See Allen and Bekoff's *Species of Mind: The Philosophy and Biology of Cognitive Ethology* (Cambridge: MIT Press, 1997). Clearly, cognitive ethology and the problems it raises for the philosophy of mind is an area of active debate.

50. See Berger, "Why Look at Animals?" 10.

51. See Scholtmeijer, *Animal Victims*, 41.

52. "'Eating Well,' or the Calculation of the Subject: An Interview with Jacques Derrida," in *Who Comes After the Subject?* ed. Eduardo Cadava et al. (New York: Routledge, 1991), 118.

53. Alistair S. Gunn, "Why Should We Care about Rare Species?" *Environmental Ethics* 3 (1980): 203, quoted in Marti Kheel, "The Liberation of Nature: A Circular Affair," *Environmental Ethics* 1985, vol. 7, no. 2, reprinted in *Beyond Animal Rights: A Feminist Caring Ethic for the Treatment of Animals*, ed. Josephine Donovan and Carol J. Adams (New York: The Continuum Publishing Company, 1996), 24–25. Kheel herself adds: "The frequent reference [in nature ethics] to an idea being 'intuitive,' 'counterintuitive,' or 'reasonable' is, at least, a partial recognition of the significance of intuition or nonrational thought in moral decisions."

54. Annette C. Baier, "Knowing Our Place in the Animal World," in Miller and Williams, *Ethics and Animals*, 61–62. See also Tom Regan, *The Case for Animal Rights* (Berkeley and Los Angeles: University of California Press, 1983), 133–40, for a discussion of intuition's role in moral judgment.

55. In a recent "road rage" incident following a minor traffic accident in San Jose, California, one of the drivers grabbed the other driver's small dog from her car and threw it into oncoming traffic—killing it—and fled the scene. Local police reported that they received more offers of reward money (totaling some $100,000) in an effort to find the perpetrator than they had received in connection with any other fugitive, including rapists and child molesters.

56. Psychologist Elizabeth Paul has surveyed the attitudes of both animal advocates and scientists who experiment upon animals, and found, among other things, that these parties generally share a common understanding of the existence of a "phylogenetic hierarchy" for mentation and sentience, but are divided over their intuitive sense of where moral lines should be drawn in this hierarchy. See "Us and Them: Scientists' and Animal Rights Campaigners' Views on the Animal Experimentation Debate," www.psyeta.org/sa/sa3.1/paul.html, 3 February 2001.

57. As animal law expert Gary L. Francione notes ("Animals as Property," 2

*Animal Law* 1 [1996], www.animal-law.org/library/anmlprop.htm, 11 November 1999], anticruelty laws almost universally contain explicit exclusions for all institutionalized forms of animal exploitation, thus leaving open the question of whether these practices can be considered cruel, or how much moral weight can be attached to the suffering they produce.

58. A 1995 Associated Press poll showed that 67 percent of the respondents agreed either somewhat or strongly with the statement "an animal's right to live free of suffering is just as important as a person's right to live free of suffering"; 71 percent of the same respondents said they ate meat, fish, or poultry frequently. See David Masci, "Fighting over Animal Rights," *CQ Researcher* 6 (2 August 1996): 676. The apparent inconsistency that this shows on the part of at least 38 percent of the respondents, whether conscious or not, invites Salt's comment: "It is of little use to claim 'rights' for animals in a vague general way, if with the same breath we explicitly show our determination to subordinate those rights to anything and everything that can be construed into a human 'want'" (*Animals' Rights*, 9).

59. Baker, *The Postmodern Animal*, 188.

60. Baier, "Knowing Our Place," 62–63.

61. Rollin, *Animal Rights*, 98.

62. Gary L. Francione, "Abortion and Animal Rights: Are They Comparable Issues?" in *Animals and Women: Feminist Theoretical Explorations*, ed. Carol J. Adams and Josephine Donovan (Durham: Duke University Press, 1995), 149–59.

63. Ibid., 156. As we will see in Chapter 6, contractarian arguments in the debate attempt to address this problem by including the animal perspective in policy matters by proxy.

64. See Scholtmeijer, *Animal Victims*, 14.

65. It is noteworthy that ecologists Paul Shepard and Paul Sears refer to ecology as a "subversive science" because it calls into question fundamental beliefs about the priority of human interests and desires. See Paul Shepard, "Ecology and Man—A Viewpoint," in *Deep Ecology for the 21st Century: Readings on the Philosophy and Practice of the New Environmentalism*, ed. George Sessions (Boston: Shambala Publications, 1995), 139.

66. Salt, *Animals' Rights*, 105–6.

## *Chapter 2: Broader Philosophical Considerations*

1. Famous examples in the Western monotheistic tradition include the first creation story in Genesis 1:26 ("Then God said, 'Let us make man in our image, after our likeness; and let them have dominion over the fish of the sea, and over the birds of the air, and over the cattle, and over all the earth, and over every creeping thing that creeps upon the earth'"), and God's proclamation to Noah in Genesis 9:2: "The fear of you and the dread of you shall be upon every beast of the earth, and upon every bird of the air, upon everything that creeps on the ground and all the fish of the sea; into your hand they are delivered."

2. See Chapter 1, note 32.

3. As R. G. Frey quips, "to everyone except rabid Cartesians (who, I expect, are an extinct species anyway), animals feel pain"; *Interests and Rights: The Case Against Animals* (Oxford: Clarendon Press, 1980), 63.

4. See Salt, *Animals' Rights*, 11–12.

5. Thomas Young (*An Essay on Humanity to Animals*, 1798, quoted in ibid., 153) makes the point plainly: "Animals are endued with a capability of perceiving pleasure and pain; and from abundant provision which we perceive in the world for the gratification of their several senses, we must conclude that the Creator wills the happiness of these creatures, and consequently that humanity towards them is agreeable to him, and cruelty the contrary."

6. Andrew Linzey, "The Theos-rights of Animals," in Regan and Singer, *Animal Rights*, 137–38.

7. James Gaffney, "Can Catholic Morality Make Room for Animals?" in Linzey and Yamamoto, *Animals on the Agenda*, 108.

8. See Aristotle, *On the Soul*, Book 2, part 1; and Sorabji, *Animal Minds*, 100.

9. Descartes makes a very clear argument of this kind: "There are two different principles causing our motions: one is purely mechanical and corporeal and depends solely on the force of the spirits and the construction of our organs, and can be called the corporeal soul; the other is the incorporeal mind, the soul which I have defined as a thinking substance. Thereupon I investigated more carefully whether the motions of animals originated from both these principles or from one only. I soon saw clearly that they could all originate from the corporeal and mechanical principle, and I thenceforward regarded it as certain and established that we cannot at all prove the presence of a thinking soul in animals. I am not disturbed by the astuteness and cunning of dogs and foxes, or all the things which animals do for the sake of food, sex, and fear; I claim that I can easily explain the origin of all of them from the constitution of their organs" (Letter to Henry More, 5 February 1649, quoted in Regan and Singer, *Animal Rights*, 18).

10. James Rachels, *Created from Animals: The Moral Implications of Darwinism* (Oxford: Oxford University Press, 1990), 174.

11. *On the Origin of the Species*, Chapter 2.

12. See Richard Ryder, "Experiments on Animals," in Godlovitch et al., *Animals, Men and Morals*, 80–81.

13. Machan, "Do Animals Have Rights?" 168.

14. There are many facets to this blow to the human ego, some with specific relevance to our relationship with other animals. To the animal's detriment, there is a discernible, reactionary intensification of misotheory in the early post-Darwinian world. For example, Maureen Duffy writes that "it's not surprising that the heyday for the circus coincided with the dissemination of popular evolutionary theories . . . We are the thing imitated, the master-copy, then our imitators are seen to be pitifully inept and our own cleverness is underlined" ("Beasts for Pleasure," 121). Further, as biologists certainly are not immune from the psychological effects of their knowledge, there may be, as Donald Griffin puts it, a "palliative" incentive "to shift attention away from the embarrassing fact of our animal ancestry by accentuating those aspects of science that are more akin to physics. This may help explain why so many appear to be so certain that consciousness and language are uniquely human capabilities" (*Animal Minds*, 253). Griffin's point may help explain the highly emotional (and apparently inconsistent) resistance that many in the scientific community have shown toward rethinking the use of animals in medical research. As Ryder argues ("Experiments on Animals," 80), for the scientist who continues to conduct research on

animals in the face of the evidence for continuity, "the only logical alternatives . . . are to admit that he is either pre-Darwinian or immoral." See also Hugh LaFollette and Niall Shanks, "The Origin of Speciesism," *Philosophy* 71 (1995): 55.

15. Hans Jonas, "Evolution and Freedom," in *Mortality and Morality: The Search for the Good after Auschwitz* (Evanston, Ill.: Northwestern University Press, 1996), 63.

16. Scholtmeijer, *Animal Victims*, 66.

17. Rachels, *Created from Animals*, 183.

18. David Hume, *A Treatise on Human Nature*, Book I, Part I, Section XVI. For Hume, the point was so fundamental that later in the same passage he considers it a test of a philosophical psychology's adequacy whether it can account for the thinking of humans and animals alike.

19. Griffin, *Animal Minds*, 12.

20. Griffin, *Animal Thinking*, 9.

21. Sorabji, *Animal Minds*, 7.

22. *Will to Power*, note 674 (Kaufmann translation).

23. Peter Carruthers, "Brute Experience," *Journal of Philosophy* 89 (1989): 258–69, quoted in Griffin, *Animal Minds*, 247–48.

24. Griffin, *Animal Thinking*, 94.

25. See Bernard Rollin, "Thought without Language," in Regan and Singer, *Animal Rights*, 50; and Peter Singer, *Animal Liberation*, rev. ed. (New York: Avon Books, 1990), 12.

26. Griffin, *Animal Thinking*, 40–41.

27. As Griffin argues (*Animal Minds*, 257): "simple human reflexes have tended to serve as 'type specimens' of instinctive behavior and to color our view of unlearned behavior as a whole. But perhaps it is unwisely anthropocentric to assume that this view accurately describes instinctive behavior in all other animals. The large genetic component underlying many sorts of animal behavior may not justify the conclusion that all instinctive behavior is a homogeneous category. In particular, the analogy to our own situation does not establish how tightly consciousness is linked to learned behavior as contrasted with behavior strongly influenced by hereditary constitution."

28. The point has been covered by several in the debate: for example, John Harris, "Killing for Food," in Godlovitch et al., *Animals, Men and Morals*, 103; Rollin, *Animal Rights*, 99; and Rachels, *Created from Animals*, 193–94.

29. Steven Sapontzis, "Aping Persons," in Singer and Cavalieri, *The Great Ape Project*, 272.

30. Leonard Nelson, "Duties to Animals," in Godlovitch et al., *Animals, Men and Morals*, 155.

31. See *Discourse on Method*, Part V.

32. Rachels, *Created from Animals*, 187.

33. Ibid., 189–90.

34. Rollin, "Thought without Language," 46.

35. Ibid., 49.

36. Rachels, *Created from Animals*, 190.

37. Scholtmeijer, *Animal Victims*, 89.

38. Berger ("Why Look at Animals?" 3–4) adds that it is precisely in being free from language that the animal is able to preserve its distinctness from humans,

to maintain its objective reality as something other than a "confirmation" of human reality. The animal's value as providing an extra-cultural perspective on human beings depends upon that perspective not being readily translatable into human language.

39. Sapontzis, "Aping Persons," 270.

40. Gary L. Francione, "Personhood, Property and Legal Competence," in Cavalieri and Singer, *The Great Ape Project*, 252–53. Fletcher's criteria include: minimum intelligence; self-awareness; self-control; a sense of time; a sense of futurity; a sense of the past; the capability of relating to others; concern for others; communication; control of existence; curiosity; change and changeability; balance of rationality and feeling; idiosyncrasy; neocortical functioning.

41. Robert W. Mitchell, "Humans, Nonhumans, and Personhood," in Cavalieri and Singer, *The Great Ape Project*, 242.

42. Ibid.

43. Griffin, *Animal Minds*, 248–49.

44. See Griffin, *Animal Thinking*, 87–94.

45. Gregory Bateson, quoted in Mitchell, "Humans, Nonhumans, and Personhood," 241.

46. See Sapontzis, "Aping Persons," 270.

47. John Rodman, "The Liberation of Nature?" *Inquiry* 20 (1977): 91.

48. Griffin, *Animal Thinking*, 28.

49. Thus, he reaches the interesting epistemological conclusion that "there are facts that do not consist in the truth of propositions expressible in a human language"; see "What Is It Like to Be a Bat?" reprinted in Thomas Nagel, *Mortal Questions* (Cambridge: Cambridge University Press, 1979), 171.

50. If they cannot yield precise answers in science or philosophy, they nonetheless provide fertile material for fiction. A noteworthy example is Barbara Gowdy's *The White Bone* (New York: St. Martin's Press, 2000), a vivid attempt to tell a story entirely from the perspective of an African elephant.

51. See Israel Rosenfield, *The Strange, Familiar, and Forgotten: An Anatomy of Consciousness* (New York: Vintage Books, 1993).

52. Heidegger (*The Fundamental Concepts of Metaphysics*, 230–31) makes this point in his analysis of an experiment in which the retinal image of a glow worm was successfully captured: "But can we infer from this what the glow worm sees? By no means. By reference to the achievement of the organ we cannot at all determine the capacity of vision or the way in which the achievement of the organ is taken into service by the potentiality to see. We cannot even recognize the problem of the connection between the organ and the capacity of vision unless and until we have determined the glow worm's environment as such. And that in turn requires elucidation of what an environment for the animal means in general. The kind of achievement pertaining to the insect eye, and thus to every organ and accordingly to every organic part of the organ, is determined by being put into the service of the visual capacity of the insect, i.e., as something which has no independence of its own and is inserted as it were between the environment and the seeing animal. It is something inserted not from without, but by the specific capacity by way of its instinctual and drive-like accomplishment."

53. Ludwig Wittgenstein, *Philosophical Investigations*, II. xi.

54. For a succinct argument for this position, see Marc Bekoff, "Common

Sense, Cognitive Ethology and Evolution," in Cavalieri and Singer, *The Great Ape Project*, 102–8.

55. See Josephine Donovan, "Attention to Suffering: Sympathy as a Basis for Ethical Treatment of Animals," in *Beyond Animal Rights*, 151–52.

56. Rollin, *Animal Rights*, 94–95.

57. See Stephen R. L. Clark, "The Consciousness of Animals," in *Animals and Their Moral Standing* (London: Routledge, 1997), 148–51.

58. Griffin, *Animal Minds*, 238.

59. Adriaan Kortlandt, "Spirits Dressed in Fur?" in Cavalieri and Singer, *The Great Ape Project*, 139–40.

60. Griffin, *Animal Thinking*, 137.

61. See Marian Stamp Dawkins, *Animal Suffering: The Science of Animal Welfare* (London: Chapman and Hall, 1980).

62. Griffin, *Animal Minds*, 23.

63. Yamamoto, "Aquinas and Animals," 89.

64. See Griffin, *Animal Minds*, 24.

65. Ibid., 254.

66. See Ryder, "Experiments on Animals," 80.

67. Scholtmeijer, *Animal Victims*, 82.

## Chapter 3: Utilitarian Arguments

1. Jeremy Bentham, *An Introduction to the Principles of Morals and Legislation*, Chapter 1.

2. Ibid., Chapter 17.

3. As he writes (*Principles of Penal Law*, Chapter xvi): "[Animal sports] necessarily suppose either the absence of reflection or a fund of inhumanity, since they produce the most acute sufferings to sensible beings, and the most painful and lingering death of which we can form any idea . . . The time will come when humanity will extend its mantle over everything which breathes."

4. John Stuart Mill, *Utilitarianism*, Chapter 2.

5. Salt, *Animals' Rights*, 47.

6. Of course, there are differences among utilitarians as to exactly which mental states must be maximized (are good) and minimized (are bad) by morally right actions, and few utilitarians today subscribe to the pure hedonism of earlier utilitarians. However important such distinctions are for ethical theory, they need not concern us terribly here, inasmuch as one would expect the capacity of nonhumans to exhibit deliberate preferences for courses of action that lead to a net disutility, or to express informed preferences about their well-being beyond what they find pleasant and painful, to be limited. Tom Regan (*The Case for Animal Rights*, 208–11) argues effectively that Singer's preference utilitarianism is subject to the same fundamental criticisms as classical hedonic utilitarianism.

7. While there is little question that the foundation of Singer's argument in *Animal Liberation* reflects his utilitarian commitments, it should be noted that he later declares "the text of *Animal Liberation* is not utilitarian. It was specifically intended to appeal to readers who were concerned about equality, or justice, or fairness, irrespective of the precise nature of their commitment." See his

"A Response," in *Singer and His Critics*, ed. Dale Jamieson (Oxford: Blackwell Publishers, Ltd., 1999), 283.

8. Singer tends to use the word *sentient* inexactly, to mean "capable of suffering pain" (see *Animal Liberation*, rev. ed. [New York: Avon Books, 1990], 7–8, 10–15). As discussed below, the moral importance of painful experience and its link to the moral category of interests is more complex than Singer's analysis allows; see Frey, *Interests and Rights*, 33–37. For a thorough analysis of the problem and its significance for utilitarian arguments about animals, see Gary Varner, "Harey Animals," www-phil.tamu.edu/gary/hareyanimals.pdf, 21 September 2003. While Singer's argument for animal suffering is largely analogical, Varner argues for an empirical approach; see the chart he reprints from his book, *In Nature's Interests? Interests, Animal Rights and Environmental Ethics* (New York: Oxford University Press, 1998), which summarizes the available empirical evidence for the capacity to suffer in various classes of animals.

9. See *Animal Liberation*, 2–9, 221. In addition to drawing inspiration from Bentham, here Singer clearly has appropriated Ryder's earlier argument: "In as much as both 'race' and 'species' are vague terms used in the classification of living creatures according, largely, to physical appearance, an analogy can be made between them. Discrimination on grounds of race, although most universally condoned two centuries ago, is now widely condemned. Similarly, it may come to pass that enlightened minds may one day abhor 'speciesism' as much as they now detest 'racism.' The illogicality in both forms of prejudice is of an identical sort. If it is accepted as morally wrong to deliberately inflict suffering upon innocent human creatures, then it is only logical to also regard it as wrong to inflict suffering on innocent individuals of other species" ("Experiments on Animals," in Godlovitch et al., *Animals, Men and Morals*, 81).

10. *Animal Liberation*, 6.

11. Ibid., 4–5. Singer later (18–22) acknowledges that such factual differences are relevant to the question of killing. See note 59 in this chapter.

12. *Animal Liberation*, 8.

13. See Chapters 2 and 3 of *Animal Liberation*. While agricultural and scientific practices are the focus of his discussion, he makes it clear (ibid., 22) that the argument covers virtually all uses of animals that impose physical or emotional suffering.

14. That some animal advocates liken the treatment of animals to the Holocaust is given dramatic treatment in J. M. Coetzee's *The Lives of Animals* (Princeton: Princeton University Press, 2001).

15. Midgley, *Animals and Why They Matter*, Chapter 9.

16. Singer himself has apparently acknowledged that there may be a biological basis to speciesism, with the result that cultural change may be insufficient to effect revaluation of the animal (interview on *Start of the Week*, BBC Radio 4, 11 May 1998). The implications of "social distance" arguments for the moral standing of animals are discussed in Chapter 5.

17. Of course, a strong case can be made that, for example, race-consciousness—as opposed to a simplistic strategy of "color blindness"—may be necessary to overcome racial injustice in a historically oppressive society. In order to do justice to my fellow human beings' individual needs and interests, I do indeed need to recognize their race and gender. This point, however, only further undermines the utilitarian's analogy between human and animal oppression.

18. See Frey, *Interests and Rights*, 41.

19. Quoted in Peter Singer, "Animal Research: Philosophical Issues," in *Encyclopedia of Bioethics*, vol. 1, 151.

20. Singer, "Animal Research," 150.

21. Singer, *Animal Liberation*, 81–85.

22. First, it is not clear why the benefits of research would need to outweigh the harm so greatly in order to meet the utilitarian standard: might not modest animal suffering be justified by the reasonable expectation of somewhat greater human benefit? Second, Singer's discussion of the chimpanzee and the retarded child overlooks the fact that the latter will have a higher emotional value for normal humans, evoking stronger empathy in most than the nonhuman animal would. (Even if we premise, as Singer does, that the child in question is orphaned so his or her exploitation would evoke no pain in family members, those conducting the research may still be pained.) Singer might argue that such feelings would be symptomatic of speciesism—which is certainly possible—but it would not be obviously irrational for a human being to be more empathetic to one of his fellows (this point is revisited subsequently in Chapter 5). Would not the violation of this empathy serve as an additional source of suffering for those who participated in the experiment, and shouldn't our deliberations take that into account?

23. Ingmar Persson, "A Basis for (Interspecies) Equality," in Cavalieri and Singer, *The Great Ape Project*, 185–87.

24. Scholtmeijer, *Animal Victims*, 81–82.

25. This argument is critiqued by Andrew Linzey ("Animal Welfare and Rights: Vegetarianism," in *Encyclopedia of Bioethics*, vol. 1, 172). He cites Frederick Ferre's argument that "life is cannibalistic on itself," and that ethics must reflect an "affirmation of the nutrient cycle," as a clear attempt to circumvent the needed ethical analysis.

26. See *Animal Liberation*, 17–20, 239, for Singer's critique of "intrinsic worth" arguments.

27. Singer makes clear (*Animal Liberation*, 21, 228–29) that his position does not rest on a prohibition against killing.

28. This and other forms of suffering imposed on animals reared for food are documented in *Animal Liberation*, Chapter 3. See also Ruth Harrison's now classic *Animal Machines* (London: Vincent Stuart, 1964) and Gail Eisnitz's more recent *Slaughterhouse* (Amherst, N.Y.: Prometheus Books, 1997).

29. The concept of adaptation may be misapplied to domesticated animals, which are creatures of millennia of selective breeding by humans, rather than natural evolutionary forces. However, while a domesticated animal almost certainly suffers less in confinement than would one of its wild counterparts, it is difficult to imagine that any sentient being with genealogical roots among wild social animals could thrive under factory-farm conditions.

30. *Animal Liberation*, 159–60. Later (in his *Practical Ethics*, 1993) he emends his position to include a utilitarian proscription against even the humane killing of mammals, on the grounds that they may have a sufficient sense of themselves and their futurity to render even their painless death a morally significant harm.

31. *Animal Liberation*, 229.

32. Linzey, "Animal Welfare," 173.

33. Bart Gruzalski, "The Case against Raising and Killing Animals for Food," in Miller and Williams, *Ethics and Animals*, 251–65.

34. Similar difficulties confound the question of whether we should eat animals that are harvested from the wild. Singer's discussion of the utility of eating crustaceans and mollusks (*Animal Liberation*, 173–74) borders on the silly.

35. See Jan Narveson, "Animal Rights Revisited," in Miller and Williams, *Ethics and Animals*, 51–56.

36. See Scholtmeijer, *Animal Victims*, 71.

37. Nietzsche writes with apparent sincerity: "I have no doubt that the combined suffering of all the animals ever subjected to the knife for scientific ends is utterly negligible compared with one painful night of a single hysterical bluestocking" (*Genealogy of Morals*, Second Essay, Section 7).

38. Hugh LaFollette and Niall Shanks, "Utilizing Animals," *Journal of Applied Philosophy* (1995): 13–25.

39. Singer, *Animal Liberation*, 90–91.

40. Carl Cohen, "The Case for the Use of Animals in Biomedical Research," *New England Journal of Medicine*, vol. 315 (1986): 868, reprinted in *Intervention and Reflection: Basic Issues in Medical Ethics*, 5th ed., ed. Ronald Munson (Belmont, Calif.: Wadsworth Publishing Company, 1996), 409.

41. Stephen R. L. Clark, "Modern Errors, Ancient Virtues," in Stephen R. L. Clark, *Animals and Their Moral Standing* (London: Routledge, 1997), 163–64.

42. Griffin, *Animal Minds*, 246, 251–52.

43. Varner, "Harey Animals," 2.

44. Peter Singer, "Not for Humans Only: The Place of Nonhumans in Environmental Issues," in *Ethics and Problems of the 21st Century*, ed. K. M. Sayre and K. E. Goodpaster (Notre Dame: University of Notre Dame Press, 1979), reprinted in *Social and Personal Ethics*, 2nd ed., ed. William H. Shaw (Belmont, Calif.: Wadsworth, 1996), 171.

45. Singer, *Animal Liberation*, 16–17.

46. Singer, "Animal Research," 152.

47. See Richard Ryder, "Painism," in Bekoff and Meaney, *Encyclopedia of Animal Rights*, 269–70.

48. Frey, *Interests and Rights*, 160. We may add that the painist and the utilitarian treat pain (and pleasure) as absolutes that are immune from the influences of socialization and culture. Since it is possible to think about what we *ought* to feel pleasure and pain at (either biologically from the point of view of health, or ethically), this assumption is problematic.

49. Ibid., 163.

50. Ibid., 49.

51. Ibid., 145. We may add to Frey's analysis this consideration: How would the utilitarian respond to the grotesque possibility of genetically engineering livestock with a diminished sensitivity to pain, veal calves with a disposition toward confinement, or laboratory animals that are even more compliant with experimental procedures? Their exploitation might serve utility more clearly, but the ugliness of the spectacle is still troubling. With our growing biotechnological prowess, the point is not entirely hypothetical. Moreover, since the sensory and communicative acuity of domesticated animals is vastly inferior to that of their wild counterparts, the utilitarian case for their exploitation is thus strengthened.

52. Ibid., 156.

53. David Degrazia, "Well-being of Animals," in Bekoff and Meaney, *Encyclopedia of Animal Rights*, 359–61.

54. As Roslind Godlovitch argues, if suffering has a disvalue but life has no intrinsic positive value, this seems to create a duty to exterminate (euthanize) all those who will certainly suffer ("Animals and Morals," in Godlovitch et al., *Animals, Men and Morals*, 168). See also Rollin, *Animal Rights*, 70.

55. Rodman, "The Liberation of Nature?" 91.

56. See Singer, "Not for Humans Only," 171.

57. Discussed by Frey in *Interests and Rights*, 41–42.

58. Nietzsche, *The Will to Power*, note 674.

59. As Singer himself argues (*Animal Liberation*, 20): "A rejection of speciesism does not imply that all lives are of equal worth. While self-awareness, the capacity to think ahead and have hopes and aspirations for the future, and the capacity for meaningful relations with others and so on are not relevant to the question of inflicting pain . . . these capacities are relevant to the question of taking life. It is not arbitrary to hold that the life of a self-aware being, capable of abstract thought, of planning for the future, of complex acts of communication, and so on, is more valuable than the life of a being without these capacities."

60. Singer's rejection of this position seems to rest on extra-utilitarian considerations; see *Animal Liberation*, 226.

61. James Gaffney, "Can Catholic Morality Make Room for Animals?" in Linzey and Yamamoto, *Animals on the Agenda*, 105.

62. Narveson, "Animal Rights Revisited," 56.


## Chapter 4: Deontological Arguments

1. Scholtmeijer, *Animal Victims*, 58.

2. *Fundamental Principles of the Metaphysic of Morals*, First Section (Abbott translation). That Kant is indeed playing on the distinction between humans and other animals is not explicit here, but is made clearer in his discussion of the same point in *The Critique of Practical Reason*, Chapter 2.

3. *Fundamental Principles*, First Section: "And, in fact, we find that the more a cultivated reason applies itself with deliberate purpose to the enjoyment of life and happiness, so much the more does the man fail of true satisfaction. And from this circumstance there arises in many, if they are candid enough to confess it, a certain degree of misology, that is, hatred of reason, especially in the case of those who are most experienced in the use of it."

4. Ibid., First Section.

5. See ibid., Preface and Second Section.

6. *The Critique of Practical Reason*, Chapter III; *Fundamental Principles*, Second Section.

7. "Duties to Animals and Spirits," in Regan and Singer, *Animal Rights*, 23.

8. Arthur Schopenhauer, *On the Basis of Morality*, trans. E. F. J. Payne, rev. ed. (Providence, R.I.: Berghahn Books, 1995), 96.

9. Notably, W. D. Ross argues that "if we think we ought to behave in a certain way to animals, it is out of consideration primarily for *their* feelings that we think we ought to behave so; we do not think of them merely as a practising-ground for virtue. It is because we think their pain a bad thing that we think we

should not gratuitously cause it. And I suppose that to say we have a duty to so-and-so is the same thing as to say that we have a duty, grounded on facts relating to them, to behave in a certain way towards them"; *The Right and The Good* (Oxford: Oxford University Press, 1930), 49.

10. Brigid Brophy, "In Pursuit of a Fantasy," in Godlovitch et al., *Animals, Men and Morals*, 127–28.

11. Paul Brett, "Compassion or Justice? What Is Our Minimum Ethical Obligation to Animals?" in Linzey and Yamamoto, *Animals on the Agenda*, 235.

12. Rollin, *Animal Rights*, 132.

13. See Marti Kheel, "The Liberation of Nature: A Circular Affair," 29; and Mary Anne Warren, "Difficulties with the Strong Animal Rights Position," *Between the Species* 2, no. 4 (Fall 1987): 433–41, reprinted in James E. White, *Contemporary Moral Problems*, 5th ed. (St. Paul, Minn.: West Publishing, 1997), 484: "This is an age in which nearly all significant moral claims tend to be expressed in terms of rights. Thus, the denial that animals have rights, however carefully qualified, is likely to be taken to mean that we may do whatever we like to them, provided that we do not violate any human rights. In such a context, speaking of the rights of animals may be the only way to persuade many people to take seriously protests against the abuse of animals."

14. Sapontzis, "Aping Persons," 274.

15. *Animal Liberation*, 8. Singer's point is ironic, inasmuch as he is often identified as an "animal rights advocate" in popular accounts of his work, despite the fact that he explicitly rejects the *philosophical* value of the concept "animal rights." Thus, environmentalist John Livingston's cynical observation: "It appears to be the inevitable fate of any once-useful term to become sloganized in the homogenizing digestive tract of the popular media. 'Animal rights,' (much like 'environment' and 'ecology') is now a code word that is more symbolic than useful, bereft of most of its original meaning, but still convenient for those whose daily task is not to produce thoughts but to fill space"; *Rogue Primate: An Exploration of Human Domestication* (Boulder, Colo.: Roberts Rinehart Publishers, 1994), 160–61.

16. As noted in previous chapters, Gary Francione has contributed significantly to the legal theory behind animal law. See also Steven M. Wise, *Rattling the Cage: Toward Legal Rights for Animals* (Cambridge, Mass.: Perseus Books, 2000); and Rollin, *Animal Rights*, Chapter 2.

17. Livingston, *Rogue Primate*, 171.

18. Berger, "Why Look at Animals?" 13.

19. See Alan White, "Why Animals Cannot Have Rights," in Regan and Singer, *Animal Rights*, 119–21.

20. Livingston, *Rogue Primate*, 163.

21. Some, such as legal theorist Ronald Dworkin, argue that the connection between legal and moral rights is tighter than these extreme examples suggest, since the application of any system of legal rules will require appeal to extralegal moral principles.

22. Machan, "Do Animals Have Rights?" 163–64.

23. See Rachels, *Created from Animals*, 143.

24. For example, see Rollin, *Animal Rights*, 36–38.

25. Harlan B. Miller has proposed that we substitute the more palatable "argument from species overlap" for "argument from marginal cases."

26. James Lindemann Nelson, "Marginal Cases," in Bekoff and Meaney, *Encyclopedia of Animal Rights*, 237.

27. Persson, "A Basis for (Interspecies) Equality," 191. See also Frey, *Interests and Rights*, 30; and Singer, *Animal Liberation*, 19–20, where he adds: "One could take the argument as showing that the severely retarded and hopelessly senile have no right to life and may be killed for quite trivial reasons, as we now kill animals . . . What we need is some middle position that would avoid speciesism but would not make the lives of the retarded and senile as cheap as the lives of pigs and dogs are now, or make the lives of pigs and dogs so sacrosanct that we think it wrong to put them out of hopeless misery." Thus, for Singer, the issue of marginal cases not only makes space for the moral standing of animals, but also provides a reason for preferring utilitarianism to the rights approach.

28. Harlan B. Miller, "The Wahokies," in Cavalieri and Singer, *The Great Ape Project*, 233.

29. See Frey, *Interests and Rights*, 28–32.

30. Livingston, *Rogue Primate*, 161. See also Kheel, "Liberation of Nature," 29: "It is only when our instincts have failed us that we turn to such concepts as rights."

31. A strong example is Evelyn Pluhar's *Beyond Prejudice: The Moral Significance of Human and Nonhuman Animals* (Durham: Duke University Press, 1995), which uses the marginal cases problem to develop a Kantian-Gewirthian animal ethic.

32. Tom Regan, *The Case for Animal Rights* (Berkeley and Los Angeles: University of California Press, 1983), especially 205–28.

33. Ibid., 235–43.

34. Tom Regan, "Animal Rights," in Bekoff and Meaney, *Encyclopedia of Animal Rights*, 43.

35. Regan, *The Case for Animal Rights*, 243–48.

36. Ibid., 264.

37. Ibid., 81. While not without controversy, our discussion in Chapter 2 shows that these claims are not implausible. The key to Regan's understanding of animal consciousness is the argument that an animal that exhibits the autonomy to fulfill its preferences is forming beliefs and desires—even though they are not articulated in language—and therefore possesses a meaningful degree of subjectivity. See ibid., 84–86.

38. Regan leaves open the possibility that other animals besides mature mammals may also qualify as subjects. See ibid., 367.

39. Regan, "Animal Rights," in Bekoff and Meaney, *Encyclopedia of Animal Rights*, 43.

40. *The Case for Animal Rights*, 351: "On the rights view, vegetarianism is morally obligatory, and . . . we should not be satisfied with anything less than the total dissolution of commercial animal agriculture as we know it, whether modern factory farming or otherwise."

41. Ibid., 394: "Those who accept the rights view are committed to denying any and all access to these 'resources' [animals] on the part of those who do science. And we do this not because we oppose cruelty (though we do), nor because we favor kindness (though we do), but because justice requires nothing less."

42. Once again, we should distinguish between the practical and the theoretical aspects of this issue. Regan maintains (ibid., 357) that our moral obligation

toward wild animals must take the form of "managing" our capacity for wrong-doing rather than managing wildlife, and that the fundamental moral right of wild animals is the right to be left alone to lead their own lives; thus, he argues (ibid., 363) that in *practice* the rights position implies an environmental ethic that should satisfy those environmentalists who are skeptical of human inter-vention in the nonhuman world. But this does not entirely set aside Livingston's criticism: that in order to respect the nonhuman world we would have to con-ceive of it in terms of the anthropocentric notion of rights is paradoxical on its face. If we content ourselves with the practical protection of animals but fail to grapple with this theoretical paradox—as I do in Parts III and IV—then we fall short of appreciating the full importance of the debate over animals.

43. See Robert W. Loftin and Ellen R. Klein, "Animal Welfare and Rights: Hunting," in *Encyclopedia of Bioethics*, vol. 1, 189–90. Adds Shepard (*Thinking Animals*, 248): "Only in one sense is the ethical argument [for animal preserva-tion] without the distortion of our human social model: that animals should be preserved because they are, as they are, because their existence itself is moral justification. But it is not a new idea and its application is ambiguous because such unlimited rights will always conflict with human interest, and there is no reason to think that people are so charitable or so good that they will yield in that conflict."

44. See Frey, *Interests and Rights*, 50–51. Other convenient examples are found in many arguments from the abortion debate: their authors construct models of personhood and rights possession with a clear view to the conclusions they will entail concerning the moral status of the human fetus.

45. Tom Regan, "The Case for Animal Rights," in *In Defense of Animals*, ed. Peter Singer (New York: Perennial Library, 1986), reprinted in White, *Contempo-rary Moral Problems*, 476. This comment leads us to ask whether Clark's criti-cism of utilitarianism, cited in Chapter 3, should be applied to rights arguments as well.

46. See his critique in *Morals, Reason, and Animals* (Philadelphia: Temple University Press, 1987), 249–59.

47. Warren, "Difficulties with the Strong Animal Rights Position," 480.

48. Tom Regan, "Animal Welfare and Rights: Ethical Perspectives on the Treatment and Status of Animals," in *Encyclopedia of Bioethics*, vol. 1, 166.

49. See Donald VanDeVeer, "Interspecific Justice and Intrinsic Value," *The Electronic Journal of Analytic Philosophy* Issue 3, Spring 1995, www.phil.indi-ana.edu/ejap/1995.spring/vandeveer.1995.spring.html, 5 September 2000: "It is one thing perhaps to claim that a chimp and a human have equal intrinsic value—though such a claim stretches the imagination and rubs against the moral intuition of most people. It strikes many as preposterous to maintain that, e.g., a paramecium, a mole rat, a congressperson, and the last panda all have the same intrinsic value. Thus, the more inclusive one's criterion of moral standing the more tempting it is to adopt some sort of inegalitarian view with the regard to possession of intrinsic value—at least if amounts or degree of value have any important bearing, *ceteris paribus*, on respective (albeit presumptive) duties to such beings."

50. Regan, *The Case for Animal Rights*, 237.

51. While Kant famously saw no contradiction between the moral respect for persons and the retributive theory of punishment—indeed, he thought the

criminal's right to respect *required* retribution—Regan is more ambivalent: while acknowledging the importance of the considered judgment that punishment is morally justifiable, he sidesteps whether his version of rights theory requires that it be rejected (see ibid., 290–91).

52. See ibid., 246, 362–63. Warren argues ("Difficulties with the Strong Animal Rights Position," 482) that Regan's failure to be more committal on the status of animals other than mature mammals is a critical flaw in his theory: "The existence of a few unclear cases need not pose a serious problem for a moral theory, but in this case, the unclear cases constitute most of those with which an adequate theory of animal rights would need to deal. The subject-of-a-life criterion can provide us with little or no moral guidance in our interactions with the vast majority of animals. That might be acceptable if it could be supplemented with additional principles which would provide such guidance. However, the radical dualism of the theory precludes supplementing it in this way. We are forced to say that either a spider has the same right to life as you and I do, or it has no right to life whatever—and that only the gods know which of these alternatives is true."

53. VanDeVeer, "Interspecific Justice and Intrinsic Value": "But moral agents cannot live as though every little creature is of great value (I speak here of their individual and not their collective value) any more than they can regularly agonize about whether a treasured wedding ring is in every bag of trash being thrown out. Until we learn otherwise (and we have some duty to learn), we have no *urgent* duty to avoid harming individual creatures whose lives are not of evidently non-trivial value." As I explore further in Chapter 7, this problem makes the strong rights position self-defeating in an interesting way: rights are political concepts which, when imposed on the nonhuman world, seem to require the dismantling of human political existence.

54. See "Why Animals Have Right to Liberty," in Regan and Singer, *Animal Rights*, 122–31; and "Do Animals Have a Right to Life?" in Miller and Williams, *Ethics and Animals*, 275–84. Rollin's argument for animal rights perhaps belongs in the same general category as Rachels's, but owing to its debt to Aristotelian concepts, it is dealt with separately in Chapter 5.

55. Rachels, *Created from Animals*, 195.

56. Rachels, "Do Animals Have Right to Life?" 278–80. See also *Created from Animals*, 178–79.

57. Rachels, "Why Animals Have a Right to Liberty," 124.

58. Frey, "On Why We Would Do Better to Jettison Moral Rights," in Miller and Williams, *Ethics and Animals*, 286. See also *Interest and Rights*, 9. Singer makes a similar argument in *Animal Liberation*, 8.

59. Livingston, *Rogue Primate*, 164.

60. Sapontzis, "Aping Persons," 275.

## Chapter 5: Aristotelian Arguments

1. A noteworthy example is Alasdair C. MacIntyre's *After Virtue: A Study in Moral Theory*, 2nd ed. (Notre Dame: University of Notre Dame Press, 1984). This point has been made explicitly by some in the debate over animals; for example, see Marti Kheel, "From Heroic to Holistic Ethics: The Ecofeminist

Challenge," in *Ecofeminism: Women, Animals, Nature,* ed. Greta Gaard (Philadelphia: Temple University Press, 1993), 256.

2. *Nicomachean Ethics* 1.3.

3. Sorabji, *Animal Minds,* 94. He makes a convincing case that this way of using the animal is not unique to Aristotle, but is characteristic of a great deal of pre-Christian Greek thought.

4. Aristotle, *On the Parts of Animals,* 4.5, 681$^a$12–14 (Ogle translation). See also his *History of Animals,* 8.1.

5. In Aristotle's case, quite literally, inasmuch as he—and the Greeks generally—conceived of *psychē* as a general principle of living things, and not something uniquely human. Thus, *On the Soul* is introduced as a contribution to natural science, not philosophical anthropology.

6. Aristotle, *History of Animals,* 8.1, 588$^a$17–30.

7. For example, see *Metaphysics* 1.1; *On the Soul* 2.3, 3.3; and *Nicomachean Ethics* 1.7.

8. Aristotle, *Politics* 1.5, 1254$^b$16–25 (Jowett translation).

9. Ibid., 1.8, 1256$^b$20–27.

10. *Nicomachean Ethics* 1.7, 13.

11. Ibid., 1.9, 1099$^b$33–1100$^a$1.

12. Ibid., 8.11, 1161$^b$3.

13. While Kant, as we saw in Chapter 4, rejects the argument that happiness is the good, Aristotle's ethics is eudemonic. And while Aristotle is no utilitarian, his attention to the place, time, manner, intention, and the like of the agent's performance when evaluating an act's moral worth stands in contrast to Kant's singular criterion of universalizability.

14. Kant's argument in "Duties to Animals and Spirits" (quoted in Chapter 4) clearly echoes Aristotle's language in *Politics* 1.8, 1256$^b$16–22: "After the birth of animals, plants exist for their sake, and the other animals exist for the sake of man, the tame for use and food, the wild, if not all at least the greater part of them, for food, and for the provision of clothing and various instruments. Now if nature makes nothing incomplete, and nothing in vain, the inference must be that she has made all animals for the sake of man."

15. See Sorabji, *Animal Minds,* 195–207 for a detailed treatment of this history.

16. See *City of God,* Book I, Chapter 20 (Dods translation): "when we say, Thou shalt not kill, we do not understand this of the plants, since they have no sensation, nor of the irrational animals that fly, swim, walk, or creep, since they are dissociated from us by their want of reason, and are therefore by the just appointment of the Creator subjected to us to kill or keep alive for our own uses."

17. Aquinas, *Summa Theologica,* Second Part of the Second Part, Question 25, Article 3.

18. Rollin, *Animal Rights,* 71. This implies, as Rollin later makes clear, that there can be no direct moral duties to valuable things that lack interests of their own, such as aesthetic objects, whole species of animals, or the inanimate natural world.

19. Ibid., 74.

20. Ibid., 75.

21. Ibid., 92.

22. Ibid., 76–77.

23. Ibid., 78. This position is dubious because, among other reasons, there would seem to be little selection pressure for animals with such brief life-spans to develop conscious experience; only among longer-lived creatures would there be an appreciable value to the learning that pain-consciousness makes possible.

24. Ibid., 75–76.

25. Ibid., 83. Rollin describes this right as "the only absolute, invariable, and inalienable right."

26. For example, on page 89 of *Animal Rights*, Rollin writes: "*if we wish* [my italics] to use Kantian terminology, we must say that *any living thing with interests is an end in itself* [his italics], worthy of moral consideration merely in virtue of its being alive." I take this to mean that Kantian language gives us a convenient shorthand for expressing the claim that animals are moral objects proper, not that Kantian ethics provides us with the necessary means of clarifying that moral status.

27. Ibid., 90.

28. Salt, *Animals' Rights*, 28.

29. Warren, "Difficulties with the Strong Animal Rights Position," 484.

30. Paul W. Taylor, "The Ethics of Respect for Nature," in *The Animal Rights/Environmental Ethics Debate: The Environmental Perspective*, ed. Eugene C. Hargrove (Albany: State University of New York Press, 1992), 109–10; Holmes Rolston III, *Philosophy Gone Wild* (New York: Prometheus Books, 1986), 111.

31. Rollin, *Animal Rights*, 99.

32. Ibid., 97. Clark makes a similar point: "Nor do I think it sensible to demand a single moral theory from which all right decisions can be easily deduced, as though we could ever relegate the pain of moral choice to pocket calculators" ("Modern Errors, Ancient Virtues," in *Animals and Their Moral Standing*, 167).

33. Rollin, *Animal Rights*, 96. Cf. Singer, *Animal Liberation*, 16–17 (quoted in Chapter 3).

34. Rollin's discussions of these practices lie somewhere in between an equivocal utilitarian approach and an unyielding animal rights position. Concerning the use of animals for food, Rollin applauds the "traditional" vegetarian argument (*Animal Rights*, 85) that meat-eating is unjustified since it requires the animal sacrifice its interest in staying alive for our more trivial interest in the taste of flesh. He concedes, however, that since other animals apparently lack a sense of death, "killing an animal is not the worst thing one can do to it," and so an animal's right to life is not perfectly analogous to a human's (ibid., 86). Of more concern to Rollin than meat-eating per se is the treatment of agricultural animals under intensive conditions that overtly disregard their telic needs and interests (see his "Animal Welfare and Rights: Animals in Agriculture and Factory Farming" in *Encyclopedia of Bioethics*, vol. 1); thus, his teleological approach provides a stronger argument for a return to extensive agriculture than for vegetarianism.

The teleological approach would seem to provide a stronger basis for an absolutist rejection of the use of animals in research, since much of this activity amounts to a perversion of the animal's biological and psychological teleology for the ends of research. However, Rollin rejects this position as "utopian" (*Animal Rights*, 137), given how entrenched the use of the animal is within scientific practice. Instead, he opts for a reformist tack, arguing that proposed research ought to meet utilitarian criteria, and be conducted with as much accommodation of the animal's *telos* as the research will allow (ibid., 137–40).

35. Ibid., 93–95.

36. Ibid., 79–82.

37. Ibid., 87.

38. Ibid., 118–19. Dworkin's arguments are found in his well-known *Taking Rights Seriously* (Cambridge, Mass.: Harvard University Press, 1978).

39. Aristotle, *Nicomachean Ethics*, 2.6, 1107$^a$9–26.

40. Ibid., 2.4, 1105$^a$27–34 (Ostwald translation): "In the arts, excellence lies in the result itself, so that it is sufficient if it is of a certain kind. But in the case of the virtues an act is not performed justly or with self-control if the act itself is of a certain kind, but only if in addition the agent has certain characteristics as he performs it: first of all, he must know what he is doing; secondly, he must choose to act the way he does, and he must choose it for its own sake; and in the third place, the act must spring from a firm and unchangeable character."

41. Ibid., 6.13, 1145$^a$5–6.

42. As Tom Regan (*The Case for Animal Rights*, 196–99) argues, the cruelty/kindness ethic is unworkable, because it requires access to the private events of the agent's mental life to determine whether his intentions were virtuous or vicious.

43. Lawrence C. Becker, "The Priority of Human Interests," in Miller and Williams, *Ethics and Animals*, 227.

44. Another noteworthy example is Rosalind Hursthouse's *Ethics, Humans and Other Animals: An Introduction with Readings* (New York: Routledge, 2000), Chapter 6.

45. Becker, "The Priority of Human Interests," 238.

46. Ibid., 231.

47. Which Becker defines as (ibid., 229) "an imprecise amalgam of relevant facts about tolerable spatial arrangements, the frequency and nature of permissible social interactions, and the roles in social structures."

48. Ibid., 232–33. Re reciprocity, "it is always reasonable for virtuous people to think that anything they have to give is more likely 'owed' to those closer than far away. Distributional preferences, given the disposition to reciprocate, will therefore be ordered in terms of social distance"; re empathic identification, "the interests of those close to us . . . have a vividness, immediacy, and indubitability that imaginatively constructed empathy can never match . . . Insofar as empathic identification produces conduct 'for' the interests of others, it will produce preferences for those with whom our empathy is strong over those with whom our empathy is weak. The consequence is preferences ordered by social distance."

49. Ibid., 234.

50. Ibid., 237.

51. Ibid., 239.

52. Ibid., 240–41; see also Midgley, *Animals and Why They Matter*, 98–101.

53. Rollin, *Animal Rights*, 81–82. The point compares with the analogy Salt

draws between racism and anthropocentrism (*Animals' Rights*, 20–21): in both cases, oppression and cruelty are founded "on a lack of imaginative sympathy"; once affinity is established, he argues, the recognition of rights is inevitable.

54. Becker, "The Priority of Human Interests," 225.

55. Ibid., 237.

56. Ibid. Becker's conclusion is comparable to Clark's position ("Apes and the Idea of Kindred," in Cavalieri and Singer, *The Great Ape Project*, 121–22): "The moral truth that lies behind the error that others have called 'speciesism' (and justly rebuked) is that we both do and should treat those 'of our kind' better . . . Species kinship rests on relationship, and not on resemblance, although there will be various similarities to reckon with within and without the kind . . . All those of one kind with us begin as equals: we are one, each one of us, a part of one long, variegated lineage, sharing enough of our habits, gestures and abilities to reveal our common source."

57. Such a more subtle analysis of speciesism is also a feature of Midgley's argument; see *Animals and Why They Matter*, Chapter 9.

58. Becker, "The Priority of Human Interests," 237.

59. Ibid., 226.

60. Ibid., 237–38.

61. Ibid., 238.

62. Baier, "Knowing Our Place in the Animal World," 74.

## Chapter 6: Contractarian Arguments

1. A strong example of using contractarianism to undermine recent extensionist arguments is Peter Carruthers, *The Animals Issue* (Cambridge: Cambridge University Press, 1992).

2. Jan Narveson, "Animal Rights Revisited," in Miller and Williams, *Ethics and Animals*, 56–57.

3. Baier, "Knowing Our Place in the Animal World," 73–74.

4. Among other modern social contract theorists, Locke (in the *Second Treatise of Government*) holds similar ideas to Hobbes on humanity's dominion over the animal, while Rousseau (discussed subsequently) acknowledges extracontractual duties to nonhuman animals.

5. While later insights into human history and sociology force us today to think of such a "state of nature" as hypothetical, it is not clear whether Hobbes does so, or envisions it as reflective of the actual state of early human existence. See *Leviathan*, Chapter 13.

6. Ibid., Chapter 13.

7. See ibid., Chapter 17.

8. In ibid., Chapter 15, Hobbes declares that the science of these natural laws is "the true and only moral philosophy. For moral philosophy is nothing else but the science of what is good and evil in the conversation and society of mankind." Thus, Hobbes denies morality its prescriptive dimension, identifying it with what human beings in fact desire for their well-being.

9. Ibid., Chapter 14.

10. Ibid., Chapter 17.

11. Hobbes rejects Aristotle's assertion (see *Politics*, 1.3–8, discussed in Chap-

ter 5) that human inequality is natural, arguing instead that master-servant rela-tionships—like all power relations—exist only by covenant (see *Leviathan*, Chapter 15).

12. Hobbes, *The Elements of Law Natural and Politic*, Chapter 22, #9.

13. *Leviathan*, Chapter 14.

14. Ibid., Chapter 26. Thus, Hobbes's position is problematic with respect to marginal cases as well.

15. This is seen straight in the opening paragraph of *Leviathan:* "NATURE (the art whereby God hath made and governs the world) is by the art of man, as in many other things, so in this also imitated, that it can make an artificial animal. For seeing life is but a motion of limbs, the beginning whereof is in some princi-pal part within, why may we not say that all automata (engines that move them-selves by springs and wheels as doth a watch) have an artificial life? For what is the heart, but a spring; and the nerves, but so many strings; and the joints, but so many wheels, giving motion to the whole body, such as was intended by the Artificer?"

16. Ibid., Chapter 2.

17. Ibid., Chapter 6.

18. Ibid., Chapter 46.

19. Ibid., Chapter 2.

20. Ibid., Chapter 3.

21. Ibid., Chapter 4.

22. Bonnie Steinbock, "Speciesism and the Idea of Equality," *Philosophy* 53 (1978): 253.

23. For example, *Second Discourse*, Preface (Cole translation): "[Man's] duties toward others are not dictated to him only by the later lessons of wisdom; and, so long as he does not resist the internal impulse of compassion, he will never hurt any other man, nor even any sentient being, except on those lawful occasions on which his own preservation is concerned and he is obliged to give himself the preference. By this method also we put an end to the time-honoured disputes concerning the participation of animals in natural law: for it is clear that, being destitute of intelligence and liberty, they cannot recognise that law; as they par-take, however, in some measure of our nature, in consequence of the sensibility with which they are endowed, they ought to partake of natural right; so that mankind is subjected to a kind of obligation even toward the brutes. It appears, in fact, that if I am bound to do no injury to my fellow-creatures, this is less because they are rational than because they are sentient beings: and this quality, being common both to men and beasts, ought to entitle the latter at least to the privilege of not being wantonly ill-treated by the former."

24. John Rawls, *A Theory of Justice*, rev. ed. (Cambridge, Mass.: The Belknap Press of the Harvard University Press, 1999), 11.

25. Ibid., 266. These quotes reflect the final statement of these principles, but they are discussed throughout *A Theory of Justice*.

26. Ibid., 15.

27. Ibid., 11.

28. Baier, "Knowing Our Place in the Animal World," 61.

29. Rawls, *A Theory of Justice*, 448–49. Here we see the complication for the justice-as-fairness position that marginal cases present. Since intelligence is one of the natural assets obscured by the veil of ignorance, the enfeebled should be

directly covered by the principles of justice; yet this quote makes clear that those sufficiently enfeebled to lack a clear sense of justice are not owed "strict justice."

30. For a full analysis of this possibility, see Mark Rowlands, *Animal Rights: A Philosophical Defence* (Basingstoke: Macmillan, 1998).

31. Rollin, *Animal Rights*, 36.

32. See Rawls, *A Theory of Justice*, 128–29.

33. Narveson, "Animal Rights Revisited," 57.

34. Ibid.

35. Ibid., 58.

36. Ibid.

37. See Rawls, *A Theory of Justice*, 111.

38. Baier, "Knowing Our Place in the Animal World," 73.

39. See Scholtmeijer, *Animal Victims*, 67: "Hospitality coming from humankind to other species would likely imply to most people treating all animals as pets. The image of the friendly pet represents its own kind of trespass against animals. As to actual pets, we welcome into our homes the smaller animals we have domesticated but could not tolerate having an untamed hyena or wild boar rushing about the house. Our mental houses are much the same: wild, or dirty, or slimy creatures throw into disarray the tidy, rational world we like to establish in our minds. Hostile animality may well have residence in subconscious hinterlands and jungles, but the civilized mind by definition wants its animals under control."

40. Livingston, *Rogue Primate*, 175. Cf. Nietzsche, *Gay Science*, Section 224; *Daybreak*, Section 333.

41. Regan, *The Case for Animal Rights*, 171–72.

42. Donald VanDeVeer, "Interspecific Justice and Animal Slaughter," in Miller and Williams, *Ethics and Animals*, 153.

43. Ibid., 149.

44. Ibid., 154.

45. Ibid., 155. Correlative to this principle is the "Creation Requirement," that "no rational being should deliberately *cause to exist* a sentient creature when it is certain or highly probable that such a creature would have a life not preferable to no life at all" (ibid., 156).

46. Ibid., 159. These benefits include protection from natural predation, elements, illness, and starvation.

47. Ibid., 162.

48. See Narveson, "Animal Rights Revisited," 56.

49. According to Singer (*Animal Liberation*, 95), there are some five billion chickens raised annually in the United States alone; other sources estimate that roughly 20 billion farm animals are slaughtered for food worldwide each year. Add to this the number of pets, draft animals, and research subjects used worldwide, and it becomes clear that domesticated animals vastly outnumber humans. (Some environmentalists have suggested that if aliens were to observe earth, they might conclude that *cattle* comprise the dominant species on the planet.) Of course, these numbers are contingent upon various social and cultural factors, and the ratio of nonhumans to humans might be smaller in a society built upon VanDeVeer's principles of Life Preferability and the Creation Requirement. Still, as these principles do not preclude a significant amount of

animal exploitation, those in the pre-original position could still bet on humans being outnumbered.

50. Compare this to Paul Shepard's position in *Tender Carnivore,* 9–16. He makes the case that the biological, psychological, and social attributes of domesticated animals are so vastly inferior to those of wild animals that, given the choice, a wild animal might well consider nonexistence preferable to the domesticated life.

51. Colin McGinn, "Apes, Humans, Aliens, Vampires and Robots," in Cavalieri and Singer, *The Great Ape Project,* 149.

52. Ibid. For a similar argument, see Leonard Nelson, "Duties to Animals," in Godlovitch et al., *Animals, Men and Morals,* 152.

53. McGinn, "Apes, Humans, Aliens, Vampires and Robots," 147.

54. Baier, "Knowing Our Place in the Animal World," 74.

## Chapter 7: Extensionism and Its Limits

1. For example, Michael P. T. Leahy, *Against Liberation: Putting Animals into Perspective* (London: Routledge, 1991).

2. The clearest example I have found comes from the libertarian thinker L. Neil Smith ("Animals Are Property," in *The Rights of Animals,* ed. Tamara L. Roleff [San Diego: Greenhaven Press, 1999], 39): "In moral terms there are just two kinds of entity in the universe: people and property. Animals are not people. Some—wild animals—are unclaimed property that would be better off with owners . . . Animals are groceries. They're leather and fur coats. They're for medical experiments and galloping to hounds. That's their *purpose.* I, a human being, declare it. Do what you like with *your* animals."

3. For example, we saw in Chapter 3 that Carl Cohen argues for the continued use of nonhuman animals in research, but his argument is tempered by such statements as: "The human treatment of animals requires that we desist from experimenting on them if we can accomplish the same result using alternative methods" ("The Case for the Use of Animals in Biomedical Research," in Munson, *Intervention and Reflection,* 410); "We surely do have obligations to animals" (ibid., 411); and "The needless killing of animals is wrong" (ibid.). Similarly, Tibor Machan—whose opposition to the concept of animal rights was discussed in the Introduction and Chapter 4—acknowledges that "reckless disregard for the life or well being of animals shows a defect of character, lack of sensitivity, callousness" ("Do Animals Have Rights?" 167), and "we know that animals can feel pain and can enjoy themselves and this must give us pause when we consider using them for our legitimate purposes. We ought to be humane, we ought to [use] them in a fashion consistent with such care about them as sentient beings" (ibid., 171).

4. VanDeVeer, "Interspecific Justice and Animal Slaughter," in Miller and Williams, *Ethics and Animals,* 162.

5. Especially those controversies that involve the treatment of marginal cases, such as abortion, euthanasic infanticide, and non-voluntary euthanasia. In these debates, one faces analogous difficulties to those in the debate over animals because—as I explore further below—the beings whose moral status is in ques-

tion are not the autonomous agents for whom traditional ethical categories were constructed.

6. One would do well not to make too much of this, but a survey of the artwork selected for the covers of many of the important books in the debate (e.g., Singer's *Animal Liberation*, Regan's *The Case for Animal Rights*, Rollin's *Animal Rights and Human Morality*, and Clark's *Animals and Their Moral Standing*) show a penchant for placid depictions of domesticated animals.

7. Baier, "Knowing Our Place in the Animal World," 62.

8. Ibid., 65.

9. Ibid., 67. But not beyond suspicion, given the preponderance of attention paid by animal advocates to "cute" or otherwise charismatic mammals.

10. Bentham (*Principles of Morals and Legislation*, Chapter 17, Section 1, iv) provides an early recognition of this problem: "What other agents then are there, which, at the same time that they are under the influence of man's direction, are susceptible of happiness. They are of two sorts: 1. Other human beings who are styled *persons*. 2. Other animals, which, on account of their interests having been neglected by the insensibility of the ancient jurists, stand degraded into the class of *things*."

11. A fact Schopenhauer (*On the Basis of Morality*, 177) decried as "unmistakably a priestly trick for the purpose of reducing animals to the level of things."

12. Midgley, *Animals and Why They Matter*, 112–14.

13. Of course, the *respect* due to persons and the *usefulness* discerned in mere things are not the only possible modes of evaluation. In Part IV, I will explore a third possibility: *appreciation*, based on the model of aesthetic experience.

14. Raymond Corbey, "Ambiguous Apes," in Cavalieri and Singer, *The Great Ape Project*, 135. Sorabji (*Animal Minds*, 215) adds: "Plato performed a service in insisting that to treasure another as akin is not the same as to treasure another as being like oneself—the unlikeness may be part of the pleasure."

15. As Steve Sapontzis writes ("Aping Persons," 271): "Focusing animal rights concern and activity on nonhuman great apes and other nonhuman primates expresses and continues this bias. We are called on to recognise that harmful experiments on nonhuman great apes are wrong because these apes are genetically so much like us or because they are so intelligent, again like us. Such calls clearly retain an anthropocentric view of the world, modifying it only through recognising that we are not an utterly unique life form."

16. To try to quantify this, E. O. Wilson (*The Diversity of Life*, 1992) estimates that all mammalian species account for a mere 0.388 percent of all the earth's animal and plant species, and other chordates a mere 3.7 percent.

17. As Rawls (*A Theory of Justice*, 448–49) states simply: "A correct conception of our relations to animals and to nature would seem to depend upon a theory of the natural order and our place in it. One of the tasks of metaphysics is to work out a view of the world which is suited for this purpose; it should identify and systematize the truths decisive for these questions."

18. Scholtmeijer, *Animal Victims*, 69.

19. "Aping Persons," 271.

20. For example, see Singer, *Animal Liberation*, 243; Regan, *The Case for Animal Rights*, 133–34; and Rollin, *Animal Rights*, 21–22.

21. Livingston, *Rogue Primate*, 171.

22. Salt, *Animals' Rights*, 106–7.

23. Of course, students of other contentious moral issues—such as the abortion controversy—will be quick to add that the complexity of the problem and weariness at finding a solution are not unique to the debate about animals, which is certainly true. I would only argue that the difficulties here are more numerous, and—as discussed in Chapter 1—of more far-ranging significance given the ubiquity of animal exploitation.

24. Sorabji, *Animal Minds*, 215.

25. Ibid., 217. See also Gary L. Francione, "Animal Rights and Animal Welfare," 48 *Rutgers L. Rev.* 397 (1996), www.animal-law.org/library/araw_ii.htm.

26. Baier, "Knowing Our Place in the Animal World," 75–76.

27. See Sorabji, *Animal Minds*, 213–15. This position is implied by Becker ("The Priority of Human Interests," 237), and developed by Midgley (*Animals and Why They Matter*). As I explore in Chapter 9, this concern with specific relationships is also characteristic of much feminist thinking about our treatment of animals and about ethics in general.

28. The point is implicit throughout *Animal Liberation*, but explicitly developed in "Not for Humans Only."

29. Of special note is his discussion of environmental ethics in *The Case for Animal Rights*, 359.

30. See *Animal Rights and Human Morality*, 101–3.

31. See Marti Kheel, "From Heroic to Holistic Ethics: The Ecofeminist Challenge," in *Ecofeminism*, 249: "Today, many nature ethicists conceive of themselves not as the owners of nature, but as the owners of value, which it is their prerogative to mete out with a theoretical sweep of their pens. Ethical deliberation on the value of nature is conceived more or less like a competitive sport."

32. *Rogue Primate*, 104. Cf. Deleuze and Guattari, *A Thousand Plateaus*, 239: "What would a lone wolf be? Or a whale, a louse, a rat, a fly? . . . The wolf is not fundamentally a characteristic or a certain number of characteristics; it is a wolfing. The louse is a lousing, and so on. What is a cry independent of the population it appeals to or takes as its witness?" See also Berger, "Why Look at Animals?" 4–5, where he argues that the consciousness of animals as revelations of their species-essence is very old, perhaps a prototype of the ontological dualism that would become Platonism.

33. *Rogue Primate*, 110.

34. Ibid., 109.

35. Experiments with single-celled organisms, sponges, and insects suggest that eusociality and collective action are selected under conditions of need; biologically, individuality appears to be a luxury that is only possible in times of plenty. Human individualism may therefore reflect the condition of agricultural surplus under which much of human civilization has existed.

36. It is an interesting possibility that the kind of consciousness the mystic experiences amounts to something like the kind of animal consciousness Livingston suggests, making the mystical something more biological than spiritual. In turn, the extra-moral character of religiosity at the mystical level would dovetail with the argument that ethics is inadequate to accommodate the animal. On the biology of religious experience, see Alex Comfort, *I and That: Notes on the Biology of Religion* (New York: Crown Publishers, 1979).

37. The point recalls Bertrand Russell's comment ("If Animals Could Talk" [1932], in *Mortals and Others: Bertrand Russell's American Essays 1931–1935*,

ed. H. Ruja [London: Allen & Unwin, 1975], vol. 1, 120–21, reprinted in *Political Theory and Animal Rights*, ed. P. A. B. Clarke and Andrew Linzey [London: Pluto Press, 1990], 92): "There is no impersonal reason for regarding the interests of human beings as more important than those of animals. We can destroy animals more easily than they can destroy us; that is the only solid basis of our claim to superiority. We value art and science and literature because these are things in which we excel. But whales might value spouting, and donkeys might maintain that a good bray is more exquisite than the music of Bach. We cannot prove them wrong except by the exercise of arbitrary power. All ethical systems, in the last analysis depend upon weapons of war."

38. Sapontzis, "Aping Persons," 275.

39. Scholtmeijer, *Animal Victims*, 52.

40. Shepard, *Thinking Animals*, 248.

41. Scholtmeijer, *Animal Victims*, 84.

## Chapter 8: The Call and the Circle

1. Raymond Corbey, "Ambiguous Apes," in Cavalieri and Singer, *The Great Ape Project*, 133. The point recalls our discussion in Part I of the English origins of the recent debate over animals.

2. Ibid., 134. As we will see below, Scheler's position prefigures some of Heidegger's reflections on the animal. This is a curious example for Corbey to latch onto, given that Scheler's phenomenology of sympathy allowed for and even advocated fellow-feeling between humans and the rest of the animal world. For analysis, see Josephine Donovan, "Attention to Suffering: Sympathy as a Basis for Ethical Treatment of Animals," in *Beyond Animal Rights: A Feminist Caring Ethic for the Treatment of Animals* [New York: The Continuum Publishing Company, 1996], 150–51.

3. "Attention to Suffering," 134–35. As discussed subsequently, this criticism of Levinas is echoed by Derrida.

4. Jean-Paul Sartre, "Existentialism," trans. Bernard Frechtman, in *Existentialism and Human Emotions* [New York: Philosophical Library, 1957], 13–15. In explaining his assertion that in the case of human beings existence precedes essence, he states (ibid., 15–16): "But what do we mean by this if not that man has greater dignity than a stone or a table? . . . Man is at the start a plan which is aware of itself, rather than a patch of moss, a piece of garbage, or a cauliflower." Sartre does not venture to make any ontological distinction between the vegetable and the mineral, and he ignores the animal entirely.

5. Baker, *The Postmodern Animal*, 12.

6. Ibid., 9.

7. Scholtmeijer, *Animal Victims*, 5.

8. See James W. Kirchner and Anne Weil, "Delayed Biological Recovery from Extinctions throughout the Fossil Record," *Nature* 404, no. 6774 (9 March 2000): 177–80.

9. One can argue that domestic animals have always been creatures of their owners' wills, but genetic engineering radicalizes this. Examples of how this new technology will expand the commodification of the animal abound: labora-tory animals with patented genomes designed for the study of specific patholo-

gies; pigs and chimpanzees genetically modified to facilitate xenotransplantation; "pharm animals" genetically modified to produce therapeutic drugs for humans; and livestock whose growth cycle is engineered and whose nutritional composition is customized at the molecular level.

10. Martin Heidegger, *The Fundamental Concepts of Metaphysics: World, Finitude, Solitude,* trans. William McNeill and Nicholas Walker (Bloomington and Indianapolis: Indiana University Press, 1995), 197.

11. Ibid., 199.

12. Ibid., 198.

13. Ibid., 264.

14. Ibid., 237–38.

15. Ibid., 238–39.

16. See ibid., 229, 233–34, 237.

17. Ibid., 188–89; this Heideggerian theme was broached in Chapter 1.

18. Ibid., 194. Cf. 255: "This does not mean that life represents something inferior or some kind of lower level in comparison with human Dasein. On the contrary, life is a domain which possesses a wealth of openness with which the human world may have nothing to compare."

19. Ibid., 270–71.

20. Ibid., 211.

21. Ibid., 273.

22. Ibid., 264.

23. Heidegger, "Letter on Humanism," trans. Frank A. Capuzzi and J. Glenn Gray, in *Basic Writings,* rev. ed., ed. David Farrell Krell (San Francisco: Harper San Francisco, 1993), 230.

24. Heidegger, *The Fundamental Concepts of Metaphysics,* 255.

25. It should be noted that the problem of the animal figures in Derrida's other critiques of Heidegger, including *"Geschlect* II: Heidegger's Hand" and *Of Spirit: Heidegger and the Question.*

26. "'Eating Well,' or the Calculation of the Subject: An Interview with Jacques Derrida," in *Who Comes After the Subject?* ed. Eduardo Cadava et al. (New York: Routledge, 1991), 104.

27. Ibid., 105.

28. Ibid., 111.

29. Ibid., 108.

30. Ibid., 104.

31. Ibid., 111–12.

32. Ibid., 113. I discuss this important phrase further in Chapter 10.

33. Ibid., 116–17.

34. For example (ibid., 104): "Can one take into account the *necessity* of the *existential* analytic and what it shatters in the subject and turn towards an ethics, a politics (are these words still appropriate?), indeed an 'other' democracy (would it still be a democracy?), in any case towards another type of responsibility . . .? Don't expect from me an answer in the way of a formula. I think there are a certain number of us who are working for just this, and it can only take place by way of a long and slow trajectory. It cannot depend on a speculative decree, even less on an opinion. Perhaps not even on philosophical discursivity." See also ibid., 109, 116.

35. Ibid., 112.

36. Ibid.; my italics.

37. Ibid., 117.

38. Ibid., 118.

39. "L'Animal que donc je suis (à suivre)," in *L'Animal autobiographie: Autour de Jacques Derrida*, ed. M.-L. Mallet (Paris: Galilée, 1999), discussed in Baker, *The Postmodern Animal*, 74.

40. Ibid., 117.

41. Ibid., 109.

42. This is not to suggest that Derrida's overall project is founded on a concern for nonhuman animals. However, the case of his reading of Heidegger is instructive: were it not for the "awkwardness" of the animal in Heidegger's discourse—exploited by Derrida to great effect—Derrida's deconstruction might have been driven in a different direction.

43. Deleuze and Guattari, *A Thousand Plateaus*, 18 (the first ellipsis is theirs).

44. Ibid., 16.

45. Ibid., 22: In arborescent systems "all individuated enunciation remains trapped within the dominant significations, all signifying desire is associated with dominated subjects."

46. Ibid., 21.

47. Ibid., 11.

48. Ibid., 294.

49. Ibid., 18.

50. Ibid., 20.

51. Ibid., 15.

52. Ibid., 10.

53. Ibid., 237.

54. Ibid., 243–49.

55. Ibid., 256–60.

56. Ibid., 240.

57. Ibid., 279.

58. Ibid., 237.

59. Ibid., 237–38.

60. Ibid., 238–39.

61. Ibid., 240–41. This distinction is not offered as an ontological distinction between fundamentally different types of species: "There is always the possibility that a given animal, a louse, a cheetah or an elephant, will be treated as a pet, my little beast. And at the other extreme, it is also possible for any animal to be treated in the mode of the pack or swarm; that is our way, fellow sorcerers."

62. Ibid., 239–40.

63. Ibid., 273–74.

64. Ibid., 248. Indeed, they write that "all becomings are already molecular. That is because becoming is not to imitate or identify with something or someone" (272); and "Although all becomings are already molecular, including becoming-woman, it must be said that all becomings begin with and pass through becoming-woman" (277).

65. Ibid., 291.

66. Ibid., 247.

67. Ibid., 242.

68. Ibid., 238.

69. "Eating Well," 107–8.

70. See Baker, *The Postmodern Animal*, 149.

71. A theme developed by Derrida in *Of Grammatology*.

72. On the "rhizomatic" nature of recent genetic science, see Deleuze and Guattari, *A Thousand Plateaus*, 10–11.

73. See Donna J. Haraway, *Simians, Cyborgs, and Women: The Reinvention of Nature* (New York: Routledge, 1991), discussed in Baker, *The Postmodern Animal*, 100.

74. "L'Animal," quoted in Baker, *The Postmodern Animal*, 186.

75. Scholtmeijer, *Animal Victims*, 54.

76. The point echoes Jonas's argument discussed in Part I. See Chapter 2, note 15.

## Chapter 9: Ecophilosophy

1. The history of recent ecological philosophy and its relationship to the debate over animals is summarized by George Sessions in "Ecocentrism and the Anthropocentric Detour," in *Deep Ecology for the 21st Century*, 156–83. There, reflecting the view of many environmental ethicists, Sessions presents recent extensionist animal advocacy as tangential to ecophilosophical thought.

2. This is not to suggest that environmentalism is entirely incompatible with European thought, which is belied by the greater influence Green politics has had in Europe than in North America. Indeed, some of the critical work discussed in the previous chapter has had a marked impact on philosophical thinking about the environment. For example, Heidegger's critique of technology in the Western tradition and his existential analysis of human mortal existence as *dwelling on earth* have been important sources of inspiration for the deep ecological perspective; see Bill Devall and George Sessions, *Deep Ecology: Living As If Nature Mattered* (Salt Lake City: Peregrine Smith Books, 1985), 98–100. And demonstrated at the end of this chapter, some the conclusions of the post-structuralists are also compatible with ecophilosophy.

3. J. Baird Callicott, "Animal Liberation: A Triangular Affair," in Hargrove, *The Animal Rights/Environmental Ethics Debate*, 47–52.

4. Aldo Leopold, "The Land Ethic," in *A Sand County Almanac and Sketches Here and There* (New York: Oxford University Press, 1989), 224–25.

5. Arne Naess, "The Shallow and the Deep, Long-range Ecology Movements: A Summary," *Inquiry* (Oslo) 16 (1973), reprinted in *Deep Ecology for the 21st Century*, 151–55.

6. Paul Shepard, "Ecology and Man—A Viewpoint," in *Deep Ecology for the 21st Century*, 137. We can think of deep ecologists as extending Yamamoto's thought experiment cited in Chapter 1 to cover the exclusion of other elements of the natural world besides animate species: Suppose (in a parallel universe) *Homo sapiens* lived on a planet with no grasslands, mountains, rivers, forests, and so on. What sense of their "humanity" would the people on *that* planet have?

7. As Callicott writes, the "ecological picture of the earth and its biota can actuate the moral sentiments of affection, respect, love, and sympathy with which we human mammals are genetically endowed. It also actuates the special

sentiment or feeling (call it 'patriotism'), noticed by both Hume and Darwin, that we have for the *group as a whole* to which we belong, the *family* per se, the *tribe*, and the *country* or *nation*. From the point of view of modern biology, the earth with its living mantle is our tribe and each of its myriad species is, as it were, a separate clan"; "The Search for an Environmental Ethic," in *Matters of Life and Death*, ed. Tom Regan (New York: McGraw-Hill Higher Education, 1986), excerpted in Shaw, *Social and Personal Ethics*, 199.

8. Paul W. Taylor makes this point with respect to the ecological interpretation of the earth as an organic system: "Its ethical implications for our treatment of the natural environment lie entirely in the fact that our *knowledge* of these causal connections is an essential *means* to fulfilling the aims we set for ourselves in adopting the attitude of respect for nature . . . Its theoretical implications for the ethics of nature lie in the fact that it . . . makes the adopting of that attitude a rational and intelligible thing to do" ("The Ethics of Respect for Nature," in Hargrove, *The Animal Rights/Environmental Ethics Debate*, 109).

9. See Naess, "Self-Realization: An Ecological Approach to Being in the World," in *Deep Ecology for the 21st Century*, 225–39.

10. See Callicott, "Animal Liberation," 49–50. Interestingly, Nietzsche's metaphor has found some support in fact: it has been demonstrated that satellite views of human urban centers and their surrounding sprawl bear a striking resemblance to melanomas as they invade surrounding healthy skin tissue.

11. See Rolston, *Philosophy Gone Wild*, 213–15. However, others, such as Naess (see "The Deep Ecology 'Eight Points' Revisited," in Sessions, *Deep Ecology for the 21st Century*, 217), hold that only individuals can possess inherent value.

12. See Callicott, "The Search for an Environmental Ethic," 197. According to the International Union for Conservation of Nature and Natural Resources' 2006 "Redlist" of threatened species, of the 16,611 species that have been identified as "critically endangered," "endangered," or "vulnerable," 2,299 are mammals and birds; the rest are cold-blooded vertebrates, invertebrates, and plants.

13. Shepard, *Thinking Animals*, 247–48.

14. Ibid., 248.

15. Callicott, "Animal Liberation," 55. Cf. Scholtmeijer, *Animal Victims*, 57, where she poses the respect for such natural acts as predation as key to avoiding nihilism in the post-Darwinian world. See also Nietzsche, *Genealogy of Morals*, Second Essay, Section 11: "*in itself*, of course, no injury, assault, exploitation, destruction can be 'unjust,' since life operates *essentially*, that is, in its basic functions, through injury, assault, exploitation, destruction and simply cannot be thought of at all without this character."

16. See Chapter 8, note 75. It should be noted that Scholtmeijer does not share the deep ecologist's appraisal of sport hunting: see *Animal Victims*, 70.

17. See Callicott, "Search for an Environmental Ethic," 202, 203.

18. Henry David Thoreau, *Walden*, "Higher Laws," which also includes the following: "Fishermen, hunters, woodchoppers, and others, spending their lives in the fields and woods, in a peculiar sense a part of Nature themselves, are often in a more favorable mood for observing her, in the intervals of their pursuits, than philosophers or poets even, who approach her with expectation. She is not afraid to exhibit herself to them"; and "There is a period in the history of the individual, as of the race, when the hunters are the 'best men'—as the Algon-

quins called them. We cannot but pity the boy who has never fired a gun; he is no more humane, while his education has been sadly neglected . . . [Hunting] is oftenest the young man's introduction to the forest, and the most original part of himself. He goes thither at first as a hunter and fisher, until at last, if he has the seeds of a better life in him, he distinguishes his proper objects, as a poet or naturalist it may be, and leaves the gun and fish-pole behind."

19. Leopold, "Goose Music," quoted in Marti Kheel, "From Heroic to Holistic Ethics: The Ecofeminist Challenge," in *Ecofeminism*, 252.

20. See Devall and Sessions, *Deep Ecology*, 188. This theme is explored further in Part IV.

21. Callicott, "Animal Liberation," 52. It should be noted that Callicott later softens this view to accommodate Midgley's argument that the integration of domestic animals into human culture runs so deep as to justify their inclusion in our natural feelings of kin altruism. See "Animal Liberation and Environmental Ethics: Back Together Again," in Hargrove, *The Animal Rights/Environmental Ethics Debate*, 256. And while his earlier position on domestic animals is shared by other environmentalists, none of this is to suggest that environmentalism encourages active disregard for the interests of extant domestic animals.

22. Callicott, "Search for an Environmental Ethic," 198. It is likely that his argument would also lead us to class so-called *r* selection species such as rats, pigeons, and squirrels—which thrive in the environmental imbalances caused by human activity—as a kind of human artifact, lacking the ecological entitlement of other wild animals.

23. Callicott, "Animal Liberation," 54. Note Livingston's comment on a related point (*Rogue Primate*, 15–16): "It is interesting that the wild antecedents of a number of our domesticated animals are either already extinct or on the edge of being so . . . It seems that we do not wish to be reminded of the original wildness of our household creatures." As I explore in Part IV, the extensionist's preoccupation with domesticated animals may be a symptom of this psychology.

24. Callicott, "Animal Liberation," 58.

25. The deep ecological approach thus seems to finesse a difficulty that Scholtmeijer (*Animal Victims*, 86) astutely observes in extensionist arguments: "Viewing animals as subjects of morality need not represent a threat to animality in general. The problem resides in the utopian vision projected by such moral ideals. The hope for a universal 'Peaceable Kingdom' in which killing has ceased and no being persecutes another certainly does exclude the habits of the natural animal. Humanitarian acceptance of animal predation would appear culturally to entail the establishment of two moral communities, one for a population of gentle, vegetarian human beings, and another for the amoral, carnivorous animal—a kind of moral 'game preserve,' as it were. In terms of ethics, there is nothing especially wrong with this vision of two worlds, except in so far as it divides species even more thoroughly than they are currently divided."

26. Or, Naess's equally counterintuitive proposal ("Self-Realization," 234) that we "conceive of reality, or the world we live in, as alive in a wide, not easily defined sense. There will then be no non-living beings to care for."

27. Rolston, *Philosophy Gone Wild*, 69.

28. Clark, "Is Nature God's Will?" in Linzey and Yamamoto, *Animals on the Agenda*, 129–30.

29. Andrew Linzey, "Animal Welfare and Rights: Vegetarianism," in *Encyclopedia of Bioethics*, vol. 1, 172–73.

30. To take the example of North America, the "state of nature" prior to the arrival of human beings on the continent is significantly different from the state of nature at the time Europeans arrived, which is in turn significantly different from the state of wilderness areas that exist today. The question of what criteria modern environmentalists should use to compare these is explored in Daniel Botkin, *Our Natural History: The Lessons of Lewis and Clark* (New York: Berkley Publishing Group, 1996).

31. It should be noted that some environmental ethicists, such as Callicott ("Animal Liberation," 48), concede the point: "there can be no value apart from an evaluator, . . . all value is as it were in the eye of the beholder. The value that is attributed to the ecosystem, therefore, is humanly dependent or . . . at least dependent upon some variety of morally and aesthetically sensitive consciousness." Some have borrowed the economic concept of *existence value* to explain why persons might desire the preservation of wild spaces they may never experience: the value of such spaces is not intrinsic to them, but lies in the human knowledge that they exist.

32. Rolston, *Philosophy Gone Wild*, 103–4.

33. Ibid., 115.

34. Rolston (ibid., 114) asserts that if a nuclear disaster were about to make all mammalian species (including humans) extinct but leave the rest of the natural world intact, the last humans would have a moral obligation not to destroy the remaining biosphere, even though the value of that reality would remain unenjoyed by any sophisticated valuing consciousness.

35. Scholtmeijer, *Animal Victims*, 5.

36. Jonas, "Evolution and Freedom," 65–66. On a related point, Joseph Campbell speculates that Paleolithic man's fascination with the enduring nature of animal species—their apparent permanence relative to the flux of the natural world, and the births and deaths of individual members—provided a foundation in primitive thought for what would later become the definitive element of Platonism: that "Forms" or general ideas have a timeless objective reality. See *The Masks of God*, vol. 1: *Primitive Mythology* (New York: Viking, 1969), 292.

37. I return to the importance of this new animal aesthetic in Chapter 11. Celebrated examples include Damien Hirst's 1991 piece, *The Physical Impossibility of Death in the Mind of Someone Living*, which consists of a whole tiger shark corpse suspended in a glass tank of formaldehyde, and Mark Dion's 1993 *Library for the Birds of Antwerp*, a mixed-media piece featuring eighteen live African finches. As Baker (*The Postmodern Animal*, 96) summarizes this animal aesthetic: "Taken out of human meaning, the animal still holds to form." He quotes from an interview with animal artist John Issacs, who, in comparing the relationship of animals and humans to time, asserts: "We're actually the displaced on this planet. Animals are almost part of the geology" (ibid., 159). Whereas the deep ecologist's concern for species and ecosystems makes the individual animal but a part of larger gestalts, this aesthetic apprehension of the animal makes human culture and its effects on natural environments the changing backdrop against which the stability of extra-cultural animal reality stands out. From this perspective, domestication, genetic engineering, and species extinction are problematic because they threaten to destabilize this contrast.

38. See Regan, *The Case for Animal Rights*, 362; Kheel, "Liberation of Nature," 20. Less sophisticated critics of nature ethics have tried to poison the well by noting Hitler's vegetarianism and Himmler's invocation of the "sacredness of the soil."

39. Callicott, "Animal Liberation," 51–52.

40. See Sessions, "The Anthropocentric Detour," in *Deep Ecology for the 21st Century*, 176. It will be noted by animal advocates that in the same breath that Naess asserts the value of biospherical egalitarianism, he cautions that it can only be recognized "in principle," "because any realistic praxis necessitates some killing, exploitation, and suppression" ("The Shallow and the Deep," 150).

41. See Naess, "The Deep Ecological Movement: Some Philosophical Aspects," in *Deep Ecology for the 21st Century*, 68; "Self-Realization," 234, 238–39.

42. As an example, Rodman ("The Liberation of Nature?" 89, discussed in Frey, *Interests and Rights*, 164–65) reflects the distinction: "I confess that I need only to stand in the midst of a clear-cut forest, a strip-mined hillside, a defoliated jungle, or a dammed canyon to feel uneasy with assumptions that could yield the conclusion that no human action can make any difference to the welfare of anything but sentient animals. I am agnostic as to whether or not plants, rocks and rivers have subjective experience, and I am not sure that it really matters. I strongly suspect that the same basic principles are manifested in quite diverse forms: e.g., in damming a wild river and repressing an animal instinct (whether human or nonhuman), in clear-cutting a forest and bombing a city, in Dachau and a university research laboratory, in censoring an idea, liquidating a religious or racial group, and exterminating a species of flora or fauna." While many can relate to the type of *experience* to which Rodman refers, one would be hard pressed to develop a coherent philosophical ethic that can establish equivalence among all these types of action.

43. Naess, "The Shallow and the Deep," 71, 78–79.

44. See Devall and Sessions, *Deep Ecology*, 188; and Dolores LaChapelle, "Ritual—The Pattern That Connects," in *Deep Ecology for the 21st Century*, 57–63.

45. See Naess, "Self-Realization," 236, where he opposes environmental ethics to what he terms "environmental ontology."

46. Josephine Donovan, "Animal Rights and Feminist Theory," in *Beyond Animal Rights*, 40–46.

47. Derrida, "Eating Well," 113–14.

48. See Chapter 8, note 66. See also Deleuze and Guattari, *A Thousand Plateaus*, 275–76.

49. Deleuze and Guattari, *A Thousand Plateaus*, 291.

50. Valerius Geist, *Life Strategies, Human Evolution, Environmental Design: Toward a Biological Theory of Health* (New York: Springer-Verlag, 1978), 321–23.

51. See Janis Birkeland, "Ecofeminism: Linking Theory and Practice," in *Ecofeminism*, 30; and Kheel, "From Heroic to Holistic Ethics: The Ecofeminist Challenge," in *Ecofeminism*, 247–48.

52. For a summary, see Lori Gruen, "Dismantling Oppression: An Analysis of the Connection between Women and Animals," in *Ecofeminism*, 65–74. Some examples: The sexual objectification of women frequently finds expression in speciesist practices, the most obvious being the marketing to women of clothing

made from animal's fur, and cosmetics that have been extensively animal-tested or, in the case of perfumes, require the exploitation of civets to produce musk. Some feminists have drawn analogies between the objectification of women in pornography and the marketing of animal products by the meat industry. Carol Adams (*The Sexual Politics of Meat: A Feminist-Vegetarian Critical Theory*, Tenth Anniversary Edition [New York: Continuum International Publishing Group, 1999]) argues that the cruelty of factory farming disproportionately affects female animals—surrounding the production of what she terms "feminized protein"—in the treatment of egg-laying hens, dairy cows, and brood sows. She also documents—echoing Derrida's comments quoted above—how Western culture rewards the virility and power of the male eater of flesh. An important example from outside the West concerns the use of animals in so-called traditional medicine; important megafauna are being driven toward extinction in part as a result of the superstitious belief that men who consume preparations that contain rhinoceros horn or tiger penis will enhance their sexual potency.

53. Kheel, "The Liberation of Nature," 18. See also Birkeland, "Ecofeminism," 18–19.

54. Birkeland, "Ecofeminism," 16. She adds (ibid., 44) that often an environmentally objectionable practice "is a function of power relations that shape institutions, laws, and economic and planning methods, and only partly a function of chauvinism toward other animals."

55. Carol Gilligan, *In a Different Voice: Psychological Theory and Women's Development* (Cambridge, Mass.: Harvard University Press, 1982). For an example of the philosophical use of this work see Kheel, "Heroic," 255.

56. Most feminists have emphasized that "male" and "female" in these contexts are social and political constructions, not biological categories; others, however, adopt a kind of "gender essentialism," based on the ubiquity of male aggression and recent insight into the differences between male and female neurology.

57. Birkeland, "Ecofeminism," 25.

58. As Gruen ("Dismantling Oppression," 80) writes, "Constructing, and then naturalizing, hierarchies has been one of the more insidious justifying mechanisms for the oppression of both women and animals."

59. Linda Vance, "Ecofeminism and the Politics of Reality," in *Ecofeminism*, 124.

60. Kheel, "Heroic," 255. A representative example of the feminist critique of extensionism is found in Donovan, "Animal Rights and Feminist Theory," 40: "Just as the natural rights theory proposed by Regan inherently privileges rationality, Singer's utilitarianism relapses into a mode of manipulative mastery that is not unlike that used by scientific and medical experimenters to legitimate such animal abuses as vivisection. It is for this reason that we must turn to cultural feminism for alternative theory."

61. Kheel, "The Liberation of Nature," 26. The term *unified sensibility* is Robin Morgan's, but as Kheel demonstrates, the theme of unifying reason and emotion is found in many feminist works.

62. This theme in feminist ethics is echoed in Sapontzis's argument that an "affective value theory" is needed to produce an unbiased ethic for the nonhuman world: "Such a theory holds that values originate with feelings, such as pleasure and pain, fulfillment and frustration, joy and sorrow, excitement and depression,

and so forth. Without such feelings there are only matters of fact and definition, i.e. physical and conceptual configurations and changes" ("Aping Persons," 271).

63. This concept receives extensive treatment in Iris Murdoch's *The Sovereignty of Good*, an influential source for feminist ethicists. See Kheel, "Heroic," 256, and Donovan, "Attention to Suffering," 163–64.

64. Donovan, "Attention to Suffering," 152.

65. See ibid., 148 on the traditional origins of the ethics of care.

66. Salt, *Animals' Rights*, 114.

67. Gruen, "Dismantling Oppression," 79.

68. Kheel, "Heroic," 256.

69. Donovan, "Animal Rights and Feminist Theory," 51–52.

70. Kheel, "Heroic," 257, and "Liberation of Nature," 27, where she writes: "Emotion easily divides from reason when we are divorced from the immediate impact of our moral decisions."

71. As Bridget Brophy ("In Pursuit of a Fantasy," in Godlovitch et al., *Animals, Men and Morals*, 126) writes: "Reason is necessarily the language of moral, political and scientific argument: not because reason is holy or on some elevated plane, but because it *isn't*; because it is accessible to all humans; because, as well as working, it can be seen to work."

72. For example, Kheel ("The Liberation of Nature," 31) writes: "Few of us . . . would relinquish the idea that we, as humans, are more important than a stone. Yet, by showing that such a thought is based, in fact, on a feeling and that it cannot be justified by rational thought alone, we may be able to detach from our egos long enough to see that we are, indeed, all part of a whole of which no part may rationally be said to be more important than another." What exactly she means by "important" is left vague, but it should be clear that there are rational grounds for considering a human life to be of greater moral significance than a stone. Any line of thought that could not express such grounds ought to be rejected.

73. Andrew Linzey, "Animal Welfare and Rights: Pet and Companion Animals," in *Encyclopedia of Bioethics*, vol. 1, 182. Cf. Berger, "Why Look at Animals?" 12–13: "The pet completes [the owner], offering responses to aspects of his character which would otherwise remain unconfirmed. He can be to his pet what he is not to anybody or anything else. Furthermore, the pet can be conditioned to react as though it, too, recognises this. The pet offers its owner a mirror to a part that is otherwise never reflected. But, since in this relationship the autonomy of both parties has been lost (the owner has become the-special-man-he-is-only-to-his-pet, and the animal has become dependent on its owner for every physical need), the parallelism of their separate lives has been destroyed."

74. Cf. Salt (*Animals' Rights*, 42): "Pets, like kings' favorites, are usually the recipients of an abundance of sentimental affection but of little real kindness; so much easier is it to give temporary caresses than substantial justice."

75. Carol J. Adams, "Feminist Traffic in Animals," in *Ecofeminism*, 210–11.

76. A problem acknowledged by Donovan, "Attention to Suffering," 157; and Kheel, "Liberation of Nature," 28.

77. Gruen, "Dismantling Oppression," 77–78.

78. Vance, "Ecofeminism and the Politics of Reality," 125, and the corresponding endnote on 143.

79. Birkeland, "Ecofeminism," 29. On a related point, Greta Gaard cautions against what she terms "cultural cannibalism" on the part of some deep ecolo-

gists, who selectively adopt individual beliefs and practices from Native American and Eastern cultures, without appreciating the larger contexts from which they emerge (Greta Gaard, "Ecofeminism and Native American Cultures: Pushing the Limits of Cultural Imperialism?", in *Ecofeminism*, 296).

80. Birkeland, "Ecofeminism," 27.

81. Vance, "Ecofeminism," 135.

82. Kheel, "Heroic," 258–59. As a cautionary note on this theme of interconnectedness, see note 13 above: since not every individual or every species is essential to the long-term health of particular ecosystems, some nature ethicists who stress the "web" metaphor for our relationship to the biosphere risk ascribing an almost mystical valuation to every living thing that is not supported by environmental science.

83. Ynestra King, "The Ecology of Feminism and the Feminism of Ecology," quoted in Gruen, "Dismantling Oppression," 80.

84. Kheel, "Heroic," 244, my italics.

85. As Alison Jaggar ("Feminist Ethics: Some Issues for the Nineties," *Journal of Social* Philosophy 20, nos. 1–2 [Spring–Fall 1989]) makes the point: "moral epistemology is an area in which feminists' critiques are better developed than their alternatives."

86. See Birkeland, "Ecofeminism," 20; Kheel, "Liberation," 22.

87. For example, Rita Manning makes the explicit argument in "Caring for Animals," in *Beyond Animal Rights*, 118; it is implicit in Donovan's "Animal Rights and Feminist Theory," which she dedicates to her dog. Ecofeminists generally argue for a biocentric respect for the wild (see Vance, "Ecofeminism," 141) but have been critical of the deep ecologists' masculinist glorification of the act of hunting. See Marti Kheel, "License to Kill: An Ecofeminist Critique of Hunters' Discourse," in *Animals and Women*, 95–104.

88. Kheel, "Liberation of Nature," 22.

89. Kheel, "Heroic," 243–44.

90. Vance, "Ecofeminism," 125–26.

91. Kheel, "Heroic," 244.

92. Gaard, "Ecofeminism and Native American Cultures," 305.

93. As Vance ("Ecofeminism," 137) writes: "Clearly, ecofeminists cannot expect to initiate huge demographic transitions within our lifetimes, or, most likely, within the imaginable future. What we can do, however, is make the need for responsible cooperation with the land known, and use our own lives to model the possibilities."

94. See Birkeland, "Ecofeminism," 46; Vance, "Ecofeminism," 138–40.

95. See Devall and Sessions, *Deep Ecology*, 18–24.

96. Deane Curtin, "Toward an Ecological Ethic of Care," in *Beyond Animal Rights*, 72.

97. See Vance, "Ecofeminism," 141; Devall and Sessions, *Deep Ecology*, 111–15.

98. As Rolston concedes (*Philosophy Gone Wild*, 70): "A fair criticism of what we have proposed is that it is impressionistic and difficult to make 'operational,' so accordingly we do also need the logic that unfolds under other models of life and responsibility."

## Chapter 10: Sacrifice and Self-Overcoming

1. José Ortega y Gasset, *History as a System*, in Walter Kaufmann, *Existentialism from Dostoevsky to Sartre*, rev. ed. (New York: New American Library, 1975), 154.

2. Scholtmeijer, *Animal Victims*, 54.

3. *Birth of Tragedy*, "Attempt at Self-criticism," Section 4 (Kaufmann translation). The question suggests the polemical theme of *Genealogy of Morals:* What is the value of value? See Preface, Sections 3 and 6.

4. *Genealogy*, First Essay, Section 17 (Kaufmann translation).

5. See *Beyond Good and Evil*, Section 186, the first section in the chapter entitled "Natural History of Morals."

6. See, for example, *Genealogy*, First Essay, Section 3.

7. See also *Daybreak*, Section 26 (Hollingdale translation): "The beginnings of justice, as of prudence, moderation, bravery in short, of all we designate as the *Socratic virtues*, are *animal:* a consequence of that drive which teaches us to seek food and elude enemies. Now if we consider that even the highest human being has only become more elevated and subtle in the nature of his food and in his conception of what is inimical to him, it is not improper to describe the entire phenomenon of morality as animal."

8. See *Genealogy*, Second Essay, Section 12.

9. For a summary, see Daniel Dennett, *Darwin's Dangerous Idea: Evolution and the Meanings of Life* (New York: Simon and Schuster, 1995), 467–93.

10. Raymond Corbey, "Ambiguous Apes," in Cavalieri and Singer, *The Great Ape Project*, 135.

11. *Genealogy*, First Essay, Section 11. The image of the "beast of prey" is discussed below.

12. *Will to Power*, note 864.

13. *Gay Science*, Section 352. Cf. Shepard, *Tender Carnivore*, 18: "The qualities derived from planting are most clearly seen in the later peasant farmers of the civilized or historical agricultural state. They adhere to the native soil, revere their ancestors, are sober-minded, and have strong codes of conduct. They are simple, industrious, tenacious, and predictable. But simplicity can mean dull wits, and industry can be a kind word for toil, the price and token of security, respect, and piety. The other virtues are euphemisms for the simplified, repetitive life of people whose bulldog grip on their humanity is misinterpreted as contentment and wise serenity."

14. *Beyond Good and Evil*, Section 44.

15. *Genealogy*, Second Essay, Section 24.

16. *Will to Power*, note 397 (Kaufmann translation). The passage later includes the line: "In order to be fair to morality, we must put two zoological concepts in its place: *taming* of the beast and *breeding* of a particular species."

17. *Beyond Good and Evil*, Section 202 (Kaufmann translation).

18. Livingston, *Rogue Primate*, 174.

19. Ibid., 164.

20. Ibid., 14.

21. Ibid., 10.

22. Ibid., 12. Cf. Geist, *Life Strategies*, 392–93: "Diversity under agricultural surplus conditions is produced by reproduction of individuals that are capable of

being skilled in only a few abilities, but that suffice to make them desirable and even prestigious members of society. Such individuals have as much a chance to reproduce as individuals who have a wide range of faculties well developed, as was demanded by Paleolithic conditions. This promotes genetic diversity, as well as an increase in the genetic load. The process can be termed self-domestication. It explains, in part, the reduction of brain size in humans since the Paleolithic. We find the very same in domestic animals."

23. Livingston, "Ethics as Prosthetics," in *Environmental Ethics: Philosophical and Policy Perspectives*, ed. Phillip P. Hanson (Burnaby, B.C.: Institute for the Humanities, Simon Fraser University Publications, 1986), 67.

24. *Rogue Primate*, 163. See also "Ethics as Prosthetics," 70.

25. *Rogue Primate*, 10. Cf. Nietzsche, *Twilight of the Idols*, "The Problem of Socrates," Section 10, in which he locates the origins of Western moral thought in the "fanaticism with which the whole of Greek thought throws itself at rationality."

26. *Rogue Primate*, 139. Cf. Shepard, *Tender Carnivore*, 18–20, where he links homocentricity with agrarian domesticity.

27. *Rogue Primate*, 100–104; "Ethics as Prosthetics," 73.

28. "Ethics as Prosthetics," 71–72.

29. Midgley, *Animals and Why They Matter*, Chapter 10.

30. Shepard, *Tender Carnivore*, 4–9. A detailed defense of this kind of explanation is developed by archeologist Kent Flannery, discussed in Christine Mary Rodrigue, "An Evaluation of Ritual Sacrifice as an Explanation for Early Animal Domestications in the Near East" (Ph.D. dissertation, Clark University, Worcester, Massachusetts, 1986), 21–25. Mythologist Joseph Campbell offers the interesting speculation that the catalyst for this process in the Near East may have been the cross-pollination of northern Paleolithic hunting cultures and southern Paleolithic planting cultures, their sharing of primitive techniques of herding and plant cultivation perhaps inspiring the creation of agriculture proper; see *Masks of God*, 401.

31. Livingston, "Ethics as Prosthetics," 70–71.

32. *Genealogy of Morals*, Second Essay, Section 16.

33. Ibid., Second Essay, Section 17.

34. The range of explanations that has been offered is thoughtfully reviewed in Rodrigue, "An Evaluation of Ritual Sacrifice," 10–61.

35. Some have even suggested that the domestication of other animals was not an intentional process, but something more akin to a gradual coevolution between humans and other species, explainable by principles of adaptation. See David Rhindos, *The Origins of Agriculture: An Evolutionary Perspective* (discussed in Rodrigue, "An Evaluation of Ritual Sacrifice," 27–34), and Stephen Budiansky, *The Covenant of the Wild: Why Animals Chose Domestication* (New Haven: Yale University Press, 1999). Michael Pollan makes an interesting argument of this type concerning the domestication of plants; see his *The Botany of Desire: A Plant's-eye View of the World* (New York: Random House, 2001).

36. See Shepard, *Tender Carnivore*, Chapter 1, "Ten Thousand Years of Crisis." His and other arguments on this point are developed by the anarcho-primitivist John Zerzan in *Elements of Refusal* (Seattle: Left Bank, 1988), 68–73.

37. See Lori Gruen, "Dismantling Oppression," 64, 85; Rodrigue, "An Evaluation of Ritual Sacrifice," 56–57, 64, 72–73.

38. The case can be made that in certain cultures particular types of animals were domesticated for specific religious purposes; for example, in religions that attach significance to the moon, the domestication and use of ungulates with curved, crescent-like horns is predominant. But this by itself is insufficient to ground sacrifice as the total explanation for domestication, and it would be unreasonable to ignore entirely the collective effect of numerous practical and economic incentives to tame wild herd animals. The strongest counterargument to the religious explanation is that sacrificial rites proper are clearly discernible only in sedentary, socially stratified cultures, a presumed *precondition* of which is domestic agriculture. See Rodrigue, "An Evaluation of Ritual Sacrifice," 169–83.

39. Shepard, *Tender Carnivore*, 143–44.

40. See Campbell, *Masks of God*, 292–93. Cf. Berger, "Why Look at Animals?" 2, where he notes that in the earliest human cultures the material exploitation of animals was something secondary to their spiritual and magical functions, and came only at the "invitation" of the animals themselves. The relationship between shaman and "master animal" in hunting mythology seems to be an archetype for one of the literary themes discussed by Deleuze and Guattari: the becoming-animal of the sorcerer, who—on the fringes of civilization—forms an alliance with the animal pack.

41. Campbell, *Masks of God*, 295–98.

42. For example, *Tender Carnivore*, 152–54.

43. Campbell, *Masks of God*, 349–50. See also Ortega, who asserts that "every good hunter is uneasy in the depths of his conscience when faced with the death he is about to inflict on the enchanting animal" (*Meditations on Hunting*, 98), an uneasiness that becomes overwhelmingly real when seeing "the frightening mystery of blood," the radical absurdity of the "purely internal made external" (ibid., 100).

44. Sigmund Freud, *Totem and Taboo*, trans. James Strachey (New York: W. W. Norton and Company, 1989), 142–44. Of course, Freud is most interested in totemic laws concerning exogamy and the incest taboo, which is of less concern here.

45. For example, Shepard, drawing on the insights of Alfred Reginald Radcliffe-Brown and Claude Lévi-Straus, interprets totemism as the attempt to model human social relations on the complex ecological relations of other animals—a way of using "animals and plants [to] mediate between culture and nature in the mental life of man"—yet he offers no interpretation of the totemic feast. See *Tender Carnivore*, 202–5; and *Thinking Animals*, 125–30.

46. Freud, *Totem and Taboo*, 174–75. The passage begs comparison with Nietzsche's analysis of the link between the enjoyment of cruelty and the festival; see *Genealogy*, Second Essay, Section 6.

47. It is noteworthy that in pre-totemic cultures *all* animal kills required attendant ceremonial rites, whereas in late totemic cultures wild animals could be hunted by the individual at liberty, and only the sacrifice of the domesticated totem was taboo (see *Totem and Taboo*, 168–70). Thus, the historical teleology of sacrifice seems to be one of increasing intensification, with single communal ceremonies ultimately having the power to sanctify the entire way of life of the community.

48. Ṣcholtmeijer, *Animal Victims*, 80, drawing on René Girard's *Scapegoat and Things Hidden since the Foundation of the World.*

49. Quoted in Sorabji, *Animal Minds*, 170.

50. How the individual becomes dependent upon and indebted to tradition is a theme developed by Nietzsche in several texts. On the role of sacrifice in this process, see *Genealogy*, Second Essay, Section 19.

51. See Shepard, *Tender Carnivore*, 9–16; Livingston, *Rogue Primate*, 16–27.

52. See Jim Mason, "Disensoulment," in Bekoff and Meaney, *Encyclopedia of Animal Rights*, 288.

53. Quoted in Freud, *Totem and Taboo*, 170.

54. Scholtmeijer, *Animal Victims*, 81.

55. Sorabji (*Animal Minds*, 170) notes that religious sacrifices provided most of the animals used for food in pre-Christian Greece, and that meat that had not been sacrificed must have been difficult for early Christians to obtain.

56. See Marti Kheel, "From Heroic to Holistic Ethics," 254.

57. Nietzsche, too, appreciated the connection between sacrifice and the anthropocentrism of ethical reasoning. He writes in *Genealogy*, Second Essay, Section 2, concerning the *sovereign individual* that domesticating culture breeds: "this master of a *free* will, this sovereign man—how should he not be aware of his superiority over all those who lack the right to make promises and stand as their own guarantors, of how much trust, how much fear, how much reverence he arouses—he '*deserves*' all three—and of how this mastery over himself also necessarily gives him mastery over circumstances, over nature, and over all more short-willed and unreliable creatures?" Then, in Section 3, he notes the power of bloody sacrificial rites to help burn the capacity for memory that a sovereign individual requires.

58. For example, see *Ecce Homo*, "Why I Am a Destiny," Section 3, and *Genealogy*, Third Essay, Section 27.

59. See Livingston, *Rogue Primate*, 32–34; and Geist's comment in note 22 above.

60. Shepard, *Tender Carnivore*, 15–16. Not that this amounts to a compliment; Shepard concludes (ibid., 16) that "man is not properly a domestic animal, although civilization has disrupted his epigenetic stability and loosed a horde of 'goofies.'" Livingston grants Shepard's point that our retention of social and communication skills marks a significant difference between humans and other domesticated animals; see *Rogue Primate*, 34–35.

61. *Will to Power*, note 684.

62. "Ethics as Prosthetics," 76 (the Shepard quote is from *Madness and Civilization*).

63. Scholtmeijer, *Animal Victims*, 82. It is not clear whether Scholtmeijer has in mind culture per se, or the domesticated culture that defines Western civilization. I take the analyses of Nietzsche, Livingston, and Derrida used in the preceding two sections to be directed at the latter, leaving open the possibility that other, less problematic cultural possibilities exist.

64. Brian Luke, "Taming Ourselves or Going Feral? Toward a Nonpatriarchal Metaethic of Animal Liberation," in *Animals and Women*, 313 (my italics).

65. This seems to be the suggestion of Scholtmeijer (*Animal Victims*, 83): "If it is true that only the uncivilized human being is alarmed at the killing of animals

and requires mechanisms for assuaging conscience, then current concern for the lives of animals does not necessarily indicate urban squeamishness over the shedding of blood. Instead of signaling an extension of pre-established ethics to accommodate animals, the present effort to find grounds for the rights of animals might originate in the subversion of known culture by as yet unarticulated and long-buried forces in the collective mind. All animals are wild animals for the pre-civilized person; all are his or her equals or superiors and demand atonement for trespass upon the sanctity of their lives."

66. Nietzsche, *The Birth of Tragedy*, Section 8.

67. *Will to Power*, note 120; later in the note he writes: "We no longer love [nature] on account of its 'innocence,' 'reason' or 'beauty'; we have made it nicely 'devilish' and 'dumb.' But instead of despising it on that account, we have felt more closely related to it ever since, more at home in it. It does *not* aspire to virtue, and for that we respect nature."

68. For example, *Genealogy*, First Essay, Section 11, where Nietzsche describes the "noble" type of human being that was superseded by the "slave revolt" in morality: "Once they go outside, where the strange, the *stranger* is found, they are not much better than uncaged beasts of prey. There they savor a freedom from all social constraints, they compensate themselves in the wilderness for the tension engendered by protracted confinement and enclosure within the peace of society, they go *back* to the innocent conscience of the beast of prey, as triumphant monsters who perhaps emerge from a disgusting procession of murder, arson, rape, and torture, exhilarated and undisturbed of soul, as if it were no more than a students' prank." See also *Beyond Good and Evil*, Section 257, where again Nietzsche equates noble human beings with natural "men of prey who were still in possession of unbroken strength of will and lust for power . . . more *whole* human beings (which also means, at every level, 'more whole beasts')."

69. As Scholtmeijer (*Animal Victims*, 68) notes, "Animals suffer for our rejection of what we consider to be the animal aspects of human culture."

70. *Will to Power*, note 124.

71. See, for example, ibid., note 660, which analyzes the human body as a political structure. In *Beyond Good and Evil*, Section 22, Nietzsche seems to acknowledge that his transposition of human political concepts to the biotic realm is problematic.

72. Anyone who has attempted to identify a thread of consistency running through Nietzsche's various invocations of the term will appreciate Deleuze's conclusion that the will to power "is an essentially *plastic* principle that is no wider than what it conditions, that changes itself with the conditioned and determines itself in each case along with what it determines"; *Nietzsche and Philosophy*, trans. Hugh Tomlinson (New York: Columbia University Press, 1983), 50.

73. For example, see *Will to Power*, note 55.

74. For example, see *Thus Spoke Zarathustra*, "On Self-Overcoming."

75. The future-directedness of Nietzsche's thought seems especially unnatural. See Livingston, *Rogue Primate*, 183–84: "The Western future-orientation is virtually total. Our self-identities as individuals and societies—maybe even as a

species—appear to be cast in terms not of what we have been, nor of *what* we are, but of what we shall *become*. But *only humans become.*"

76. Ibid., 45–51.

77. These are only known to have occurred outside of Africa—presumably because early *Homos* evolved within the continent's ecosystems—notably in North America and in Polynesia and New Zealand. See R. N. Holdaway and C. Jacomb, "Rapid Extinction of the Moas (Aves: Dinornithiformes): Model, Test, and Implications," *Science* 287 (24 March 2000): 2250–54. It should be noted that some biologists are skeptical of the "blitzkrieg" hypothesis, arguing that these extinctions may have been simply the result of the inability of prey species to recognize the new predators as such, rather than evidence of a will to dominance on the part of Paleolithic humans.

78. *Rogue Primate*, 89.

79. Ibid., 182–83.

80. Ibid., 167: "We know in our tissue and bone and viscera that order and peacefulness are good, and natural, and that their absence is neither. We know that not as academicians but as biological beings. It is that inherent knowledge that prompts us to construct legal, moral, and ethical systems. It is usual to credit such constructions to 'innate human decency.' I believe it to be, rather, our vestigial inherent animal compulsion to comply."

81. Luke, "Taming Ourselves or Going Feral?" 313.

82. Ibid., 302.

83. Ortega, *Meditations on Hunting*, 112.

84. Livingston, "Ethics as Prosthetics," 68.

85. *Rogue Primate*, 10.

## Chapter 11: The Child, the Hunter, and the Artist

1. Livingston, *Rogue Primate*, 10.

2. See *Will to Power*, note 871; *Beyond Good and Evil*, Section 188.

3. *Rogue Primate*, 196–97.

4. Midgley, *Animals and Why They Matter*, 145.

5. Ortega, *Meditations on Hunting*, 124.

6. Ibid., 121.

7. Ibid., 125. He adds (ibid., 127) concerning the exploitation of these availabilities in the present: "The hunter is, at one and the same time, a man of today and one of ten thousand years ago. In hunting, the long process of universal history coils up and bites its own tail."

8. Shepard, *Tender Carnivore*, 146.

9. Ortega, *Meditations on Hunting*, 125.

10. Ibid., 125–26.

11. Quoted in Gaffney, "Can Catholic Morality Make Room for Animals?" in Linzey and Yamamoto, *Animals on the Agenda*, 111.

12. The one favored by humane animal advocates is that the mastery of fire by early *Homos* was more fundamental than hunting, for it made possible the cooking of otherwise indigestible vegetable foods (meat does not need to be cooked to be digested by humans); the gathering of cookable roots and tubers requires social organization and the development of tools, their high carbohydrate con-

tent could have provided the caloric intake necessary for the development of large brains, and the institution of cooking would have favored monogamous family structures.

13. Geist, *Life Strategies*, 354–55.

14. Campbell, *Masks of God*, 397–98.

15. For a review of the important interpretations that have been offered of Upper Paleolithic cave art, and a compelling argument for their shamanic function, see David Lewis-Williams, *The Mind in the Cave* (London: Thames & Hudson, 2002).

16. Shepard, *Tender Carnivore*, 241.

17. Ibid., 144–45.

18. Rollin, *Animal Rights*, 92.

19. Compare Ortega with Deleuze and Guattari on this point. Ortega writes (*Mediations on Hunting*, 132): "*hunting is an imitation of the animal* . . . In that mystical union with the beast a contagion is immediately generated and the hunter begins to behave like the game." In strikingly similar language, Deleuze and Guattari (*A Thousand Plateaus*, 242) write that "animals are packs, and that packs form, develop, and are transformed by contagion. These multiplicities with heterogeneous terms, cofunctioning by contagion, enter certain *assemblages*; it is there that human beings effect their becomings-animal. But we should not confuse these dark assemblages, which stir what is deepest within us, with organizations such as the institution of the family and the State apparatus. We could cite hunting societies, war societies, secret societies, crime societies, etc. Becomings-animal are proper to them."

20. Ortega, *Meditations on Hunting*, 132.

21. See Paul S. Martin and Christine R. Szuter, "War Zones and Game Sinks in Lewis and Clark's West," *Conservation Biology* 13, no. 1 (February 1999): 36–45.

22. Geist, *Life Strategies*, 390.

23. Ortega, *Meditations on Hunting*, 128–29.

24. See ibid., 106, where Ortega likens the need for the hunt to end in death to a *religious mystery*.

25. Gruen, "Dismantling Oppression," 62.

26. Geist, *Life Strategies*, 321–23.

27. Ibid., 390–91: "The discovery of animal milk as food, and its consequent husbanding as a reliable supply of high-quality protein, must have led to fundamental restructuring of a society in which agriculturists previously depended on domestic plants plus the meat and eggs of wild animals for food. First, animal milk can be used directly to feed the human infant, relieving the male of the necessity to structure a supportive psychological milieu for his wife or wives . . . The role of the *mother per se* is degraded. In her absence or inability to produce milk the infant can still be raised on animal milk. The availability of animal milk permits an increase in reproduction, an increase in phenotypic development of individuals, and thus production of more and better soldiers to protect the society. It also increases the expendability of males and permits warfare to flourish more frequently and with greater loss of life; warfare can be less ceremonious. The availability of animal labor, of course, also aids warfare as well as permitting greater exploitation of the soil for crop production." It should be noted, however, that Gruen is well aware of the androcentrism of agrarian culture; see "Dismantling Oppression," 63.

28. Shepard, *Tender Carnivore*, 135–37.

29. See Olga Soffer et al., "The 'Venus' Figurines," *Current Anthropology*, August–October 2000, vol. 41, Issue 4, 511–38.

30. Quoted in Nicholas Wade, "What's It All About, Alpha?" *New York Times*, 7 November 1999, Section 4, 1–2.

31. Geist, *Life Strategies*, 395.

32. Ortega, *Meditations on Hunting*, 131.

33. Shepard is guilty of such utopianism. In *The Tender Carnivore*, Chapter 6, he outlines an alternative to our current cultural and ecological crises that he terms "techno-cynegetics": a turn to chemical-based food production; the relocation of human population centers to the peripheries of continents, thereby allowing for the maximization of wild space; the use of intensive city planning to reduce the size of human communities and encourage a return to tribalism—all as the means resurrecting the hunting culture that was overthrown by agriculture. Even if the steps necessary to effect such radical cultural, economic, and geographic transformations can be rationally justified, one could not reasonably expect them to be implemented quickly enough to save the animal—if they could be accomplished at all.

34. Berger, "Why Look at Animals?" 9–10, 15–17.

35. Indeed, this is already a reality. There is a variety of genetically modified organisms commercially available, ranging from pet fish that have been "designed" to glow in the dark, to the infamous "Oncomouse," whose patented genetic design makes it vulnerable to contracting cancers, and therefore useful in medical reseach.

36. Berger, "Why Look at Animals?" 26: "That look between animal and man, which may have played a crucial role in the development of human society, and with which, in any case, all men had always lived until less than a century ago, has been extinguished. Looking at each animal, the unaccompanied zoo visitor is alone. As for the crowds, they belong to a species which has at last been isolated. This historic loss, to which zoos are a monument, is now irredeemable for the culture of capitalism."

37. See Baker, *The Postmodern Animal*, 164–65.

38. See Shepard, *Tender Carnivore*, 222; Geist, *Life Strategies*, 321–22.

39. The importance of aesthetic considerations in the appreciation of the non-human world has been a prominent theme in environmental thought. For example, we saw in Chapter 9 that Leopold lists "beauty"—what is "esthetically right"—among the biocentric criteria of his land ethic. Because beauty and other aesthetic concepts can apply to non-sentient elements of nature more smoothly than traditional moral categories, many subsequent environmental ethicists have addressed the usefulness of aesthetic considerations in spelling out limits to human behavior vis-à-vis the natural world. See, for example, Norman H. Morse, "An Environmental Ethic—Its Formulation and Implications," in Hanson, *Environmental Ethics*, 28–29; Eugene Hargrove, "The Aesthetics of Wildlife Preservation," in *Earth Ethics: Introductory Readings on Animal Rights and Environmental Ethics*, 2nd ed., ed. James P. Sterba (Upper Saddle River, N.J.: Prentice-Hall, 2000), 132–38; and Lily-Marlene Russow, "Why Do Species Matter?" *Environmental Ethics* 3 (Summer 1981): 103–12. For examples of extensionist animal advocates who recognize a supplemental value to aesthetic

considerations, see Rollin, *Animal Rights*, 103–4; and Clark, "Modern Errors, Ancient Virtues," in *Animals and Their Moral Standing*, 167–68.

40. Often compared by its practitioners to that of sexuality, as the dual senses of the word *venery* reveal.

41. Maureen Duffy, "Beasts for Pleasure," in Godlovitch et al., *Animals, Men and Morals*, 120–21.

42. *Critique of Judgment*, Section 5.

43. Among Kant's followers, one may cite the poet Friedrich Schiller, who argued that in the aesthetic we find the operation of a "play drive" that reveals our full humanity by integrating our sensuous and rational dimensions; see his *On the Aesthetic Education of Man in a Series of Letters*. A stronger example is to be found in John Dewey's *Art as Experience*; although no Kantian, Dewey offers an analysis of human aesthetic experience aimed at revealing its continuity with animal sentience.

44. "The wolf shall dwell with the lamb, and the leopard shall lie down with the kid, and the calf and the lion and the fatling together, and a little child shall lead them. The cow and the bear shall feed; their young shall lie down together; and the lion shall eat straw like the ox. The suckling child shall play over the hole of the asp, and the weaned child shall put his hand on the adder's den. They shall not hurt or destroy in all my holy mountain; for the earth shall be full of the knowledge of the lord as the waters cover the sea."

45. See Scholtmeijer, *Animal Victims*, 42–43.

46. Baker, *The Postmodern Animal*, 19.

47. For a full analysis, see Marjorie Hope Nicolson, *Mountain Gloom and Mountain Glory: The Development of the Aesthetic of the Infinite* (Seattle: University of Washington Press, 1997).

48. Kant, *Critique of Judgment*, Sections 24–29; I here gloss over Kant's distinction between the "mathematically" and "dynamically" sublime. It is noteworthy that in Section 26 Kant asserts that the aesthetic apprehension of the animal form cannot occasion the sublime; his point becomes clear in Section 58, where he argues that the elegance of these forms is unnecessary for the animals themselves, and thus they seem to have been chosen by nature "with an eye to our taste." Thus, for Kant the animal form evidences the conformity of nature to human sensibility, and so cannot give rise to the intuition of human transcendence.

49. See Scholtmeijer, *Animal Victims*, 56–57.

50. "Why Look at Animals?" 14 (italics added).

51. See Ortega, *Meditations on Hunting*, 103–5; Shepard, *Tender Carnivore*, 151. Their point is echoed by environmental aestheticist Allen Carlson: "Thus aesthetic appreciation of the environment is not simply a matter of looking at objects or 'views' from a specific point. Rather, it is being 'in the midst' of them, moving with regard to them, looking at them from any and every point and distance and, of course, not only looking but smelling, hearing, touching, feeling. It is being in the environment, being a part of the environment, and reacting as a part of it. It is such active involved aesthetic appreciation, rather than the formal mode of appreciation nurtured by the scenery cult and encouraged by photographs, that is appropriate to the natural environment" (*Aesthetics and the Environment: The Appreciation of Nature, Art and Architecture* [London and New York: Routledge, 2000], 35).

52. Some examples are discussed in Chapter 9, note 37.

53. Baker, *The Postmodern Animal*, 81–82.

54. Scholtmeijer, *Animal Victims*, 91. Livingston ("Ethics as Prosthetics," 75) echoes her point, arguing that our dealings with animals today should not depend on the rational calculations of ethicists, but instead require the poet's ability to "perceive without recourse to archetypes (or, more often, stereotypes)."

55. Kant, *Critique of Judgment*, Section 42. As Rolston reads such experiences (*Philosophy Gone Wild*, 108), the fact that deception can destroy the aesthetic satisfaction of natural objects imbues our aesthetic appreciation of nature with epistemological and ontological significance.

56. Rolston writes (*Philosophy Gone Wild*, 99): "We can be thrilled by a hawk in the wind-swept sky, by the rings of Saturn, the falls of Yosemite . . . All these experiences come mediated by our cultural education; some are made possible by science. An Iroquois would have variant experiences, or none at all. But these experiences have high elements of givenness, of finding something thrown at us, of successful observation." I am suggesting here that the "givenness" is more profound in the case of our experience of animals than other elements of the natural world.

57. As Carlson's *Aesthetics and the Environment* shows, the search for such an alternative has been prominent in environmental aesthetics. Comparable work on the aesthetics of animals is still needed.

58. See Sarah Boxer, "A Memorial Is Itself a Shaper of Memory," *New York Times*, 27 October 2001, Section A, Column 1, 11.


## Conclusion

1. *Daybreak*, Section 333. Cf. *Gay Science*, Section 224; and Livingston, *Rogue Primate*, 174–75 (see Chapter 6, note 39).

2. Shepard, *Tender Carnivore*, 265.

3. Deleuze and Guattari, *A Thousand Plateaus*, 240.

4. Ortega, *Meditations on Hunting*, 138.

5. Ibid., 140.

# BIBLIOGRAPHY

Adams, Carol J., and Josephine Donovan, eds. *Animals and Women: Feminist Theoretical Explorations.* Durham: Duke University Press, 1995.

———. *Beyond Animal Rights: A Feminist Caring Ethic for the Treatment of Animals.* New York: The Continuum Publishing Company, 1996.

Allen, Colin, and Marc Bekoff. *Species of Mind: The Philosophy and Biology of Cognitive Ethology.* Cambridge: MIT Press, 1997.

Aquinas. *Summa Theologica.* Trans. Fathers of the English Dominican Province. Westminster, Md.: Christian Classics, 1981.

Aristotle. *Historia Animalium.* Trans. D'Arcy Wentworth Thompson. Oxford: Clarendon Press, 1910. .

———. *Metaphysics.* Trans. Richard Hope. Ann Arbor: University of Michigan Press, 1960.

———. *Nicomachean Ethics.* Trans. Martin Ostwald. Indianapolis: Bobbs-Merrill, 1962.

———. *On the Parts of Animals.* Trans. William Ogle. New York: Garland Publishing, 1987.

———. *On the Soul.* Trans. Hippocrates G. Apostle. Grinnell, Iowa: Peripatetic Press, 1981.

———. *Politics.* Trans. Benjamin Jowett. Mineola, N.Y.: Dover Publications, 2000.

Augustine. *City of God.* Trans. Marcus Dods. New York: Modern Library, 1983.

Baker, Steve. *The Postmodern Animal.* London: Reaktion Books, 1999.

Beauchamp, Tom L., et al. *The Human Use of Animals: Case Studies in Ethical Choice.* New York: Oxford University Press, 1998.

Bekoff, Marc, and Carron A. Meaney, eds. *Encyclopedia of Animal Rights and Animal Welfare.* Westport, Conn.: Greenwood Press, 1998.

Bentham, Jeremy. *The Works of Jeremy Bentham.* Vol. 1. Ed. J. Bowring. New York: Russell & Russell, 1962.

Berger, John. *About Looking.* New York: Pantheon Books, 1980.

Cadava, Eduardo, et al., eds. *Who Comes After the Subject?* New York: Routledge, 1991.

Campbell, Joseph. *The Masks of God*, vol. 1: *Primitive Mythology.* New York: Viking, 1969.

Carlson, Allen. *Aesthetics and the Environment: The Appreciation of Nature, Art and Architecture.* London and New York: Routledge, 2000.

Cavalieri, Paola, and Peter Singer, eds. *The Great Ape Project: Equality Beyond Humanity.* New York: St. Martin's Press, 1993.

Chapple, Christopher Key. *Nonviolence to Animals, Earth and Self in Asian Traditions*. Albany: State University of New York Press, 1993.

Clark, Stephen R. L. *Animals and Their Moral Standing*. London: Routledge, 1997.

Clarke, Paul A. B., and Andrew Linzey, eds. *Political Theory and Animal Rights*. Winchester, Mass.: Pluto Press, 1990.

Darwin, Charles. *On the Origin of the Species*. Washington Square: New York University Press, 1988.

Dawkins, Marian Stamp. *Animal Suffering: The Science of Animal Welfare*. London: Chapman and Hall, 1980.

Deleuze, Gilles, and Félix Guattari. *A Thousand Plateaus: Capitalism and Schizophrenia*. Trans. Brian Massumi. Minneapolis: University of Minnesota Press, 1987.

Dennett, Daniel C. *Darwin's Dangerous Idea: Evolution and the Meanings of Life*. New York: Simon and Schuster, 1995.

Devall, Bill, and George Sessions. *Deep Ecology: Living As If Nature Mattered*. Salt Lake City: Peregrine Smith Books, 1985.

Eisnitz, Gail. *Slaughterhouse: The Shocking Story of Greed, Neglect and Inhumane Treatment inside the U.S. Meat Industry*. Amherst, N.Y.: Prometheus Books, 1997.

*Encyclopedia of Bioethics*. Rev. ed. New York: Simon & Schuster Macmillan, 1995.

Francione, Gary. "Animals as Property." 2 *Animal Law* 1 (1996).

———. "Animal Rights and Animal Welfare." 48 *Rutgers L. Rev.* 397 (1996). www.animal-law.org/library/araw_ii.htm.

Freud, Sigmund. *Totem and Taboo: Some Points of Agreement between the Mental Lives of Savages and Neurotics*. Trans. James Strachey. New York: W. W. Norton and Company, 1989.

Frey, R. G. *Interests and Rights: The Case Against Animals*. Oxford: Clarendon Press, 1980.

Gaard, Greta, ed. *Ecofeminism: Women, Animals, Nature*. Philadelphia: Temple University Press, 1993.

Geertz, Clifford. *Local Knowledge: Further Essays in Interpretive Anthropology*. New York: Basic Books, 1983.

Geist, Valerius. *Life Strategies, Human Evolution, Environmental Design: Toward a Biological Theory of Health*. New York: Springer-Verlag, 1978.

Godlovitch, Stanley, Roslind Godlovitch, and John Harris, eds. *Animals, Men and Morals: An Enquiry into the Maltreatment of Non-humans*. New York: Taplinger Publishing Company, 1972.

Griffin, Donald R. *Animal Minds*. Chicago: University of Chicago Press, 1992.

———. *Animal Thinking*. Cambridge, Mass.: Harvard University Press, 1984.

———. *The Question of Animal Awareness: Evolutionary Continuity of Mental Experience*. New York: The Rockefeller University Press, 1976.

Hanson, Phillip P., ed. *Environmental Ethics: Philosophical and Policy Perspectives*. Burnaby, B.C.: Institute for the Humanities, Simon Fraser University Publications, 1986.

Hargrove, Eugene C., ed. *The Animal Rights/Environmental Ethics Debate: The Environmental Perspective*. Albany: State University of New York Press, 1992.

Harrison, Ruth. *Animal Machines*. London: Vincent Stuart, 1964.

Heidegger, Martin. *Basic Writings: From* Being and Time *(1927) to* The Task of Thinking *(1964)*. Rev. ed. Ed. David Farrell Krell. San Francisco: HarperSanFrancisco, 1993.

———. *The Fundamental Concepts of Metaphysics: World, Finitude, Solitude*. Trans. William McNeill and Nicholas Walker. Bloomington and Indianapolis: Indiana University Press, 1995.

Hobbes, Thomas. *The Elements of Law Natural and Politic*. Ed. J. C. A. Gaskin. Oxford: Oxford University Press, 1999.

———. *Leviathan*. Ed. J. C. A. Gaskin. Oxford: Oxford University Press, 1998.

Hume, David. *A Treatise of Human Nature*. Ed. Ernest C. Mossner. Baltimore: Penguin Books, 1969.

Hursthouse, Rosalind. *Ethics, Humans and Other Animals: An Introduction with Readings*. New York: Routledge, 2000.

Jaggar, Alison. "Feminist Ethics: Some Issues for the Nineties." *Journal of Social Philosophy* 20, nos. 1–2 (Spring–Fall 1989): 91–107.

Jamieson, Dale, ed. *Singer and His Critics*. Oxford: Blackwell Publishers, Ltd., 1999.

Jonas, Hans. *Mortality and Morality: The Search for the Good after Auschwitz*. Evanston, Ill.: Northwestern University Press, 1996.

Kant, Immanuel. *The Critique of Judgment*. Trans. J. H. Bernard. Amherst, N.Y.: Prometheus Books, 2000.

———. *The Critique of Practical Reason*. Trans. T. K. Abbott. Amherst, N.Y.: Prometheus Books, 1996.

———. *Fundamental Principles of the Metaphysic of Morals*. Trans. T. K. Abbott. Buffalo, N.Y.: Prometheus Books, 1988.

Kaufmann, Walter. *Existentialism from Dostoevsky to Sartre*. Rev. ed. New York: New American Library, 1975.

Kellert, Stephen R., and Edward O. Wilson, eds. *The Biophilia Hypothesis*. Washington, D.C.: Island Press, 1993.

LaFollette, Hugh, and Niall Shanks. "The Origin of Speciesism." *Philosophy* 71 (1995): 41–60.

———. "Utilizing Animals." *Journal of Applied Philosophy* 12, no. 1 (1995): 13–25.

Leahy, Michael P. T. *Against Liberation: Putting Animals into Perspective*. London: Routledge, 1991.

Leopold, Aldo. *A Sand County Almanac and Sketches Here and There*. New York: Oxford University Press, 1989.

Linzey, Andrew, and Dorothy Yamamoto, eds. *Animals on the Agenda: Questions about Animals for Theology and Ethics*. Urbana and Chicago: University of Illinois Press, 1998.

Livingston, John A. *Rogue Primate: An Exploration of Human Domestication*. Boulder, Colo.: Roberts Rinehart Publishers, 1994.

Machan, Tibor. "Do Animals Have Rights?" *Public Affairs Quarterly* 5, no. 2 (April 1991): 163–73.

MacIntyre, Alasdair C. *After Virtue: A Study in Moral Theory*. 2nd ed. Notre Dame: University of Notre Dame Press, 1984.

Masci, David. "Fighting over Animal Rights." *CQ Researcher* 6 (2 August 1996): 675–92.

Midgley, Mary. *Animals and Why They Matter*. Athens: University of Georgia Press, 1983.

Mill, John Stuart. *Utilitarianism*. Ed. Roger Crisp. Oxford: Oxford University Press, 1998.

Miller, Harlan B., and William H. Williams, eds. *Ethics and Animals*. Clifton, N.J.: Humana Press, 1983.

Munson, Ronald, ed. *Intervention and Reflection: Basic Issues in Medical Ethics*. 5th ed. Belmont, Calif.: Wadsworth Publishing Company, 1996.

Nagel, Thomas. *Mortal Questions*. Cambridge: Cambridge University Press, 1979.

Nicolson, Marjorie Hope. *Mountain Gloom and Mountain Glory: The Development of the Aesthetic of the Infinite*. Seattle: University of Washington Press, 1997.

Nietzsche, Friedrich. *Basic Writings of Nietzsche*. Trans. Walter Kaufmann. New York: Modern Library, 1968.

————. *Daybreak*. Trans. R. J. Hollingdale. Cambridge: Cambridge University Press, 1982.

————. *Thus Spoke Zarathustra: A Book for All and for None*. Trans. Walter Kaufmann. New York: Penguin Books, 1978.

————. *Twilight of the Idols* and *The Anti-Christ*. Trans. R. J. Hollingdale. Harmondsworth, England: Penguin Books, 1968.

————. *Will to Power*. Trans. R. J. Hollingdale and Walter Kaufmann. New York: Vintage Books, 1968.

Ortega y Gasset, José. *Meditations on Hunting*. Trans. Howard B. Wescott. 1972. Reprint, Bozeman, Mont.: Wilderness Adventures Press, 1995.

Paul, Elizabeth. "Us and Them: Scientists' and Animal Rights Campaigners' Views on the Animal Experimentation Debate." www.psyeta.org/sa/sa3.1/paul.html. 3 February 2001.

Pluhar, Evelyn. *Beyond Prejudice: The Moral Significance of Human and Nonhuman Animals*. Durham: Duke University Press, 1995.

Quammen, David. *Monster of God: The Man-Eating Predator in the Jungles of History and the Mind*. New York: W. W. Norton and Company, 2003.

Rachels, James. *Created from Animals: The Moral Implications of Darwinism*. Oxford: Oxford University Press, 1990.

Rawls, John. *A Theory of Justice*. Rev. ed. Cambridge, Mass.: The Belknap Press of Harvard University Press, 1999.

Regan, Tom. *The Case for Animal Rights*. Berkeley and Los Angeles: University of California Press, 1983.

————, and Peter Singer, eds. *Animal Rights and Human Obligations*. 2nd ed. Englewood Cliffs: Prentice-Hall, 1989.

Rodman, John. "The Liberation of Nature?" *Inquiry* 20 (1977): 83–131.

Rodrigue, Christine Mary. "An Evaluation of Ritual Sacrifice as an Explanation for Early Animal Domestications in the Near East." Ph.D. dissertation. Clark University, 1986.

Roleff, Tamara L., ed. *The Rights of Animals*. San Diego: Greenhaven Press, 1999.

Rollin, Bernard E. *Animal Rights and Human Morality*. Rev. ed. Buffalo: Prometheus Books, 1992.

Rolston, Holmes, III. *Philosophy Gone Wild*. New York: Prometheus Books, 1986.

Rosenfield, Israel. *The Strange, Familiar, and Forgotten: An Anatomy of Consciousness*. New York: Vintage Books, 1993.

Ross, W. D. *The Right and the Good*. Oxford: Oxford University Press, 1930.

Rothschild, Miriam. *Animals and Man*. Oxford: Oxford University Press, 1986.

Rousseau, Jean-Jacques. *A Discourse on the Origin of Inequality; A Discourse on Political Economy; The Social Contract*. Trans. G. D. H. Cole. Franklin Center, Pa.: Franklin Library, 1982.

Rowlands, Mark. *Animal Rights: A Philosophical Defence*. Basingstoke: Macmillan, 1998.

Rudrum, Alan. "Ethical Vegetarianism in 17th Century Britain: Its Roots in 16th Century European Theological Debate." *The Seventeenth Century* 18, no. 1 (Spring 2003): 76–92.

Salt, Henry S. *Animals' Rights Considered in Relation to Social Progress*. 1892. Reprint, Clarks Summit, Pa.: Society for Animal Rights, 1980.

Sapontzis, Steve F. *Morals, Reason, and Animals*. Philadelphia: Temple University Press, 1987.

Sartre, Jean-Paul. *Existentialism and Human Emotions*. New York: Philosophical Library, 1957.

Scholtmeijer, Marian. *Animal Victims in Modern Fiction: From Sanctity to Sacrifice*. Toronto: University of Toronto Press, 1993.

Schopenhauer, Arthur. *On the Basis of Morality*. Trans. E. F. J. Payne. Providence: Berghahn Books, 1995.

Sessions, George, ed. *Deep Ecology for the 21st Century: Readings on the Philosophy and Practice of the New Environmentalism*. Boston: Shambala Publications, 1995.

Shaw, William H., ed. *Social and Personal Ethics*. 2nd ed. Belmont, Calif.: Wadsworth, 1996.

Shepard, Paul. *The Tender Carnivore and the Sacred Game*. Athens: University of Georgia Press, 1973.

———. *Thinking Animals: Animals and the Development of Human Intelligence*. New York: The Viking Press, 1978.

Singer, Peter. *Animal Liberation*. Rev. ed. New York: Avon Books, 1990.

Sorabji, Richard. *Animal Minds and Human Morals: The Origin of the Western Debate*. Ithaca, N.Y.: Cornell University Press, 1993.

Steinbock, Bonnie. "Speciesism and the Idea of Equality." *Philosophy* 53 (1978): 247–56.

Thoreau, Henry David. *Walden* and *Civil Disobedience*. Ed. Sherman Paul. Boston: Houghton Mifflin, 1960.

VanDeVeer, Donald. "Interspecific Justice and Intrinsic Value." *The Electronic Journal of Analytic Philosophy* Issue 3 (Spring 1995).

Varner, Gary. "Harey Animals." www.phil.tamu.edu/~gary/ hareyanimals.pdf. 21 September 2003.

White, James E., ed. *Contemporary Moral Problems*. 5th ed. St. Paul, Minn.: West Publishing, 1997.

Wise, Steven M. *Rattling the Cage: Toward Legal Rights for Animals*. Cambridge, Mass.: Perseus Books, 2000.

Wittgenstein, Ludwig. *Philosophical Investigations*. Trans. G. E. M. Anscombe. Cambridge, Mass.: Blackwell, 1997.

# INDEX

abortion, 22, 27, 253n44, 263n23
absolute speciesism. *See*
  dominionism
Adams, Carol, 180, 271–72n52
*Aesthetics and the Environment*
  (Carlson), 284n57
agriculturists, 219
Allen, Colin, 241
"alpha predators," 238n10
animal aesthetics, 223–28, 270n37,
  282–83n39, 283n51; aesthetic
  power of animals, 230; and
  aesthetic satisfaction, 224–25; and
  the discourse of the divine in
  nature, 225–26; and performance
  art, 231. *See also* Romanticism
animal debates: analysis of, 4–8,
  233–36; philosophical implications
  of, 5; shortcomings of, 124–26;
  success and consensus in, 6, 122–24
animal exploitation, 12, 13, 102, 127,
  194; logic of, 21–22, 65, 136; for
  medical and scientific research, 13,
  63, 67, 69, 249n51, 261n3
animal liberation, 58–59, 60–63, 165;
  and analogies to human liberation
  movements, 60–61, 173; criticism
  of, 62
*Animal Liberation* (Singer), 60–62; as
  a utilitarian document, 246–47n7
*Animal Machines* (Harrison), 22
animal rights, 42, 58, 154, 189,
  251nn13, 15, 252n41; and the
  concept of "marginal cases," 79–82,
  112, 261–62n5; deontological
  arguments for, 73–76, 127–28; and
  the great apes, 262n15; legal rights,
  97–98; moral individualism and the

value of rights, 86–87; moral rights,
  94, 252–53n42; and the subversion
  of known culture, 278–79n65;
  "theos-rights," 35–36. *See also*
  *Case for Animal Rights, The*
  (Regan)
animal suffering, 27–28, 63, 69–70,
  241n55, 242n58, 247nn8, 13;
  compared to human suffering,
  249n37; denial of, 35; lack of
  scientific knowledge of, 68
animal welfare movements, 21, 53,
  66, 239n36
animality, 18, 152–53, 233, 269n25;
  and domestication, 192; human,
  166, 193; transformation of, 17
animals: ambiguity of, 129;
  anthropomorphizing of, 4, 40, 179;
  consciousness of, 15, 24–25, 43–44,
  51–52, 94–95, 241n49, 252n37,
  256n23, 263nn32, 36; cruelty
  toward, 98–99; and culture, 15–16;
  "Disneyfication" of, 77; as
  empathetic objects, 14, 16;
  endangered species, 268n12;
  equality of to one another, 3; as
  food for humans, 57, 64–66;
  instinctive behavior of, 44, 244n27;
  institutionalization of, 16; in a
  laboratory environment, 27–28,
  240n41, 241n56; legal protection
  for, 3; legal standing of, 28,
  241–42n57; as metaphors for
  human emotional requirements,
  13, 14; otherness of, 14, 17–18;
  philosophical importance of, 53–54;
  physiology of, 22; population of,
  262n16; as property, 2, 30, 261n2;

virtue/virtue ethics, 98–102, 104, 128,
132, 178; constituents of virtue of
character, 99; and cruelty to
animals, 98–101; virtue-based
animal ethic, 99–102
vivisection, 21, 235

Wallace, Alfred, 41
Warren, Mary Anne, 95
Wegman, William, 15
"What Is It Like to Be a Bat?" (Nagel),
50, 245n49
*White Bone, The* (Gowdy), 245n50
wildlife management, 28, 221
wildness, 164, 165, 166, 209–10;
experience of in parks and wildlife

refuges, 221–22; human wildness
and ferality, 205–7; impact of
human wildness on other life
forms, 205–6, 208; "legitimizing,"
204–5
*Will to Power, The* (Nietzsche), 193,
207, 275n16
Wilson, E. O., 238n14

Yamamoto, Dorothy, 11, 12, 18, 53,
170

zoology, 150
zoos, 222
Zuntz, Gunther, 201, 292

MARC R. FELLENZ is an associate professor of
philosophy in the Department of Arts and Humanities
at the Grant Campus of Suffolk County Community
College. He is the author of articles on "Animal
Rights" and "Animal Experimentation" in *The
Encyclopedia of Science, Technology and Ethics*
(Woodbridge, Conn.: Macmillan Reference USA,
2005).

WITHDRAWN

*The University of Illinois Press
is a founding member of the
Association of American University Presses.*

---

*Composed in 9.5/12.5 Trump Mediaeval
by BookComp, Inc.
for the University of Illinois Press
Manufactured by Thomson-Shore, Inc.*

*University of Illinois Press
1325 South Oak Street
Champaign, IL 61820-6903
www.press.uillinois.edu*